Mike Torrez

Mike Torrez

A Baseball Biography

JORGE IBER

McFarland & Company, Inc., Publishers

Jefferson, North Carolina

LIBRARY OF CONGRESS CATALOGUING-IN-PUBLICATION DATA

Names: Iber, Jorge, 1961–
Title: Mike Torrez : a baseball biography / Jorge Iber.
Description: Jefferson, North Carolina : McFarland & Company, Inc.,
    Publishers, 2016 | Includes bibliographical references and index.
Identifiers: LCCN 2016029385 | ISBN 9780786496327 (softcover : acid
    free paper) ∞
Subjects: LCSH: Torrez, Mike. | Baseball players—United States—
    Biography.
Classification: LCC GV865.T65 I44 2016 | DDC 796.357092 [B]—dc23
LC record available at https://lccn.loc.gov/2016029385
BRITISH LIBRARY CATALOGUING DATA ARE AVAILABLE

ISBN (print) 978-0-7864-9632-7
ISBN (ebook) 978-1-4766-2445-7

Front cover image of Mike Torrez, 1969, pitching against the Royals
reprinted with permission from *Topeka Capital Journal*

Printed in the United States of America

McFarland & Company, Inc., Publishers
  Box 611, Jefferson, North Carolina 28640
    www.mcfarlandpub.com

For my father, Manuel Iber, who taught me to love the wonderful game of baseball!

For my wife, Raquel, and our son, Matthew, thank you both for all of your love and support during the time I was so distracted while finishing this book.

For Mike Torrez and the rest of the Torrez clan. I very much appreciate how you welcomed me into your family and the Oakland community.

Acknowledgments

As always, there are many individuals to thank upon completion of a book manuscript. First off, I thank my wife Raquel and our son Matthew for their love and support. I also thank Mike Torrez and his family for allowing me the opportunity to tell their story. The Torrez story is more than just about "the pitch" to Bucky Dent in 1978. It is a tale of courage and determination of a *familia* from Mexico that came to Kansas and worked diligently to fulfill the American Dream. For my colleagues in the profession who encouraged me to pursue sports history (in no particular order): Arnoldo De Leon, Samuel O. Regalado, José Alamillo, Richard Santillan, Paul Carlson, Alwyn Barr, Larry Gerlach, and Monte Monroe. To the wonderful "crew" of the Student Division of the College of Arts and Sciences at Texas Tech University; my thanks to all for being understanding with me when I seemed a bit distracted with you while finishing up this project.

Table of Contents

Introduction
Mike Torrez, from the Barrios of Kansas to the Major Leagues and Beyond

The passing in August 2010 of Bobby Thomson, the man who hit what is now acknowledged as having been the tainted "shot heard round the world" in 1951 for the Giants, and the publication of an autobiography by the "goat" in that confrontation, Dodgers pitcher Ralph Branca, doubtless stirs vivid memories among aficionados of our national pastime's storied past.[1] While there are a plethora of such moments in baseball lore, a similar event has ties to an aspect of game's chronicle that has only recently started to draw academic and mainstream interest: the participation and historical significance of Latino[2] athletes in American sport. The pitch of interest in this work was thrown by a son and grandson of Mexican-born railroad workers from the Oakland *barrio* of Topeka, Kansas, Mike Torrez (then pitching for the Red Sox after having been with the Yankees), to light-hitting Yankees shortstop Bucky Dent at Fenway Park on October 2, 1978. While this round-tripper did not end the playoff contest in dramatic fashion, as did Thomson's, it did erase a 2–0, late-inning Boston lead and sparked New York to an improbable 5–4 victory, completing a frenetic rally by the Bronx Bombers to a division championship after trailing Boston by 14 games as late as July 19. While the responsibility for blowing this huge lead cannot be placed on one player, Mike Torrez bore a disproportionate and unfair brunt for the Red Sox's late-season collapse. He was so spurned in Boston, for example, that Celtics fans booed when the Garden's public address announcer called out his name during a game.

That pitch forever linked Torrez and Dent, and the men have, over the intervening decades, made sport and money off fans eager to discuss and relive the instant.[3] Indeed, almost 40 years removed, Torrez still garners attention from Yankees fans (after all, he did win two games for them in the 1977 World Series) and is a regular attendee at "old-timer" events and fantasy camps in the New York City area and Florida. While that campaign garnered him a championship ring and a huge, by the standards of the day, free agent contract, Torrez toiled but one season in the Bronx, with the majority of his time in the Majors spent with the St. Louis Cardinals, the Montreal Expos, and the Red Sox. Boston fans were far less forgiving after "the pitch," and he endured a great deal of ill-treatment until leaving to play for the Mets in 1983. It was not until the centennial celebration of Fenway Park in 2012 that he was invited back for an event at the facility. He has never returned.

Writing about the lives, experiences and significance of Latino ballplayers has increased markedly over the past two decades. Non-academic writers such as Nick C. Wilson, Noe Torres, Tim Wendel, Mark Kurlansky, Rafael Hermoso and many, many others have researched interactions between Latinos and baseball, here in the United States and in the players' various home countries.[4] Not surprisingly, the story of Pittsburgh Pirates legend Roberto Clemente leads this list, with David Maraniss' masterful 2006 work, *Clemente: The Passion and Grace of Baseball's*

Mike Torrez, Mike Cordaro, and Bucky Dent at a recent team-sponsored fantasy camp in Florida. Courtesy of Mike Torrez.

Last Hero, an excellent integration of biography and social history.[5] On the academic side of the ledger are noted scholars such as Samuel O. Regalado, Adrian Burgos, Richard Santillan, and Roberto Gonzalez Echevarria.[6] While there are many parallels between this project on Mike Torrez and the players discussed in the works cited above, the majority of the projects cited tend to focus upon individuals born outside of the contiguous United States. A key argument here is that Mike Torrez's life in a Kansas barrio will flesh out different nuances about the relationship of Latinos and sport than does a focus on the experience of foreign-born athletes. For example, while many authors recount the problems faced by non-native Latinos navigating their way through the minor leagues, not much has been written about a person of Spanish-surname who, because of circumstances extant in the United States during the time he attended school, did not speak much Spanish. How did such an athlete deal with playing winter league baseball in the Dominican Republic where it was simply assumed he spoke Spanish? Further, as this work will show, Torrez, while putting together an overall record of 185–160 in the Majors for a .536 winning percentage and winning one World Series title, never garnered the same attention and adulation as a Fernando Valenzuela, whose overall regular season mark was 173–153, for a .531 winning percentage and two World Series titles. Was Torrez, who was born in the United States, viewed differently from the Mexican-born Valenzuela, and if so, why? Addressing the question of which man was a "better" pitcher is not the objective, although Torrez did pitch the Mets to a 7–1 victory over Valenzuela and the Dodgers on August 31, 1983. He also had a no-decision in another contest versus "El Torito" that year. What is of interest, however, is to examine how these individuals, both of Mexican backgrounds, were perceived by their communities and the broader population.

The story of Michael Augustine Torrez provides an entry into three important strands of Mexican American/Latino history. First, his story is part of a growing body of biographical literature now being generated for this group. Recent works include accounts of the lives of a federal judge, an academician, a medical doctor/civil rights activist, and a mayor of El Paso.[7]

Second, a perusal of the pages of Torrez's home-state historical journals, *Kansas History* and *Kansas Quarterly* (and other periodicals), reveals a not-insignificant assemblage of items dealing directly with the Mexican American role in the history of Kansas and the Midwest. A number of theses, dissertations and books have examined topics such as the arrival of *traqueros* (track laborers) and *betabeleros* (beet workers) from Mexico in the early 1900s, the movement of Mexicanos and other Spanish-speakers into locales such as Garden City in the later decades of the twentieth century, and the positive and negative aspects of the processes involved with integrating *recien llegados* (recent arrivals) into a community with a long-standing Mexican American populace.[8] This work on Torrez, his career, and his community is in line with arguments articulated and discussed in such works and follows the call made by Rita G. Napier in a *Kansas History* article entitled "Rethinking the Past, Reimagining the Future." At the very end of the essay, Napier noted that increasing the awareness of "other" groups in the state's history (and in the Midwest as well) would make it possible to include "different stories, new actors, fresh images.... This new knowledge has yarn of many colors with which to weave our future."[9] Torrez's story, hopefully, will add to this emerging tapestry for sports history, the history of the Sunflower State and beyond.

Finally, while projects concerning Spanish-speakers throughout the nation have generated insight into various aspects of their history, such as labor, religion and education, one area that has been almost completely ignored is the role of sport. Numerous ethnic groups, such as African Americans, Jews, Native Americans and Italian Americans, have garnered substantial coverage from historians of sport.[10]

A quick perusal of the pages of *Kansas History* and *Kansas Quarterly* revealed that both publications have published a fair amount concerning athletics; but no article has yet focused specifically on Latinos/Mexican Americans. Recent publications include a biography of a legendary official, an overview of Wilt Chamberlain's Jayhawks years, the development of six- and eight-man football on the plains, interracial baseball in Wichita, and the significance of the Haskell Institute's football team to Native American identity.[11] Further, a search of sports history-focused publications such as *Journal of Sport History* and the *International Journal for the History of Sport* contain only a limited number of U.S.-based Latino-themed articles, though the number is increasing. Among the offerings are articles by Jorge Iber, Fernando Delgado, Alan Klein, Hilary A. Braysmith, José Alamillo, Benita Heiskanan, and Enver M. Casimir.[12]

The most active journal in detailing the story of Latinos in baseball (mostly at the Major League level) is *Nine: A Journal of Baseball History and Culture*, with recent works by Gilberto Garcia, Kevin A. Johnson and Joseph W. Anderson, Roberta Newman, and Larry Gerlach, to mention just a few.[13] In addition, there are two works from this publication that deal with topics that are significant to Torrez's career: one on the positives and tensions associated with the integration (whites, Latinos and African

Americans) of clubhouses, another on Latino identity in the Major Leagues.[14] The story of Mike Torrez provides a vehicle for examining similar stories in the past of Kansas and the Midwest. In reality, such accounts are only now being researched and integrated into the broader historical literature of both Spanish-speakers and U.S. sport.[15]

Research on the topic of this population and athletics in Kansas is extant, however. For example, two important works, though not by historians, shed light on the significance of sport in the lives of Latinos in the state, both focusing on Garden City. The first is from the early 1990s, when Mark A. Grey, an anthropologist, studied how recent arrivals in this community were alienated by the broader population of the local high school, in part because they did not participate in "traditional" American sports (most significantly, in football).[16] At the start of his essay, Grey counters an often accepted notion that sports helps immigrants assimilate into the broader culture with a more nuanced approach. Instead, he argues that since (at the time he conducted his research) most Latinos at Garden City High School (GCHS) did not play "conventional" athletic endeavors, focusing instead on soccer, that "sports in schools ... actually work to marginalize immigrant and other minority students in both the school and the community."[17] Actually, Grey contends, because of the existence of a more "established" (long-standing) Spanish surnamed community (which did participate in sports like football), it was possible to further segregate/separate new arrivals from the social mainstream, both on campus and off.[18] As a sop, the school permitted the formation of a soccer club (not at the varsity level), though support, at least at this time, was lukewarm. The net result was that most of the Spanish-surnamed (and Asians as well) at GCHS were generally perceived as "outsiders" and not among the "accepted" segments of the population.[19] In summary, Grey argues that it was necessary to provide support for a soccer club, and even to make it a varsity sport. By permitting the new arrivals such an outlet, they would feel like they "belonged" at the institution, and some would even begin to gravitate toward other activities, such as football.

> Clearly, the interest in playing common American games was present among immigrant and other minorities. What was lacking was any mechanism to accommodate their athletic interests in the school. On the contrary, by narrowly defining the range of athletic (and related) activities recognized by the school, these students were given few legitimate opportunities to demonstrate their willingness to become integrated members of "American" society on their own terms.[20]

An important follow-up is presented by Sam Quinones in his book *Antonio's Gun and Delfino's Dream: True Tales of Mexican Immigration,* in a chapter entitled "A Soccer Season in Southwest Kansas."[21] Here (as of 2003), the author notes that some Latinos had moved into football, though still perceived as outsiders, sometimes being referred to by teammates not by name, but rather as "Kicker." While not fully accepted, Quinones argues that one of these youths, Juan Torres, by "joining the football team, ... had been allowed into a special club, the benefits of which he'd been only partially aware of until then."[22] The potential to change the perception of Latinos at GCHS through sports was present, though still not fully realized. The leap forward would come from an unexpected source: *futbol*.

Grey's suggestion from the late 1980s became reality in 1996, when GCHS fielded its inaugural varsity squad. While the institution had a "product," it did not attract much interest (or generate a positive vibe in the community or on campus). While head coach (and academic counselor) Joaquin Padilla started each campaign with high hopes, these wilted as, invariably, athletes left with families who moved on to other jobs/locales or when individual students were declared academically ineligible. At GCHS, soccer was almost exclusively a Latino endeavor (in 2003, when Quinones visited, there were 17 immigrant students—16 Latinos and one Vietnamese—and one Anglo on the roster). Unlike elsewhere, where soccer is the sport of children who hail from swanky suburbs, in this part of Kansas it "was as foreign to the native white residents as the immigrants who played it."[23] If there was any hope of establishing support and gaining a greater measure of acceptance for the players (and the newcomer Latinos in general), it was necessary to win and win big (particularly since the football team's appearance in the 1999 state title game was still fresh in the town's collective memory). The result would be, hopefully, more positive interactions with the rest of the student body, perhaps even a chance to move on to a college squad and become the generation that escaped the toil and limitations of work at nearby meat processing plants. Until that happened, the local Spanish-surnamed peoples, Padilla correctly surmised, were perceived just as "meat-plant workers [who] never made the papers, no student ... had ever been recognized or popular because he played soccer."[24] The breakthrough occurred in 2003.

To the surprise of many, the Buffaloes became a force and, more astoundingly, Garden City took notice, with white students and teachers attending matches in substantial numbers for the first time. As GCHS continued this season, the "team was something for immigrant kids to be proud of ... [and] one result was that some of the Latino students gradually began to lose their fear of participating [in other school activities]."[25] The squad finished with a record of 15–1–1, losing to Wichita Heights High in the state semi-final round. While denied a "Remember the Titans" ending, the GCHS Buffaloes enlightened many locals as to certain possibilities from the dramatic demographic changes that had taken place since the 1980s.

Sport has played a not-insignificant role in breaking down some, though not all, barriers to challenging stereotypes for the sons (and later, daughters, as GCHS added girls' soccer in 2001) of the *recien llegados.* As Quinones summarized, "the Garden City High School team had diverted the attention of a town obsessed with football. Immigrant kids puffed with pride, and more than a sport emerged from the shadows on the High Plains ... [the season] 'opened the eyes of a lot of guys on the team, to let them dream a little bigger.'"[26]

An examination of how Mike Torrez made his way from the "wrong side of the tracks" to the Major Leagues and the social and historical significance of his experiences provides a broader understanding of Mexican American and Latino social history. That is the primary goal of this work. The account of this ballplayer's story, through a recounting of the circumstances of his life and career, provides unique insights on topics such as the differences in experiences between native and non-native Latinos in the various levels of baseball; the racial issues extant as the number of players with Spanish-surnames increased, thus further diversifying the sport's clubhouse; and the process of the ending of the reserve clause and the coming of free agency.

This study contains nine chapters in what may be thought of as sections of three chapters each. The first contextualizes the circumstances for arrival of Mexican Americans into Kansas in the early parts of the twentieth century, and covers a time period through the end of Torrez's high school athletic career in 1964. Chapter 1 notes the arrival of Mexicanos in the Sunflower State in general, and Topeka in particular, between the time of the Mexican Revolution of 1910 and the end of World War II. What attracted Spanish speakers to this area? What type of work did they do and what was life like? Available materials document the rise of important institutions in the barrio of Kansas' capital city and elsewhere in the state and region. Among the topics covered will be the development of early churches, mutual aid societies, labor organizations and more. Into this milieu arrived Torrez's paternal and maternal grandfathers, Mariano Torrez (in 1911) and Calixto Martinez (in 1922).

Chapter 2 examines the role of sport in these communities as a mechanism for enjoyment, resistance, and developing ethnic identity, pride and solidarity. The development of "Mexican" baseball and basketball throughout the Midwest demonstrates the vital role sport played in the daily barrio life. Teams and tournaments became important touchstones for workers and their families, and strengthened fraternal and cultural ties across state lines. Further, beginning in the 1930s, a few Mexican Americans began to appear on the pages of Kansas papers as athletes for local high schools.

For Chapter 3 the focus returns to the Torrez family and details their daily experiences in Oakland. Through extensive oral history interviews and other sources, the trials and tribulations of the clan are documented between Mike's birth in 1946 and the end of his high school athletic career (caused, in part, because of his participation in a Mexican American basketball tournament in Omaha, Nebraska). In many ways, the story of Mike Torrez parallels that of most other Mexican Americans in Oakland and elsewhere in the U.S. The role of these individuals, for the most part, was to work hard for relatively low wages in industries such as the railroads, agriculture, and mining. The Torrez family was not outside the norm in this regard. They also mirrored the love that other Mexican Americans had for the game of baseball (and sports in general). The key element that differentiated Mike Torrez from others in his barrio was that he could throw a better fastball than just about anyone else. The God-given talent, and his family's assistance in teaching him the fundamentals of the game, were what dramatically altered the path of Torrez's life and career choice.

The next three chapters, 4 through 6, detail the signing of this "diamond in the rough" by the Cardinals organization, his years in the minor leagues, arrival in the Major Leagues, and trades and moves through various franchises and cities. Among some of the key issues examined are his ties to other Latinos both on the squads (particularly with the Cardinals) and in the winter leagues. Further, during his first full season (1969) in St. Louis, Torrez had an opportunity to spend time with Curt Flood and witnessed first-hand his teammate's valiant struggle to attack the dreaded reserve clause. Finally, after spending time with the Expos and Orioles, Torrez was exiled to another Oakland, the one in California, to play on an A's squad being decimated by Charlie Finley. After one season of butting heads with the cantankerous owner, Torrez was traded to the Yankees at the start of the 1977 campaign and walked right into the heart of what has been described as the "Bronx Zoo"; well-documented tensions were created by the interactions of the cadre of George Steinbrenner, Billy Martin, Thurman Munson and Reggie Jackson. All the while, with the rise of the Chicano Movement in the Midwest and elsewhere in the nation, Torrez had become a symbol of Mexican American pride and a role model to barrio youths long before the arrival of another famous pitcher of Mexican descent in the early 1980s.

The final three chapters of the work document the 1977 season, Torrez's free agent signing with the Boston Red Sox in 1978, his final years in the Majors, and his post-retirement life. Chapter 7 covers Torrez's role during the 1977 Yankees season, and his contributions, both on and off of the field, to maintaining some semblance of normalcy in the midst of New York's tumultuous season. Further, it will refer back to his hometown of Topeka and the importance of this Chicano/Mexican American role model at the heart of the national pastime, to the rising tide of "Brown Pride" in the community. The chapter concludes with a discussion of Torrez's signing with the Red Sox. There are several unique contextual issues connected with his arrival at Fenway Park. First, he was one of the early, major free agents and was thus construed as a "savior" for a team that, at that point, had not won a World Series for 60 years (as all of the team's fans know, this number would grow to 86 years, with the "curse" finally ending in 2004). Also, the Boston of the late 1970s was a city in turmoil, with the recent civil disturbances concerning forced busing for local students. Finally, given that Torrez, a Latino, stepped into a starting rotation with another, and very popular individual, Luis Tiant, how did the Fenway faithful react? As will be noted, Tiant was most likely the first (openly acknowledged) Latino who was well embraced by the Fenway faithful. It is evident from my research that Torrez never was, particularly after the loss in the one-game playoff. Chapter 7 also fleshes out the 1978 campaign, which started with so much promise for the team and for Torrez, only to end in heartbreak on October 2.

Chapter 8 examines how things were never the same in Boston after that bitter disappointment, though Torrez did have a couple more good campaigns before finally moving back to the National League in 1983. Of note during that season, however, was a victory over Valenzuela, in which the two "Mexican" pitchers in the majors at the time locked horns. In 1984, with the Mets in full rebuilding mode, Torrez was released, spent a bit of time with the A's and finally signed with an unaffiliated and woebegone Class A team in Miami known as the Marlins.

Chapter 9 covers Torrez experiences since his retirement, including a problematic stint as general manager of the Newark Bears. This chapter concludes with a summary of Torrez's life and career and its significance to the broader study of Latino athletes in the United States. While Torrez and his brothers had access to a substantial structure of Mexican American athletics throughout the Midwest in their youth, the number of Spanish-surnamed athletes in the region has grown dramatically over the past three decades. The state of Kansas is an interesting place to study this trend. The state (and, indeed, much of the Midwest) has undergone a dramatic demographic transformation since the 1980s. While Spanish-speakers have been residing in this region for more than one century, there has recently been a dramatic increase in their numbers due to the relative attractiveness of jobs in the meat processing and other agricultural industries prevalent in the region. This pattern has been ably documented by various authors. One interesting facet of this story, however, has been the dramatic increase in the number of Spanish-surnamed students who are attending local schools, and are now representing their communities on the gridiron, the basketball court, baseball diamonds and elsewhere.[27] Torrez's story clearly demonstrates that there is a historical precedent for this and that it is not merely a current-day phenomenon. Given the historical perspective presented in this work, how is sport impacting social relations and the interactions of the extant inhabitants with this "new" group in middle-America? Stories such as those of Mike Torrez can provide a solid foundation for understanding both the chronological and current aspects of this question.

Mike Torrez, a Mexican American from Topeka, Kansas, took advantage of his individual talents, which were nurtured through existing community organizations in his and other barrio communities, to reach the pinnacle of American sport: pitching in the World Series at Yankee Stadium. His story bears witness to the importance of athletics to an ethnic community, and how this endeavor can be utilized to challenge assumptions about an ethnic group. Further, it provides entry into stories that are only now beginning to be told about Latinos in the United States, in biographies and sport, which shed much light into the history of this people. Such neglected tales are worth telling and add nuance and texture to the overall story of the Spanish-speaking population of our nation.

1

Riding the Rails and Shooting for Their Supper

Early Mexican American Life in Kansas, 1900–1950

When Mike Torrez signed with the Boston Red Sox prior to the 1978 season, he joined the last Major League team to incorporate an African American onto its roster (Pumpsie Green in 1959). Even by the early to mid–1970s, the team still had difficulties integrating non-white players into their clubhouse. There were some Latino athletes on the squads before the late 1970s, however. The franchise did bring up Mel Almeda, the first Mexican-born individual to play in the big leagues, in 1933, for example. Later, Puerto Rican José Santiago contributed greatly to the 1967 pennant run and even started in Game 1 of that year's World Series. Finally, the Sox's all-time great, Ted Williams, was of Mexican descent, though he certainly did not make it well known during his playing days. During the 1960s and beyond, there were several talented African Americans who starred and confronted varying degrees of racial difficulties at Fenway Park and in the city, such as Reggie Smith (1966–1973), Cecil Cooper (1971–1976), and Hall of Famer Jim Rice (1974–1989). As reporter Howard Bryant articulated in his 2002 work, *Shut Out: A Story of Race and Baseball in Boston*, New England's MLB representative and its fans, had, for many decades, created a less-than-welcoming atmosphere for athletes who did not fit a specific racial or ethnic type. Other works by and about Celtics legend Bill Russell, for instance, indicate that the issue of race in professional sport in Boston was not unique to the Red Sox.[1]

One example Bryant discussed was the experiences of Tommy Harper, who played in Boston between 1972 and 1974 and then returned to coach for the periods of 1980–1985 and 2000–2002. During his stint as a player,

Harper complained about how the Elks Club of Winter Haven, Florida (the team's spring training base), would often invite white players to visit their facilities, but not so the African Americans. Harper discussed this issue with management in the early 1970s and upon his employment as a coach. In 1985, he once again brought up the matter and was ultimately fired. As Bryant argued, the Harper situation "was an embarrassing, revealing moment, [but] the true racial tension that existed within the framework ... would be in the team's atmosphere, [and was] always a more difficult problem to corral."[2]

One player who transcended some, though certainly not all, racial issues surrounding the Red Sox was the black Cuban American pitcher, Luis Tiant, Jr. (also known as "El Tiante," 1971–1978). The son of a Negro Leagues legend, in Bryant's view, Tiant was key to "the most sustained, hopeful period of recent Red Sox history" (Bryant's book was published two years before Boston finally broke the "curse" in 2004).[3] Tiant's success in Boston, particularly from 1972 through 1976, endeared him to New Englanders; he even pitched the team to victory against the Toronto Blue Jays (5–0 on October 1) on the final day of the 1978 regular season and temporarily staved off the epic collapse, only to have the Torrez-Dent events transpire the following day. In the middle of an era that saw great racial tensions in Boston, however,

> Tiant would always be conflicted about race; he was the leader on the mound but was savvy enough to avoid incendiary statements to the press that could have turned a hot city against him. That didn't mean he was anybody's fool, he just tried not to swim in the hot water. That's how it would be in Boston, though. Tiant would spend the days downplaying the effects of the club's history of race ... yet couldn't give an interview without returning to how blacks and whites got along. Race never went away.[4]

Thus, Mike Torrez entered into this setting of extant racial animosities and history, both inside and outside of the clubhouse, after signing a lucrative free agent contract shortly after the 1977 World Series.

At first, Red Sox fans were thrilled to welcome their former rival. Having a player with World Series and playoff experience, in addition to being a pitcher who "ate up innings" (with over 243 innings pitched in 1977), Mike Torrez would help bolster the effectiveness of returning starters Tiant and Bill Lee. Going into the 1978 campaign, Boston had jettisoned three members of the previous rotation: Reggie Cleveland, Ferguson Jenkins, and Rick Wise. The squad finished tied for second in its division in 1977 with a record of 97–64 had a team ERA of 4.12 and could not keep up with the Yankees in the American League East. In addition to Torrez and Tiant, the Red Sox also pinned their playoff hopes on former

(1975) Rookie Pitcher of the Year Dennis Eckersley (who came over from the Cleveland Indians) and 27-year-old rookie Jim Wright. Given the substantial offensive firepower in a starting lineup which featured Carlton Fisk, Fred Lynn, Jim Rice, Dwight Evans, and Carl Yastrzemski, it was expected that the team would have little difficulty in scoring runs; they did not, tallying 796 to finish second in the American League in 1978.[5] Thus, it was logical to assume prior to the season that improved pitching would allow Boston to surpass New York and Baltimore in the standings.

One of the earliest, and most enlightening, articles written about Torrez shortly after his move to Boston appeared in the *Herald American*. Reporter Bill Liston presented Torrez as the epitome of the American dream, stating that he "has come a long way from the days of his youth when he literally had to shoot for his supper." The scribe quoted Torrez concerning certain circumstances of his upbringing when he hunted to keep food on the table, worked in gas stations, and was part of "a poor, though not impoverished family." This was the reality for most of the Mexican American families in Oakland and barrios like it throughout the nation. Hunting for your supper (which Torrez and his brothers did fairly regularly), and coming up with a variety of methods (such as having children work at an early age) to better family finances, were simply part of daily existence.

The set-up presented Torrez as worthy of loyalty and respect from temperamental Boston fans not yet accustomed to cheering for or accepting Spanish-surnamed athletes (in certain ways his story mirrored aspects of Luis Tiant's). Liston chastised aficionados who begrudged Torrez his now substantial salary. "Those baseball fans who might resent big money contracts free-agents have been getting ... certainly have to have second thoughts when thinking about Mike Torrez ... [to say he] has paid his dues in achieving his lofty financial peak is putting it rather mildly."[6] Thus, the stage was set for Torrez and the Red Sox, both underdogs, to achieve baseball immortality. Here was the joining of the son and grandson of humble railroad workers who had left their native Mexico in hope of a better life with a team that had waited six decades for an opportunity to overcome the arrogant and insufferable Yankees dynasty. This enchanting tale would certainly end with the triumph of the downtrodden, no?

To understand Mike Torrez and his background, it is necessary to examine the conditions and locale in which he spent his childhood—the Oakland barrio of Topeka.[7] Like the story of many persons of similar ethnic descent throughout the United States, the tale of the Torrez family has ties to both the railroads and to agriculture; indeed, these were the key occupational sectors responsible for drawing Latinos to Kansas. How and why did Mexicans and Mexican Americans come to Kansas during the early part of the twentieth century? What jobs did these men and women do, where did such *familias* live, what circumstances did Spanish-surnamed persons confront in places of employment and schools, and what type of organizations did they establish in their communities? Over the past several decades, academics and graduate students have researched such questions, and a not-unsubstantial literature exists on the topic. Further, there are collections in the region which contain contemporary accounts, further documenting aspects of this history. It is to these materials that we now turn, first covering the whole of Kansas and then moving on to more narrowly focused information dealing of the Topeka (and eastern portion of the state) area.

An important start for this discussion comes from the Sunflower State's historical journal, *Kansas History*. In a 2002 article, James N. Leiker noted the extant gaps in the narrative of the territory's racial and ethnic groups. In regard to Hispanics (the term Leiker used), the story is quite complex and not sufficiently researched. In some parts of the state, Latinos were considered the same as African Americans and faced segregation. Thus, some Kansas-based, Spanish-surnamed students shared segregated classrooms, and families attended "colored" wards of local hospitals. Oral histories conducted by researchers have revealed examples of "Mexicans" not being permitted to eat in certain restaurants, swim in public pools, or utilize local parks.[8] Elsewhere, less formal separation occurred, and some employers and individuals stood up to prejudice and asked their fellow Kansans to give members of this group a "fair shake." Leiker, for example, mentioned circumstances in which the Santa Fe Railroad refused to comply with state government demands to remove and repatriate Mexican workers.[9] Another source also stated that Mexican laborers felt "the Santa Fe was more considerate with workers.... It provided better wages ... provided the immigrants with boxcars and a place to settle in Topeka, and it also donated materials for the building of the [Catholic] Parish."[10]

A newspaper article from the late 1920s called upon the broader Topeka community to assist barrio-dwellers in a neighborhood already known as "little Mexico." While parts certainly sound condescending to our twenty-first-century sensibilities, a 1928 essay from the *Topeka Journal* indicated that local elites were concerned for "less fortunate" Mexicans in their midst. N. Van Dyke encouraged people in the capital to "crawl from beneath their warm, luxurious and comfortable homes and just take a trip thru 'our little Mexico.'" Further, the author sought to dispel the notion that Mexicans were in dire circumstances due to their own laziness. "Yes! The Mexican men work.... But for the wages they work and the many children they have, the board doesn't balance." Van Dyke clamored for donations of food, clothing and bedding to "see if we can find anything that will make these striving people more comfortable this winter. Let's have more of our missionary work among our home folks."[11]

Among the most thorough efforts to document the arrival of Latinos to the state of Kansas in the early twentieth century is a 1980 project by Cynthia Mines entitled "Riding the Rails to Kansas."[12] From the very beginning, Mines notes the impact of railroad labor upon the establishment of Mexican barrios throughout the state. "If the Mexican colonies in Kansas are connected as in a dot-to-dot game, the resulting lines would form an absolutely accurate map of the main and branch lines of the Atchison, Topeka and Santa Fe Railroad." Since many jobs were seasonal, it was necessary to supplement employment at locales such as in the beet fields near Garden City, salt mines in Hutchinson and Lyons, and meat packing in Kansas City, thus creating barrios in those places as well.[13]

The recruitment for laborers usually commenced in the El Paso and Laredo areas with the work of an *enganchista* (labor recruiter), and both of Torrez's grandfathers reached Topeka through such arrangements. By the time of the 1910 census, there were an estimated 8,400 foreign-born Mexicans in Kansas, and approximately 80 percent worked for the railroad. The pull of the railroad jobs was so substantial that by the start of the Great Depression this ethnic group was the second largest non-native populace in Kansas, trailing only Germans.[14]

While such workers certainly earned more than they would have in their home country, conditions were difficult in the Midwest, in this way little different from other parts of the nation. First, many were assigned to work for section crews and track gangs, the lowest paid labor, averaging around $1.25 per day in the first decade of the 1900s; by the 1920s this figure was up to around $2.20. This pattern existed for substantial numbers of Mexicans in Kansas during the early decades of the 1900s, but research for a project called *Generations United* in the early 1990s has indicated that the laborers in Topeka's communities tended to concentrate in still low-paying, but more stable, jobs such as "the shops and yards and not on track sections and extra gangs. This led them to settle permanently in the capital city.... [Most of these] laborers were broken down into section hands, helpers, painters and water carriers."[15] Next, there was little opportunity for promotion. This too was the case in Torrez's family as both grandfathers remained as helpers for 30+ years. As historian Richard

Santillan has noted, such longevity, with very limited increases in pay and status, was not at all unusual for Mexican railroad workers during the first decades of the twentieth century.[16] Mike's father, Juan Torrez, was the first member of the clan to earn elevation beyond this status, moving up to carman (working on upholstery) after more than 20 years of service.

Such diligence did not generate great accolades for the Spanish-speaking in Kansas, but garnered some grudging (and again, condescending-sounding) respect. As one Santa Fe engineer noted, the "Mexican cannot be driven like the Negro, but anyone who knows how to manage the Mexicans can get more work out of them than any other class."[17] In summary, in regard to their work on the railroads, Mexicans had carved an important, if not well-paying or highly respected, niche in the state of Kansas. This argument even reached the highest levels of state government when one letter writer in 1929 expanded upon some of Van Dyke's themes to the governor by stating:

> I wish to get in a good word for the Mexicans. They are much less trouble than other aliens, and there are not many of them. They do the hard track work, which American citizens do not seem to care for, probably because the employment is not steady; even in the summer time they seldom find work six days in the week, and in the winter time many weeks pass without even one day's work. The Mexicans are mostly employed on seasonal labor, where they are needed [in areas] such as [the] back-breaking work in the sugar beet fields.[18]

If circumstances were rough before the start of the downturn, they became even more arduous during the 1930s. Whereas *trabajadores* (workers) and their families were grudgingly tolerated during good economic times, there were direct calls for expulsion during the Great Depression. The slowdown caused railroads to reduce expansion, directly impacting the section gangs. Researchers who have examined this topic indicate that in addition to not finding work, those who were not American citizens were not eligible for relief, and even the native-born of this descent endured chastisement and criticism for participating in work programs. In addition, there were calls from labor organizations to expel "Mexicans" from Kansas because they were competition for scarce employment, and their lower living standards were a danger to "real" Americans. As E. L. Jenkins of the Topeka Federation of Labor argued, his organization commended the governor's call for the railroads to expel the group, as it was their "belief that the Mexican immigrant has been one of the major contributing causes of our present condition of unemployment." Similar circumstances were repeated in other parts of the state.[19] Even with such discriminatory practices, one of Santillan's sources noted that Mexicans and Mexican Americans did participate in programs like the WPA and helped construct many facilities in and around Kansas' capital city:

> As I drive around Topeka today, I see many buildings we helped build during the Depression including libraries, hospitals, housing for senior citizens, and schools. After the war, we were denied entrance to certain buildings that we built during the Depression as a result of racism. Also, we constructed bridges, dams and canals. The contributions of Mexicans in the development of Topeka is (sic) everywhere.[20]

Still, there were examples of positive experiences for Mexicans and Mexican Americans during the years of the Depression in Kansas. For example, as one researcher has noted, some families did manage to purchase homes due to depressed housing prices, as well as developing contacts outside of their neighborhoods through participation in government programs and becoming "increasingly a part of the state's society. As more contact took place, some Anglos began to change their views ... [and this] would be a factor that contributed to the post World War II integration process."[21] As will be noted later, participation in sports was another apparatus used to increase connections with Anglos as well as with other Spanish-speakers elsewhere in Kansas and the Midwest.

The work of the late University of Kansas historian Robert Oppenheimer sheds more light on working conditions and educational issues confronting Mexicans in the state before 1950. In addition to the railroads, the area of agriculture provided steady, if not well-remunerated, employment prior to the start of the Great Depression. As was the case for the Torrez clan, it was a family affair to make ends meet. "In some cases wives and children of railroad workers supplemented the family income.... Workers labored daily from dawn to dusk for wages of two to nine dollars per acre for a season's work. In the decade 1931 to 1940 wages for sugar beet laborers in Kansas were the lowest among the fifteen major sugar-beet producing states."[22] Railroads also often hired young boys to work as translators and to bring water to the gangs. Oppenheimer noted that, while Mexican and Mexican American laborers for lines such as the Santa Fe were paid the same wages as whites, the number of hours the Spanish-surnamed employees worked per pay period was approximately 20 percent less. Thus, during the 1930s, "as the Depression worsened..., Mexicans ... clearly received less than their Anglo counterparts."[23]

The necessity for children to help support the economic wherewithal of families made it quite difficult, if not impossible, to complete the course of study required for a state-issued diploma or certificate. Again, Oppenheimer is instructive. For example, he noted that the first Spanish-surnamed person to graduate high school from a Topeka-area public or Catholic institution was in the later part of the 1920s. In Garden City, the first Latino male did not complete such studies until 1950. In various parts of the state, children from barrios were segregated into classrooms supposedly designed to make them fluent in English, though teachers almost never had the necessary pedagogical training or even spoke Spanish in order to communicate effectively with their charges or parents. In Topeka, this pattern was exemplified by the establishment of the Branner Annex School, located in "little Mexico." The facility was described as "four portable rooms and two old brick toilet buildings." The Spanish-surnamed children were supposed to attend this institution for the first three grades, with the intention of their "gaining sufficient mastery of English to proceed in the regular rooms at Branner or Lincoln [this is the school that Torrez and his siblings attended] Schools." As a result, parents from the neighborhood presented several petitions concerning the segregation of their children, and the separate school was finally closed in 1942.[24] Ultimately, members of the community actually sued the area's school district in an effort to force the local high school to enroll their offspring. Such activities created a backlash from various sources. As Santillan noted, the Ku Klux Klan, in some cases, "threatened to harm Mexican children who attended white schools ... [the barrio community] wrote directly to federal officials ... and the Kansas Governor for protection, but never received a reply from either office."[25]

In general, more females graduated because of "the tendency for males to leave school to find work ... [and because] families allowed young women to work only in the fields or as domestics." This pattern had a dramatic impact upon the possibility of improving economic circumstances, particularly since certain jobs for the railroads, such as apprenticeships for skilled positions or foreman posts, required at least an eighth-grade education.[26] In regard to scholastic athletics, not surprisingly, the financial necessities of individual families made participation in such endeavors quite rare, though not impossible. As a result, and as will be detailed in the next chapter, most Mexicans/Mexican Americans in Topeka and other parts of the Midwest who enjoyed and sought out competitive sports before the end of World War II tended to satisfy their quest for competition within an extensive structure of community or church-based/sponsored events.

While conditions in the schools and in the world of work were less than ideal, this did not mean that the "little Mexico" and Oakland sections of Topeka were completely destitute and devoid of homegrown organizations and a vibrant Mexican culture. Indeed, the "deprived" areas of the

Kansas capital (and other colonies of the state) were home to a variety of associations, businesses, and churches that sought to improve conditions for their people, worked to better relations with whites, and helped preserve key elements of ethnic traditions. In other words, the Spanish-speakers of the region were not victims, but worked diligently to better prospects for themselves, their children and barrios. While not referring specifically to Topeka in the following passage, Santillan's extensive research in the region provides an effective summary of the situation extant in many colonies when he states:

> Mexican communities were cloistered near the industries of their employment, and the people found living conditions socially unbearable. People still [in the 1980s, when Santillan conducted these interviews] vividly recount the social hardships of sub-standard and overcrowded housing, including the lack of hot running water, the discomforts of outdoor bathrooms, near the city dumps, the inadequate housing space to accommodate their large families, unpaved and unlighted streets and sidewalks, and the frigid cold during the winter months.[27]

There existed a substantial variety of organizations in the barrios of Topeka, in Kansas, and elsewhere in the Midwest, with some catering to the needs of the working class and others to the more elite. This brief section is presented to provide an overview of the vitality of these entities, even against difficult odds, and to support the argument that the Mexicans/Mexican Americans of the region were not passive bystanders in the face of discrimination and other such issues; indeed, they aggressively sought mechanisms to improve daily life in their communities and to better relations with the broader society.

In nearby Kansas City, for illustration, an organization known as El Casino Mexicano consisted mostly of foreign-born medical and legal professionals and had a membership list of approximately 100 individuals by the early 1920s.[28] Among the inhabitants of this pocket of concentration were two U.S.-educated brothers, Manuel and Juan Urbina, who published a newspaper known as *El Cosmopolita* starting in 1914. When the siblings failed to make the paper profitable, they sold out to a Mexicano, who then transferred operations to a Spanish-speaking Anglo, Jack Danciger.[29] Although under different owners, a perusal of the tabloid's five-year run provides readers an in-depth examination of the scope of Mexican life in the Missouri/Kansas border region. There were several key themes present within *El Cosmopolita*'s pages, no matter who operated the enterprise. Importantly, the paper's management always sought to challenge negative perceptions of Mexicanos.

A 1913 report by the city's Board of Public Welfare painted barrio life in very broad and bleak strokes, arguing that "their standard of living is so much lower than ours, the landlord ... [lowers] the standard housing to that which they are accustomed.... Needless to say, everything is filthy."[30] While acknowledging poor conditions and criminal activity among some of the Spanish-surnamed, the newspaper most often highlighted positive elements such as the establishment of community centers, activities of religious/beneficent groups and the local Mexican consulate, and events surrounding national holidays such as the *Fiestas Patrias* (Mexican independence day, September 16). The paper served as an active voice against police harassment as well. The pages also document the existence of an extensive number of businesses owned and operated by persons of Mexican background in and around Kansas City. The management included a weekly section devoted to art, history, literature and sports, while constantly stressing the necessity for improving overall educational levels.[31]

Other organizations extant in the Midwest during this era included *La Comision Honorifica Mexicana* (the Mexican Honorific Commission), which was tied to the network of Mexican consular offices throughout the United States, and included a branch in Topeka.[32] Finally, a number of youth-based associations designed to sustain Mexican culture and traditions existed. Among the key elements of such entities were varied offerings in sports. The *Diamante* (Diamond) Club in Topeka (there was a branch in Wichita), for example, began in 1920 and provided lectures and discussions on national literature and history, sponsored dances, and fielded competitive teams in baseball, football and boxing. In his research, Santillan argued that part of the reason for creating such operations was because of a lack of access to local parks and recreational centers. Indeed, it was not until after World War II that, in general, such barriers were broken down.[33]

The religious component was also significant to the daily life of the "little Mexico" and Oakland not merely for spiritual reasons, but for fraternal and cultural purposes as well. While not all members of the community were (at least nominally) Catholic, it is reasonable to begin this discussion with that denomination, given its prevalence among individuals of Mexican (and other Spanish-speaking) backgrounds. Santillan's research has documented the existence of many Catholic institutions serving Mexicanos throughout Kansas in the early decades of the twentieth century. For example, services for such congregations occurred on a fairly regular basis in places such as Newton, Emporia, Kansas City, Wichita and Deerfield by the later part of the 1920s. A substantial number of the parishes/missions were named in honor of the patron of Mexico, Our

Lady of Guadalupe, as was the one that took shape in the corner of Crane and Branner Streets, near the Santa Fe shops in Topeka.[34]

The genesis of what is acknowledged as a key building block of Mexican life in Kansas' capital city occurred in 1914, when an area resident, Pedro Lopez, encountered a clergyman, Father Epifanio Ocampo, at the nearby train station. Lopez informed Ocampo of the existence of a Spanish-speaking concentration in the vicinity and the urgent need for masses and other religious services to support the spiritual needs of approximately 20 families. The two men contacted pastors at nearby Assumption and St. Joseph parishes about assistance, and the first tentative steps toward establishing a congregation took place. Through donations generated by providing baptisms and praying rosaries with Mexicanos along the Santa Fe route, Ocampo raised funds to rent a storefront at the intersection noted previously. Here, the flock struggled to sustain its house of worship over the next few years, until the construction of a more permanent structure in 1921, built to house both the church and a school. A parish house and a recreation hall were added by the late 1920s. Much of the labor for the buildings was contributed directly by congregants. In addition to tangible facilities, Our Lady of Guadalupe housed religious organizations such as the St. Vincent de Paul Society, Apostleship of Prayer, and the Knights of Columbus. By the late 1930s, the congregation had expanded from the original 20 families to nearly 300, with a total of 1,500 people accounted for on the church's rolls. Approximately 275 children attended the institution's school.

From this humble chapel emanated some of the earliest attempts to introduce the rich Mexican culture to the broader community. Among the undertakings used to share ethnic traditions with fellow Topekans were the *Fiesta Mexicana*, started in 1932, and the Christmas tradition of *Las Posadas*, first held in 1936. The Fiesta ultimately became not only a mechanism for displaying cultural pride, but also a substantial moneymaker. By the 1940s this enterprise was the principal fundraiser for the parish and helped pay for the construction of a new building, completed in 1948. The Fiesta Mexicana has now become a city-wide event that includes a golf tournament, a downtown parade, and other happenings.[35] One individual who has played a significant role in the Fiesta's history is Louis Torrez, Mike's uncle.[36] Also, the Guadalupe School, in addition to providing a well-rounded Catholic education to many youths in Oakland, housed various sports teams that permitted Mexican youths an opportunity to test their mettle against, and interact with, athletes from other sections of the city and region.

Other religious denominations reached out to assist and proselytize the Mexican population in the barrios of Topeka. As noted in the Van Dyke article from 1928 referred to earlier, some Protestants perceived the newly arrived Spanish speakers as potential converts. Sources indicate that entities such as the Redden Chapel and the Third Presbyterian Church were active among this population from the days of the earliest arrivals into "little Mexico." The most substantial undertaking (and best documented), however, was by Baptists, through the efforts of various pastors at a mission started in 1924 that eventually became the Mexican Baptist Church. This entity existed at least through the 1970s.[37]

By the late 1930s, the Mexican/Mexican American community of Topeka and other parts of Kansas housed a not insubstantial number of organizations, secular and religious, designed to help mitigate difficulties confronted by many in daily life. While certainly not eliminating all vestiges of discrimination, racism and poverty, the entities extant in barrios and colonies attested to the vitality, drive and cultural pride of this population. The coming of World War II, however, presented new prospects to solidify and expand the push for equal rights, opportunities and greater participation in all aspects of American society.

For many years, historians maintained that the war did indeed break down significant barriers to improved circumstances for the Spanish-surnamed. As Dionicio Valdez argued in his book, *Barrios Nortenos* (about Mexican life in the Midwest, primarily in the St. Paul area), the Spanish-surnamed managed to get hired into "more permanent and higher paying jobs in meatpacking, steel mills, defense plants, railroads, textile shops … [and became] an increasingly permanent segment of the region's industrial proletariat."[38] Similar positive outcomes can be seen in the military, the employment of women, and other aspects of life. More recently, however, the tone in the literature has been more tempered.[39]

Research conducted on this topic in Kansas provides examples of both improvements and limitations of the war (and the early post-conflict) years to Mexican life in locales such as Oakland. One of the earliest works documenting the impact of the conflict upon Mexicanos in the state is a dissertation by Hector Franco for the Department of Religious Education at the University of Wichita (now Wichita State University) in 1950. Franco's assertions, while overly positive in light of recent research, paints a buoyant picture of the war's effect upon the Spanish-speakers (both soldiers and in industry) of the Sunflower State. For example, he articulates how the military provided such youths with specialized training that improved employment opportunities. Further, Franco argued that participation in the war had a beneficial psychological impact and increased the barrio dwellers' connection to the United States (thereby lessening ties to "the old country"). Finally, the Latinos' noble service and heroism on the battlefield challenged, and often changed favorably, how whites perceived the Spanish-surnamed. Two examples provided are noteworthy. First, the author quoted a recently discharged soldier who stated, "In the army I get a break, in Wellington I am just a Mex." In other words, while in the military he was judged strictly "as a man and a fighter." Next, Franco generalized (over-generalized) this trend and believed it would improve life for Spanish-speakers throughout the state:

> We recognize that some of the changes the Mexican people in Kansas are undergoing are part of the transition taking place in the nation, as it becomes conscious of racial minorities and is trying to deal fairly with them now ... through the FEPC [Fair Employment Practices Committee] which may soon become a permanent factor in the nation. We also sense an awakening to the stupidity of race prejudice which we see receding.[40]

As further proof of the changes that took place, Franco also hinted at the power of sport to change perceptions of Mexicanos as well. For example, he indicated that in Garden City (after the war) it became acceptable for youths of this background to swim in the local municipal pool and that this "would have been unthinkable before the war." For the folks in Wichita, he cited how a local (graduate of Wichita North High School) made his community proud by being named all-state in football, representing Kansas at an all-star game in Texas, and, most significantly, is "now one of the football luminaries at Wichita University." If a Mexican/Mexican American could help "us" win on the gridiron, should he not be considered a "real American"? If "they" contributed to the war effort, perhaps it was acceptable to allow them in city pools and parks?[41]

Other sources documented changes in how Mexicanos were perceived in the city of Topeka. In a collection housed at the archive of Indiana University Northwest, historian Richard Santillan has gathered an extensive array of newspapers, pamphlets and other materials collected during field work in the region. Among the materials are articles from local tabloids that demonstrate the "progress" and "contributions" of this community to the war. For example, there are several stories that trace the activities of Oakland residents serving in various military theaters. One citation, dated December 6, 1942, made note of the patriotism of the Barrientos family of 230 North Branner (near the Our Lady of Guadalupe Parish) which had three sons serving in the military. Particularly, the essay mentioned that one of these brave lads (the oldest son, Manuel) was an area celebrity who had served "as master of ceremonies of the Mexican fiesta." Another (the youngest, Joseph) served his homeland in the Army Air Corps, after he lettered in football at Topeka High. Finally, the father, Jake, was a member of the city's police force.[42] Another family that more than contributed was the Rangels clan, which had six sons serve in World War II and Korea, two of them making the ultimate sacrifice within a one-week period in the Philippines.[43] Other narratives documented the activities of local young women (through a group affiliated with the YWCA called the *Y Señoritas*) who did their part as well, performing tasks such as entertaining troops, producing items to support the YWCA's Emergency War Fund, and sponsoring first aid training.[44]

While what has been noted so far has been positive, there are certainly items that impart a bleaker picture of race relations during the war (and after) in Kansas. For example, right next to exposés on the heroism and contributions of barrio members was a letter to the editor by Mrs. McDade, a local activist, entitled "Justice and Fair Play." This commentary, from April 1943, indicated that, at least in Topeka, persons of Mexican descent were not yet granted the opportunity to sit where they pleased in local theaters or swim in city pools. Indeed, McDade argued, it was an even worse situation for Spanish-speakers because "the Negroes have one [park] of their own but the Mexicans have none." The most dramatic part of her critique was when she recounted how a Spanish-surnamed wife and mother, who had recently passed away, implored her husband as a final request to have his "parents move into our lovely home, and take care of our baby. You enlist in the United States Army, [as] our country needs your help, to restore peace to our nations (sic)."[45] If this sacrifice and attitude did not merit "fair play" from the majority, what would? It is fair to say that by the end of the conflict, the Spanish-speakers of Kansas felt that "they had earned the right to be treated as first-class citizens, since they had fought and worked side-by-side with the Anglos on the battlefield and in the defense plants."[46] Confidently, one of Santillan's subjects summarized such sentiments when he stated that as a result of being tested in battle and in the factories, Mexicans and Mexican Americans "were no longer afraid like our parents to confront local officials regarding these terrible problems. Our battle for elimination [of] social discrimination was less when compared to the horrors of war we had recently experienced overseas."[47]

Though circumstances had improved, there were still illustrations of grave injustice. Examples documented in research from southeast Kansas in the early post-war years included Catholic congregations that did not permit individuals of Mexican descent to attend services, insisting that those worshippers go instead to an "ethnic" facility. In Chanute, a Mexican American soldier was not permitted to sit next to his Anglo wife at a local movie theater. Spanish-surnamed veterans were refused haircuts in Emporia as late as 1949. In McClure, near Wichita, residents of an apartment building circulated a petition to keep a *familia* from renting in the facility. Finally, and appallingly, the Veterans of Foreign Wars and the American Legion posts of Newton excluded Mexican American members until the late 1960s. In Wellington, *veteranos* (with the support of many Anglos, who were just as outraged) gained entrance to the organizations much sooner: in 1946.[48]

If many individuals who lived and worked in barrios had been willing to stand up and challenge discriminatory practices before the war, then they were even more disposed to do so after World War II. Through the efforts of organizations such as the American GI Forum (AGIF), the League of United Latin American Citizens (LULAC), and other entities, a more empowered and self-assured Spanish-surnamed population sought redress of grievances for their people in regard to social, economic and educational inequality. In matters of schooling, for example, LULAC and AGIF supported notable lawsuits which challenged inequitable procedures resulting in rulings such as *Mendez v. Westminster School District* (Orange County, California) and *Delgado v. Bastrop Independent School District* (Bastrop County, Texas) in the late 1940s. Both cases made it possible to improve educational opportunities for children of Spanish-speaking descent.[49]

Enhanced prospects in the schoolhouse not only portended better economic and social circumstances in those aspects of Latino life, but also had nearer-term effects on scholastic athletics. As more and more barrio youths managed to stay in school, an increased number began taking their talents to the fields, courts, and diamonds to represent local institutions. As this trend escalated, just as had happened with interethnic cooperation in the military during World War II, barriers to inclusion fell.[50] As one Santillan interviewee noted,

> Many doors opened after the war in sports. Mexican youths were very visible in all aspects of school and community sports whereas few Mexican Americans youths played school sports or community [sports] prior to the 1940s. The young men and women of our community now had an opportunity to excel in many sports.[51]

In addition to increased participation in scholastic athletics, there already existed a substantial "Mexican" tradition of sports participation and competition in the Midwest (and elsewhere in the nation). Among the offerings for such undertakings were baseball, softball and basketball *ligas* (leagues) and *torneos* (tournaments), which provided opportunities to demonstrate Mexican culture and individual talents before other Spanish-speakers as well as the broader society. As one community member noted in an interview, "It was an entire community affair which took on political and social importance. Sports acted as a vehicle for us to plan how to confront the discrimination facing all of us."[52] This topic has not been thoroughly covered by historians until recently. Mike Torrez, born right after the end of the war, was in a position to take advantage of both sets of athletic activities, cultivated his talents, and began the developmental process that would eventually lead him to the heights of professional sport as a member of the Major Leagues and on its grandest stages—Yankee Stadium and Fenway Park.

2

"*Winning a Place on the Varsity Has No Attraction for Them*"
Mexican Americans, Sports and Community in Kansas and Other Parts of the Midwest, 1920–1965

In October of 1967, right after Mike Torrez had his first "cup of coffee" with the St. Louis Cardinals in the Major Leagues, the young right-hander was given an opportunity to play winter ball in the Dominican Republic. Before then, however, he returned home for a brief respite to spend time with family and friends in the Oakland neighborhood. A local sports writer from the *Topeka Capital Journal* caught up with Torrez and discussed the upcoming trip to the Caribbean, as well as his chances for making the Cardinals' rotation in the upcoming spring. As part of the discussion, Torrez was asked about what he would miss most while away from the heartland toiling for the Licey squad. Torrez responded that he would regret not being able to hunt and play "some basketball. I should be able to get back by January and I hope to play some then—maybe some city league and some Mexican tournaments."[1] It is noteworthy that, even as he neared reaching "the show," sporting events in his home region, and with co-ethnics, remained of vital importance. While not widely known, an examination of the history of the Spanish-speaking colonies in Kansas and other parts of the Midwest reveal the existence of an extensive Mexican American, community-based athletics program. The presence of such leagues and tournaments helped hone Torrez's physical gifts and provided him (and others in his family as well) with a level of celebrity among "his" people. In addition, such undertakings granted the broader, Spanish-surnamed populace opportunities for camaraderie, relaxation, and networking. This chapter will discuss the story of such programs, as well as proffer a sense of how Latinos/Mexican American athletes used their talents on and off the diamonds, gridirons and courts to challenge certain negative assumptions about their athletic and organizational abilities.

While most baseball fans (especially) are familiar with the current-day exploits of Spanish-surnamed athletes at the different levels of the national pastime, any account of both the extended chronology and broad diffusion of Latinos'/Mexican Americans' participation in baseball and other sporting activities (at all echelons) in the United States still comes as a bit of a surprise to the majority population. As will be noted, there is substantial historical evidence that counters this assertion, both in Kansas and in other sections of the nation. The following two points are presented to highlight how "unusual" many in the broader society would have considered the likelihood of individuals of such backgrounds participating in athletics—contrary to historical reality.

First, it is of value to flesh out the entire quote from which part of this chapter's title is drawn. The author, Professor Elmer D. Mitchell, was one of the leading scholars on physical education and intramural sports during the early decades of the twentieth century. In 1922 a series of essays titled "Racial Traits in Athletics" appeared in a leading academic journal, wherein Mitchell expounded upon the positive and negative physical capabilities of numerous groups. Not surprisingly, the articles were presented with the subjects in descending order, therefore the "highest" troupes then represented in American sport were discussed first. The individuals of backgrounds worthy of placement in the upper stratum were the American, English, Irish and German "races." This tier was the most vigorous, competent and powerful, and consistently led American squads to victory in competitive events on national and international stages.[2] It is necessary to skip down to the final paper in the series to find the lowly "South American," which, it seems, included the Mexican and those of similar background born north of the Rio Grande. As Mitchell saw it, this group faced an abundance of obstacles in order to compete in vigorous pursuits:

> The South American has not the physique, environment, or disposition which makes for a champion athlete. In build he is of medium height and weight, and not rugged.... [He] has inherited an undisciplined nature. The Indian in him chafes at discipline and sustained effort, while the Spanish half is proud to a fault.... [His] disposition makes team play difficult ... the steady grind and the competition involved in winning a place on the Varsity has no attraction for them.[3]

Therefore, in the informed opinion/research of an august scholar, basketball coach (at what is now Eastern Michigan University) and administrator (at the University of Michigan), Spanish-speakers in general, and those in the United States, had little, if any, compunction or aptitude to participate in sports. Surely seeking out evidence of a role for athletics in the lives of such weak-willed and non-competitive people would be fruitless endeavor, correct?

Second, approximately 20 years after Professor Mitchell's enlightened contributions, a similar-themed, though much more dangerous, instance of the inability of some whites to recognize the role of athletics in Mexican American/Latino life took place outside a high school gymnasium in Texas. In the early 1940s, the community of San Marcos (located between San Antonio and Austin) was set to host a regional basketball tournament, and the Lanier High School squad from San Antonio had qualified for the event. The team and its coach, Nemo Herrera, hailing from the mostly Spanish-speaking West Side, had quite a reputation throughout the state for achieving excellent results on the court. Unfortunately, this information had not reached into every nook and cranny of Texas. As described in the work *When Mexicans Could Play Ball: Basketball, Race and Identity in San Antonio, 1928–1945*, historian Ignacio M. Garcia recounts how Coach Herrera and others were confronted by a shotgun-toting bigot who asked why some "goddam Mexicans" were trying to enter the facility. When the adults informed the irate citizen that this was one of the teams invited to play in the competition, the "gentleman" insisted that there had to be another (most likely nefarious) reason, as it was common knowledge that "Mexicans don't play basketball." After a bit more discussion, and the intercession of a local school official, Herrera and his associates were permitted entry into the facility.[4] These are but two illustrations of the receptions that many Spanish-surnamed, particularly Mexican Americans, confronted when attempting to participate in competitive athletics, principally of the scholastic variety. Other writers have noted many more such occurrences.[5]

It is also important to point out, however, that if whites paid attention, there were ample instances which demonstrated both the desire and ability of Mexicans and Mexican Americans to compete in athletics in the United States, sometimes right alongside, or before large numbers of, the majority population. The athletic contests covered a variety of sports, including football, baseball, basketball and boxing. Below are a few examples from newspaper and other contemporary accounts from the first decades of the 1900s through the 1960s.

The game of American football was not unknown in Mexico by the later part of the nineteenth century, though it was not particularly popular. One of the earliest examples of a U.S.-based newspaper noting the existence of the game south of the border comes from the *Dallas Morning News* which, in late 1896, noted that a tour guide from the Lone Star State was to bring two football teams to play an exhibition in Mexico City around Christmas. No information as to the results of the contest between some University of Texas students and an all-star team was noted. Shortly thereafter, in January 1897, an article from the *Los Angeles Times* indicated that Missouri State University and Texas State University played another game, which ended in a scoreless tie, before a crowd of mostly American and English spectators; there were some Mexican elites (referred to as "club men") present as well. In this second essay, however, many of the stereotypes that Mitchell would repeat in 1922 were evidenced as "the opinion [is] that the Latin race is too hot-blooded to play the game without losing temper. Football is a great novelty in Mexico ... but it is not likely that it can be acclimated in the country."[6]

Novelty in the "old country" or not, the rise of football in Texas (the first high school game took place in 1892 in the Galveston area) eventually made its way into the sectors of the state where large pockets of Mexican Americans lived. By 1895, the game was played in El Paso, in Laredo by the early 1900s, and in the Rio Grande Valley of southern Texas by 1911.[7] Not surprisingly, given the educational and economic circumstances this population faced in this period, very few Spanish-surnamed athletes played for local elevens. It was only in the later part of the 1920s that a few such individuals participated at this level. Similar stories can be found elsewhere concerning the gridiron history of New Mexico and in the Cuban American concentration of Ybor City (near Tampa) in Florida.[8]

Beginning in the late 1920s, however, the *Dallas Morning News* contained a string of articles that chronicled an on-going series of games between Mexican collegiate and high school teams against U.S. institutions. For instance, in November of 1929, Mississippi College travelled to play against what the article referred to as the "University of Mexico" (most likely, UNAM-Universidad Nacional Autonoma de Mexico) in the national capital. No information as to the result of the contest was found. About one year later, the same Mexican squad came to Alexandria and lost to Louisiana College, 33–0. Many of the contests between the "University of Mexico" and American teams finished with lopsided tallies: St. Mary's University won, 57–0, and Tulsa University triumphed, 89–0, for example. On the high school side of the ledger, Jefferson High School of San Antonio defeated a Mexican secondary school, 41–7, in 1933 and San Antonio Tech defeated Mexico City Tech, 13–0, in 1935.[9] The results of such encounters did little to bolster the perception of the average American as to the athletic capabilities of Mexicans or Mexican Americans in regard to football. In a 1938 essay, William Berlin Goolsby argued matter-of-factly that the game "has a certain hold, but the Mexican is a notoriously bad player as a general rule."[10] This notion was so widespread that a legendary Texas high school coach, Earl Scott (who led the 1961 Donna Redskins to the AA Texas Title—the only team from the Rio Grande Valley ever to claim this honor) was advised not to waste his time taking the Donna post, as "the Valley was 80% Mexican American, and everybody knew Mexican Americans were poor football players."[11]

Although there were individuals in various parts of the country who challenged these assumptions, including a few who reached the collegiate and professional levels (such as Eddie Saenz and Joe Aguirre, both of whom played for the Washington Redskins), there was a fairly widespread assumption that Latinos, and Mexican Americans in particular, were not capable of playing football at high levels. Still, historians have chronicled several examples of competitors whose careers and success impugn such assertions.[12] Among those who contested perceptions of the capabilities of the Spanish-surnamed on the gridiron in the state of Kansas was John Torrez, Mike's older brother. His exploits and their significance will be discussed in Chapter 3.

Given the more extensive history of baseball south of the Rio Grande and in the Caribbean, Berlin-Goolsby was more diplomatic in regard to his assessment of the sport's role in Mexico and did not pass summary judgment on the innate talents of Mexicanos, but simply noted that "beisbol—has its immense following and there are a growing number of clubs and … parks throughout the country."[13] Again, while not presenting an exhaustive listing, there are a few ready examples from throughout the U.S. which demonstrate the impact of baseball on the lives of Mexicans and Mexican Americans.

One of the most important researchers on this topic, José M. Alamillo, has published articles detailing the significance of baseball to these groups in southern California. In one essay, which focuses primarily on the Corona Athletics Baseball Club, he argues that the team's on-field success transcended merely improving the won-loss column; rather, victories were utilized and internalized by the players and the broader cultural group to promote "ethnic consciousness, build community, solidarity, display masculine behavior, and sharpen their organizing and leadership skills."[14] In a later expose, dealing with the transnational nature of sport among many Mexican Americans (in other words, Mexican American teams would visit Mexico and Mexican teams would reciprocate in California and elsewhere, including throughout the Midwest), Alamillo asserts that baseball, and other "American" sports, were tools which Spanish-speakers in the West utilized as mechanisms to "prove" themselves to the broader population and garner a modicum of respect.[15]

Another scholar who has documented the impact and success of Latino ballplayers in the United States before the end of World War II is Alan Klein, in his work, *Baseball on the Border: A Tale of Two Laredos*. Specifically, Klein recounts the story of the 1935 barnstorming season of the La Junta Baseball Club from Nuevo Laredo, a tour that took the squad all the way up to North Dakota to challenge the great Satchel Paige, then pitching for Bismarck.[16] Although the team hailed from Mexico, it contained Cubans and included various dark-skinned athletes. Among the recollections of players interviewed were incidents of racism, such as not being allowed to enter restaurants and having to stay in "colored" sections at various tour stops, primarily in Texas. On the other hand, sources

Mexicans and Mexican Americans faced much discrimination in Topeka between the 1930s and 1950s. Juan Torrez (middle row, second from right) and his teammates rarely competed against white teams, instead playing other Mexican American ball clubs from nearby communities and even teams from Mexico which happened to be touring the Midwest. Courtesy Torrez family.

recounted many incidents where playing baseball, and demonstrating a talent in the American "national" game, helped mitigate racial hostility. The 1935 tour of La Junta provided many whites (one game in Illinois attracted an estimated 10,000 fans) in locales not used to seeing substantial numbers of Latinos (of whatever hue) an opportunity to witness a talented group of competitors who could more than hold their own in strategy and athleticism with local whites. The ability level on this team was such that one member, Chile Gomez, drew the attention of scouts and eventually became the first Mexican/Latino to play for the Philadelphia Phillies.[17]

A final example of the ability to utilize baseball to challenge assertions of lack of athletic skill can be found in an excellent article by Alexander Wolff in *Sports Illustrated* recounting the state title in baseball by the 1949 El Paso Bowie High School Bears. Here, the author recounts the struggles of the players on this fairly new program (Bowie began its baseball team in 1946) under the leadership of Nemo Herrera. If the name is familiar, it should be, as Herrera was the basketball head coach at Lanier High School in San Antonio through the end of World War II. There, he guided his charges to four state title games, winning two. Through 2015, Herrera is the only individual in Texas who has led two different high schools in two different sports to state championships.

Given this track record and the Bears' success throughout the season and playoffs, it is logical to assume that the El Paso newspapers would have sent reporters to Austin to cover the state finals; but no regional scribe made the trip to the Texan capital. The community instead was updated via collect calls from Herrera to a local radio station. Along the way, the Bears faced segregated facilities and ugly crowds who often asked why the players "spoke Spanish" and wondered aloud how "greasers" hoped to compete successfully against whites on the diamond. Even after their victory over Stephen F. Austin High School (from Austin), state officials did not grant the Bears a proper ceremony or presentation of the championship trophy. Instead, some unruly fans pelted Bowie's bus with rocks as the squad left town. The *Austin American-Statesman* almost insinuated that "Mexicans" had stolen the title. As Wolff quoted, "Amigo, the Bowie Bears have come and gone. And they have taken with them the state baseball championship. They took it Wednesday through a weird assortment of hits, errors, jinxes and other sundry items." Even when Mexican Americans played clean and inspired games, many whites chose not to give them the credit deserved.[18] These types of circumstances existed in many parts of our nation in regard to Spanish-surnamed athletes well into the 1950s.

Contrary to the assertion by the bigoted individual from San Marcos noted earlier, Mexicans and Mexican Americans did play basketball, and almost from the sport's genesis. For example, as part of outreach efforts, the YMCA brought the game to various sectors of Latin America, teaching attendees to play at facilities in Mexico City by 1902. By the middle of the 1910s and early 1920s, the Y sponsored several teams in Los Angeles as part of Americanization efforts. As early as 1921, there existed an all-Mexican five called Bohemia (later changed to *El Club Deportivo Los Angeles*) that participated in tournaments against challengers visiting from south of the border. As early as 1932, a lineup from Mexico competed against, and defeated, a side comprised of local law enforcement officers. In the years after the first Los Angeles Olympics, the Mexican government, in conjunction with local associations, established the Mexican Athletic Association of Southern California (MAASC) which worked with city officials and sponsored leagues, secured the use of recreational facilities, and worked to showcase the leadership and athletic skills of Spanish-speaking youths. In 1937, the winning team in the MAASC competition, the Centinelas Athletic Club, played the varsity from Occidental College and was victorious by 14 points. One member of this squad, Joe Placentia, competed in the 1936 Olympics for Mexico and later played in the American Amateur Union.

Concurrently in Texas, barrio-based basketball teams in El Paso played under the auspices of neighborhood entrepreneurs. One of the early participants in such events was future community organizer and labor leader Bert Corona, who recalled that in the early decades of the 1900s, El Paso was "'a hot basketball town' with plenty of opportunities to play outside of local schools." Elsewhere in the Lone Star State, civic, fraternal and civil rights organizations such as the League of United Latin American Citizens (LULAC) fielded teams in locales such as San Antonio and Corpus Christi by the early 1930s. Another hotbed of Mexican/Mexican American basketball was the city of Laredo, where crossing the border to play games and tournaments was a regular occurrence. As previously noted, while there was a great deal of *talento* (talent) on the hardwoods and blacktops throughout Texas before 1950, no other team or program matched the success and notoriety of Nemo Herrera and his Lanier High School Volks. In Arizona, a mostly Mexicano team from Miami won the state title in 1951 and dominated high school hoops for several years. Finally, not to be outdone by their Protestant competition, the Catholic Church, through the auspices of Catholic Youth Organization (the CYO, established in 1930), fielded teams in cities and towns with substantial

Mexican/Mexican American concentrations, including locales in the Midwest such as Chicago.[19] Mike Torrez and his siblings participated for many years at such "Mexican" leagues/tournaments throughout the region. Indeed, involvement in such events got him into trouble with the agency in charge of administering Kansas scholastic athletics, and cost Torrez a part of his senior season for the Topeka High School Trojan basketball team.

Many whites might have expressed surprise at the notion of Mexicans/Mexican Americans competing and succeeding in basketball or football (and even baseball), but the story of the group's participation in pugilism was certainly known broadly by the majority. From as early as the 1920s, boxers of this background had been making a name for themselves in Los Angeles, El Paso, the Rio Grande Valley, and elsewhere. Fighters such as "Mexican" Joe Rivers, Joe Salas (the first Latino to win an Olympic medal while competing for the U.S., with silver in the bantamweight division at the 1924 Games in Paris), Bert Colima, Alberto "Baby" Arizmendi, Art Aragon, Humberto Barrera (who was part of the 1960 Olympic boxing squad, along with Cassius Clay), and others, were successful representatives of Mexicans/Mexican Americans in the professional squared ring from the 1920s through the early 1960s. In addition, Hollywood brought attention to the successes and plight of such boxers with important films such as "The Ring" and "Requiem for a Heavyweight." In an excellent new book, historian Troy Rondinone details the significance of the life and career of one of the earliest Mexican-born, Friday-night fighters to grace American television, Gaspar "Indio" Ortega. At the high school level, El Paso Bowie High School also featured a boxing team during the 1930s that helped keep many of their youths in school and out of trouble with local authorities. Finally, as Alamillo has noted in regard to baseball in southern California, pugilism also provided at least one important leader of the Chicano Movement, the late Rodolfo "Corky" Gonzales (he won Golden Gloves titles in 1946 and 1947), with the opportunity to gain a degree of acceptance from the Denver and Colorado political establishment, which he then channeled into his earliest days of entrepreneurism and political activism.[20]

While providing a sense of accomplishment for the athletes and strengthening ethnic identity, boxing often imparted a reinforcement of negative stereotypes. A 1958 *Sports Illustrated* article by writer Gilbert Rogin provides an effective summary of this trend. The essay, which featured interviews with individuals associated with the management of Los Angeles area arenas, provided a sense of why boxing was so popular with this group of Spanish-speakers. Aileen Eaton, co-manager of the Olympic Auditorium, noted that "there are no Mexican football players and no Mexican baseball players to speak of.... Boxing is their sport here because there is no bullfighting or soccer."[21] One year later, in another backhanded comment (along the same lines as the summary of Bowie High's state title in baseball in 1949), another *Sports Illustrated* writer, James Murray, recounted that Mexicans and Mexican Americans simply could not control themselves after one of "their own," José Covarrubias Becerra, won the bantamweight title. The event, Murray argued, "reduced a crowd of 15,000 largely Mexican spectators to the state of gibbering hysteria." The success of this fighter, while important for a "Mexican," really did not amount to much in the grand scheme of American sport, as the author argued that "being a bantamweight is a little like being a left-handed third baseman. There's just no future in it. But in Mexico ... it is enough to be *el campeon del mundo* (world's champion)."[22]

Given all of the examples in the preceding pages, it should not be unanticipated that by the time Mike Torrez and his siblings were of an age to play competitive sports in the late 1950s, there already existed a substantial, long-standing tradition of "Mexican" athletics, both community and church-based, in Topeka and elsewhere in the region. The chance to play baseball through the CYO was an important avenue not only for developing skills on the diamond, but could also lead to other opportunities. Among these were the prospect of competing against ethnic sides comprised of Irish, Italians, Poles and others. In this way, the "Mexicans" had a vehicle with which to demonstrate individual skills before a wider population, as well as giving talented players a mechanism for eventual entry into American Legion, high school and industrial leagues.[23] A 1950 report for the University of Kansas further documented the direct connection between the Catholic Church and many athletic (and other) programs designed to benefit colonies in locales such as Emporia and Wichita.[24]

It is to a more specific discussion of such offerings that we now turn. Through extant research, it is possible to recount the story of some of the teams, leagues, and tournaments that provided rest, relaxation, competition, and community building opportunities for Mexican Americans. Such endeavors, many of which date back to before 1920, and the expanded opportunity to remain in school and participate in scholastic athletics in the post–World War II era (and the move into "mainstream" community programs, such as Little League baseball), afforded Mike Torrez with a fertile training ground to develop his abilities and made it possible for him to come to the attention of Major League scouts (also known as "bird-dogs") by the early 1960s, even though, for reasons that will be covered in Chapter 3, Torrez never got the chance to play baseball for Topeka Senior High School.

Santillan's examination of newspaper and other records, plus a substantial collection of oral history interviews, documents the existence of "Mexican" baseball teams in the Midwest as early as 1916. By 1919, there were also squads playing in cities such as East Chicago, Gary, and Kansas City. The games and tangential events were not small affairs but rather, in some cases, attracted 1000 *fanaticos* (fans) or more to watch teams compete and socialize. These clubs had affiliations with numerous companies, Catholic and other churches, and civic organizations. One of the most consistent issues faced during the first decades of the twentieth century was in finding a place to stage contests. As one interviewee from Newton, Kansas, noted, "most public parks in the Midwest did not permit Mexicans to play organized sports. When we were allowed in the parks, we were given the worst diamonds and undesirable times to play." Such circumstances called for efforts on the part of the men and women of the communities to find a locale in which to stage the event, clear the field of rocks and debris, and then provide the basic implements of the game, such as bases. Santillan found that players and spouses often "made their own ball fields ... in vacant lots or in pastures near the railroad tracks, roundhouses, or steel factories." Attendees recalled occasions where the diamond's bags consisted of dried cow dung patties or sewed-together, worn-out pillow cases.

Even with less-than-ideal conditions, games were important touchstones wherever and whenever they took place. The oft-repeated pattern on Sundays was "residents first went to church and then to breakfast before heading to the game. The players ... ran home after church, changing quickly into their uniforms before the fans arrived.... The baseball games started at around one in the afternoon. The people wore their Sunday best to the games." These were not merely athletic competitions, but also fundraising efforts for specific causes as well as networking opportunities. In many cases, teams charged admission to purchase equipment and cover traveling expenses; some clubs even had business agents arrange schedules and accommodations. Overall, the most important aspect of such events was as a way to help individuals who toiled long hours for low pay to "forget about work and problems and just have a good time." In addition to attracting competitors from other parts of the Midwest, the network stretched to states such as Texas and even into Mexico. Santillan's sources recalled that nines from Morelos, Monterrey, Mexico City, and Guanajuato regularly traversed the region seeking competition and camaraderie.[25]

While not all discriminatory practices ceased in the years after World War II, there were improved opportunities for Spanish-speakers in regard to playing the national pastime at the broader community level. Many of Santillan's interviewees stated that by the late 1940s and early 1950s, it became more common for Mexican American squads to play "white" teams on a regular basis and for barrio-based entries to be granted admission into city/community leagues. Additionally, more and more Latino children from the Midwest commenced participating in Little League, Pony, Colt, and American Legion programs. Not surprisingly, Mike Torrez would prove his worth on such squads, and his father became a highly successful and sought-after coach with various Oakland-area teams. A few locales even hired Spanish-surnamed umpires and league officials. As Ramon Pedroza from Newton stated, "we felt this was a step in the right direction." Greater access to "mainstream" city leagues and programs did not mean the extinction of ethnic-specific teams, however, and the post-war era marked the genesis of several important "Mexican" athletic organizations and tournaments that would continue to provide competition and barrio pride throughout the rest of the twentieth century.[26]

Softball proved very popular, particularly as the generation that went off to fight World War II and in the Korean War returned and started families. One of the oldest and most important of these competitions began in Newton in 1948, though the roots go back to the late 1930s. In 1988, as a tribute to the 40th anniversary of the Holy Name Softball Tournament, Paula Jasso-Wedel interviewed some "old timers" in hope of capturing information concerning the event's establishment and significance. Not surprisingly, the impetus was twofold: first, in response to Spanish-surnamed competitors not being granted the right to compete against whites, and second, for a chance to demonstrate athletic abilities before co-ethnics and, hopefully, the broader community. One of Jasso-Wedel's sources recalled that during the late 1930s, "whites and blacks had teams and now the brown boys had formed an 'unbeatable force' called Cuauhtemoc, a name of an Indian tribe in Mexico. They had a strong desire to prove themselves and show they could win."

Over the years of the military conflict, this squad played other Kansas "Mexican" teams. By 1946, sides from Hutchinson and Wichita expressed interest in participating in a more well-defined and structured program, and two years later, in cooperation with pastor at the local Our Lady of Guadalupe Church, the actual tournament began operation. Ultimately the event attracted opponents from other Midwestern states and even from Texas. The parish was the beneficiary of the myriad tamale sales, entry fees, and other fund-raising endeavors, and by 1959 the monies generated proved sufficient to cover the cost of the local congregation's new and enlarged building. Shortly thereafter, by 1963, a softball facility named in honor of the patroness of Mexico and paid for entirely by community-raised endowments became the host site. By the late 1980s there were regularly 20 different clubs competing in the event and, even though it was possible to participate readily in other "mainstream" leagues, the hope was for the program to continue being "all Chicano or as close to all Chicano as possible."[27] Various leagues and tournaments in places such as Topeka, Chanute, and Omaha continued operation well into the later stages of the twentieth century, based on this model. It is interesting to note that one of Santillan's sources argued that it was important for Mexican Americans/Latinos in the Midwest to participate in both types of offerings—in order to both maintain ethnic identity and claim their rightful place in the broader society.

> Prior to the war, the Mexican community established its own sports network of clubs, centers, teams and tournaments. The second and third generations have continued this rich tradition into the 1990s [when Santillan interviewed this source]. There is, however, a significant difference. Unlike before, the second and third generations became directly involved with Little League, Pop Warner, summer sports programs, high school sports, and other mainstream sports activities. We felt that, as taxpayers and citizens, our community and children were entitled to these recreational benefits.[28]

Mike Torrez and his siblings benefitted greatly from such community activities/programs. John, Mike's older brother, for example, continued to ply his trade on the mound and in the field for various squads on this circuit well into the early 2000s.

The basketball court was another site of Mexican/Mexican American athletic endeavors in the Midwest as early as the 1920s. By 1926 a multi-squad Mexican Basketball League operated in Kansas City, and just a few years later, in 1934, Tony Tabares played hoops for Emporia High School. A perusal of newspapers in locales such as Garden City, for example, reveals that Spanish-surnamed athletes were playing for local high schools and junior high schools in various communities in the western regions of Kansas. Similarly, individuals of this background were playing for industrial league teams such as Tri-Motors by the late 1930s. In Topeka, a team made up entirely of Mexican Americans won the city championship in 1939.[29]

The pattern established with baseball and softball is also evident in hoops. Initially, many of these squads were unable to schedule more than just a few games against "white" squads, and tournaments featuring exclusively "Mexican" teams became the norm in the years after World War II. One of the oldest such competitions, which started in the middle of the twentieth century and was still active in the early 2000s, was headquartered in Omaha. While initially an exclusively Nebraskan affair, with teams coming from locales such as Grand Island, North Platte, and Lincoln, by the late 1950s and early 1960s clubs from Illinois, Iowa, Kansas and Missouri attended. One of the most successful teams over the history of the Omaha event is the Topeka 7-Ups, which usually featured, either as player or coach, John Torrez, and often his younger brother Mike (baseball permitting), with a total of three titles to their credit. All told, fives from Topeka had claimed Omaha championships on nine separate occasions as of the early 2000s. A review of this event's history and program advertisements evidences the close ties between area Mexican American entrepreneurs, the local Catholic *parroquia* (parish), veteran's groups, and mutual aid societies. A similar project also commenced in Topeka in 1964. While not in continuous operation like its Nebraskan rival, by the early 1990s the now renamed Mid American International Hispanic Basketball Classic featured 20 teams from across the region. In 1991, a team from Juarez, Mexico, attended and claimed the title from a quintet sponsored by a local, Mexican American-owned law firm. More than 2,000 fans attended the competition.[30]

When Victor Ortiz of Garden City entered the ring against Floyd Mayweather, Jr., on September 17, 2011, to defend his welterweight title, it marked a highlight in the long and distinguished history of Midwestern Mexican American pugilism. While the results were not what fans of the native Kansan had hoped for (he lost in the fourth round via knockout), Ortiz is just the latest in a long line of fighters from the region (indeed, another Garden City native, Brandon Rios, was also recently a titlist—in the bantamweight classification). Richard Santillan's research has noted that Ortiz and Rios are but the latest *campeones* (champions) who have earned acclaim for themselves and their barrios since the early decades of the twentieth century. For example, during the years of the Great Depression, most of the Golden Gloves champs from the Kansas City area were of Mexican descent. In 1941 the team representing Garden City in the same competition featured two Spanish-surnamed youths, Pedro Orozco and Nacho Avila. That same year, Avila was a featured attraction for the broader community, participating in a boxing exhibition during "Old Settlers Days." This positive notoriety came during a time when the most common mention of a "Mexican" in the *Garden City Telegram* dealt with their involvement in criminal activity. By the 1970s, another member of the Avila clan, Ignacio "Buck," proved instrumental in keeping the sport alive for Mexican American youths in the community up through the late 1990s. Among young pugilists who trained at those facilities were Ortiz and Rios. Other Mexican American fighters of note from this region during and after the years of World War II were Ray Herrera and Joe Garcia, both from Iowa, who garnered multiple Golden Gloves titles in the late 1940s.[31]

In summary, Mexican American participation in athletics has been a key and extensive component of daily life in barrios throughout the Midwest since the very early part of the twentieth century. Wherever Spanish-speaking workers and their families settled, and no matter how difficult the jobs they did or the circumstances endured, there was always a sustained effort to establish and provide for recreational activities. While competition was a significant aspect of the undertakings, it was done for much more than mere victory on the fields of athletic endeavor. The social activities which surrounded baseball, basketball, softball and other sporting events were a mechanism to associate with family and friends in faraway locales and as a way to demonstrate physical and organizational acumen. Sports were a ubiquitous manner to celebrate cultural and ethnic traditions. In addition, as the civil rights struggle bore greater fruit in the years after World War II and Korea, the skills developed in community and church-based sporting activities made it possible for an increased number of Mexican American youths to earn opportunities to compete at the scholastic level. Now, the Spanish-surnamed were not merely "others" who did the "difficult work" and lived "across the tracks" in Midwestern communities, rather, they bore proudly the name and colors of community institutions in competition against rivals. By the time that Mike Torrez and his siblings reached their teenage years in the early 1960s, not all barriers to social equality had been eliminated; however, it was possible for both the Oakland neighborhood and the broader Topeka society to take note, and eventually take pride in, the accomplishments of a son and grandson of Mexican-born railroad workers who had come to the Sunflower State seeking greater opportunity for themselves and their families. In Mike Torrez's case, it would lead to the very heights of professional sport and pitching in the confines of some of the most historic ballparks in Major League Baseball.

3

"I'm Just Thankful That God Gave Me a Good Arm"
Childhood, Family Life and Athletics in the Oakland Barrio, 1946–1964

No matter how successful, wealthy, or long-tenured individual Major Leaguers become, it is not surprising to note that most of these men consider their first appearance in a ballpark at the sport's pinnacle to be among the greatest thrills of any career. After long bus trips, limited pay, and quite often less-than-opulent accommodations in small-city stadiums and hotels, it is no doubt awe-inspiring to finally see what day-to-day life is like at "the show." For position players who have done well in the more advanced levels of the minors, first MLB game reminiscences may include the ball with which they got their first hit; for pitchers the memento might be a bit of dirt from a mound, or the ball with which he recorded his first strikeout. Regardless of position played, a common scenario is the "call up" toward the end of a particular campaign. For teams out of contention, the goals are to provide youngsters an opportunity to play and get acquainted with the ambiance and speed of the game at this echelon, as well as for management to consider whether the new crop of athletes can help improve the future fortunes for also-ran squads. For novices fortunate enough to get "the call" to a clubhouse involved in a late-season pennant race, the atmosphere is even more exhilarating than merely playing out the last meaningless games of a late summer's schedule. While not likely to remain with the squad for the post-season play, the rookie is introduced to the camaraderie of the locker room, as well as the pressures surrounding witnessing, and participating in, highly meaningful contests.

The fall of 1967 provided but a preview of Mike Torrez's dream to make it to the majors (if but temporarily at this point). This quest, which started by pitching to his father and siblings in the dusty streets and back alleys of the Oakland barrio, became a reality in September as the Cardinals summoned Torrez from their AAA Tulsa affiliate to share lockers with players of the caliber of Orlando Cepeda, Curt Flood, and Bob Gibson, and others, during St. Louis' drive toward a National League pennant (and eventually, a hard-fought victory over the Boston Red Sox in the World Series). For Torrez, the moment he and his family had waited, prayed, and longed for finally came on September 11, when manager Red Schoendienst asked him to warm up and enter a game against the Pittsburgh Pirates. His task was to get the final out of the contest in the person of the dangerous slugger, Donn Clendenon. Torrez accomplished his mission, striking out Clendenon. Almost two weeks later (on September 22), he earned his first starting assignment against the Braves. As he recalled, "I really didn't have time to get nervous. But it was different at Atlanta. I'm always a little nervous when I start. This was worse, but it was a great feeling just being out there." Bob Hurt, from a Topeka paper, noted that the young Kansan did struggle a bit, loading the bases, but he was saved from calamity by his infielders via a timely double play. Overall, his statistics for the game were respectable: five innings pitched, three hits surrendered, one earned run, one walk, one strike out, and a no-decision (the Cardinals eventually won, 5–4, in 12 innings). Torrez got very little work beyond these two games and finished the 1967 season with a loss and an ERA of 3.00 (having pitched six total innings in three games) and did not earn his first MLB win until early in the 1968 season, against the Chicago Cubs.[1]

This chapter will detail Torrez's first steps toward becoming a Major Leaguer by focusing on the daily life of his family in Oakland, elucidating the clan's ties to athletics, various neighborhood institutions, and also links to the extant Mexican American sports teams and tournaments, and how such undertakings provided opportunities for Torrez to develop his talents prior to signing with the Cardinals just out of high school in the spring of 1964. Another area of focus will be a recounting of some of the discriminatory events/practices family members confronted during these years as part of day-to-day reality in and around Topeka.

The Torrez family came to Kansas seeking refuge from the violence of the Mexican Revolution as well as an opportunity to earn a better living. In many ways, their story is representative of many tens of thousands of their fellow countrymen in the first decades of the twentieth century.[2] Mariano Torrez (Mike's paternal grandfather) was born in Leon, Guanajuato, on July 26, 1890, and crossed into the U.S. via Laredo, Texas, on March

3, 1911. There he was recruited by an *enganchista* (labor recruiter) and eventually moved to Pauline to work, initially as a railroad laborer. By the time he arrived in the Sunflower State, Mariano was already married to Refugio Valdivia (born August 23, 1891). The pair would have ten children (five boys and five girls), and one of them, Juan P. Torrez (Mike's father, who was born June 26, 1911), arrived just months after his father's trek across the Rio Grande. Mariano spent several years living in Kansas, supporting his family and returning to Mexico whenever possible. According to Juan's younger brother Louis (the lone surviving sibling, and a wonderful source of family lore over a series of interviews), sometime in 1917 Mariano's supervisor at the Santa Fe, impressed with his work ethic, advised the young Mexicano to bring his spouse and children north. The family lived in Pauline until around 1926 or 1927, then moved to an area just outside of the Oakland neighborhood, taking up residence at 118 North East Chandler. Louis recalls that Juan actually went quite far (by the standards of the day for a Mexican American youth from a working-class family) in regard to educational attainment, and attended school until around age 16. However, it appears that by the mid 1920s, he was no longer particularly interested in academic pursuits, and Mariano proffered his son a simple choice between school and work. As a result of this bit of encouragement, Juan lied about his age and was hired by the Santa Fe.[3]

The early life story of Mary, Mike's mother, and her family is comparable. Her father, Calixto Martinez, hailed from San Julian de Logos, Jalisco, and was born on October 13, 1892. He married Concepcion Marquez, who was born August 9, 1894, on October 9, 1910. The couple had 11 offspring (five boys and six girls), with the majority of the Martinez children being American citizens, though Mary was born in Mexico on May 25, 1921. The family crossed into the U.S. in April of 1922. Not surprisingly, both of Mike's grandfathers worked for the Santa Fe Railroad. In a pattern that would predominate in Oakland, Calixto, for example, toiled as a laborer for 36 years. Initially, the Martinezes lived on 235 Klein Street, which was a couple of blocks from the Torrezes' domicile.[4]

During childhood, Mary did as most of her siblings did, working the fields when the family travelled (picking potatoes in North Dakota, for example), cleaning houses for more well-to-do Topeka residents, and having little opportunity to attend school. In a 2012 interview, Mrs. Torrez noted that she did manage to go to school in Kansas for roughly three years, but had difficulty learning English and how to read. Another element that limited Mary's schooling was that, being the second oldest daughter (and fourth child overall), and since older sister Panfila had already married, by age 14 Mary took on the responsibility of producing the family's daily tally of tortillas, starting at 5:00 each morning. Until she completed that task, her parents would not permit Mary to leave for school. Ultimately it was determined simply to keep the young woman home and end all efforts regarding her formal education.[5]

Calixto and Concepcion were quite traditional and strict, and worked diligently to ensure that Mary did not become too "Americanized" (particularly in regard to dating practices) as she entered her later teenage years. Such efforts, however, did not prevent Mary and Juan from meeting. The initial connections between the Martinez and Torrez families started as a result of Louis' interactions with his future sister-in-law and other

Mary Torrez (standing in back) is pictured here with her parents, Calixto and Concepcion Martinez, and cousin Concepcion. As a child, Mary worked the fields and cleaned the homes of wealthy families in addition to helping at home (primarily, making the family's daily quota of tortillas). Courtesy Torrez family.

young people in the barrio. Juan's younger sibling was very jovial and out-
going, and when traversing the neighborhood often engaged in friendly
chats with Mary. As the Fiesta at Our Lady of Guadalupe Church became
a regular affair in the middle of the 1930s, they saw each other at the fair
and sometimes at Mass. Louis often asked Maria to join him and some of
his sisters to attend the movie theater or to go dancing, but Calixto never
acquiesced. As a result of Louis' interactions with Mary, and probably
with some coaxing about there being a pretty young lady only a couple of
blocks over, Juan soon started visiting the area nearby 235 Klein. He was
quickly smitten. Mary recalled that her future spouse complimented both
her attire and physical beauty, and eventually left notes declaring an interest in becoming better acquainted. Given her difficulty with reading, Louis

Mary and Juan Torrez had eight children, of whom Mike was the fifth. They
are pictured here with Ernestine, Evelyn, Johnny, Mickey, Mike (seated on
far left), Stella, and Richard. Yolanda not pictured. Courtesy Torrez family.

usually read his older brother's messages on her behalf. Not surprisingly, Calixto rebuffed Juan's request to court formally, and the pair was not permitted any interactions.[6]

There matters stood until one morning in April of 1938. As usual, Mary awoke early to begin making the quota of tortillas. That day, however, through the intercession of a friend, the couple met clandestinely and took off to nearby Kansas City, where they wed on April 28, never having been on an actual date. Juan and Mary returned to Topeka and ultimately consecrated their marriage at their local Catholic parish. The Torrezes had eight children: three boys (John, Mike and Richard) and five girls (Ernestine, Evelyn, Mickey, Stella and Yolanda), with Mike being their fifth. The family lived at 208 North Lake Street in the Oakland area, at first renting, but ultimately purchasing their domicile, in part because Juan received a settlement from the Santa Fe when he lost an eye as a result of an industrial accident in the early 1940s.

As the various children grew, they attended public schools; first State Street Elementary, then Holliday Junior High, and finally, Topeka High School (except Richard, who was given an opportunity to play basketball at Hayden High School, a Catholic institution). While the barrio provided a warm, familial environment, with plenty of relatives and children to play with, the Torrez offspring were not immune from confronting some of the discriminatory practices extant in Topeka and other parts of

Although they never formally dated because Mary's parents disliked American courtship practices, Juan Torrez began seeing Mary after his younger brother Louis spoke to her at community events and mass. Mary and Juan eloped to Kansas City on April 28, 1938, and later consecrated their marriage at Our Lady of Guadalupe parish in Oakland. Courtesy Torrez family.

Kansas. Research by scholars has documented the myriad difficulties the Mexicano populace in this neighborhood faced during the early decades of the 1900s.[7] While the barrio dwellers in Oakland did tough, physical labor that others did not wish to do, they also endured low wages, limited educational and economic opportunities, and segregated facilities. As one historian noted, "in virtually every Kansas town and city, Mexicans and Mexican Americans remained segregated in movie theaters and were restricted from some sections of city parks, churches and other public facilities."[8] In discussions with family members, it becomes clear how many of these customs impacted their daily lives. Such practices influenced many aspects of existence, from social activities, to the workplace, and beyond.

Sport was one area in which whites often chose not to interact with the Spanish-surnamed population in Kansas, at least before the 1950s. Juan Torrez, for example, was an avid baseball fan and player, but Mary recalls he seldom had a chance to play on the diamond against whites.[9] Mostly, teams of Mexicanos in this part of Topeka played at the Santa Fe and Ripley Parks and almost exclusively competed versus squads from other Mexican American communities, such as from Kansas City and elsewhere in the Midwest. Other members of the family, for example Juan's younger brother Perfecto, also played baseball. While not given many opportunities to challenge the majority population, this generation of Torrezes passed down a knowledge and love of the game to the next, and John, Mike, and Richard benefited greatly from their expertise. Perfecto helped both John and Mike with pitching technique, and cautioned the boys against throwing curves before reaching a certain age. According to Louis Torrez, his brother was also an excellent boxer who did, on occasion, fight white pugilists. As a result of the older generation's love for sports, the brothers were encouraged to pursue a plethora of athletic activities. They hunted, fished, and played baseball, football, and basketball. Because of this support and the younger generation's athletic abilities, all of the Torrez boys had educational and other opportunities not common to the broader Mexican American population during the years before the Chicano Movement of the late 1960s and early 1970s.

As documented in Chapter 2, by the time of Mike's birth, baseball and basketball teams were an established part of Mexican American life in this region. For the Torrez boys, the variety of athletic endeavors provided an outlet for youthful exuberance and local pride, and for Mike, eventually led to a chance to play baseball at the grandest stage of all: the World Series within the confines of Yankee Stadium. Beyond the plethora of the community-based sports, the years after World War II also witnessed expanded prospects for Mexican youths to play at the high school level and in citywide programs. This was due, in part, to increased agitation by returning veterans to improve conditions for their *hijos* and *hijas* (sons and daughters) in the public schools. As more and more *estudiantes* (students) reached high school, some found their way on to gridirons, diamonds, and courts to represent local institutions.[10] Mike Torrez and his older brother John took full advantage of such offerings, excelling in various sports at Topeka High School (THS). As one of Richard Santillan's sources noted, "many doors opened after the war in sports. Mexican youths were very visible in all aspects of school and community sports whereas few Mexican American youths played school sports ... prior to the 1940s."[11] The on-field and court successes enjoyed by the three Torrez brothers attest to this trend.

Mike, John and Richard Torrez all played sports in their community, as well as for their respective high schools. The existing structure of Mexican American sports provided the young men an opportunity to prove their mettle in athletic competition before their barrio neighbors, as well

PONY LEAGUE

JETS

Sponsored by:
CARPENTER LOCAL 1445

FIRST ROW: Clarence Simpson III, Mascot. SECOND ROW, (LEFT TO RIGHT): Mike Hernandez, John Eagan, Danny Foster, Joe Herman, Mike Herman, Don Sloyer, Steve Eagan. THIRD ROW: Tony Herman, Coach; Clarence Simpson, Sr., Coach; Danny Ramirez, Larry Bainbridge, Mike Torrez, Jim Kamer, Ronnie Hansard, Rodney Hahn, Clarence Simpson, Jr., Manager.

Even in Pony League, Mike Torrez stood out. Here he towers over his teammates (and coaches) in a photograph from the late 1950s. Courtesy Torrez family.

as the broader society. Juan taught his sons how to throw, catch, and hit, and sometimes took them to see professionals in action via the games of the local class A minor league team, the Topeka Reds. One of Mike's recollections was that he won a pitching contest staged by the club, and Jim Maloney, then the local nine's star pitcher, encouraged and gave the youth tips to improve his delivery.[12] Further, Juan managed his boys in the Cosmopolitan as well as Little Leagues and gained a great reputation as a wonderful coach, even guiding his charges to citywide titles. Contrary to Juan's experiences of having to play exclusively against other "Mexican" teams during the 1920s and 1930s, by the time he started coaching in the 1950s, John recalls that there were no "ethnic" teams in the youth leagues of Topeka. "Everybody signed up in grade school, and the players were divided up into teams." It turns out that Juan Torrez proved very popular with his charges, and not just because of his teams' successes on the field. John stated that part of his dad's appeal to area children was that "win or lose, we always got ice cream" after each ball game.[13]

As the oldest boy, John became the first in the family to compete on behalf of THS and was among the first Mexican Americans to play basketball for the Trojans. He played football for the school from 1958 to 1960 as well, and pitched for the final team (from that era) fielded by this institution. The reason for THS dropping baseball was, John noted, because the sport interfered too much with the track team's schedule. Since many athletes competed on both squads, there were often conflicts. "I guess the track coach just had more pull!" One of the football coaches recognized John as an excellent running back, but more importantly believed, "he's the type of boy you really get a kick out of coaching. The other kids really like him. He's just a good team man." As a result of his athletic abilities, John had the opportunity to attend a junior college (Cowley County Community College in Arkansas City, Kansas) and completed a technical degree in printing. He then moved on to try out with the New Mexico State University Aggies, but did not make the gridiron team. As a result of not earning an athletic scholarship with NMSU, John returned to Topeka, where was drafted in 1963 but not accepted into the military. Subsequently, he began a lengthy career working for the Santa Fe. In addition to toiling for the same employer, John followed in his father's footsteps in being both a player and coach in Mexican American-organized athletics, remaining active until the late 2000s. For example, he was associated with the Topeka 7-Ups for many years. The squad was involved in numerous tournaments throughout the Midwest, including one of the most important, based in Omaha, Nebraska, which commenced in the mid–1950s.[14]

Beginning in 1964, John was also part of a group of local Mexican American leaders who commenced a similar undertaking in Topeka. Not surprisingly, the 7-Ups were also a dominant team in that competition, with John and Richard both helping lead the squad to an impressive number of victories by the early 1970s.[15] Mike also played on the squad after he turned professional right after high school. In an ironic twist, by the late 1970s and early 1980s, due to intermarriage and other social changes, many whites were asking to for the opportunity to play in some of the highly competitive "Mexican" or "Hispanic" tournaments in the area. This created a debate among sponsors, many of whom wanted to keep the events "strictly" for the Spanish-surnamed. John was one of the organizers who argued that with so many individuals (including members of the Torrez family) who now were the offspring of "mixed" ethnic relationships, it made sense to include a number of "non–Latino" athletes on squads. When some whites continued to complain to John, he poignantly reminded his fellow athletes that "now you know how we felt," back in the 1940s and 1950s.[16]

The Omaha tourney was, by the early 1960s, an impressive example of Mexican American, community-based sports initiatives, and attracted teams from Iowa, Nebraska, Missouri and elsewhere in late March or early April of each year. In 1964, Mike attended and participated in the event. Though cautioned by his older brother not to play, Mike did, and garnered a write-up about his participation in the local paper. While such notoriety is usually welcomed, this story created a problem for Torrez. When the Kansas State High School Activities Association (KSHSAA) got wind, it ruled him ineligible for further participation in school-sanctioned athletics. In a 1968 article, Torrez summarized his hardwood career at THS by stating that, "I was hurt some because we didn't have a baseball team in high school. I played a lot of basketball. I was a good outside shooter and got a lot of rebounds."[17] The organization's ruling ended Mike's time on the hardwood for the Trojans, but allowed him to focus all of his athletic attention on pitching. Youngest brother Richard also was a fine athlete and played basketball at Hayden High. When asked why he decided to attend the Catholic institution instead of Topeka High, Richard expressed grave concerns about how the KSHSAA dealt with his brother, and felt the public institution would not afford him fair treatment.[18]

Mike's amateur athletic career was primarily focused on the sports of baseball and basketball. As younger brothers are prone to do, he looked up to his older sibling and, seeing that John had played football from an early age, he too wanted to participate. Neither Juan nor Mary opposed the notion of their middle son playing on the gridiron, but it was John who urged Mike not to do so. John, who had injured his shoulder as a senior, cautioned his brother, who was comparatively taller and thinner of build and frame, that the hardwood would be a safer option to protect his pitching arm. An arm which, by Mike's mid-teens, had started to garner attention from knowledgeable baseball personnel.

Torrez made a name for himself playing baseball in local leagues in and around Topeka by the late 1950s. He played at the Cosmopolitan, Little, and Colt levels, and eventually moved on to play higher caliber American Legion baseball with the Topeka Caps. When Mike took to the mound, he got noticed, and not just because of his 6'4" stature. John recalls that it was not uncommon for his younger sibling to strike out as many as 15 or 16 batters per outing, and this led to another concern—overworking a potential professional prospect. Once again, the older sibling stepped in. John noted that in one tournament, after Mike has pitched a complete first game of a doubleheader, the coach for his squad ordered Torrez to warm up for the second contest. John refused to allow his brother to continue and actually threatened to take him home rather than continue.[19]

It was not just men in this family who broke barriers in regard to sport and other athletic endeavors. One of Mike's cousins, Gloria Torrez de Corona, was one of the first Spanish-surnamed cheerleaders at Highland Park High School, where she also played on the softball team in the early 1950s. One of her recollections from this era concerned the negative reception given her family when first they arrived in Highland Park. As soon as it became known that a group of "Mexicans" was moving in, a petition drive commenced to prevent them from building a "shack" in the neighborhood. Although some members of the community were prejudiced, Gloria noted that at least one local Methodist minister asked those in his flock who had signed the document to leave the congregation. At another time in 1952 or 1953, Gloria recalled that a white classmate refused to remain seated at a Highland Park restaurant that would not serve the two young women at their table.

Louis Torrez, who greatly enjoyed going to dance halls and attending movies in his youth, revealed other details of the impact of discriminatory practices on the social life and activities of Mexican Americans in Topeka from the 1930s through the 1950s. Torrez recalls being refused service at local restaurants and dance clubs, which, he noted, was not an issue during his time in the military throughout the World War II years, even while stationed in various Southern states for training. One of the reasons for excluding individuals of Spanish-speaking backgrounds at such facilities in the Topeka area was that, managers argued, members of this group would "always" start fights, and that white customers did not want to share the dance floor with them. Louis does recall being turned away from the Rainbow Room, the Lucky Five, and the Playboy before the late 1950s. Even though initially denied entrance at these facilities, Louis kept trying and did manage to convince several owners to allow him, and later, family members and friends, in.[20] Although some clubs did not allow Mexican Americans entry, there were several options for Spanish-surnamed youths to have a good time during the 1940s and 1950s in the Kansan capital. Among those were the Metropolitan Hall and Meadows Acres, which featured both big band, and local Mexican bands such as the Don Juan Band and Los Nocturnes.[21]

Similarly, Louis indicated that even after returning from the service, he was often asked to sit in the balcony of local movie theaters. Both Mike and John confirmed the existence of such discriminatory practices at the Jayhawk Theater as well as at public swimming pools during the early 1950s. One incident John recalled exemplifies the absurdities often created through the implementation of such policies. John, who is fairly light-skinned, went to Gage Park one summer afternoon with a darker-skinned friend named Teddy Ariza. At the entrance, the lighter complexioned youth calmly paid his admittance fee and was permitted entry without incident, while his friend was not allowed in. John thought it hilarious that he got in while Teddy did not. Torrez remembered having to dive constantly under the water, as Teddy, who was yelling from beyond the fence separating him from the swimming pool, called out to the lifeguard and administrator that something had to be done, as they had inadvertently permitted "a Mexican in the pool." Ariza eventually gave up on the quest to have his friend evicted.[22] This situation, while in some ways comical, does relate to a very tragic story in Torrez family annals. Gloria Torrez de Corona stated that the lack of opportunity to visit local parks and pools often led Mexican American youths to swim in nearby rivers, sometimes with tragic consequences. In 1947, her ten-year-old brother Richard drowned in the Kansas River in part, she argued, because he had been turned away from Gage Park.[23]

In order to survive economically, all members of the clan contributed to sustaining the household. Mary worked at an egg factory and, like many other Mexican American women, cleaned houses. Another moneymaking endeavor Juan utilized was the production and transportation of bootleg wine and beer to Kansas City, bringing back whisky to connections in Topeka. In this endeavor, he often utilized some of his children or their cousins as props to make it appear as if the family was merely on an outing during the clandestine runs across the Kansas/Missouri border. According to Louis, John handled all aspects of the production of his illicit beverages: growing grapes, turning them into wine, brewing beer in the basement of the family's domicile, and hiding the contraband under chicken coops in the backyard. Mariano never approved of his son's endeavors in this regard and indeed, one of Juan's siblings, Perfecto, served approximately one year in jail for bootlegging. According to family lore, Perfecto took the rap in place of his older brother, since Juan was the only person employed at the time of the incident.

The Torrez children did not just serve as props for bootlegging trips but also actively chipped in to support the domicile's budget. In addition to hunting and fishing to provide protein for the family table, Mike and John recall efforts to raise fiesta money by picking potatoes in the early 1950s. During one of these periods of employment, Mike created a bit of a stir (and got himself, his older brother, and several cousins fired) in an early demonstration of the capabilities of his pitching arm. As John recalls, Mike was upset because he believed his tally of potatoes picked was not totaled correctly. In a fit of youthful rambunctiousness, he hurled (and hit) his foreman with a rotten tuber. The youths were summarily dismissed, but the event foreshadowed some of the "stuff" that Mike would demonstrate on a much grander stage later in life.[24]

Juan and Mary's many years of diligent effort and toil had, by the very early 1960s, provided a modicum of success; they owned their home (in part, because of a $1,000 settlement Juan received when he lost his eye) as well as the adjacent lot. Juan had also been promoted over his years of service beyond "common" laborer status to carman, and later, coach carman (working on upholstery). While a step or two above many friends and neighbors, such assets did not radically alter the family's financial wherewithal. The Cardinals, however, proffered an opportunity to utilize the love of the game, and Mike's innate talent, into a transformative event. In the months after high school graduation Torrez and his family worked to make this dream a reality.[25] The 18-year-old had just concluded a 13–1 campaign with the Van-T American League team, hurled the Eastern Kansas All Stars to victory over a similar squad from the western regions of the state, and wrapped up his third (and final) year of American Legion baseball by striking out 18 hitters, leading Kansas to victory over the Nebraska Legion Stars (their only hit was a bunt single). From this moment, there was a sense that Mike Torrez had the opportunity to become a professional, and possibly make it to the majors. In a 1978 interview, Mike recalled that one of his coaches in Legion, Marvin Bonjor, advised him to look at pitching as a job and "When you go out there to pitch, think of dollars. Just think every game that you pitch, you are pitching with a purpose. In other words, take it seriously."[26]

While success on the diamond brought recognition and a modicum of approval in the local media, as discussed elsewhere, such exploits also highlight that while Latino athletes from this era were able to compete, they still faced reminders that sport could not break down all barriers or stereotypes. For example, Torrez noted on several occasions that the father of a blonde girl from Topeka West High School refused to allow them on a second date because he "thought Mexicans belong on the other side of the tracks." Later, after Torrez made the Majors, the young lady he had hoped to date while a teenager (and her husband) shared a nice visit with Torrez while he was in Chicago along with his teammates.[27]

The prospect of trying out for an MLB organization was a chance to impact positively both the personal and familial circumstances for the Torrezes. Even before free agency, earnings of non-front-line players in "the show" dwarfed take-home pay of a "typical" Oakland resident. As an example of the disparity, it is interesting to quote from a story in a Topeka paper just three years after Torrez's entry into professional baseball. As Bob Hartzell noted in his "Prep Parade" article in the fall of 1967, "Mike probably will draw somewhere around $12,000 from the Cardinals next season. The two friends he was with Tuesday night don't make that much between them."[28]

As was common practice for MLB teams, there were individuals known as bird-dogs who scouted in specific locales for the organizations. This was standard operating procedure before the start of the amateur draft in 1965. In fact, Mike Torrez was one of the final "bonus babies" from the years under the previous model. In eastern Kansas, that person on behalf of the St. Louis Cardinals was former Washburn University coach Marion McDonald. Shortly after Torrez's victory in Game 6 of the 1977 World Series for the Yankees, the bird-dog proudly recalled, "What really sold me on Torrez was an American Legion game at Lawrence. The Lawrence players could hardly get their bats around fast enough to hit a fair ball."[29] Another story which made a similar point appeared in 1968 as one of the Cardinals' scouts spoke glowingly about Torrez in the last days of his American Legion career. In a contest against a Nebraska squad, the opposition did not hit the ball out of the infield. Torrez stated, "I should have had a no-hitter, but two fielders collided."[30]

Such reports to the Cardinals' leadership set the stage for a closer

A picture of another close friend from the Cardinals, Julian Javier and wife.
When Torrez, his father and John visited the Cardinals and Branch Rickey in
1964, Javier warned the senior Torrez (in Spanish) that the team and its general manager would try to short-change the young pitcher when it came to a
signing bonus. It turns out he was absolutely correct in this assertion. Photograph courtesy Southwest Collection/Special Collections Library, Texas
Tech University, Lubbock, Texas, Mike Torrez Scrapbook Collection, Binder
11012.

examination. To pursue his professional aspirations, Juan, John and Mike
traveled beyond the familiar landscape of Topeka, east to the other end
of the Show Me State, for a tryout at Sportsman's Park. It was there that
Mike first interacted with several well-known baseball personages. After
warming up, the 18-year-old pitched to Vernon Benson, who advised the
young man to "open it up." When Mike complied, he impressed the Cardinals' personnel so much that they summoned Branch Rickey to pass
judgment upon the potential of this purported "diamond in the rough."
Benson, a third baseman/outfielder during his playing days, eventually
called upon a "real" catcher to sit behind home plate and handle Torrez's
tosses. The man drafted for the job was the soon-to-be celebrated backstop
(turned actor and broadcaster), Bob Uecker. Rickey was taken aback, so
much so that he refused to believe that Torrez was a Mexican American.
The legendary executive thought that the young Kansan was, instead, a
Native American because, purportedly, "he had not seen a Mexican that

tall." Another interesting detail from this event that Torrez noted in an interview was that Julian Javier, already playing for the Cardinals, poignantly and directly advised Mike and his father (in Spanish) that Rickey's scout would probably low-ball his offer. This was one example of the camaraderie among the Latinos and African Americans that often personified clubhouse relations among the Cardinals teams of the 1960s.[31]

Rickey's statement is significant for two reasons. First, as noted elsewhere in the historical literature, it provides credence to the acceptance of the perception that Mexican Americans could not be gifted athletes. Second, it shows a tremendous lack of awareness on Rickey's part that is perplexing as, just two years prior to Torrez's tryout, the ERA leader for the American League (with a 2.21 average and an appearance in the All-Star Game) was another "tall Mexican," Hank Aguirre of the Detroit Tigers.[32] While showing diffidence as to Torrez's potential, Rickey was intrigued. The Cardinals did not sign Torrez after the tryout, but promised to get back to him soon.

In the meantime, the Detroit Tigers also gave Torrez a tryout (while they were in Kansas City playing the Athletics) and, as he recalls, it was Bill Freehan who sat behind home plate in the bullpen to catch his offerings. Again, the organization showed interest. The Tigers were so impressed that their personnel soon visited the Torrez domicile and asked Mike not to answer calls from other clubs. Shortly thereafter, however, the Cardinals' representatives, Charley Frey and George Silvey, offered the princely sum of $20,000 for Mike's signature. This was more money than Juan would earn over multiple years of labor at the Santa Fe (he was then making around $5,000 per year)! Not surprisingly, he and Mary advised their son to pursue his professional career with St. Louis, but for different reasons. Juan was a lifelong Cardinals fan, and the thought of his son donning that MLB uniform probably influenced his advice. Mary, on the other hand, was predominantly concerned about who would feed and support Mike. After all, she argued, "he can't go, he doesn't know how to cook, he doesn't know how to do nothing!" Once Cardinals personnel promised her that they would take care of Mike's room, board and similar needs, Mary was more than willing to give her blessing as well. Finally, as Mike noted in a 1968 interview, the "$20,000 was a lot of money anyway. My parents didn't know anything about contracts. With eight kids to support, there never was any money. I'm just thankful that God gave me a good arm."[33]

Soon thereafter, however, the Tigers called and offered Torrez $75,000 to sign, but it was too late. While not demonstratively bitter about these circumstances, it appears such a harsh introduction to the "realities" of baseball economics was a lesson that he drew upon in the future as he dealt with notoriously difficult owners such as Charlie Finley of the Oakland A's and George Steinbrenner of the New York Yankees. Given that in the early 1960s the infamous "reserve clause" was still in place, Torrez was now officially the "property" of the St. Louis Cardinals.

In 2011, the *Topeka Capital Journal* featured two stories that touched upon the experiences of the Torrez family and which provide an effective summation for many of the materials covered in this chapter. One article, which appeared in November, focused on the historical experiences of children of diverse backgrounds in Kansas' capital city. Among the lives highlighted, and not surprisingly given his extensive work in the community and at Our Lady of Guadalupe Church, was the lone surviving child of Mariano and Refugio, Mike's uncle, Louis. When asked to recall his childhood, the octogenarian reiterated some of the points developed and discussed herein. In Topeka, there was opportunity for Mexican Americans in the Oakland neighborhood, but there they also encountered racism and other difficulties. "We knew we weren't able to go everywhere. We played in Ripley Park. We couldn't go swimming, but we went there for picnics and things like that. We struggled, but thank God my dad always had a job [with the Santa Fe]."[34] A few weeks prior, in a late August edition of the daily, sportswriter Kevin Haskin concluded a series of essays designed to highlight the careers of the top 100 athletes in the history of Shawnee County. The catalog is impressive, with noted competitors such as former Major League All-Star Ken Berry (who now runs a youth baseball league in Topeka), wrestling and coaching great Melvin Douglas (inducted into the National Wrestling Hall of Fame in 2013), and basketball player and coach (currently serving as the head coach at the University of Oklahoma) Lon Kruger, comprising part of the final four. The individual ranked in first place in this august lineup, however, was Mike Torrez. In his interview with Haskin, Torrez did an effective job of connecting some of his uncle's experiences with his by contemplating how his life would have been different without baseball. Though he commenced his career in the era before free agency and endured often difficult yearly haggles with general managers and owners in order to get his financial due, he recognized that playing baseball was his ticket to a better life instead of having to go "work at Santa Fe with all of my buddies and my family and my dad. Back then, they all worked there. Or at Goodyear, with my cousins."[35]

The combination of innate talent, citywide, scholastic, and Mexican American-based athletics, as well as the contributions of family members, helped make it possible for Mike Torrez to leave the Oakland barrio and eventually reach the Majors. How far he had come from his childhood days! Upon making the St. Louis roster to start the 1968 campaign, he recalled, "my father has only one eye and I was throwing so hard [by age ten] that he couldn't follow the ball." So the catching chores were turned over to older brother John. Shortly after signing on the dotted line with the Cardinals, he was off to Hollywood, Florida, for a couple of weeks of instruction along with other recent signees of the organization. Before leaving Topeka, however, he did allow himself one indulgence. "I had always wanted one of those 1915 Model T roadsters with six carburetors, 40 coats of red paint and all that stuff, and I bought one."[36]

After his unorthodox automotive purchase, Torrez began a minor league career that took him to North Carolina, Arkansas, and Oklahoma (followed by a later stint in Manitoba). His experiences in these lower echelons of the sport are revealing for several reasons. First, they highlight some of the changes that had taken place in the lower levels of professional baseball by the mid–1960s. For example, at all of his stops along the way to St. Louis, he had more than a few Spanish-surnamed teammates. Second, although he played in locales with few Latinos in the area's population at that time, his Mexican American background did not seem to cause any issues with fans or the local media. It is this part of the story to which we now turn.

4

"A Bit Wild, but a Great Fastball"
Torrez's Time in the Minor Leagues and His Arrival in St. Louis, 1964–1969

Shortly after graduating from Topeka High School, Mike Torrez realized the dream of a good number of young men of his, and many other, generations by signing a contract to begin playing professional baseball. The front page of his hometown newspaper's sport section for May 18, 1964, proclaimed in large type that the "Cardinals Sign Topeka's Torrez," and that the young man from the Oakland neighborhood was scheduled to receive a "substantial bonus" for his signature to become the franchise's property. As noted previously, the compensation for his autograph was not as generous as portrayed in the media, but the payment was significant enough to provide important benefits to the Torrez clan. Still, the issue of money bothered Mike, and this point would play an important role in decisions later in his career. As he stated in 1968 when he was playing AAA baseball for the Cardinals' affiliate in Tulsa:

> My bonus was reasonably good. It was better than some, but like everyone else I would have liked to have had more. If I had waited another day or two I think Detroit would have come through with more money ... that didn't concern me, because I expect to be making big money in St. Louis pretty soon, anyway. Real soon, in fact.[1]

Having competed successfully at Cosmo, Little, Pony and American Legion leagues in his home town and state, Torrez now embarked upon the often arduous and lengthy process that could lead to his ultimate goal: pitching at the Major League level. Torrez summarized his goals in the game by noting that, even though he was offered scholarships by schools in the Big Eight (now the Big 12) in basketball, "I messed around too much. So I never really considered college. I figured my best chance was to play professional baseball."[2] The photo which accompanied the article when he inked his pact showed a beaming Mary smiling broadly as Mike held a copy of his contract and a St. Louis cap, parent and offspring both full of hope and expectation for what lay ahead.

Fast-forward four years. Heading into the start of the 1968 season (after defeating the Detroit Tigers in the most recent World Series), Cardinals manager Red Schoendienst discussed how St. Louis hoped to repeat their previous season's success. In part, he argued, it was imperative that the "young pitchers come through to help the bullpen so that we won't have to go out and make a deal." The team had high hopes for a new bumper "crop" of hurlers coming up through their minor league system. General Manager Bing Devine perceived his squad as having so much depth that it seemed

> like the old days when the Cardinals had surplus talent. I remember one season— 1941, I believe it was—that Hank Gornicki pitched a one-hitter in the National League and was still optioned out. It is nice to have such spirited job competition, and from the boys' standpoint the good thing is that with expansion certain in one major league and possibly the other, their chance of being here next year are bright.[3]

Among the youths in the mix at camp in St. Petersburg, Florida, was Torrez (who already had logged a few appearances with St. Louis at the close of the 1967 campaign). The conclusion of spring training is a strenuous time for the athletes near the end of a team's depth-chart and at the back of a pitching rotation or bullpen. Torrez had shown some flashes over the preseason, but would it be sufficient to stick with the "big" team? Had he shown enough potential to remain with a staff that had just helped claim a world championship, or would he be assigned again to the minors for further "seasoning"?

The Cardinals ultimately decided to keep Torrez as part of their 1968 Opening Day roster in place of a more experienced pitcher named Jack Lamabe (optioned to the team's affiliate in the Pacific Coast League), whom they had acquired previously in a trade from the New York Mets. There were two significant reasons for retaining the young Topekan. First, Torrez had showed both grit and competiveness as he recovered from a rough start for the Tulsa Oilers to finish the previous season at AAA with a mark of 10–10. While certainly not a sterling won-loss record, Torrez had an excellent second half of the campaign, even earning praise in an extended article in the bible of baseball, *The Sporting News.* Second, as Juan, John and others in the Oakland barrio could readily attest, Mike, quite simply, threw hard. Schoendienst was particularly impressed with Torrez's fastball because "even though he is a bit wild, I can envision him coming in … with a runner on third base, where a walk can't especially hurt, and giving us a good chance for a strikeout."[4] This statement is supported by a quick review of Torrez's key 1967 statistics: he struck out 155 batters, but issued a troubling 108 walks (leading the league in that category) over a total of 190 innings pitched.[5] While still early in his career, the points discussed by General Manager Devine (expansion and its impact upon the talent level and increased opportunities in the Majors) and his on-field skipper Schoendienst (streaks of wildness and many strikeouts), both presaged critical elements in the subsequent years of his professional career.

This chapter will detail Torrez's minor league career as he moved through the Cardinals' system, with stays in North Carolina (two teams in the A level—the Raleigh and the Rock Hill Cardinals), Arkansas (AA level—Arkansas Travelers), and Oklahoma (AAA level—Tulsa Oilers) along the way to Busch Stadium in St. Louis. It will discuss how, when Torrez began his time in the lower levels of professional ball, players of Latino backgrounds were not the rarity they had been as recently as the 1950s. As will become apparent, while the trials and tribulations of living and playing in the minor leagues are never easy, it was certainly less problematic for a Mexican American such as Torrez in the mid-to-late 1960s than it was for some of the Spanish-surnamed players who had preceded him (particularly in the South). Further, when Torrez reached the majors to stay in 1969 (except for a brief stay in AAA Winnipeg after his trade to Montreal), the St. Louis team that he pitched for early in his career was also an anomaly, one that had effectively integrated athletes of three groups: whites, African Americans and Latinos, to an extent not widespread until later years. Finally, during the time he was away from Topeka in the minors, the Chicano Movement became an important element in the lives of Mexican Americans in his hometown and neighborhood. The *movimiento* was a direct political challenge to some of the difficult circumstances that Spanish-speakers confronted in Oakland and elsewhere in Kansas. This era of social fervor was looking for heroes to present to barrio youths, and Torrez's participation (and eventual prominence) in the national pastime helped make him a role model for other Mexican Americans.

The story of the treatment of African Americans in the minor leagues has generated substantial research. The story of Latinos in these leagues, however, has received far less attention.[6] In a 1987 essay, historian Samuel O. Regalado effectively documented the trials and tribulations confronted by the likes of Juan Marichal, Minnie Minoso, Felipe Alou, Luis Tiant, and others, on their way to "the show."[7] The most interesting aspect of Regalado's study examines the disparity of treatment of Latino ballplayers playing as lower-level professionals in different sections of the country. In brief, Regalado argues that individuals who wound up in places such as Yakima and Tacoma, Washington, and Portland, Oregon, might have missed Latino companionship and cuisine, but they were far better off than colleagues ill-fated enough to wind up in places such as Lakeland, Florida, and Lake Charles, Louisiana. Some athletes were even more fortunate and wound up plying their trade in locales such as San Diego, California, and Phoenix, Arizona (at that time still minor-league cities), and interacted with Spanish-speaking communities that often welcomed them with open arms.[8]

An examination of Torrez's minor league career does not indicate that he faced situations such as those Regalado described for mulatto players. There appear to be two key differences in Torrez's journey toward the Majors from that of many of his Spanish-surnamed predecessors. First, and not surprisingly, by the mid–1960s, there were more Latinos in the minors and the "novelty" of their presence on teams had been mitigated. For example, the first team for which Torrez played in the Cardinals' system (1965 for Raleigh in the Carolina League) included several other Latinos. Among these were Cuban-born José Arcia (who played with both the Cubs and Padres between 1968 and 1970), Puerto Ricans Marty Beltran and Felix De Leon, and a Dominican, Bobby Diaz.[9] Further, later in his career in the lower levels of professional baseball, other Spanish-surnamed individuals, such as catcher Pat Corrales (who would go on to become the first Mexican American to manage a Major League squad—the Texas Rangers in 1978—and with whom Torrez worked during his time at Tulsa), were present on teams to "show him the ropes" both on and off the field. At St. Louis, another important person for Torrez's professional education was Julian Javier, who, as noted in a previous chapter, was present at Torrez's tryout with the Cardinals and forewarned Juan Torrez that Branch Rickey would try to lowball any offers for his son's services (which, it appears, he did). Julian became a good friend and confidant during Torrez's stint with the Cardinals. Second, Torrez, having been born and raised in the United States, spoke fluent English, and, though not necessarily exposed to the circumstances of Southern-style race regulations and traditions, was not perceived in the same way as were mulatto or black Spanish-speakers.

After signing his contract, Torrez was assigned for a couple of weeks of orientation at a camp based in Hollywood, Florida. He then reported to the A-level Raleigh Cardinals of the Carolina League, managed by Ray Hathaway, for the start of the 1965 campaign. In his first outing, the young pitcher got off to an impressive start, pitching his squad to a 10–3 victory over the Burlington Senators and earning high praise from his catcher. In a statement reminiscent of some of Mike's appearances in Kansas, battery-mate Bart Zeller noted that "he was throwing the ball right by the batters.... I expected him to be throwing all over the place, but he was right on the plate. Even when we were ahead by the big margin, he never lost his poise. That is what you hope for in a young pitcher." Manager Hathaway was, not surprisingly, less effusive in his assessment, stating, "Torrez is a surprise. All during spring drills he threw nothing pitches. Tonight he was right." As befits a novice in his professional debut, Torrez focused more on what he did wrong and found plenty to criticize, stating, "I began to wear down in the fifth inning. I was throwing the ball from the side instead of overhead." Still, it surely must have been an encouragement to hear his manager note that he had "the potential to become a major league pitcher in a couple of years."[10]

A follow-up performance was even more notable, as Torrez defeated Winston-Salem later that season, 7–3. He pitched a complete game, struck out nine, and most impressively, retired 15 consecutive Red Sox hitters. Part of what made this game significant was that Torrez made use of another part of his arsenal, a curve ball, to secure several of his strikeouts. After this victory, his overall record was level at 3–3.[11] While showing occasional flashes, Torrez and his Raleigh Cardinals teammates struggled. By the end of the 143-game campaign, Torrez had achieved an unspectacular mark of 4–8, with a high 4.79 ERA, on a fourth-place squad that was mediocre at the plate (a .245 average) and on the mound (team ERA of 4.18) and completed its season 19 games out of first (with an overall record of 64–79). In his first professional season, Torrez struck out 81 hitters but also surrendered 75 walks over only 94 innings pitched.[12]

For the 1966 season, the Cardinals transferred Torrez from Raleigh to their Rock Hill affiliate in the Western Carolina League (also an A-level circuit, but with a slightly shorter season—only 122 games) and there he showed significant improvement, finishing with a record of 7–4 (starting 11 games), and more importantly, substantially lowering his ERA to a much more respectable 2.50. This campaign featured two notable events for the young Kansan. First, he pulled off a rare pitching feat against the Salisbury Astros: earning two victories in one day. In the initial triumph, he pitched two innings to complete an earlier game that had been called with the squads deadlocked at five runs each. The projected starter for the regularly scheduled contest, he struck out four of six batters he faced. Torrez was involved in bringing home the decisive run, hitting a grounder that was misplayed by the Astros' second baseman that permitted the winning tally to cross the plate. This turn of events evened his season record at 2–2. Next, he followed with a sterling nine-strikeout, seven and two-thirds innings pitched performance, as the Cardinals won the nightcap of this unusual doubleheader, 6–4. In this game, Torrez surrendered only four hits and two walks.[13]

Torrez's time with Rock Hill was positive. Not only did he have a winning record for the first time as a professional, he also cut down significantly on the number of walks per inning from his year at Raleigh (a total of only 37 in 90 innings pitched, along with scattering only 65 hits). As a result, he was named to the Western Carolinas League All-Star team. Though this Cardinals squad did not have much more success than did Raleigh (finishing 59–63, 13 games behind Salisbury in the standings), the organization's management was sufficiently intrigued to award the 19-year-old a promotion to the next rung of the minor leagues, to the Arkansas Travelers of the AA Texas League.[14]

Torrez's late-season stint at this level of competition proved instructive in a different way. Instead of toiling for second division squads, as he had during his time in both North Carolina circuits, the Travelers, under the direction of Vern Rapp, were on their way to winning the Texas League championship in 1966, giving Torrez a chance to experience life at the top of the standings for the first time as a professional. He struggled a bit in his first four outings at this new and higher echelon, went 0–2 and did not last beyond the fifth inning, prior to an impressive mid–July appearance against the El Paso Sun Kings (affiliates of the California Angels). As manager Rapp noted after the game, "It just took him a little time to get his feet on the ground. A game like this can do wonders for your confidence." Against El Paso, Torrez was dominant, tossing a complete-game, 5–2 victory (with both runs unearned). He gave up the first Sun Kings hit in the fourth inning and controlled his opponents with an array of breaking balls which made his blistering fastball even more efficient. Seven of the outs recorded were simple pop-ups to various Travelers infielders.[15]

Inconsistency, however, plagued Torrez while in Little Rock. Later that season, he was pulled after only three innings in another contest against the Sun Kings, for, as the local paper noted, "Torrez continued to be plagued with unearned runs.... He wasn't throwing as hard last night as he has been ... (and El Paso) had five hits off of the strapping Kansan."[16]

Another example of his bouts of wildness occurred when the young pitcher took the eighth of his defeats with the Travelers. In a game against the Amarillo Sonics (affiliates of the Houston Astros, and the second-place team in the league that year), he endured a nightmarish third inning where he gave up six runs, though only two were earned. Several walks helped fuel the Sonics' rally. Rapp removed Torrez after he had completed only 2⅔ innings with the less-than-impressive statistical line of three hits surrendered, five walks, and only one strike out. Reporter Bob Howell expressed the concern on the mind of many in the Cardinals' organization when he stated, "Perhaps no pitcher in baseball has been victimized by unearned runs more than big Mike Torrez ... in 64 innings, he has now allowed 39 runs, only 20 earned."[17] In summary, while enjoying the success that comes with being part of a winning team, there were concerns about Torrez's performance in the Texas League. First, his overall record was an unimpressive 3–9, and the curse of too many walks was the major cause for apprehension. His totals for 1966 at AA were as follows: 14 starts, two complete games, 79 innings pitched, 65 strikeouts and 42 bases on balls. On the other hand, there were positives as well. He produced a more-than-respectable ERA of 2.62, which was below the Travelers' staff's overall ERA of 3.00. For the entire season (split between A and AA levels), his numbers were: a 10–13 record, a 2.56 ERA, 30 games started, and 169 innings pitched.[18] At this point, his minor-league won-lost record was a pedestrian 14–21. Would the promise that the Cardinals foresaw back in 1964 ever bear fruit for Torrez and the organization?

Torrez did demonstrate some development from his first year in the Cardinals' system: particularly impressive was the fact that he almost halved his 1965 ERA at Raleigh. From management's standpoint, however, there were still far too many free passes permitted. To provide supplementary instruction and an opportunity to further refine some troublesome aspects of his mechanics, the St. Louis front office, at the conclusion of the Texas League term, sent Torrez to the Instructional League in Florida for the fall. Under the tutelage of the Cardinals' principal braintrust for hurlers—Barney Schultz, minor league pitching coach, George Kissell, pitching instructor, and Billy Muffett, pitching coach for the big league club, Torrez regained his aura of promise within the organization. At this level Mike shined and finished this short season with a record of 6–1 and an ERA of 1.20. Never doubting his abilities, Torrez argued that all he needed was to improve his delivery, stating, "they changed my follow through, so I would be more relaxed and not get so tired, and they got me to concentrating more on where I wanted to get the pitch. These things really helped me." Now, it appeared to him, he was finally ready to let his talents carry him all the way to St. Louis.[19]

This performance led to an invitation to the Cardinals' 1967 Major League spring training in St. Petersburg. Just three seasons removed from pitching American Legion baseball, Mike Torrez was attending a Major League camp. Bob Hentzen of the *Topeka Capital Journal* gleefully shared with the readers back home some of the sights and sounds that Torrez experienced. As is evident from the passage below, the hometown-based scribe was more than willing to drop names in order to impress his public about Torrez' new big league acquaintances/teammates:

> Fishing with Roger Maris. Listening to Bob Gibson play the guitar. Going on steak cookouts. And trying to win a job in the big leagues. These are the things that Topekan Mike Torrez is doing.... It's the first big league camp for the 20-year old Torrez who would have been there last year except that he was finishing a six-month stint in the Marine Corps then. With that size ... he's the biggest Cardinal-and a strong right arm, Torrez is considered a sure-fire bet to pitch in the majors. When, that is the question.

Torrez was upbeat about his chances to head north with the big club. "If they go by how everybody is pitching, I'd have a pretty good chance right now. Everything has been going real good so far. I've been throwing strikes. And getting the ball where I want it ... keeping it down."[20] While he remained positive as the team moved toward final cuts, the 20-year-old faced a daunting task in making the grade with a squad that featured front-line talents in its starting rotation such as the great Bob Gibson (who finished with a 13–7 record and a 2.98 ERA in 1967), Steve Carlton (14–9, 2.98), Dick Hughes (16–6, 2.67), Larry Jaster (9–7, 3.01) and Ray Washburn (10–7, 3.53), all of whom started at least 23 games in that championship year. The bullpen, led by Ron Willis (65 total appearances, with a 2.67 ERA and ten saves), Nelson Briles (14–5, 2.43, and six saves), and Joe Hoerner (4–4, 2.59 and a club-leading 15 saves), was solid as well (as a unit, the staff had an overall ERA of 3.05). With a substantial core of more "seasoned" talent ahead of him, it was likely that Torrez would have had limited opportunities to pitch. Thus, it was not a complete surprise that he was one of the last players demoted before the start of the season. While no doubt disappointed, Torrez took solace that he was not reassigned to the Texas League. How he pitched in fall ball and spring training in St. Petersburg had showed the franchise's leadership sufficient promise to promote him to the next level of the professional ladder with the AAA Tulsa Oilers of the Pacific Coast League.[21]

At Tulsa, Torrez benefited from the tutelage of one of the all-time great pitchers, Warren Spahn, his manager with the Oilers, as well as the advice

Tulsa Oilers-1968

Courtesy Oil Capital Newspapers

Back row left to right: Danny Breeden, Jerry Robertson, Chuck Taylor, Iedro Gonzalez, Steve Huntz, Sal Campisi, Gary Geiger.
Middle row left to right: Clay Kirby, Jim Hutto, Jim Cosman, Mike Torrez, Dick LeMay, Bob Sadowski, Joe Hague.
Front row left to right: Ramon Hernandez, Elio Chacon, Coco Laboy, Warren Spahn (mgr.), Jack Boag (trainer), Dave Pavlesic, Billy Wolff, Stu Miller.

Torrez (center of middle row) as part of the 1968 Pacific Coast League champions Tulsa Oilers squad. The ability to improve his craft under the tutelage of Warren Sphan was a definite boost to his career, and helped him move on to the Major League club the following season. Photograph courtesy of the Southwest Collection/Special Collections Library, Texas Tech University, Lubbock, Texas, Mike Torrez Scrapbook Collection, Binder 6010.

of battery-mate Pat Corrales. Just as at the A classification, this season was not stellar for the young Kansan's AAA squad, which struggled to a 65–79 finish. This result was a disappointment, as the Oilers had won the East Division of the PCL with a record of 85–62 the previous year. Torrez mirrored his team's 1967 travails, sputtering to an overall 3–8 record with a 4.54 ERA during a first half that featured what, by now, could be considered a characteristic mix of excellent and frustrating outings. One of the first half highlights came in his initial assignment of the year (only the team's fourth game of the campaign); though he took a hard-luck 3–2 loss (with Phoenix completing an opening four-game series sweep over Tulsa). In the Giants' victory, Torrez pitched an impressive 10⅓ innings and was charged with all three Phoenix runs. He also struck out five, scattered eight hits, and walked only two. Unfortunately, one of those hits came in the bottom of the 11th after the Oilers had taken a 2–1 lead in the top of the frame on an RBI double by catcher Pat Corrales. Torrez was unable to hold the lead, giving up a leadoff double to Bob Burda and a single to Frank Johnson which tied the game. Reliever Wayne Granger took the mound and promptly wild-pitched Johnson to second, walked the next batter, and surrendered a single to Bobby Etheridge that plated the winning run. Just like that, Torrez's splendid endeavor went by the wayside.[22]

In another game, this time against the Seattle Angels (affiliate of the California Angels), Torrez's performance encapsulated both the positive and the negatives that summarized this part of the season. While earning an 8–1 victory, he walked the bases loaded twice, and a free pass accounted for the opposition's lone tally. After the victory (which increased his season mark to 2–3), Spahn discussed his hurler's travails at length, stating that the young man was:

> … going to school on the mound. I want him to profit by his mistakes and that is the only way he'll realize his tremendous potential. He has great stuff, but he needs to find the strike zone. When you're wild one bad pitch can take you and the team out of the game. I took him out after six innings even though he had a five-run lead because I suspected he was tiring … he had made a lot of pitches.[23]

Torrez followed up this victory, taxing though it may have been, with a better effort against Denver (affiliate of the Minnesota Twins) in his next start, defeating the Bears, 8–3. It appears that the tutelage of an all-time pitching great was having some impact, for after the contest Torrez noted, "Warren has been working with me all week on those two problems and I was pleased I cut the free passes down to four." In this complete-game triumph, Torrez scattered eight hits, struck out six, and was charged with only two earned runs.[24]

While feeling confident, this would be Torrez's final victory over the first part of the year, as he followed up this effort with a short (2⅔ innings) and disastrous appearance against the Oklahoma City 89ers (affiliate of the Houston Astros), losing, 9–1.[25] Later, he reached his nadir for 1967 with a severe wild streak in a game against San Diego (affiliates of the Philadelphia Phillies). The Oilers lost, 7–3, as the Padres shelled Torrez in the bottom of the eighth for four of his six earned runs. Again, too many walks were his downfall as he issued eight free passes (while giving up only four hits).[26] Not surprisingly, there was renewed concern that the supposed prodigy from Oakland might not achieve his full potential. As noted in an article detailing Torrez's second-half surge, the first part of 1967 left room for serious doubt for, "Although Torrez had flashes of brilliance in the early part of the Pacific Coast League season, he struggled with nightmarish control problems. Torrez still has the dubious distinction of leading the league in walks with 93."[27] During the remainder of the campaign, however, his results improved dramatically, and the turnaround commenced with a complete-game four-hitter against the Spokane Indians (affiliates of the Los Angeles Dodgers) in a 3–1 victory by the Oilers. Manager Spahn noted that for Torrez this was "probably his best [outing] of the year."[28]

This triumph, the first of six consecutive, would eventually boost Torrez's overall mark to 9–8. The streak earned Torrez some major national recognition in the form of an extended article by John Ferguson in *The Sporting News.* The essay discussed some of the concerns Cardinals management had about his control, but crowed that Torrez was currently the "Pacific Coast League's most exciting pitcher." In the September 2, 1967, issue of the weekly, Ferguson cited Torrez's statistics during this impressive roll: just five earned runs allowed over 58⅓ innings and a superb ERA of 0.77. Included were 34 consecutive scoreless innings pitched in the Oilers' home park. Two highlights of the successful run included a 1–0 shutout against Oklahoma City on July 28 and a three-hit, 11 innings-pitched outing against Hawaii (affiliate of the Washington Senators) on August 9.

Now, instead of expressing consternation, assistant Cardinals farm director Fred McAlister stated, "Torrez can pitch in any league, including the National, the way he pitched against the 89ers." Torrez cited two important reasons for his dramatic improvement. First, Spahn continued to work with him and "showed me how to get more wrist snap on my curve." This made his fastball even more effective, as long as he could place it where he wanted. To remind himself of the importance of maintaining the good mechanics drilled into him over the Instructional League fall in Florida, Torrez wrote, "think, concentrate, and throw strikes" on his glove. Second, Spahn roomed the two Mexican American batterymates together on the road. Torrez noted that Corrales provided his teammate with constant reminders that helped him focus on the proper mechanics, even when he became tired on the mound. This forced Torrez to continue to throw overhand, instead of from the side. As the season wound down, Torrez looked forward to taking the next step in his professional career. "I know I've got one of the best arms in the organization. I know the Cardinal staff is pretty well set, but if you are good enough, you will make it." Overall, Torrez completed the campaign with a 10–10 record and a more-than-respectable 3.32 ERA. His minor league record was looking more positive, and George Silvey, director of the Cardinals' farm system, noted, "I only wish we could bring him up now, but the way the staff is going, it will be a chore getting Bob Gibson back on the active list."[29]

Over the span of his triumphant stretch, the *Tulsa Tribune* featured one of the few articles during Torrez's minor league career that made direct mention of his ethnicity. In a piece entitled "Oilers Streak to Latin Beat—Cha-Cha-Cha," sportswriter Dick Suagee specifically identified both Torrez and Pat Corrales as being of "Mexican descent." Perhaps this was a sign of the growing familiarity of Latinos in the minor leagues by the later part of the 1960s. While the reporter may have gotten his musical influences a bit mixed up (given that the Cha-cha is of Cuban origin), he made no other commentary as to the heritage of the two players.[30] Shortly after the end of the Oilers' 1967 season, Torrez was summoned to the parent club. He was called up on September 10 and made his debut the following day.

The results of Torrez's first efforts at the Major League level were detailed briefly at the start of Chapter 3. In the article cited in that chapter, Torrez came across as being just mildly uneasy regarding his first appearance, but in the *Sports Illustrated* article from 1968 he expanded upon what can only be the natural nervousness that a rookie pitcher feels upon approaching the mound for his first appearance with the big club:

> I remember when I pitched for the first time in the majors last season. Somehow we had blown a lead, and the call went to the bullpen for me to start throwing. I came in with runners at first and second and two outs and struck out Donn Clendenon of the Pirates. The way it happened, it was the best thing for me, because I didn't have too much time to think. But later on, I was told that I was going to start a game it was totally different. I had time to think about what could happen to me and I got nervous. You look around, and all of a sudden you are in the major leagues. They were all there—Cepeda, Maris, Flood, Brock, and I know they were yelling for me. But you feel so alone.[31]

After his relief stint on September 11, the Pittsburgh bench was effusive in its praise of the young Torrez. "What are the Cardinals trying to do, start another dynasty?" said Coach Smith, with tongue in cheek. "If the kid had had a little work, he might have been rough out there. Come to think of it, he did throw one ball."[32] While Torrez did not win his first start against the Atlanta Braves later that 1967 season, writer William Leggett noted that "Manager Red Schoendienst liked what he had seen, and Torrez began to figure quite high in his plans for the future." A recent work on this Cardinals team summarized the franchise's hopes for Torrez stating, "Torrez gave the Cardinals' coaching staff yet another option from their deep stable of pitchers."[33]

After the triumphant conclusion of the World Series, the Cardinals asked Torrez to pitch in a winter league. In this era it was not at all unusual for MLB teams to send talented prospects to sharpen their skills in

Caribbean-based associations. In addition to potential future stars, many current Latino players participated to stay in shape and play before "their people." For Torrez, however, his background created issues as, due to his surname, it was assumed he was fluent in *Español*. Given the era during which he grew up, it was not uncommon for Mexican American families not to encourage children to speak Spanish, beyond just a few words as ethnic markers. His lack of fluency led to some awkward situations. It turns out that he had not wanted to play for Licey. However,

"This guy called me from Santo Domingo. He was speaking Spanish and I was trying to tell him I didn't want to pitch there. But he must have misunderstood me. I don't speak Spanish too well. Anyway, he sent me a contract, and I thought, what the heck, so I signed." Mike also had trouble in an interview with a Spanish-speaking radio station. "The guy asked me in Spanish how tall I was and I told him 220 pounds. It really cracked him up."[34]

The language barrier notwithstanding, he performed well, finishing with a record of 6–7 and an ERA of 2.20 in 106 innings. One highlight of this campaign occurred on December 17, as he was on the mound the entire game and pitched the Tigers to a 2–1 11-inning victory over the *Aguilas* (Eagles).[35] Such impressive performances raised his stock among Cardinals management. As one Topeka reporter argued, "word siphoning down from Busch headquarters indicates Torrez stands a good chance of becoming the fifth starter for the Cards. At least, he'll get a good look in spring training."[36]

Torrez pitching for the Licey club early in his career. While in Santo Domingo, he faced some troubles with local media as they simply assumed he was fluent in Spanish because of his ethnic background. He would return to the Dominican Republic after his release by the A's in 1984 and help lead the Tigers to a title that winter. Photograph courtesy Southwest Collection/Special Collections Library, Texas Tech University, Lubbock, Texas, Mike Torrez Scrapbook Collection, Binder 21019.

It is interesting that in this interview, Torrez discussed how playing in the Caribbean had forced him to miss two things he most enjoyed during Kansas winters: hunting and playing "some basketball. I should get back by January and I hope to play some then—maybe some city league and some Mexican tournaments." Even as Torrez neared reaching "the show," sporting events among, and with, co-ethnics remained of vital importance.[37]

The opportunity to join the starting pitching rotation of a Major League squad is very difficult, and was a particular predicament for Torrez as he reported for spring training in 1968. For example, Dave Groat of *The Sporting News* argued that the "toughest roster to crack would be that of the.... Cardinals ... [but that they would] take a long look at several promising pitchers including.... Mike Torrez."[38] *Sports Illustrated* seconded this assertion by including Torrez in an article (and cover) about "hot rookies" for the upcoming 1968 season that featured other future stars, such as the Cincinnati Reds' catcher, Johnny Bench, and the California Angels' Mexican-born third baseman, Aurelio Rodriguez. In the article, William Leggett noted, like Groat, that Torrez had a tough road before him. "Mike Torrez, the tall, handsome kid pitcher for the St. Louis Cardinals, is being counted on to step into a pitching rotation that already includes Bob Gibson, Nelson Briles, Steve Carlton, and Dick Hughes, and this is a very high step to climb."[39]

Torrez had turned some heads, though there was continued trepidation concerning his bouts of wildness. Still, his potential, and fastball, were difficult to overlook, and he headed north with the team. Torrez earned his first Major League victory against Chicago on April 19, helping the Cardinals defeat the Cubs, 9–2. He had an impressive line, with 5⅔ innings pitched, seven hits allowed, four free passes, one strikeout and two earned runs surrendered. In addition to Torrez's performance, another young hurler, Hal Gilson, pitched the remaining 3⅓ innings, allowing only one hit. Cardinals historian Doug Feldmann summarized the evening as a "night [that] belonged to the youngsters," which boded well for St. Louis' continued dominance in the National League.[40]

By late May, Torrez sported a 2–1 record with a 2.64 ERA. However, the starting rotation for the Cardinals had been so efficient—and in Bob Gibson's case—thoroughly dominant, that there had been little opportunity to utilize Torrez except out of the bullpen. As a result, nearly seven weeks into the season, he only had 17⅓ innings under his belt. After a problematic relief appearance against the Phillies (he walked three batters in only 1⅔ innings), management had seen enough. Larry Harnly of the Springfield, Missouri *State Journal-Register* summarized the situation by

stating that Red Schoendienst confronted a problem most baseball managers would dearly love to have, that of fielding such a superb starting
staff that a prized rookie languished by only working in relief. After not
having pitched Torrez for almost three weeks, General Manager Bing
Devine determined that the prospect would be better off at Tulsa with a
steady spot in a starting rotation. "Anybody is going to suffer when he
hasn't worked in 18 games or so. I know he would rather start than relieve."
Even though Torrez had been effective at the Major League level, he
packed his bags for the return trip to the minors. Still, there was the expectation that this would be the final journey "down" the professional ladder.
As Harnly noted, with the approach of Major League expansion for 1969
(with the Seattle Pilots and the Kansas City Royals entering the American
League, and the Montreal Expos and the San Diego Padres joining the
National League), "the hunch here
is that when the Cardinals have to
protect 15 of the 40 players on
their major league roster prior to
the ... draft on Oct. 15, Torrez will
be one of the 15."[41]

Although disappointed, Torrez responded with a solid effort
in his first performance for the Oilers, a 9–1 victory over the Spokane
Indians.[42] After not having pitched
for an extended period, the work
with Tulsa produced the exact
results that Torrez (and the Cardinals) had hoped for. "I pitched
five innings against the Giants the
first week in May, but have had little work since. There's one quick
way back to St. Louis, and that's

Torrez in his home whites while with the Tulsa Oilers. While he was disappointed to have been sent back down to AAA after a very solid spring training
in 1968, Torrez's success with this team helped attract attention and eventually led to his participation in the Cardinals' tour of Japan after the World
Series. He would finally earn a spot in the St. Louis rotation in 1969. Photograph courtesy of the Southwest Collection/Special Collections Library, Texas
Tech University, Lubbock, Texas, Mike Torrez Scrapbook Collection, Binder
21022.

to do the job here in Tulsa." In this outing, his full arsenal of pitches was on display. As Jesse Owens from the *Tulsa World* noted, the young pitcher was no longer relying merely on a blazing fastball to get batters out, but rather mixed his pitches well and kept opponents off-balance with breaking balls. Buoyed by the result, the ever-confident Torrez was convinced that his stay in Oklahoma would be brief. "If you look at my averages, I should still be there [in St. Louis]. Later in the season when the hot weather and the doubleheaders set in, they might need me."[43] He followed this victory with an even better accomplishment, pitching a complete-game, two-hit shutout against the Oklahoma City 89ers in his next time on the mound.[44]

The opportunity to start regularly was exactly what Torrez needed as he completed the campaign with an 8–2 mark and a 3.24 ERA, bringing his overall minor league record to 29–26. Manager Warren Spahn noted "when he goes back [to St. Louis], he will be a starter." He did not start more games for the Oilers because of a stint in the Marine reserves, plus an injured arm that sidelined him until the end of July. The time away from the rotation led him to overthrow his pitches upon his return, and that led to a trip to St. Louis, not to start Major League games, but rather to receive therapy. As he noted ruefully, "I tried to make up for what I missed, figuring the Cardinals might need me in August.... I got to St. Louis all right, but for arm treatment, not to pitch." Now four years beyond his signing, Torrez found it hard to be patient and continue to wait for his chance to join the big club's rotation.[45]

The opportunity to pitch at AAA also afforded Torrez participation in playoff action, as Tulsa, rebounding from a last-place finish the previous campaign, was the dominant team in the circuit and won the PCL title in 1968 with a record of 95–53, then defeating Spokane, 4–1, in a best-of-seven championship round.[46] At the conclusion of the year, Torrez came to accept that the time in Tulsa had been a positive for his overall professional development:

> I never dreamed I would be sent down. I hadn't pitched bad enough to merit being sent down. I told them I didn't think they gave me a chance. I was mad about the whole thing. But now as I look back I know it may have been the best thing. Pitching every fourth or fifth day has really helped me. My control is better, my curve is better, and I feel good and strong.[47]

Torrez had little time to enjoy the success, or to even to rest his arm, from the just concluded 1968 season, for shortly after the Oilers' triumph in the PCL title series, the parent organization asked him to join the reigning National League champions on a month-long tour of Japan. In part, this

Although Torrez did not get to play in the 1968 World Series for St. Louis, his impressive performance for the AAA Tulsa Oilers merited him an invitation to the Cardinals' tour of Japan after the Fall Classic. Here, he pitches against the Yomiuri Giants. Photograph courtesy of the Southwest Collection/Special Collections Library, Texas Tech University, Lubbock, Texas, Mike Torrez Scrapbook Collection, Binder 6001. Reprinted with permission from the St. Louis Cardinals.

was a reward for a sterling second half of the campaign in Tulsa. In addition, with the expansion draft, retirements, and a series of trades, the team's roster was reduced and this opened the possibility of taking some rookies on the junket. The selection of Larry Jaster by the Montreal Expos in the expansion draft, Roger Maris' retirement, and the Cardinals' trading of John Edwards, Bob Tolan and Wayne Granger made it possible to include Torrez and first-base prospect Joe Hauge on the tour.[48]

Torrez excelled in these exhibitions, both on the mound and at the plate. He was the losing pitcher in the second game of the trip, 3–2, giving up a single to Shozo Doi of the Tokyo Giants after coming on in relief in the bottom of the ninth.[49] Later, he picked up a victory in a complete-game performance, 5–3. He scattered seven hits and struck out six over a combined squad made up of Yomiuri Giants and Hiroshima Toyo-Carps players.[50] A true highlight, however, was when Torrez hit a home run as part of a 3–2 victory over another combined team made up of Yomiuri Giants and Chunichi Dragon squads on the next-to-last game of the schedule. Overall, Torrez was ecstatic as he wound up the leading hitter for the Cardinals during their Japanese stint to go along with a 3–1 record on the mound, pitching 26 innings, yielding 18 hits, and striking out 13 batters.[51] As a beat writer noted, while, like many rookies, he had initially carried the bags of team leader Orlando Cepeda, by the end of the visit, Torrez boasted that "When we get back, I'll be the pitching ace."[52] After an impressive second-half turnaround with the Tulsa Oilers and good success during the Japanese exhibitions, Torrez looked forward to 1969 as his chance to make it to, and stick with, the St. Louis Cardinals.

Before that happened, however, several important developments regarding player-management relations occurred that would play significant roles in the remainder of Torrez's professional career. First, with the hiring of Marvin Miller in 1966, the Major League Baseball Players Association (MLBPA) entered a new phase in its interactions with team owners. As noted by baseball historian Benjamin G. Rader, by the end of 1966:

> the owners had learned more about Miller's intentions. They now knew that he planned nothing less than a fundamental reordering of the relationship between management and the players. No longer would the owners be able to decide unilaterally on minimum salaries, working conditions, or the size of their contribution to the pension fund. In the future, such issues would be decided at the bargaining table.[53]

Opposite, bottom: **Torrez is congratulated by teammates after circling the bases after his home run in Japan. Photograph courtesy of the Southwest Collection/Special Collections Library, Texas Tech University, Lubbock, Texas, Mike Torrez Scrapbook Collection, Binder 6004. Reprinted with permission from the St. Louis Cardinals.**

Mike Torrez enjoys a bit of camaraderie with Orlando Cepeda, while traveling via coach during the team's tour of Japan in 1968. Photograph courtesy of the Southwest Collection/Special Collections Library, Texas Tech University, Lubbock, Texas, Mike Torrez Scrapbook Collection, Binder 6005. Reprinted with permission from the St. Louis Cardinals.

Torrez getting off of the bus at a stop in Japan. His most vivid memories of this trip concerned his ability to make long distance calls to Mary and John in Topeka on the team's dime. Photograph courtesy of the Southwest Collection/Special Collections Library, Texas Tech University, Lubbock, Texas, Mike Torrez Scrapbook Collection, Binder 6007. Reprinted with permission from the St. Louis Cardinals.

In 1968 the players and team owners signed the first "basic agreement" in professional sports, part of which stipulated an increase in the minimum salary for players at the Major League level from $7,000 to $10,000 per season. Additionally, the union earned the right for agents to represent players as well as the establishment of a formal grievance process. The months just before the start of the 1969 season produced other key occurrences, such as owners easing out General William Eckert from the Commissioner's office and replacing him with Bowie Kuhn. Miller, believing that owners were dragging their feet in regard to another key issue, player pensions, asked veterans to boycott camps just prior to the start of spring training. Almost 400 members of the union complied with this request.[54]

This turn of events presented Mike Torrez with a twofold opportunity. First, with many of the "known commodities" in the Cardinals' lineup not in camp, young players/pitchers had a greater likelihood to show what they could do (for example, Orlando Cepeda did not report to camp that year until the day before the first exhibition game). In conjunction with this, Red Schoendienst's preference for utilizing five starters meant that the Cardinals were looking for someone to solidify the back end of the rotation as Dick Hughes (who had gone 16–6 in 1967, but who had a troublesome 1968), the previous occupant of that post, was no longer perceived as a starter. Thus, the final slot would come down to a battle among younger pitchers, such as Santiago Guzman, Jerry Reuss, Chuck Taylor, Dave Giusti (recently acquired from the San Diego Padres), and Mike Torrez. If the team could find a solid fifth hurler, Curt Flood argued, St. Louis was likely to achieve a third consecutive trip to the post-season (now under the new division setup, which started in 1969).[55]

Second, with overall working conditions and earnings potential improving for players, it now meant that the hoped-for "big money" Torrez wanted for himself and his family might finally be there for his taking. In one of the first articles from St. Petersburg that year, *The Sporting News* columnist Bob Broeg noted, "Mike Torrez wasn't about to let the players' dissatisfaction with pension terms keep him out of the camp of the National League champion Cardinals. Not when he had a good chance to make the pitching staff and a pretty fair shot at a starting assignment."[56]

Initially, it seemed as if Torrez had the inside track for the final spot on the rotation, given his record in Tulsa and Japan. Other than the injury he had suffered after returning from the Marines, the past one and one-half seasons had been highly successful. As the Cardinals headed to camp for 1969, George Silvey, the man who signed Torrez, sounded very upbeat about the Kansan's chances. "We picked Torrez's record apart.... He was

8–2 the last half of '67 … and 8–2 this year at Tulsa. Counting the 2–2 with the Cardinals, that makes him 18–6…. Those are pretty good credentials when you remember that he hadn't even been regarded as having arrived." Torrez held up his end of the bargain by pitching well during the club's time in Florida. Among the highlights were a three-inning scoreless appearance on March 13 and a sterling five-inning performance against the Royals in early April, leading the squad from the eastern part of the Show-Me State to a 1–0 victory over Kansas City in the expansion team's first home appearance. After this contest, both manager and catcher were very complementary of Torrez, particularly concerning his control. As Schoendienst noted, "He was real good. His trouble before always was control, but he's had that all spring." Battery-mate Tim McCarver noted that Torrez's mechanics had also improved. "Of course, he pitched good last year…. But he'd be a little too strong … and had a tendency to be high all the time. Sometimes he gets to standing up too straight, instead of bending over when he pitches. He likes me to remind him." The victory over the cross-state squad pushed Torrez's final spring record to 4–1 and made it possible for him to go north with the Cardinals again. The difference would be that this time, even with some troubles at the start of the season (for both Torrez and the team), his stay in the majors would last the entire campaign.[57] As he went north with the club, he not only joined one of the most successful teams in the game, but also one of the most diverse locker rooms in all of the majors.

By the middle of the 1960s there was an increased presence of Latinos on the rosters of teams in baseball's pinnacle circuit. One of the most notable popular media discussions of this topic appeared in a 1965 *Sports Illustrated* article entitled "The Latins Storm Las Grandes Ligas," by Robert H. Boyle.[58] In this essay the principal focus was on foreign-born players: mostly Dominicans, Puerto Ricans and Cubans. Much of the commentary included within this essay would sound a bit offensive to early 21st-century sensibilities, with Doyle (and others) noting that some players had "strange" customs relating to their religious beliefs and practices, for example. Further, there was a liberal amount of stereotyping in regard to the players' emotional dispositions based on their nationalities, with terms such as "fussy and noisy extroverts" (as regards Cubans) bandied carelessly about. On the other hand, Dominicans were classified as "more reserved and formal, though their politics may be tumultuous." Finally, Puerto Ricans were perceived to be "as reserved as Dominicans but more sensitive to slights." Perhaps this reflects the national media's reactions to some of Roberto Clemente's interactions with reporters. Doyle noted that it was quite rare for a Mexican to make it to the majors and pointed out that Mexican-born Ruben Amaro (then with the Phillies) was among the few who had done so (though the writer also mentioned that Amaro was half–Cuban). No distinguishing character traits were mentioned or recognized concerning players of Mexican American backgrounds, such as Mike Torrez or Pat Corrales.[59] In sum, this article was instructive regarding the existence of a new dynamic in Major League clubhouses, the effervescent, prideful, and sometimes difficult Latino. How such character traits made Latinos different from other ethnic/racial groups (such as Italian Americans and Irish Americans, for example) that had been in the majors for generations was not addressed. Further, how would such players ultimately fit into MLB locker rooms? Would this trend have any impact on how Mike Torrez would fit in with his Cardinals teammates?

Torrez pitching in an exhibition game in Kansas City against the expansion Royals in 1969. This was the culmination of a dream for the Torrez family. Not only did Mike make it to the big leagues this season, he also pitched in the first home (not regular season) game of the franchise located nearest to his home town. Photograph courtesy *Topeka Capital Journal.*

Researchers have noted that some franchises adapted well to such circumstances, while others struggled. Recently, historian John N. Ingham, in an article detailing the trials and tribulations of the 1967 Pirates, noted how difficult this balancing act could be.[60] Ingham examined the problems that existed within the Pittsburgh clubhouse as the team, which already included white ethnic heroes (such as local boy made good, Bill Mazeroski), African American stars (such as Willie Stargell), and Spanish-surnamed luminaries (such as the incomparable Clemente), struggled to coalesce into a cohesive unit, particularly after the arrival of Maury Wills in 1967 and the naming of Harry "the Hat" Walker (brother of Dixie Walker, he of the petition against Jackie Robinson among the Brooklyn Dodgers in 1947) as manager prior to the start of the 1966 season. Also troubling (as far as African American athletes were concerned) were Walker's ties to another individual with a nefarious history regarding baseball's reintegration: Ben Chapman. The Alabama-born field general, so prominently and disgustingly displayed in the recent movie "42," had been Harry's manager with the Phillies at the time of Robinson's debut. While many teams were guilty of mistreating Robinson in his rookie season, most contemporary observers (and historians) have concluded that the club from the City of Brotherly Love was particularly obnoxious and went above and beyond the pale of other squads in the National League in its harassment.

Obviously, the personalities and backgrounds of each player, field general, the press and the city's ethnic composition have to be taken into consideration (and Ingham does, in wonderful detail). Ingham's research, however, indicates that the Pirates of 1967 split along three fault lines: with the Latinos and most whites backing Walker, most of the African Americans opposed to "the Hat," and the remaining whites being quite ambivalent about the whole situation. The key issue discussed in the essay, however, was that the arrival of players from Spanish-speaking nations/backgrounds did, at least in this circumstance, helped create or intensify cleavages among the players on a particular team.[61]

The squad that Mike Torrez joined seems to have been one that did manage to establish a better rapport among the various groups and focused primarily on continuing their winning ways (having won a World Series and two consecutive National League pennants going into 1969). A May 25, 1968, article in *The Sporting News* noted that a great deal of the reason for this level of geniality among the various racial and ethnic groups in the St. Louis locker room was due to the presence and leadership of Orlando Cepeda. This contrasted dramatically with Cepeda's previous experiences with the San Francisco Giants. As reporter Neal Russo noted:

> There had been cliques in San Francisco. There were Negroes and the Latins and the American whites. Juan Marichal, in a magazine article, charged that there was even more bigotry toward Latins than toward Negroes in America. Cepeda prefers not to talk about the Giant problem. He feels that sort of situation has been vanishing fast. "First, there now are many more Latins in the majors than when I was breaking in.... We know the other players, the fans, the writers and broadcasters and the club officials better, and they know us better. We understand each other more. Years ago, many Americans didn't understand us Latins and often they didn't try."[62]

In addition, Cepeda worked constantly with players of different backgrounds to help create a cohesive unit both on the field and off. As an *Ebony* writer noted, going into 1968, "El Birdos may not have players all of the same feather, but, countering the old adage, they flock together. In spring training, a coach called them 'the loosest team I've ever seen.'"[63] Further evidence of the team's ability to cross ethnic lines can be seen in how the teammates socialized, even during the World Series of 1967, with players of the various contingents gathering at the house of Celtics great Bill Russell while visiting Boston.

There is no doubt that Orlando Cepeda helped institute a fairly positive and socially accepting atmosphere among all of the groups in the Cardinals' clubhouse, but Mike Torrez did not get to spend much time to interact with him for, in a surprise move, the St. Louis front office traded the popular Puerto Rican to the Atlanta Braves for Joe Torre just before the start of the 1969 season.[64] Still, it appears that, from the perspective of interracial/interethnic relations, the team that Torrez joined was much more accepting of individuals of diverse backgrounds than others in the majors at this time. As long as an athlete contributed to a continuation of the winning tradition of recent campaigns, his background was not much of a concern in the Busch Stadium clubhouse. A recent work on the history of the 1967 and 1968 Cardinals summarized the team's racial/ethnic relations:

> The Cardinals had ... proven something—how a team and a city could stay together. Cepeda's "El Birdos"—with their eclectic mix of races, personalities, demeanors, and abilities—modeled a camaraderie, togetherness, and stability that was absent from most other sectors of American life in the 1960s. "I enjoyed the city and my teammates," Cepeda said of his years in St. Louis. "I've never seen a team that had so many different individuals hold the same approach to the game, and to life. I've never seen a group work together so closely."[65]

While the players on the Cardinals (and those who followed baseball in general) may not have been mindful of Torrez's ethnic background, the folks back home in the barrios of Topeka certainly were. As in other parts of the nation with an abundant Mexican American presence, Kansas' capital city experienced its own version of the Chicano Movement in the later part of the 1960s (and through the 1970s). This social movement looked for heroes, and as Mike Torrez gained greater and greater notoriety in the majors, many came to view him as a role model for community youths to emulate. This aspect of Torrez's story is important because, until very recently, there had been little effort to link the Chicano-era drive for Mexican American rights with sporting endeavors. Two recent studies of this time period proffer effective overviews of the plethora of undertakings associated with the *movimiento* in the areas of unionization, religion, legal struggles, politics, and other topics; however, neither provides much of a discussion of the connection of the era's efforts with Mexican American participation in sports.[66]

As regards the Chicano Movement in the Midwest (and Kansas, in particular), the activities of groups there mirrored much of what occurred in California, Texas and elsewhere. It is important to provide a brief overview of their activities here. For example, Richard Santillan's research notes that activists "utilized demonstrations, sit-ins, school walk-outs, boycotts, marches, picket lines, and other forms of civil disobedience" in the region. These methods were used to confront police abuses, discriminatory practices, and racial gerrymandering, and to push for greater political representation, better educational opportunities, and bilingual education. A prime example of the movement's efforts in Topeka is demonstrated by a student walk-out (or "blowout") to protest conditions at Torrez's alma mater, Topeka High School, in April 1970. Here, "about 125 Mexican Americans walked out of classes ... and marched to the Board of Education Building," to seek better circumstances and more Spanish-surnamed instructors for barrio youths. Likewise, in the Sunflower State, the La Raza Unida Party (an alternative, ethnic-based, Mexican American political party which started in southern Texas in the mid–1960s) held political workshops for *estudiantes* at Wichita State University. The very next year, over 1,000 Chicano students attended a conference on the campus of Kansas State University in Manhattan to express their grievances and clamor for redress. Likewise, institutions such as Washburn University (in Topeka) and the state's flagship entity for higher education, Kansas University, saw the establishment of Mexican American/Chicano-based student organizations (both for undergraduates and for law school pupils) by the late 1960s or very early 1970s. Indeed, there were even Brown Beret (a more militant group under the general umbrella of the Chicano Movement) chapters in Wichita, Topeka, and Kansas City, Kansas, though these were quite small.[67]

A more direct discussion of Chicano-era events in Topeka can be gleaned from the recollections of a native of a barrio known as "the Bottoms" (right next to Oakland) named Thomas Rodriguez in his book, *Americano: My Journey to the Dream.*[68] Here, the author discusses some of the efforts undertaken in the capital city to improve conditions for Mexican Americans. For example, Rodriguez notes the development of job and life-skills training efforts, increased medical services for the elderly, the rise of advocacy groups (such as LULAC—the League of United Latin American Citizens), and veterans organizations (the American GI Forum—AGIF—which commenced operations in Topeka in 1954). Another key undertaking, Justicia, Inc., began operation in 1970 with the goal of assisting "the Spanish-speaking population ... in areas of law, education, law enforcement, the courts, economic development, and other endeavors." The Catholic Church sponsored a unit, *El Centro de Servicios Para Mexicanos* (The Center for Services for Mexicans), operated by the Archdiocese of Kansas City, Kansas.[69] This association had direct ties to Our Lady of Guadalupe, as the first director was the pastor for the parish, Father Ramon Gaitan. The associate director for El Centro was Mike's cousin, Gloria Torrez de Corona.

As noted previously, while there has been a great deal of discussion and research on the myriad organizations and efforts of the Chicano era, until recently, there had been little attempt to connect this period's undertakings with sport. In a 2011 work entitled *Latinos in U.S. Sport: A History of Isolation, Cultural Identity, and Acceptance*, historians Jorge Iber, Samuel O. Regalado, José M. Alamillo, and Arnoldo De Leon provide a preliminary effort to examine such ties.[70] At the level of the majors, of course, it is not surprising to discuss the undertakings of men such as Roberto Clemente, Orlando Cepeda, Juan Marichal and Felipe Alou to better conditions for Latino players and the broader Spanish-surnamed population. What makes the work noted above important is that the authors provide concrete examples of how sports were now recognized as a direct challenge to negative perceptions of the intellectual and physical capabilities of Spanish-speakers of all backgrounds. Just one example will suffice to illustrate this point. In a section on basketball, the authors noted the social importance and significance of the success of an athlete named Chuy Guerra, who played on the hardcourt for the Roma (Texas) High School Gladiators and the University of Texas–Pan American (now University of Texas, Rio Grande Valley) Broncos, to the broader Mexican American populace of this section of the Lone Star State. A quote by an area resident who was a teen during the Chicano Movement era, and who is now a professor at Texas Tech University Law School, Jorge Ramirez, connects directly the success of these teams with increased pride among the denizens of the mostly Mexican American communities of this region:

> I remember Chuy because I went to Pan American basketball games. The biggest sporting events that happened in the Valley revolved around Pan American University.... I remember when Coach Abe Lemons was hired to start coaching the team, he brought quite a bit of fame for the team and one of the players I remember was.... Guerra. I remember this because ... [he] was somebody I could look up to, somebody that I, as a Mexican American kid, could be proud of, somebody who was like me, somebody who was perhaps paving the way for those of us who were coming behind.[71]

In many ways, much of what Professor Ramirez indicates here mirrors points articulated by Mike and John Torrez, as well as some of the individuals interviewed by Richard Santillan in discussing Mexican American baseball and basketball leagues and teams in the Midwest. To an extent, Torrez's success would serve as an inspiration similar to that of Chuy Guerra in southern Texas.

After a series of frustrating bouts of wildness as he moved up the farm system through stints in North Carolina, Arkansas and Oklahoma, by the start of the 1969 season, Mike Torrez had achieved his goal of reaching the Major Leagues. Now that he shared a locker room (hopefully, on a more permanent basis than in late 1967 or early 1968) with pitching greats such as Bob Gibson, Torrez wanted to learn as much as possible from the veterans in the Cardinals clubhouse in order to help him remain in the majors. "When I first got up to the big leagues, I wanted to find out what made these guys successful. I wanted to pattern myself after these guys. I figured if they were successful with what they had done, it had to help me. So, I was always asking questions. I always wanted to learn."[72] The Cardinals seemed poised to continue their dominance in the National League as the majors moved in to the new era of divisional play (with St. Louis now located in the Eastern Division along with the Cubs, Mets, Pirates, Phillies and the newly-birthed Expos). Everything seemed to be in place for Mike Torrez to fulfill the promise that he started demonstrating when tossing pitches to Juan and John back in the Oakland neighborhood. The 1969 season, however, did not start well for either Torrez or the Cardinals due to issues both on and off the field.

5

"I Was Surprised They Gave Up on Me So Quick"
Torrez's Time in St. Louis and Montreal, 1969–1974

Mike Torrez's first full season with the St. Louis Cardinals, 1969, was impressive as he finished with a record of 10–4 and a respectable ERA of 3.59 (the team's overall ERA for that year was 4.06). While individually successful, the overall campaign was a setback for a squad that had won a World Series and two National League pennants over the previous two years. That season, the Redbirds slipped to a record of 87–75, finishing in fourth place, toward the lower echelons of the newly created National League East Division. For many in the Gateway City, this downturn, though disappointing, appeared but a bump in the road; after all, with the addition of promising young pitchers such as Torrez, Jerry Reuss, and Santiago Guzman to an established stable of talent featuring the likes of Steve Carlton, Nelson Briles and the already legendary Bob Gibson, St. Louis' mound corps, it seemed, was well positioned for a return to postseason glory in 1970. Additionally, the trade of Orlando Cepeda (to Atlanta) just prior to the start of 1969 had brought the potent bat of Joe Torre (he would hit .289 with 18 home runs and 101 runs batted in his first season with the Redbirds) to Busch Stadium, joining the likes of Lou Brock, José Cardenal, and Joe Hague in the daily batting order. Finally, the controversial trade of Curt Flood to the Philadelphia Phillies in October 1969 procured yet another legitimate power hitter, Dick Allen (he would hit 34 homers and drive in 101 runs in 1970), to the Cardinals' fold.

The highlight for Mike Torrez in the 1970 campaign took place on April 15 as he came tantalizingly close to pitching the first St. Louis-based National League no-hitter since 1924 against the second-year Montreal

Expos (leading his team to a 10–0 victory). Neal Russo of the *Post-Dispatch* summarized the young hurler's brush with immortality in a column on April 16. Not only was Torrez dominant on the mound, he also had a perfect day at the plate, going three-for-three, scoring two runs and driving in one. Russo conducted an interview with Mike's wife, Connie, whom he had married in May of 1969, to get her impressions of the action after the contest. In regard to her spouse's plate appearances, "they were all like home runs to me," she said. This victory was impressive for yet another reason: it was Torrez's 11th consecutive triumph for the Cardinals (he finished with nine successive wins in 1969 and this game raised his record for 1970 to 2–0). It seemed that the promise envisioned by organization back in 1964 was finally being realized. "'I wasn't even going to go to the game because I was thinking that this can't go on forever,' said jinx-minded Connie of … [the] winning streak." Only a leadoff single in the top of the eighth inning by center fielder Adolfo Phillips marred Torrez's effort. The performance even garnered praise from Bob Gibson, someone not normally effusive in offering admiration. The fault for the hit was not Torrez's, Gibson stated, but was rather that of the man behind the plate. "Don't ask Torrez about that pitch. Ask Joe Torre. He called the pitch." The backstop agreed, stating that, "Mike's fastball was really quick tonight. He was consistent with it, even with all of the walks. It sounds funny, but he wasn't as wild as he had been." A summary of Torrez's statistics from this game provided room for great optimism, but as Torre articulated, control remained a problem (with six walks allowed). No matter, this day was joyous for all concerned in the St. Louis clubhouse. At this early point in the season, the Cardinals were in an accustomed spot: first place.[1] But the rest of the 1970 season would not be as rosy as this mid–April exhibition.

Indeed, within little more than one year from this performance, Torrez's life and career path had turned a full 180 degrees away from that euphoric day. By mid–1971, he was no longer property of the St. Louis organization, he would be back in the minors (toiling for an awful AAA team affiliated with the Expos, the Winnipeg Whips), and his brief marriage would be on the verge of divorce. This chapter, then, will focus on the early years of Mike Torrez's career in the Major Leagues, highlighting his time in the National League cities of St. Louis and Montreal. During these seasons, he would come in contact with individuals who would play key roles in the remainder of his athletic career, primarily Curt Flood and Gene Mauch. Both men would reinforce for the young Kansan the vagaries of life in professional baseball, even at its highest levels. Flood would help to break down the shackles of the reserve clause, and eventually help to lead major leaguers to the promised land of free agency (of which Torrez would be an early beneficiary). The African American center fielder would also reinforce for Torrez and his teammates the importance of standing up for one's beliefs, as well as fighting to improve one's lot against difficult odds (similar to the efforts of many Mexican Americans back in Oakland and "the Bottoms"). After Torrez's trade to the Expos, new skipper Mauch would further solidify in Torrez's mind the need for security; for even though he pitched well for a poor team, it was not enough to remain in a city he grew to love. Meanwhile, back in Kansas, the barrio community continued its efforts to improve circumstances and began to focus more intently upon the success of a native son as a role model for the youth of the area.

After reaching the World Series in 1967 and 1968, the St. Louis Cardinals expected to continue their winning ways under the new divisional format that commenced in 1969. Given the competition in their division, which featured an expansion team (Montreal), a squad that had never had a winning season (New York Mets), and a traditional cellar-dweller (Philadelphia), it appeared that the Cardinals would feast regularly upon such weaklings and be in position to challenge the better nines (the Cubs and the Pirates) in the East. In pre-season prognostications, *The Sporting News* quoted Red Schoendienst as being confident in his returning pitchers, and happy to have a young player with plenty of upside. "I think that Mike can make it as one of our regular starters, and if he does, we'll have quite a pitching staff."[2] Other positive reviews of Torrez's potential to join the back end of the starting rotation came from coach Billy Muffett who, after seeing the young Kansan pitch consecutive scoreless performances in the first half of March, noted, "I have never seen him better."[3] Things looked even more positive when Dave Guisti, with whom Torrez was competing for the fifth starter spot, was ineffective in an exhibition outing against the Mets, retiring only one batter.[4] Torrez punched his ticket north with the big club by shutting down the Kansas City Royals in one of the final tune-ups before the start of the regular season, pitching five shutout innings to help St. Louis defeat the expansion club, 1–0, in the Royals' home debut at Municipal Stadium.[5]

While shining in various spring training assignments, Torrez did not get off to a fast start. Most of his early-season outings were of the middle-inning relief variety. One of his first appearances was in a 1–0 Cardinals defeat at the hands of the Cubs on April 16, wherein he pitched the top of the ninth inning in relief of hard-luck loser (against Ferguson Jenkins), Steve Carlton. This pattern continued for the next several weeks. In some games, he was certainly roughed up; for example, just four days later, he surrendered two earned runs and five hits in just two innings in a lopsided defeat to the Mets. A similar problematic performance followed on May 2 as he again gave up five hits and two earned in two innings, this time against the Phillies.[6] Torrez finally chalked up his first win in a relief appearance against expansion San Diego on May 9, coming in during the sixth inning, surrendering only one hit, and getting out of trouble with a double play. St. Louis scored five runs in the bottom of the frame, and he was credited with the victory. On the previous day, with his club having time off, he had married Connie Reisinger. He followed up his win with two more shutout innings versus the Padres on the tenth.[7] Perhaps this would be the start of another streak similar to that with the Oilers in 1968 that helped catapult him into his spot with St. Louis.

It was not to be, however, as the situation for the pitcher and the club got progressively worse as the first half of the season unfolded. Between his victory in early May and the start of July, Torrez, inserted into the regular rotation, failed to register another triumph over four less-than-impressive starts. Once again, walks were a problem. On May 24, he gave up only two hits to the Dodgers, but walked five and was replaced after 5⅔ innings, trailing, 1–0; the Cardinals lost, 5–0. A particularly poor performance during this skid came on June 5, when he was roughed up by the usually light-hitting Houston Astros in a game the Cardinals lost, 11–6. As the starter, Torrez gave up five runs, six walks, and four hits, lasting only through the fourth frame. An even more problematic outcome occurred in a St. Louis victory against the Cincinnati Reds on June 11. Although his offense staked him to an early 5–0 lead, he failed to last through the third inning, giving up three runs and being replaced by Mudcat Grant, who was credited with the 10–5 win.[8]

Toward the end of June, however, Torrez began to turn around his performance, even though he would lose one more game. On June 22, the Cardinals lost to the Mets and the great Jerry Koosman, 1–0. Torrez went stride for stride with the New York pitcher, giving up only seven hits and striking out five over seven innings pitched. Back-to-back extra-base hits in the bottom of the sixth by Bud Harrelson (triple) and Tommy Agee (double) doomed St. Louis, and dropped Torrez's season record to 1–4. After this start, he returned to the bullpen, coming on in relief on June 28 and 29 in two more Cardinals defeats (to the Cubs, 3–1 and 12–1).[9]

Although not an overwhelming outing, Torrez finally got his second victory against New York on July 1, pitching eight innings and allowing five earned runs on eight hits and three free passes. He followed that with a stronger start against the Phillies on the tenth; earning a 9–3 victory. He then reported for Marine Reserve duty. He returned to the mound on July 17 and again dispatched the Phillies, 11–3. As the majors approached the All-Star break, it seemed that Torrez had regained his momentum. It had been a difficult first part of the season, but his record was now even at 4–4 (though his ERA stood at a hefty 4.60). The defending National League champions, likewise, limped into the brief mid-season hiatus with a resoundingly mediocre 49–48 record, and trailed the blazing Chicago Cubs by 11 games.

As do many players who are not involved in the celebrations surrounding the mid-summer classic, Torrez took the break to return to Topeka to visit with family and friends back in the Oakland and surrounding neighborhoods. In an article for the *Daily Capital*, reporter Bob Hentzen visited with the hometown major leaguer to get a better sense of how things were unfolding in St. Louis. Of course, one of the key elements of the interview focused on the Cardinals' unexpected on-field struggles. Like any good team member, Torrez expressed optimism and argued that his squad, though having endured a difficult first part of the campaign, would get back in the divisional race. "I think we are starting to get things put together. The guys are hitting the ball harder and we're getting more runs. At the first of the year, we couldn't get a fly ball when we needed it. Everything just went bad at once." Torrez argued that the team was playing better just before the break, and both players and fans were hoping for a repeat of St. Louis's performance from five years earlier when the Cardinals had a similar record (actually one game below .500 at the All-Star Game), yet caught and passed the Phillies on the last day of the season to earn the National League title. Given that many of the players from that team, such as Flood, McCarver, Brock, and Gibson, were still around, there was hope that another strong stretch run was possible. Further, after the break, the Cardinals were going on a western swing and Torrez argued, "we usually do pretty good against the Western ball clubs.... Our guys know what it is to win and they'll be giving a little extra."[10]

In regard to his individual performance, Torrez indicated that he had exhibited decent control of his pitches, and "I haven't been all over the place, just missing a little. With a few breaks here and there and a few runs, it might have been different." Additionally, he believed that the various pitching changes instituted for the 1969 season, particularly lowering the mound from 15 inches to ten inches in response to the dominance of pitchers such as Bob Gibson the previous campaign, as well as a smaller strike zone, had had a detrimental impact on hurlers:

It seems like on your curve ball you don't get it to bite off the lower mound. Briles (Nelson) has had a lot of trouble. His curve was breaking flat—like a slider. The hitters rare back and hit that as far as they want to. Most all of the pitchers seem to be throwing higher. Even Gibson. He was in and out (with his deliveries) last year. This year he's up and down. It seems like they have us throwing underneath the ground ... in a foxhole.[11]

While this article served as an interesting first-hand synopsis for Topekans of how the Redbirds were doing, the essay is also important for yet another reason. It is one of the very first exposés to present a chronicling of this major leaguer's participation in an event that had significance for the denizens of the barrios of Kansas' capital city. In particular, the photo that accompanied the piece provides a very meaningful narrative. The photo shows Torrez sharing some of the "tricks of the trade" with an almost exclusively African American and Latino youth audience. Here, the still implies, was an example of the possibilities extant for these young men. Their fathers and other family members might work in low-paying, difficult occupations, but here was "one of their own" who had utilized the opportunities provided by baseball in order to improve both his own financial standing as well as that of his family. Here is not only a general "hometown boy makes good" story, but one that can be particularly embraced by the residents of Oakland, the Bottoms, and elsewhere. As the Chicano Movement era continued to unfold in Kansas, such demonstrations of pride became more common.[12]

While the latter half of 1969 did not produce another pennant, as the "Amazing" Mets surprised the rest of the National League and claimed the crown, the Cardinals did improve dramatically in the waning months and eventually finished a respectable 12 games over the break-even mark. Torrez, who after a 1–4 start did not lose another game all season, was a major factor in this development. Torrez had numerous highlights during this nine-game winning streak. Among them, three performances, all complete games, stood out. First, in a game against the San Francisco Giants on July 27, he allowed only two walks during an 8–2 triumph. Next, on August 7, he allowed only five hits and three walks (with six strikeouts) in a 2–1 defeat of the San Diego Padres. Finally, in a game on September 19 in Wrigley Field over the by-then-fading Cubs, he gave up only seven hits and four walks as part of a 7–2 win. This defeat was part of a painful tail-off by Chicago toward the end of this season. In response to the fine outing by the Cardinals' young pitcher, Cubs manager Leo Durocher could only grumble that "we beat their good pitcher (Gibson) and then let this guy (Mike Torrez) get away."[13]

As occurred during his stay with the AAA Tulsa Oilers, *The Sporting*

News took notice of Torrez's post–All-Star Game turnaround, and Neal Russo generated a piece on how the 22-year-old figured prominently in the Cardinals' resurgence. Russo noted that St. Louis produced a strong 20–8 record for July and substantially cut into their deficit versus Chicago (which had been 15½ games at the end of June and getting as close as 7½ games back). During this month, Torrez and Carlton were both 4–0, Chuck Taylor was also unbeaten at 3–0, and Briles was "only" 4–2. Simultaneously, the offense benefitted from sustained periods of production by Joe Torre (18 RBI), Vida Pinson (22-game hitting streak) and Julian Javier (.333 average and 14 RBI). Not surprisingly, what helped Torrez during his own winning streak was getting the ball over the plate consistently. In one of his final defeats of 1969, the young Topekan admitted, he had put too much pressure on himself because Juan and Maria were in attendance at Busch Stadium. "I wanted to do good so badly because my folks were in from Kansas." Once he regained his command, however, things improved substantially, including the three complete games described above. Another aspect of the turnaround came from Torrez seeking advice from Bob Gibson. "I've learned so much from him on the bench, especially on how to pitch certain hitters. Gibby reminds me I've got to get ahead of the hitters … and when they guess, they lean in on pitches instead of sitting back and waiting."[14]

Even with their torrid pace from July, the Cardinals were unable to catch the Cubs; though they got as high as second place before the Mets cruised past both St. Louis and Chicago to earn the inaugural National League East division title. As the season headed toward its conclusion, recriminations about this "failure" became prevalent. One line of thought argued that management had made far too many changes to the roster from the team that had earned back-to-back National League titles. Further, there were other arguments that focused on how realignment had "punished" the Cardinals by placing them in the East, as opposed to the West division. After all, the Gateway City is further West than both Cincinnati and Atlanta, no? Given how well the Mets and the Cubs played that season, St. Louis would have been closer to first place in the NL West than they ever achieved in the NL East. Toward the end of August, with approximately one-quarter of the season left, as Neal Russo noted, St. Louis had dominated western rivals (36–21), while they were sub-break-even against divisional foes (31–32). If only they had been in the "right" division, the Cardinals would have been only one game out of first place heading into September.[15]

Although putting up a valiant, if uneven, fight, St. Louis was eliminated from contention on September 21, but the "rigor mortis had set in some time back and the patient had been ailing right from the start, with three straight losses to the Pirates [on] April 8–9–10." It turned out that the changes to the lineup, even with the fine season by Torre, simply did not generate sufficient scoring punch. "As season's end neared, the Cardinals were still engaged in a hot battle with.... Montreal for 11th place in scoring in a 12-team league." Such a putrid offensive output is not what division titles are made of. While the offense sputtered, however, the mound staff certainly did its part for the cause. As the end of September approached, the threesome of Carlton, Gibson, and Torrez had notched an overall mark of 44–26. Indeed, it appeared that this side of the Cardinals' equation was ready to go for 1970. After winning nine consecutive decisions, Torrez appeared on his way to being an important cog in the rotation for years to come. The Cardinals acted quickly and resigned Torrez for what was termed "a modest raise."[16] Shortly after the end of this season, one of his teammates, Curt Flood, would be traded to the Philadelphia Phillies after an excellent decade, both on defense (center field) and at the plate, with St. Louis. Flood's reaction to this trade started a process that would make the phrase "signed for a modest raise" after a year such as Torrez had just completed into an anachronism by the later part of the 1970s.

There have been many authors, both popular and scholarly, who have detailed the timeline and significance of Curt Flood's personal story, his refusal to report to the Phillies, as well as the changes unleashed because of this heroic stance (of which Mike Torrez would certainly become a beneficiary). In addition, Flood himself penned a personal narrative of his life and the circumstances that commenced in October of 1969 and continued through the Supreme Court decision of 1972, *Flood vs. Kuhn.*[17] If it is possible to recap the argument the center fielder presented to the average baseball fan, as well as to the ownership of Major League baseball, it can be summarized by his response to a query by Howard Cosell in a television interview. When Cosell argued that $90,000 per year was an excellent salary and that the majority of Americans would settle gladly for such as amount of money, Flood replied presciently that, "A well paid slave is still a slave."[18]

In addition to Flood, the Cardinals included Byron Browne, Joe Hoerner, and Tim McCarver as part of the October 1969 transaction with Philadelphia. McCarver's reaction to the trade was similar to that of most ballplayers of this era. The athletes were the property of the various franchises, and this was how the game (both on the field and off) was played.

At this point, there was little if anything that individuals could do about such circumstances. "I really hate to leave St. Louis because I have enjoyed playing there…. The fans were as good as any … in the big leagues…. Maybe Curt Flood and Joe Hoerner and I can make the Phillies a live team again. They'd been going bad for quite a time."[19] Cardinals historian Doug Feldmann noted, "the other Cardinals were naturally stunned by the news of the situation," meaning both to the trade as well as Flood's "unusual" reaction to what was then merely standard operating procedure on the part of a club. Still, the locker room was seemingly pleased that "a bona fide power hitter was coming to the team as a result of the transaction." In return, the Cardinals were to receive slugger Dick Allen, the prime motivation for the deal in the first place, as well as infielder Cookie Rojas and pitcher Jerry Johnson.

Torrez was, like many on the squad, disappointed that a good friend such as Flood was leaving. Still, given how he had been treated by the franchise when he signed in 1964, Torrez's principal focus was not on the implications of Flood's battle against the majors and the reserve clause, but rather was on building upon his positive second half of the 1969 season to cement a permanent spot on the starting rotation and to further increase his earnings. The Cardinals were in a rebuilding mode, and the young Kansan was expected to "continue to develop in the absences of Briles, Washburn and Hughes, men who had quickly fallen from memory after being key components of the recent pennant-winning years."[20] By the end of November of 1969, Neal Russo projected that the starting rotation for St. Louis in the coming campaign would be: Gibson, Carlton, Briles, and Torrez.

To improve his standing with the organization, Torrez had a solid winter ball season (with the Licey Tigers), finishing his tour with an ERA of below 3.00, a 4–4 record, and two wins in the league playoffs.[21] Once again, director of player personnel George Silvey crowed about the young pitcher's performance. "Mike benefitted a lot because our pitching coach…. Billy Muffett, was managing the Licey club … [he] worked hard on his control … but the big thing was he got a lot of action against top hitters— like the three Alou brothers and Rico Carty."[22] A final positive from the 1969 season came when Torrez earned acclaim from the St. Louis chapter of the Baseball Writers' Association of America just before heading off to spring training in St. Petersburg, when he and Chuck Taylor shared the "Rookie of the Year" Award presented by the organization at a dinner staged on January 26, 1970.[23]

In anticipation of this upcoming campaign, Neal Russo provided insight for local fans as to the growing number of Latinos on the Cardinals: a total of ten "Latin Americans" now populated the team's pre-season roster. Interestingly, the article provided a stark differentiation between the "south of the border men" and Mike Torrez. Players such as Santiago Guzman, Julian Javier, and the newly acquired Cookie Rojas were presented as valuable cogs in the team's machinery, but also as individuals who might require the need for translators. "Too bad old Mike Gonzalez, the helpful coach of more than a generation ago, isn't around to help Schoendienst with his translating." Torrez, though it was noted that both of his parents were from Mexico, was not encompassed into the same category as were those players who hailed from the Dominican Republic, Cuba, and other Spanish-speaking nations. Thus, this article provides some support for the argument that Torrez, as a Mexican American, was not viewed in the same way as were other Latinos on the team.[24]

The 1970 season got off to a promising beginning as Torrez twice defeated the second-year Expos, 7–3 on April 9 and again on the 15th as noted at the start of this chapter. These two games ran Torrez's tally of victories to an impressive 11 consecutive, but the streak ended with a thud at Wrigley Field on April 22 when the young pitcher lasted a mere 1⅔ innings against the Cubs, giving up four runs and, more ominously, four walks. By the time he left the mound, Chicago led, 4–0, and a valiant St. Louis rally fell short in a 7–5 defeat. Two more losses followed, one a hard-luck loss versus the Braves (3–2, pitching 8⅔ innings); the other a less-than-impressive 7–3 outing against the Reds in which he gave up six runs and six hits in only five innings.[25]

Between the middle of May and the All-Star Game (on July 14) the only constant regarding Torrez's performances was inconsistency. Instead of becoming a reliable starter, he floundered, some days pitching well (for example, he held the Cubs scoreless for seven innings in a 1–0 Cardinals victory on May 15), and on others faring quite poorly. One lowlight for the first half of the season occurred on June 20. In a contest at Wrigley Field, he produced the shortest stint in his career up to that time, getting shelled for six earned runs in only ⅓ of an inning. He gave up but three hits in this barrage, but compounded his troubles with four walks. While not giving up many hits, he endured a severe lack of control that (as of the middle of June) had caused almost half of the runs given up to be the result of walks and hit batsmen (16 runs out of 34 earned). This debacle looked particularly poor as Carlton and Gibson followed up with 3–0 and 3–2 triumphs, moving the Cardinals closer to the East Division lead.[26] Maddeningly, just two days after his less-than-stellar outing, Torrez pitched nine innings of shutout baseball versus the Pittsburgh Pirates in a game that the Cardinals lost in extra innings, 1–0. A final example of his troubles came on July 2 against the Expos, when he lasted but ⅔ of an inning and surrendered a grand slam as part of a six-run first at Park Jarry. As the Cardinals headed into the break, his early 2–0 record had skidded to a lackluster mark of 6–8.[27]

Matters did not improve much after the All-Star Game, though Torrez produced a solid outing in his first appearance of the second half, a 3–1, complete-game victory over the Braves in which he walked only two batters. Even with this solid effort, his ERA was at 4.22 for the season toward the end of July.[28] Torrez's final victory of 1970 came on August 3 against the Phillies, 4–1, a complete-game five-hitter. This raised his record to 8–9. He had five more starts (four non-decisions and one loss—on September 24, 7–1 against the Cubs), and two relief stints over the rest of the campaign. His final record was a highly disappointing 8–10 with an ERA of 4.22. The entire Cardinals squad, even with the arrival of Dick Allen (in his first, and only, season in St. Louis), faltered badly and finished a woeful 76–86, 13 games behind the division-winning Pirates. A post-mortem of the season by Neal Russo noted that Gibson was his usual brilliant self (finishing 23–7), but that there was another pitcher who was now the apparent apple of management's eye: Jerry Reuss. Russo described Reuss' season as being one where he was "displaying brilliance over and over and putting himself high in the Cardinals' plans for 1971." This statement is a bit confusing, as Reuss, though younger than the "other" youthful hurler on the staff, Torrez, had a similar season: 7–8 with an ERA of 4.10. A final hint about the club's disappointment in Torrez occurred when he sought permission to pitch winter ball yet again, but this time was denied the opportunity. Overall, with the exception of Gibson, the mound staff for 1970 proved a major disappointment. As Russo noted, "the bullpen was a bust most of the season; the starting crew flopped, especially Steve Carlton (10–19) ... and Mike Torrez (from 10–4 record to 8–10)."[29]

After enduring a sub-.500 season for the first time since 1965, St. Louis fans and management looked forward to improved fortunes in 1971. Bing Devine did not sit idly by over the winter and quickly began to reshuffle the Cardinals' roster. Only four days after the end of the 1970 campaign, the general manager traded Dick Allen to the Dodgers for 1969 "Rookie of the Year" infielder Ted Sizemore and catcher Bob Stinson. Sizemore, in particular, had impressed Devine because he batted an even .500 (8-for-16) for Los Angeles during the team's visits to Busch Stadium. These additions, as well as a trade for Matty Alou (who had 231 hits in 1969), in hope of finally dispelling the ghost of Curt Flood, supposedly would help the overall offensive output and provide protection in the lineup for Joe Torre, who hit .325 in the just concluded season. Over the spring, Schoendienst took "a lot of time in March to sort out yet another new-look batting order, trying to settle on an opening-season lineup from among all of the new players."[30]

On the mound, opinions differed as to how the Cardinals' staff would perform. Former catcher Tim McCarver argued that St. Louis would bounce back as contenders in a Bob Broeg article which appeared just days prior to opening day. "They still got Gibby and they've got two good young ones in Mike Torrez and Jerry Reuss. And anybody who has seen him knows that big Steve is back."[31] Others, however, were not as certain. Neal Russo, in a piece that appeared just two weeks later in *The Sporting News*, noted that St. Louis was "loaded with 'ifs,'" and that much of this uncertainty centered upon the pitching staff, particularly the starters after Gibson and Carlton. He specifically noted that "Torrez, after scrapping the no-windup routine partly at the suggestion of Gibson, faltered and was dropped back" from being the fourth starter. This gave Reggie Cleveland, who had been used as a reliever in 1970, the opportunity to step into Torrez's slot.[32] The pressure was on again for the Topekan to regain his form and reclaim a spot in the rotation. Overall, things went surprisingly well for the team, as the Cardinals finished 90–72, in second place in the National League East, only seven games behind the division-winning Pirates.

From the moment that 1971 started for Torrez, however, things spiraled into both a professional and personal void. After the season (and after being traded to the Expos), Torrez spoke with Bob Hentzen of his hometown paper and stated that an accident in the Windy City during the opening series helped set the negative tone for the year. "I was getting a glass of water and it slipped. Like everybody, I think I have good hands and I tried to catch the glass. But it hit the sink and I cut the heck out of my hand. I had three stiches … and there was also a big gash on my wrist." By overcompensating for the injury, he developed a sore arm, and later, a similar ailment in his shoulder. "I had never had one (sore arm) before and I didn't say much about it. I kept thinking it would go away, but it didn't."[33]

Even with his injury, Torrez had a few effective performances. His first start, against Houston, was not terribly successful as he pitched 8⅓ innings and allowed five earned runs and five free passes. Torrez was charged with the Cardinals' 8–4 defeat. His next outing was better, with another eight innings pitched and only two earned runs in a 4–2 win against the Padres. At the end of April, Torrez suffered his second (and, it turns out, final) defeat for St. Louis, 9–1, against the Mets. This was an ineffective start as New York roughed the Kansan up for four runs in only three innings. After this stint, Schoendienst relegated Torrez mostly to middle relief until early June. He had two more starts in a St. Louis uniform, neither particularly successful. His final appearance for the organization that signed him shortly after high school came on June 12 against the Pirates. Torrez's final line as a Cardinal was two innings pitched, three earned runs, and most damagingly, five bases on balls.[34] Three days later, he was traded to the Expos for pitcher Bob Reynolds.

Neal Russo summarized Torrez's performance for the truncated season by stating, "Torrez, now 24, has struggled with a control problem that was accentuated by his absences for military reserve duty. In 36 innings ... he walked 30."[35] Torrez's final statistics for St. Louis were a 1–2 record and a hefty ERA of 6.00.[36] It is interesting to note that Russo did not mention any injury and arm troubles, but seemed to blame Torrez's ineffectiveness on his military service in the Marine Corps reserve. After concluding the transaction, Montreal assigned Torrez to their International League (AAA) team, the Winnipeg Whips. If things had been bad in the majors with the Cardinals, they quickly turned worse in Manitoba.

The Montreal Expos' first campaign in 1969 resulted, not surprisingly, in a horrid record of 52–110. One of the few highlights that season occurred when Bill Stoneman pitched a no-hitter against Philadelphia in only the franchise's ninth game. Beyond that, there was precious little to cheer for. Under the guidance of Gene Mauch, however, the Expos improved dramatically in 1970 and increased their victory total by 21 games to finish a more than respectable 73–89. This dramatic improvement generated aspirations of reaching the "coveted" .500 mark for 1971 (it did not happen, as the team actually fared just a bit worse, finishing 71–90). By the trading deadline, management was searching for more pitching depth to back up Stoneman, Steve Renko, and Carl Morton, who had a combined 20–17 record, while the remaining starters were but 1–8. It was in hope of unearthing extra firepower for their mound corps that Montreal sought out Torrez.[37]

Upon reaching Winnipeg, Torrez donned not a Whips uniform, but rather that of the Expos for an exhibition game between the parent club and its top affiliate. On June 18, Torrez was welcomed unceremoniously to the organization as his soon-to-be AAA teammates teed off on his offerings in an 11–3 victory. Not wanting to put too negative a spin upon their new acquisition's rough first innings, both managers, Mauch and Whips skipper Clyde McCullough, dutifully argued that Torrez "looked good." As when he was with the Tulsa Oilers, Torrez believed that if he was given the ball on a regular basis, that he would do well. "I needed this work. I'll be better if used regularly." Shortly after his arrival, the Whips were in next-to-last place in the IL with a record of 27–39 (for a .409 winning percentage). The rest of the season would not go anywhere near as well as Winnipeg collapsed and went 17–57 to finish a horrid 44–96, 42 games behind the Rochester Red Wings. Not surprisingly, the Whips finished last in the association in hitting (.248), runs per game (3.87), and pitching (5.97 team ERA).[38]

Torrez made a respectable impression over his first two starts, however, winning on June 21 against Toledo, 8–6, and stopping Richmond, 4–3, on June 26. On both occasions, he appeared to tire in the later innings and needed assistance from his bullpen. Now with a different organization, Torrez opened up to the press concerning his frustrations with how the Cardinals had treated him. After the game against the Mud Hens, he argued that the continued control problems stemmed from a lack of use during his stint in St. Louis. While demonstrating a fair amount of bitterness, he nevertheless remained confident in his abilities. "I had pitched a three-hitter against San Diego, went on a weekend with the military and when I rejoined the St. Louis team, I found I was no longer in the starting rotation. I was surprised they gave up on me, but I have no doubt that I'll be back in the majors soon with the Expos."

Although he struggled with the Whips (his final record was 2–4, with an ERA of 8.16), Torrez was given a chance to come up to Montreal at the end of the season. As Gene Mauch noted, this was part of a master plan by the organization, and patience was an important requirement for fans. "I am not interested in the number of games we win this year, whether it's 81, 71 or 91, I'm concerned only with the development of players who will win a lot of games for me one of these years." While Torrez endured a nightmarish 1971 at both the major league and AAA levels, the trade ultimately proved of benefit. After all, he was now the property of a third-year team, and perhaps the expansion trend in the majors might have been the opportunity the Topeka native needed to finally stick with, and develop into, a consistent starter at this level. Ironically, when the Expos called up Torrez for the last month, his initial appearance with his new club was against St. Louis in a 7–2 Cardinals victory. Although not in a winning effort, a now slimmer (he dropped almost 25 pounds after the trade) Torrez handcuffed his former team over three shutout innings of relief during his first appearance at Park Jarry.[39] Montreal general manager Jim Fanning, with only three reliable starters, hoped that the addition of Torrez and others would provide added strength for the following season. Part of this effort to further develop the 24-year-old prospect called for another assignment to a winter league, this time not in the Dominican Republic, but rather to Caracas, Venezuela, where Torrez was productive and had an ERA below 3.00.[40]

While still at Winnipeg, Torrez visited by phone with Topeka reporter Bob Hartzell and, in a lengthy discussion for the hometown folks, went into substantial detail about his issues during the campaign. In this article, the conversation focused mostly on on-field circumstances, such as being traded by the organization that thought so much about him in 1964. The *Topeka Capital Journal* essay provided an extensive summary of Torrez's travails, noting that at the time of the phone interview, "he isn't feeling at the top of the world at the moment." Torrez described the lack of talent on the Winnipeg squad and said, given the youth in the Montreal organization, the Whips were not really as talented as a typical AAA team. As for his own situation, he noted, "my arm has been weak from lack of throwing.... I don't know the hitters in this league, and they've been hitting me pretty good. The spot starting and all at St. Louis kind of messed me up." Further, he believed that leaving for his military commitment also stalled his progress. "I would throw pretty good and then leave for the Reserves. I would ... not throw for four or five days. Then I'd come back and work the first day back and my arm would stiffen up." Still, he professed a dogged determination to return to the majors. "They're waiting (at Montreal). They need help, and said they want me up there.... This is the worst year I've ever had, ... a lot of players go through it, and I think I'll bounce back."[41] In a later interview, this time with Expos beat reporter Ian MacDonald, Torrez focused on issues of a more personal nature (and the impact they had on his concentration): troubles with his marriage to Connie. "I use to lie awake at night wondering what to do about my marriage.... I didn't know if I should be there and forget baseball. Finally, I decided that the marriage was finished and started divorce proceedings." During their short marriage, Mike and Connie had a daughter named Christiann.

After making the difficult determination about his personal life, Torrez refocused on baseball. It was at this time that Jimmy Bragan replaced Clyde McCullough as manager of the Whips. It was Bragan who, on the suggestion of Mauch, asked Torrez to lose weight. While Torrez had a solid performance in his first appearance for Montreal, his new manager was not yet convinced of his value to the club. MacDonald even noted in one of his essays for *The Sporting News* that, as the Expos finalized their roster for the coming season, they considered cutting or trading the young Kansan. Because of his high ERA with Winnipeg, however, Montreal could not find a team with which to consummate an exchange. Ultimately, the Expos retained Torrez, not because they felt he would be of great value, but mostly because "his market value was low."[42] By the start of the 1972 season, then, Torrez was once again a single man and had another, albeit tenuous, opportunity to prove his worth at the Major League level. This season, however, would be radically different from the travails endured in 1971.

Some of the doubts Mauch harbored about Torrez's ability to improve his rotation were allayed during 1972. In his first five appearances, for example, the recent acquisition hurled two-thirds of a shutout inning in relief of Steve Renko, a no-decision (with seven innings pitched and only two earned runs against the Padres) and three victories (including two complete games and eight innings in the other outing). No doubt, the highlight of the campaign before the All-Star Game came against Torrez's former team on June 27, when the Expos defeated St. Louis, 11–3. Here,

Torrez takes a swing at the plate as Gene Mauch and his Expos teammates look on at Park Jarry. Photograph courtesy of the Southwest Collection/Special Collections Library, Texas Tech University, Lubbock, Texas, Mike Torrez Scrapbook Collection, Binder 4069.

Torrez pitches against the Philadelphia Phillies in Park Jarry during the 1972 season. Photograph courtesy of the Southwest Collection/Special Collections Library, Texas Tech University, Lubbock, Texas, Mike Torrez Scrapbook Collection, Binder 16025.

Torrez not only earned the victory (scattering ten hits and three runs over seven innings), but also scored twice and drove in one run.[43] This triumph brought his record up to an impressive 9–3. Even more notably, this total was for a team that was only 28–36 at this point of the season. This defeat was the only Cardinals loss during a stretch where they won 12 of 13.[44] By the mid-year hiatus, Torrez's record stood at 11–5. His final appearance prior to the break was also impressive, as the Expos defeated San Diego, 2–1, on a complete-game effort (allowing only four hits and striking out six).[45]

The difference from the previous season could not have been more stark. Whereas in 1971 the Cardinals were concerned whether Torrez was good enough to fill in the back part of their rotation, by the following summer he was now described as Montreal's "tiger," who was "the ace of the mound corps—a killer-type fighter who genuinely hates to lose." Never bashful about his abilities, the Topekan believed he could become the first Expos hurler to win 20 games in one season. "When I'm right I can beat anybody, I know that…. I think shutout every time I start. I just don't want anybody to score on me. I know they will sometimes, but not if I have my best stuff."[46] What had made such a difference? After all, the Expos were not a particularly high-scoring team that could outgun opponents on a nightly basis. In part, the change of scenery and the divorce helped, but Torrez also developed an effective slider to complement his fastball. After defeating the Braves, 2–1, in mid–June, Henry Aaron noted that the Kansan was now more of a threat because "I don't recall seeing Torrez throw a slider in the (five) years he was with St. Louis. He's came [sic] up with a good one."[47]

Torrez on the mound for the Expos at an early 1970s home game. Photograph courtesy Southwest Collection/Special Collections Library, Texas Tech University, Lubbock, Texas, Mike Torrez Scrapbook Collection, Binder 4073.

Although he would not reach the 20-victory plateau, this was a highly satisfying season for Torrez who, for his final victory on September 10, went the route and defeated the defending World Champion Pirates, 8–2. Although stumbling a bit over his final four starts, with three losses and a no-decision, Torrez's record for the year was an impressive 16–12 with a career-best (to this point) ERA of 3.33 and 13 complete games. He started 33 games, pitched 243⅓ innings, and had an ERA of 3.33. Overall, the Expos finished with a record of 70–86 (.449 winning percentage), and Torrez was the only non-reliever to post a winning mark. Balor Moore and Bill Stoneman were the next best members of the rotation, finishing with records of 9–9 and 12–14, respectively. Out of the bullpen, however, the young franchise had found a gem in Mike Marshall, who finished 1972 with a 14–8 tally, 18 saves, and an impressive ERA of 1.78 (though he would pitch only two more seasons north of the border).[48]

Over Montreal's first four campaigns, there had been some signs of progress, but the team still had not come close to the break-even mark on the field. Indeed, it could be argued that the on-field performance had stagnated since the 21-game improvement between the expansion year and 1970. In 1971 and 1972 the Expos won only 71 and 70 games, not even matching their sophomore output of 73. Right after the completion of the 1972 season, manager Gene Mauch proclaimed loudly that it was time to take a hard look at the roster and perhaps trade some of the more valuable current pieces, à la the Rusty Staub deal consummated with the Mets. That transaction brought three solid additions to the daily lineup: Tim Foli, Mike Jorgensen, and Ken Singleton. Now, the skipper and front office were on the hunt for even more talent. "We have to get better quickly and we aren't in a position where we can bring up help from our farm system."

Torrez was one of the players he singled out as possible trade bait during the off-season. Indeed, some of Mauch's comments were fairly lukewarm. "If Mike Torrez puts another year in like he did ... there are several teams who would want him. Right now, most teams are taking that 'show us you are for real' attitude. They're not certain that they believe." Later in a December piece, the Expos' English-language beat writer, Ian MacDonald, referred to Torrez as a pitcher who "bounced from the obscurity of a Triple-A has-been in 1971 to a 16-game major league winner."[49] While providing a modicum of faint praise at the close of 1972, just before spring training Mauch stated that Torrez was one of the individuals he would count on for 1973 to help achieve better results. After notching 16 wins, the manager argued, "Torrez is capable of winning more."[50]

Contradictory statements coming from his manager were not what

Torrez expected after his dramatic turnaround. In January, the now 26-year-old pitcher boldly proclaimed that he was "predicting 23 (wins) for '73." He saw himself as a potential ace of a Major League starting rotation and believed, "any time I go out to the mound I have a good chance of beating the other team." Further, Torrez was active in promoting his new club to the broader region as, unlike most of his Expos teammates, he stayed in Quebec over the off-season and made many personal appearances on behalf of the team's speaker's bureau. As a result of his on-field success and off-season work, Torrez, reaching back to notions developed in the Oakland barrio, expected to earn proper compensation:

> I think I deserve a credible increase. I'm sure that management sees it the same way. I figure if I did the job, I deserve to get paid for it. I haven't discussed salary yet. I have mentioned that I would like to be among the first to sign—or at least among the first group ... [last year] they wanted me to take a pay cut because of my poor season the year before.... Eventually, I did not have to take a cut. This time, I expect a raise. Then I'll get that 23 wins and go for the big salary. You have to keep producing in order to get that big money.[51]

Torrez had a great deal riding on the 1973 season. Would he prove himself a genuine Major Leaguer, indeed, someone who could be at the top of a rotation, and earn the money of a front-line starter? Or would he suffer a "sophomore jinx" with Montreal, as occurred in his second full season with the Cardinals? In contract negotiations with Jim Fanning, the Expos' general manager, just before spring training, Torrez's representative, Alan Eagleson (a new element in team–player negotiations), indicated that the Torrez camp and the club "had established a mutual understanding." Eagleson also noted that the main issue for this contract was to provide a good increase in recognition of a fine 1972, but ultimately, "Torrez will have to

A photograph of Torrez signing autographs and greeting the Expos' faithful before a game in Montreal. Photograph courtesy Southwest Collection/Special Collections Library, Texas Tech University, Lubbock, Texas, Mike Torrez Scrapbook Collection, Binder 12001.

"Faites équipe avec nous" / "Team up with us"

Torrez on the cover of the 1973 Expos Media Guide. He was coming off of a bounce-back season in which he went 16–12 with a mediocre club. He forecasted that he would win 23 games in 1973, but his overall record instead dropped to only 9–12 and led to some heated exchanges with his manager, Gene Mauch. Photograph courtesy Southwest Collection/Special Collections Library, Texas Tech University, Lubbock, Texas, Mike Torrez Scrapbook Collection, Binder 14002.

come back with a good year so that he can go after the big money." Ultimately, the team signed Mike for around $40,000 for the 1973 season.[52]

Unfortunately for Torrez, after boasting about winning more than 20 games during the off-season, this campaign turned out very frustrating. Given the doubts expressed previously by Mauch, tensions between the two men only increased over Torrez's final two years with the Expos.

The first five starts for 1973 once again highlighted the control problems that had plagued Torrez. After successive loses to the Cubs, Phillies, and Pirates, he had provided opponents 16 free passes. Further, he was not striking out anywhere near as many batters as the year before, with only eight Ks registered over those outings.[53] Even as he claimed his first victories of the season, 6–5 against Philadelphia on April 19 and 7–2 against Cincinnati on April 24, Torrez continued to have trouble finding the plate, with eight walks and four strikeouts over six innings versus the Phillies and six more free passes (though with eight strikeouts) against the Reds.[54] By his final start before the All-Star Game (which took place on July 24), a 4–0 loss to Cincinnati, he sported a less than impressive 5–9 record.[55]

**Torrez works on his bunting during a spring training session while with the
Expos. Photograph courtesy Southwest Collection/Special Collections Library,
Texas Tech University, Lubbock, Texas, Mike Torrez Scrapbook Collection,
Binder 8033.**

After the break, Torrez continued to lose, dropping his next two decisions,
11–3 to the Mets and 2–0 to the Cardinals. It was in this loss to St. Louis,
however, that he had one of his better performances of the season. While
Reggie Cleveland handcuffed the Expos offense in a complete-game 5-
hitter, Torrez matched his opponent almost stride for stride and allowed
the same number of safeties over eight innings.[56]

Over the next eight appearances, however, Torrez reeled off another
substantial positive streak, giving the Expos a chance to win every time
he took the mound, just as he had accomplished during his time at Tulsa
and St. Louis. In a one-month span between early August and September,
the Kansan notched four victories, three no-decisions, and a one-inning
relief appearance to raise his record to a more respectable 9–11. The highlight of this stretch was a 12–0, complete-game victory over the Phillies
on September 2.[57] Although he did not earn another victory for 1973, he
continued to pitch well with two more no-decisions of over six innings
and only two hits allowed. Finally, he faltered in his last two starts, failing

to hold a 5–0 advantage against Chicago and surrendering seven earned runs in 4⅔ innings against the Pirates.[58] Overall, Torrez finished this year with a record of 9–12 and a 4.46 ERA. His innings pitched declined to 208, but his walks increased to 115, with only 90 strikeouts. Even with both Torrez and Bill Stoneman (who went 4–8 with a 6.80 ERA) not producing as they had in 1972, the Expos had their most successful season to date, finishing 79–83.

The development of Steve Renko (15–11, ERA of 2.81) and Steve Rogers (10–5, ERA of 1.54), and the continued sterling work of Mike Marshall (14–11, 31 saves, ERA of 2.66), provided the fans in Quebec a chance to experience their first taste of competitive, playoff-significant baseball in a season's waning days. In mid–September, with the Expos part of a three-way log-jam with Pittsburgh and New York, Montreal was actually in second place in their division with a 75–74 mark. Over the final 14 games, however, the squad limped across the finish line with a 4–10 record. Ultimately, the Mets won the National League East that year with a mediocre record of only 83–79. One of the more painful defeats in that span occurred when Torrez was unable to hold a five-run advantage against the Cubs in an 8–6 loss on September 19. It was a total team collapse, as Mike Marshall added to the misery by giving up two two-run home runs. In early October, Gene Mauch referred to the span as his team's "one black week." This slide cost the franchise a chance to reach the playoffs for the first time, as the Expos fell just short on 1973's final regular-season day.[59]

After the campaign's conclusion, Mauch expressed apprehension that Torrez's 16–12 record from the previous year may have been, indeed, nothing more than a fluke. In addition, the Expos skipper, a stickler for discipline and known to favor "more seasoned" players, had concerns about Torrez's off-the-field partying. A discussion with two individuals involved with the team that season, broadcaster Jacques Doucet and outfielder (and Torrez's friend and confidant) Ken Singleton, shed light on some of the issues dividing the two men. In an interview with Doucet, the veteran announcer indicated that he did not perceive undue tensions between Torrez and Mauch over the 1971 and 1972 seasons. Starting in 1973, however, Torrez's performance did not meet his manager's expectations, particularly during a stretch between July and August. After several ineffective outings, Doucet recalled the field general snarling that he "may not pitch him again for the rest of the season."[60]

A quick review of this time period lends substantial support to Doucet's recollections. Starting on July 1, Torrez pitched against the

Pirates, Astros (July 6), Reds (July 10), Braves (July 15), Reds (July 20), and Mets (July 28). In all six outings, he failed to make it out of the fourth inning on four occasions and had a record of 1–5 (dropping him to 5–10 for the season). Even in the victory over Houston, Torrez surrendered six earned runs over eight innings. Not exactly the type of stretch that Mauch had expected from someone who claimed he would win 23 games in 1973.[61]

Adding to Mauch's strain was a sense that Torrez took to the night-life in the city a bit too well. Ken Singleton noted in his interview that both he and Torrez were single at the time (Christiann was living with his mother, Connie) and Montreal was "a great party town" for unattached and successful young men. Singleton's recollections are that Torrez (as well as other teammates) greatly enjoyed the local scene.[62] This trend was not a secret to people in the clubhouse for, even before Torrez's trade north of the border, one St. Louis reporter had dubbed him a "knight of the neon." Certainly for an "old school" manager such as Mauch, such goings-on were easier to stomach if a player performed well on the field. A 16-win season in 1972 may have made this tolerable, but a 9–12 record the following year most likely did not. By the time the Expos were ready to report for camp in Daytona Beach, Florida, for 1974, however, Torrez was in a serious relationship with a Quebec-born model/celebrity, Danielle Gagnon, whom he would marry in late October of that year. One benefit of this connection to a local was a further strengthening of his ties to the franchise.[63]

Even with all of his work promoting the club, there were doubts about Torrez's value heading into the upcoming campaign. After boasting that he would win over 20 games in 1973, Bob Dunn's article summarized the club's concerns about Torrez's future when he noted, "a year ago, there was a question of whether another Expo right-hander, Mike Torrez, could win 20. Now, 20 is 10." Determined to redeem himself, the 27-year-old countered that he would not give up his spot in the rotation without a fight. "They tell me it's like two years ago when I had to beat somebody out of a job. Well, I think … somebody had to beat me out of a job. I'm going to come out smokin' the first day."[64]

Torrez was true to his word, at least over his first three starts: all wins. In this span, his most effective outing occurred on April 23 at Candlestick Park against the Giants. He pitched five innings and gave up only one earned run and two walks as part of an 8–4 Expos triumph.[65] These initial victories were followed in succession by three defeats, evening his record by the middle of May though his ERA hovered around a hefty

4.13.[66] From that moment until the All-Star break, the Kansan continued to win and actually equaled his 1973 victory total with a record of 9–6 by the arrival of the mid-season hiatus, though his ERA increased still further to 4.29. Among his subsequent thirteen appearances were some excellent performances, such as a complete-game victory over the Braves, 7–3, with only two free passes allowed to Atlanta hitters. Other outings, however, were not as efficient, the most concerning being a one-inning stint against the Cubs in an 8–7 loss on June 28.[67] Indeed, in an early August article for *The Sporting News*, Dunn indicated that Torrez had almost lost his slot in the starting rotation.[68]

The interview with Ken Singleton provides further background concerning the increasing tensions between Torrez and his manager. While not recalling the specific date, Singleton noted that after what Mauch considered a less-than-sterling start, the Montreal skipper knocked a post-game meal table all over Torrez, ruining his clothes.[69] During a stretch in August, Mauch did not start Torrez for more than three weeks, until a game against the Braves on the 27th, which resulted in a 6–1 Expos win (raising his record to 10–8). By this point in the season (roughly 125 games played), Montreal was seven games out of first place and below .500.

Mauch, Singleton recalls, was very frustrated with the club's overall performance, particularly with Steve Rogers, who dropped from an excellent 1973 record (10–5 with a 1.54 ERA) to 15–22 with an ERA of 4.47, and with Torrez.[70] Even with the situation brewing within the clubhouse, Torrez finished the season in good fashion, winning five more games down the home stretch. His best performances were complete-game victories over the Reds, 2–1 on September 1, and a 2–0 triumph over the Phillies September 27.[71] Overall, this season was another turnaround, as Torrez tied Rogers for most victories by a starter and dropped his ERA to 3.57 (below the overall staff mark of 3.60).[72] The Expos, who had come close to winning the division in 1973, stagnated, with an almost identical record of 79–82, good only for fourth place in the National League East. With lofty expectations prior to the season, recriminations and reshuffling of team personnel seemed the order of the day.

In reality, a clubhouse purge started even before the end of the season. The first to go was Ron Hunt, who was waived in September. Bob Dunn's article from September 21 indicated that this was just an initial move. Torrez was the other player named specifically in this article as being on the block. Even the six consecutive victories toward the end of 1974 were not expected to be sufficient to save his job with Montreal. "Torrez, winner of two straight complete-games since being released from the bullpen …

is one of the Expos who expects he'll be playing elsewhere in 1975." The beat writer described the situation succinctly, stating, "Mauch lost faith … in some of the veterans, notably first baseman Ron Fairly and right-hander Mike Torrez."[73]

Or had he? An essay in *The Sporting News* that appeared in the middle of October seemed to indicate that the Expos might not move Torrez after all. Team sources appeared to indicate that Torrez and his manager had patched up their relationship and were looking forward to what they might accomplish as a tandem in 1975. The theme of the piece was that Mauch had not really lost confidence in Torrez, but rather that the skipper inadvertently sent mixed signals to his pitcher. That mistake, hopefully, would not reoccur in the upcoming season.

> Mauch knows what the problem was with Torrez. He knew that Torrez was spending too much time and effort worrying about what Gene Mauch was thinking that he wasn't keeping his mind solely on what he was doing. Torrez knew it too. He fought it, but didn't lick it until he got so mad at Mauch that he really did not care whether no. 4 liked his pitching or not. To be comfortable, Torrez has to feel Mauch has confidence in him. Mauch is responsible for giving Torrez that feeling, and Torrez is responsible for making Mauch confident.[74]

Even opponents stated that Torrez was pitching well toward the end of 1974. No less of a competitor than Larry Bowa of the Phillies crowed (after Torrez shut out Philadelphia), "I saw him when he was a rookie … and tonight's the best I've seen him pitch. I'm talking about location, and the variety of pitches." Why trade away someone who engenders such praise from other players? In his conclusion, Dunn also noted that there were going to be important changes in Torrez's life shortly: he was marrying Danielle in late October. It seemed as if all was in place for yet another positive campaign: Torrez was solidifying his ties to the area by marrying a local, and Mauch was, apparently, willing to give him a chance to be a part of the Expos' rotation once again.[75] That is, until the Baltimore Orioles came calling with an offer for both Torrez and Ken Singleton. In exchange, Montreal received Dave McNally, Bill Kirkpatrick, and Richie Coggins.[76]

Jacques Doucet argues (and he is not alone) that this was probably one of the most lopsided (negative) deals the Expos ever consummated. The key piece of the transaction supposedly was McNally, a left-hander who had gone 16–10 with a 3.58 ERA in 1974 with Baltimore. Since his numbers were similar to Torrez's, and he was a southpaw, the deal made sense for, in addition to Torrez, Steve Rogers, Steve Renko, Dennis Blair, and Ernie McAnally, the principal starters for Montreal, were all right-handers. General Manager Jim Fanning did his best to paint a positive picture, stating, "I'm not disappointed with what we got at all." Unfortunately, as Doucet notes, Kirkpatrick never reached the Major Leagues, and Coggins (in his one partial season with Montreal) played in only 13 games, hit .270, and drove in four runs. The supposed crown jewel of the transaction, Dave McNally started only 12 games, went 3–6 with a 5.24 ERA, and pitched just 77⅓ innings in an Expos uniform before calling it a career in June of 1975.[77]

For the departing Torrez and Singleton, who had both married French Canadians, leaving town was a disappointment, but still, at this moment

After the Cardinals gave up on him, Torrez spent several years toiling for the Montreal Expos. After the 1974 season, he was traded, along with Ken Singleton, to the Orioles in exchange for Dave McNally and two other players. It is considered one of the most lopsided, and detrimental, trades in Expos history. Photograph courtesy Southwest Collection/Special Collections Library, Texas Tech University, Lubbock, Texas, Mike Torrez Scrapbook Collection, Binder 3018.

in time, just "part of the game." As Singleton noted, "In a way I am happy, but in other ways, I'm sad. The fans here have always treated me with respect, no matter how bad or good things were going, and I'll never forget that." Torrez argued that his now former team had gotten the short end of the transaction. "Singleton really didn't have a bad season this year.... But they were so desperate for a left-hander that I guess they had to make a deal." It seems that Mauch's discussion and contemplation about "next year" had proven merely a ploy on management's part to improve their bargaining position with potential trade partners, though it did not turn out that way. For the newlywed Danielle, it was a rude introduction to something that Torrez was too familiar with since 1964: the vagaries of life in professional baseball. As the new Mrs. Torrez said after the couple received "the call" from General Manager Fanning, "I looked up at Mike. For the first time since we'd met, he was crying. His pride was hurt. They didn't believe in him anymore ... yet he had worked so hard."[78] Although somewhat surprised and disappointed, Torrez was now moving on to a squad that had a great deal more talent than did the Expos. Instead of floundering around the break-even mark, the Orioles were consistent winners with legitimate possibilities of playing deep into the post-season. Perhaps this third franchise would finally be the place where Torrez's career would blossom.

Over his first five seasons in the majors, Torrez continued to make regular stops back in Topeka to visit family and friends. During the first half of the 1970s, there was much activity that took place in Oakland and surrounding neighborhoods (as well as in other parts of the Midwest). During this era, the community became much more active in seeking redress of grievances in the areas of education, political representation, and economic development. In addition, there continued to exist a vibrant Mexican American sporting culture/program throughout much of the region, and John Torrez was an important player in some of these efforts. Another member of the Torrez clan who was very active in the Chicano movement's political side was Mike's cousin, Gloria.

A 2004 book by local activist Thomas Rodriguez provides an extensive discussion of a vast array of federally funded programs, local endeavors, and civic associations of various stripes active in the Kansan capital during the early 1970s. Among the organizations mentioned were ventures such as the Jobs for Progress Program, the first undertaking using money from Washington with the specific goal of helping improve employment possibilities for Mexican Americans in Kansas. A Chicano veterans group (American G.I. Forum), a civic organization (the League of United Latin

American Citizens—LULAC) and the local Catholic Archdiocese were among the strongest supporters of this endeavor.

On the political front, the assistant director of Jobs for Progress (Rodriguez was the director), Jasper "Jay" Garcia, threw his hat into the ring to run for the city commission, the first Mexican American to do so in the history of Topeka. While he did not win in 1973, Garcia garnered an impressive 46 percent of the general vote. Now, it seemed, it was possible for a Spanish-surnamed person to run, and garner support, from areas outside of the traditional barrios. These and other efforts led to unprecedented growth and activism among Mexican Americans throughout Kansas, and by 1975 there were 20 organizations and agencies, with Justicia, Inc. and El Centro de Servicios Para Mexicanos (Gloria was the Assistant Director of this program—sponsored by the Kansas City, Kansas, Archdiocese) being most prominent, working to improve conditions for this sector of the population. Finally, all of this effort culminated with the establishment of a state-government entity, the Kansas Advisory Committee on Mexican American Affairs (KACMAA) in 1974. One of the earliest leaders of this unit was Ruben Corona, Gloria's husband. In 1980, KACMAA spun off another office, the Kansas Council of Hispanic Organizations (KCHO). Looking back at all of this activity in the political, economic, and social realm, Rodriguez noted:

> The Hispanic organizations and agencies of the 1970s inspired many young people to get involved in helping to make things better for Hispanic people. In doing so they promoted the value of education and emphasized the importance of maintaining their cultural roots ... the Hispanic "pathfinders" of the 1970s, laid a strong foundation for future generations of Hispanic leaders and raised consciousness of all of the people of the City of Topeka and in the State of Kansas, about the problems facing the Hispanic population.[79]

In the area of sports, some of the efforts that commenced during the 1940s and 1950s flourished during the heyday of Chicano-era activism. Not only did the Newton-based softball event mentioned previously continue to thrive, but basketball leagues and tournaments began in the mid- to late 1960s and expanded. For example, the Topeka Mexican Basketball Tournament of 1973 took place in early January. A total of 16 squads, from Kansas, Nebraska, Illinois, Missouri, and Iowa, attended the event, which was organized by a committee headed by John Torrez. In addition to his duties for the whole undertaking, John also continued to lead and play for the 7 Ups. At the school level, Our Lady of Guadalupe School also placed greater emphasis upon its athletic programs, with both boys and girls teams winning multiple tournaments and championships over the 1960s.[80]

While Guadalupe's teams had met with some success over the years, it is interesting to note the impact that Chicano activism had on the appearance of the school's teams. As noted in *Generations United*, a work that recounts the story of the institution, during earlier periods, "uniforms for the athletes were almost nonexistent, or if present they were handed down from another school." The increased pride, and improved economic opportunities for some, brought about a concerted, in-barrio effort to remedy this situation.

> Things began to change after the Booster Club was organized under the leadership of Paul Griego and Manuel Chavez, Sr. in 1975.... The organization devoted much time encouraging youngsters and raising funds for the sports program.... It took a long time to get enough money for the uniforms, but little by little, this was accomplished; and today the teams of Our Lady of Guadalupe have beautiful uniforms for each sport they participate in.[81]

Overall, Thomas Rodriguez argues, the primary thrust of the Mexican teams and tournaments in Topeka and elsewhere in the Midwest over the decades was to instill pride in the members of the barrio communities, whether they were players, organizers, or fans.[82]

One final aspect of all of these efforts was endeavors to present success stories of Mexican Americans, in a variety of fields, to barrio denizens as well as the broader Topeka community. Examples of these undertakings can be seen in the pages of a publication created by the members of Our Lady of Guadalupe parish (and saved by Mike's uncle Louis) in conjunction with the Fiesta celebrations. These documents provide a wonderful overview of efforts in education, mutual aid, and support of ethnic pride extant in Oakland over many decades. For example, the 1973 pamphlet showed pictures of area children graduating from the parish's middle school (including a picture of the 1954 graduating class featuring John Torrez), as well as photos of the Sociedad Mutualista Del Santo Nombre (Mutual Aid Society of the Holy Name) that supported members with death benefits during the Great Depression. More recent offerings revealed local children dressed in costume performing traditional dances. The document also demonstrated the extensive ties between Guadalupe and many organizations established during the early 1970s, such as Centro de Servicio Para Mexicanos (for which Gloria worked), Justicia, Inc., the G.I. Forum, the Latin American Student Service Organization (LASSO) at Washburn University, and Topeka Jobs for Progress. Featured prominently in the 1974 document were interviews with candidates for Fiesta queen, and pictures of the inaugural Fiesta Parade held in downtown Topeka in 1972.

There are two interviews featured in the later pamphlet that provide interesting political commentary and context. First, there is a discussion with one of the older residents of the barrio, Don Tomas Hernandez, who harkened back to the arrival of Mexicanos in the area, and decried the decline in traditional music, dance and the speaking of Spanish in barrio households. "The kids cannot sing in Spanish, because many of them don't even know how to speak Spanish. The first thing we need to do is to teach them, because it is part of our culture." In response to Hernandez's plea, a second interview with Silvia Rivera Martinez documented how the Chicano-era inspired generation was working to reverse such trends. Silvia, who was attending California State–Los Angeles, majored in fine arts and minored in Spanish. Her goal, she indicated, was to work as an educator in Topeka and improve conditions in the barrio. In this interview, she enumerated effectively many of the goals and aspirations of the *movimiento* in Kansas and elsewhere:

> Silvia's belief in sharing of culture and customs demands proper awareness of the people, their heritage and culture. A positive self image results from a better understanding of who we are, where we came from, and what we are capable of becoming ... so that having an understanding of who we are, we may continue to revitalize and enhance that heritage which is so psychologically needed and culturally desired by a people who is proud of their background and culture.[83]

All told, the brochures for the annual Fiesta captured the interrelationship between the parish and the efforts on a variety of fronts to improve Mexican American life. In future editions, Torrez would be featured prominently, particularly in 1978 (after the Yankees won the 1977 World Series).[84] Though he was apolitical, his trade to an American League team that would visit nearby Kansas City provided area Chicano leaders with another opportunity to showcase him as well as highlight some of the talent (athletic and intellectual) that existed within the barrios.

As Mike Torrez headed to Miami for Orioles camp in 1975, he and Danielle were disappointed to leave Montreal, but the couple travelled with a sense of the possibilities available in Baltimore. In a January essay for *The Sporting News*, beat writer Doug Brown noted that the leaders of other American League clubs thought that the Orioles would be "tough to beat." The scribe quoted former Orioles great Frank Robinson (who had just been named manager of the Cleveland Indians), who asserted that Torrez would be a key player in the upcoming season. "Torrez can win. He proved that last season (15–8) and he should do even better with a great Baltimore infield behind him."[85] In a 1976 interview with his hometown paper, Torrez summarized how he felt going to what was certainly the best team (at least on paper) that he had been a part of since moving up to the majors. "You can win games, but you need more than that. Especially after you have been around a few years. You need to know that what you are doing is accomplishing something."[86] Over the next few years, with three more teams, he would certainly do that, and both he and the denizens of Oakland would find much to savor in the experience.

6

"I'm One of the Best in the Business Right Now"
Torrez's Seasons with Baltimore and Oakland, 1975–1977

Upon his departure from Montreal, Torrez kicked off a nine-year stint in the American League with his two best Major League seasons. He reached the peak of his career while playing with athletes and owners at the epicenter of the many changes that altered the game's business and labor structure in the mid–1970s. Prior to his move to the junior circuit, he had teamed with Curt Flood, the man who helped start the process of ending the reserve clause. Eventually, Torrez would also have to interact with another man who would help bring about free agency—Oakland Athletics owner Charlie Finley—and the man who would take greatest advantage of player freedom, New York Yankees owner George Steinbrenner.

At the conclusion of the bicentennial season, Mike Torrez faced a disconcerting situation. He had just completed two highly successful campaigns with different organizations (Baltimore and Oakland) and established career-best marks for both victories (20) and ERA (2.50). Still, he was on the roster of an Athletics team being dismantled in response to the new dynamics in Major League baseball. After 1975, a year in which the A's won their fifth consecutive AL West title and finished with a 98–64 mark (they were swept in the playoffs by the Boston Red Sox, the team which outlasted the seemingly invincible Orioles to win the East), owner Charlie Finley began to unload talent, starting with Reggie Jackson and Ken Holtzman going to Baltimore in exchange for Torrez, Don Baylor and Paul Mitchell. In addition, the franchise that had dominated the early part of the 1970s by winning three consecutive World Series had already endured the loss of another one of its all-time greats, Jim "Catfish" Hunter, after he went 25–12 with a 2.49 ERA in 1974. In part, Torrez was expected to fill in a portion of the void left after Hunter's transition into Yankees pinstripes.

The 1976 Athletics were not of the same caliber as the squads that had earned three championships, but neither were they wholly devoid of talent. While many of the athletes were less than thrilled to be toiling for a stubborn and prickly proprietor, the Kelly green and gold still fielded Gene Tenace, Phil Garner, Bert Campaneris, Sal Bando and Joe Rudi, and now Don Baylor in the starting lineup. In addition to Torrez, the pitching staff retained Vida Blue in the starting rotation and Rollie Fingers coming out of the bullpen. While Finley crowed about the deal (and probably, the savings), veterans were less sanguine about the exchange. Joe Rudi, for example, argued, "I don't think that the guys we got from Baltimore are as good as Kenny or Reggie. Torrez isn't as good a pitcher as Kenny.... I don't want to take anything away from the guys we got, but...."[1]

While Rudi had his doubts, Torrez was coming off of what would turn out to be the best single season of this career (20–9 with an ERA of 3.06). Further, though his record with Oakland in 1976 was a more pedestrian 16–12, his ERA was an excellent 2.50. Even with all of the turmoil going on in the A's locker room, Torrez's one complete season in the Bay Area would be one of his best, including his finest stretch at baseball's pinnacle as, toward the end of the season, he pitched three consecutive shutouts.[2] While the Athletics had lost a lot of talent due to Finley's transactions, they made a surprise run for the AL West title; falling just short (2.5 games behind) of catching the Kansas City Royals.

To a great extent, Mike Torrez became as dominant a pitcher as he had been in American Legion back home in Kansas, just on a bigger stage. As players cleaned out lockers in October, manager Chuck Tanner (who would be traded to the Pittsburgh Pirates before the start of the following year as part of a deal for Manny Sanguillen) argued that the Torrez and Blue pairing comprised the "best lefty-righty combination in baseball."[3]

By this point of his career, Torrez had demonstrated the capabilities of a front-line starter. He had won while with the mediocre Expos (40–32 overall), and over 1975 and 1976 fashioned a 36–21 mark. Now, with more lucrative dynamics in place (and entering the final year of his contract for 1977), Torrez looked to gain the financial windfall of which he had dreamed while pitching to his father and brother in the backyard of the family home in the "other" Oakland—that of his youth. Unfortunately, he was in the worst locale to achieve that goal, though that would change shortly after the start of the 1977 season. Almost overnight, he would move from what had become a Major League backwater to the penthouse of the baseball universe: Yankee Stadium.

After departing from Montreal, Torrez spent the next nine seasons in the American League with Baltimore, Oakland, New York, and finally, Boston. This chapter will examine his first two-plus seasons in the junior circuit. As had occurred with the Expos, he was in the midst of clubhouses with athletes who were at the epicenter of the changes taking place in baseball in the mid–1970s. He spent time with the man who helped start the process that ended the reserve clause, Curt Flood in St. Louis; was a teammate of Andy Messersmith, who was eventually declared one of the first "free agents" under the Seitz decision in December of 1975, at

Montreal; was acquired as a potential replacement for Catfish Hunter in Oakland; was part of a deal that sent Reggie Jackson to the Orioles, and ultimately, Torrez himself became a millionaire after signing with the Red Sox just after his success in the 1977 World Series.

In his hometown, Torrez was acknowledged as a symbol of pride for Mexican Americans, and would realize a level of recognition and status that no other Spanish-surnamed individual had achieved previously in Kansas. On the occasions when the Orioles or Athletics played in nearby Kansas City, a Torrez start against the Royals was feted as an

En route to his best ERA in his Major League career, Torrez pitches on behalf of the Oakland A's. After his one full season by the Bay (1976), Charlie Finley would trade his disgruntled hurler to the New York Yankees. Photograph courtesy Southwest Collection/Special Collections Library, Texas Tech University, Lubbock, Texas, Mike Torrez Scrapbook Collection, Binder 1049. Reprinted with permission from the Oakland Athletics.

occasion for the Spanish-surnamed to show off ethnic pride and the vibrancy of Topeka's barrios. In many ways, when Torrez and his teammates visited, it was cause for smaller-scale version of the celebrations held during the annual Fiesta at Our Lady of Guadalupe parish.

The trade, while a surprise to Mike and Danielle, was initially perceived as a positive. Though leaving behind the warmth and familial ties of Quebec, the new organization offered Torrez a realistic chance to make it to the playoffs for the first time. In an interview with his hometown paper prior to the 1975 season, Torrez crowed about the prospect of pitching with an infield that included Mark Balanger, Bobby Grich, and, of course, the legendary Brooks Robinson, behind him. "I've never been on a team this good, even when I was with the Cardinals.... The guys here get along together beautifully and have a lot of fun. I can see why they have been so successful."[4] With other members in the rotation such as Jim Palmer (though he was only 7–12 in 1974), Mike Cuellar, and Ross Grimsley, it appeared that Baltimore had the makings of formidable group of starters, especially if Palmer had anything resembling a "normal" year in 1975. A fifth, and spot, starter was a young Doyle Alexander, though manager Earl Weaver primarily worked with a four-man corps.

All of these developments were very much to Torrez's liking. Unlike his last two seasons with Gene Mauch, the Orioles, he noted, "weren't pushing me. They told me I'd be pitching every fourth day. It gave me confidence that they had confidence in me."[5] He did have some arm trouble over the spring and did not pitch more than five innings in any start in Florida. Still, management felt fairly confident that Baltimore could defend its AL East title from a challenge expected to come, primarily, from the revamped New York Yankees.[6] While there was much optimism, 1975 proved a great disappointment for Baltimore and led to another trade of Torrez, even after he was one of the few positives (along with Jim Palmer, who won 23 games) on the underperforming squad.

Over the first two months, the Orioles struggled in many aspects of the game, and by late May were mired in last place of the AL East, ten games under the break-even point. As *The Sporting News* beat reporter Jim Henneman noted, it had been almost one decade since the Birds had been so far out of first place at this point in the season. The cause of the early-season futility lay in all areas: the relievers did not record a save in the first 57 games; Brooks Robinson had barely cracked the .200 mark; Lee May was hitting at around the same figure; and Bobby Grich had had no luck at the plate, as many line drives off of his bat were caught for outs instead of falling in for hits. Ever the philosopher, manager Earl Weaver argued that he was "a firm believer that these things even out in the course of a season. We haven't gotten a break, but if we don't now, we'll get them later." Roughly a quarter into the schedule, Jim Palmer (7–3) and Mike Torrez (5–2) were the lone bright spots on the mound. Indeed, Torrez should have sported an even better record as the bullpen failed to hold two three-run leads for victories after he left the mound in the late innings.[7]

Among the most notable of Torrez's starts over this span were complete-game victories over Luis Tiant and the Red Sox, 11–3, on April 13 (his first American League start); twice against Cleveland, 3–2 on the 26th and 11–1 on May 4; and, finally, a 3–2 victory against the White Sox on May 14. His final turns before the arrival of June, however, were very frustrating and indicative of the problems the Orioles faced. On May 18, he pitched 7⅔ innings against California, losing 5–1. However, he surrendered only one earned run as the Birds' vaunted defense committed three errors (including one by Torrez).[8]

The game that caused Torrez the greatest consternation, however, was his next start on May 24 against the Royals in Kansas City. This was the first time he had pitched near his hometown since a 1969 exhibition game with the Cardinals. Not surprisingly, the Oakland community turned out in full force to support a fellow Chicano. While there are no documents that relate directly to the activities surrounding the May 24 game, later in the season (when he again started in Kansas City), there are materials that specify local efforts to assure a Mexican American presence at Royals Stadium.

> John and Mary Torrez of Topeka are indeed proud of their son's ... great achievement(s).... Most of us remember Michael when he was just a youngster and played ball with the Cosmopolitan League in Topeka, of course, Michael had a good coach and supporter in his dad, John. Two times the Orioles played in Kansas City, the Torrez clan and friends chartered a bus to see him play. He dropped the first game [actually a no decision], but the second he was determined to win and did.[9]

In addition such articles articulate clearly how Torrez's successes on the mound were contextualized as part of the barrio's quest for greater acceptance. Another local publication made a direct connection to Torrez's significance to the community, stating that he "has been an inspiration to thousands of Chicano kids all over America who hope to follow in his footsteps into the majors."[10] Unfortunately, the bullpen once again let him down. He pitched eight innings, and led 4–2 when taken out of the game, but the relievers failed to quell the Royals' rally in the bottom of the ninth, and the Orioles lost, 5–4.[11] Still, as the team approached the middle of June, the tandem of Palmer and Torrez were about the only two players having notable seasons, accounting for 16 of the club's first 22 (nine for Palmer and seven for Torrez) victories.[12] By the time of the All-Star break, Torrez sported a 10–5 record, with his final start before the hiatus being a shutout versus the Oakland Athletics, 4–0. In this game, he was dominant: only two free passes, nine strikeouts, and just four hits permitted.[13]

After the mid-summer classic, Baltimore began to move up the AL East standings and entering the final two months, still had a chance to compete against the surprising Boston Red Sox. By this point in the season, the locals had come to the realization that many of General Manager Frank Cashen's moves were paying off. Indeed, if he had not brought some of this talent, "this season would already be a disaster. Without the acquisition of Lee May, Ken Singleton and Mike Torrez, the Orioles would already be into a rebuilding program for 1976."[14]

Torrez more than proved his worth over the final 70 games of the season as in his final 17 starts he posted a record of 10–4, with three no-decisions. In his one bad start, he lasted only two innings against the Texas Rangers (though not taking the loss) on August 15. In addition, during this stretch, Torrez pleased his Topeka fans with a complete game, 4–2 victory over the Royals on August 27. The final, and most significant, highlight occurred on September 21 with a two-hit shutout of the Milwaukee Brewers in which the Kansan recorded his 20th win of the season. A final game versus the Yankees resulted in a 3–2 loss to Catfish Hunter. After all of the doubts by the Cardinals and Gene Mauch, Torrez had achieved a milestone that has been a gold standard for pitchers over many decades: 20 victories in one season. In addition, he pitched a total of 270⅔ innings (trailing only Palmer) and finished tied for fourth in victories and tenth in games started in the American League.[15] Although Baltimore got close, they did not manage to catch the Red Sox and finished 4.5 games behind the division winners with a record of 90–69. Surely, the tandem of Palmer and Torrez would return for 1976 to help reclaim the division title for the Birds?

After the conclusion of the season, it was clear that Cashen had pulled off a major coup via the trade engineered with Montreal; the transaction netted both a 20-game winner and a .300 hitter. "In fact, both Cashen and Manager Earl Weaver must shudder to think where the Orioles would have been without Torrez and Singleton. Certainly it would not have been a contending year." While enjoying champagne to celebrate his momentous victory in Milwaukee, Torrez gave a lot of the credit to his teammates, and an infield defense that did eventually live up to pre-season billing. "It's a nice feeling. I'd felt that there were times in the past when I pitched well enough to win 20 games. I always felt I could do it if I was pitching for a team as good as this one."[16] Torrez helped the defensive cause by throwing 35 double-play balls, leading the league in that category.

While there were certainly many positives to the Orioles roster, the team did not have sufficient offensive punch (batting average of .252 and only 124 HRs), especially to compete with a Boston outfit that featured Jim Rice, Freddie Lynn, Carlton Fisk and others. So, by the start of 1976, new General Manager Hank Peters (Cashen moved into sales and marketing for a brewing company after the season), had "his sights set on big game in the American League. His target was Reggie Jackson ... who could more than alleviate the Orioles' need for a left-handed power hitter." In order to trade for such a prized athlete, Charlie Finley asked a great deal in return from Baltimore. As early as January, Torrez's name was bandied about as possible trade bait and a deal was still rumored even after he re-signed with the Orioles late in spring training.[17] Given the quality of young pitchers in the Birds' organization, "like Paul Mitchell and Mike Flanagan ... the Orioles would no doubt be willing to sacrifice a pitcher with Torrez's ability if it meant getting Jackson in return."[18]

The Oakland Athletics of the early 1970s were one of the best teams ever assembled. The outfit included several future members of the Hall of Fame, and in 1974 won a third consecutive World Series title, a feat unmatched since the Casey Stengel-led dynasty of the New York Yankees. As detailed in two important works on this era, *Champagne and Baloney: The Rise and Fall of Finley's A's*, by Tom Clark, and *Charlie Finley: The Outrageous Story of Baseball's Super Showman*, by G. Michael Green and Roger D. Launius, the efforts of Curt Flood and Marvin Miller in the early 1970s set in motion a series of events that would end the reserve clause and, eventually, bring about free agency. Finley, given his irascible nature and bargain-basement ways, helped move this process along because of his dealings with Catfish Hunter.[19]

Before the last title run, Hunter's representative had inserted a clause in Hunter's contract with Finley so as to shelter part of his client's salary ($50,000) via the purchase of a ten-year annuity. By August, Finley noted that he would not execute the clause due to tax considerations (as he could not claim the salary as an expense for 1974). This led to a protracted battle concerning whether Finley's failure to procure the financial instrument had voided Hunter's contract and made him a free agent. The dispute ultimately wound up in arbitration. The three members of the panel were

Miller, John Gaherin (representing the owners), and Peter Seitz. Obviously, Miller and Gaherin would vote in support of their respective interests, and that meant that Seitz would cast the deciding ballot. On December 13, his decision shocked the baseball world: Catfish Hunter was declared free from his ties to the Oakland Athletics. "Seitz said it was clear ... that Hunter's objective was to avoid taxation on current income and that Finley made no statement that the deferral was conditioned on ... the right of Finley to claim the deferred salary as a business expense." A Superior Court denied a later appeal by the owner, and Catfish Hunter signed eventually with the New York Yankees for a total package of approximately $3.5 million. Green and Launius summarize the event as follows:

> Charlie Finley's refusal to execute Hunter's deferred-salary clause cost him the game's most prized starting pitcher—all because Finley wanted to write Hunter's deferred $50,000 salary off as a business expense in 1974. Hunter was the glue of Finley's heralded pitching staff. The A's "big-game" pitcher had few equals in all of baseball. His loss hurt the A's future chances immeasurably. Finley's penny-pinching and tightfisted ways had finally caught up with the wily owner.... Baseball was on the brink of a new era, all thanks to ol' Charlie Finley.[20]

This was not the end of the acrimony in the Athletics' clubhouse. After the 1974 season, 13 players filed for arbitration, with Finley settling seven cases before the hearings took place. Of the remaining six, the owner won four (against Sal Bando, Joe Rudi, Ken Holtzman, and Reggie Jackson). Still, the team had talent, and their mutual hatred of their owner helped fuel them to one more AL West title. "They already hated Finley and channeled this hatred to their advantage as a unifying force."[21]

After being swept out of the playoffs by the Red Sox, however, further critical events transpired both within the Oakland organization and in the broader world of baseball. Specifically, Peter Seitz struck again in December of 1975 and declared both Andy Messersmith and Dave McNally free agents. Finley's reaction to the arbitrator's decision was as expected. For the 1976 season, the following group of his players were eligible to play out their contracts and become free agents: Reggie Jackson, Joe Rudi, Bert Campaneris, Bill North, Sal Bando, Gene Tenace, Rollie Fingers, Ken Holtzman and Vida Blue. This meant that (since there was not a new labor agreement in place by the start of the season) Finley might lose this talent without getting much, or even anything, in return. It was time for the showman to act; and Mike Torrez would be in the middle of the hornet's nest.[22]

With the realities of the new era, plus personal issues such as an impending divorce, the miserly Finley was strapped for cash. Among his moves in March of 1976 was a decision to cut the salaries of players by 20 percent, the maximum allowed by league rules.[23] Further, on April 3 he pulled the trigger on the expected transaction involving Reggie Jackson. The trade sent the outfielder and pitcher Ken Holtzman, plus a minor leaguer, to Baltimore in exchange for Mike Torrez, Don Baylor and Paul Mitchell. Charlie Finley argued that the "deal was made because it will lead us to another world championship. I would have made the deal even if all three of the players were signed." Not surprisingly, fans in the Bay Area were not quite as enthusiastic. One common, though unfair, assessment was that "Finley had exchanged the Golden Gate Bridge for three crabcakes."[24] The owner was not done in gutting his squad, as in June he would sell (though that would be negated by Commissioner Kuhn) the services of Rudi, Blue and Fingers to the Yankees and the Red Sox.

Torrez's reaction to having to make another move was not a surprise, given that this was the second time the he was traded in two years. "What must I do to stay with a team?"[25] Danielle, on the other hand, was happy to leave Maryland behind. "For me, the trade was a good thing, too. I abhorred Baltimore, with its desolate downtown and high crime. I always felt I saw panic on the faces of its people. The city's whole atmosphere seemed so old and crumbling."[26] Although the Athletics were not what they were in earlier years, perhaps they still had a run left in them; if only to spite their owner.

The season did not start off too poorly, and Oakland had a winning record (9–8) at the end of April, just one game out of first place. There were two principal reasons for the decent start: Chuck Tanner emphasized the running game (the team would steal 341 bases that season—a Major League record), and the pitching of Mike Torrez (who had three wins and a 2.88 ERA over his first six starts).[27] An early season highlight for Torrez took place on April 30, when he pitched the Athletics to an 11–1 triumph over the Orioles in Baltimore, besting Jim Palmer. Torrez went the route in defeating his former teammates, and allowed just two hits to go along with six strikeouts.[28]

The early bounce did not last, however, and by the end of May, the A's had plummeted to fifth place in the AL West with an 18–24 record, already 7.5 games out of first.[29] During the last half of the month, Oakland endured a horrific road trip that was documented in painful detail by beat writer Ron Bergman. Even with their owner providing a pep-talk prior to a doubleheader against Chicago, the Athletics finished the trip 0–8. The local scribe argued that things went so unsuccessfully on the swing that it "made the 1972 McGovern campaign look like a Democratic landslide." By the start of July, things were worse, even though the team actually had a winning record (6–5) during the two-week stretch it took to resolve the Rudi, Blue and Fingers issue. While almost at the break-even mark (33–35), the A's were still 7.5 games out as the All-Star Game approached.[30]

Although his ERA remained low, Torrez struggled to win games before the mid-season hiatus. His final three starts prior to the mid-summer classic provide a nice synopsis of the issues he faced with Oakland's struggling offense. On June 30, against the Texas Rangers, the Athletics managed ten hits off of Gaylord Perry and a reliever but lost, 3–2. This defeat lowered Torrez's record to 6–9. In his next two starts, against Baltimore and Cleveland, however, he pitched impressively, giving up only two earned runs over 15⅓ innings. With 4–1 and 2–1 victories, Torrez headed into the break with a mark of 8–9.[31]

Before Oakland traveled to Cleveland to face the Indians, the team visited the Kansas City Royals over the Fourth of July weekend. Here, the importance of Torrez to the Chicano community in Topeka was on full

Mike Torrez is welcomed by Topeka dignitaries for "Mike Torrez Day" over the July 4 weekend in 1976. The success that this local hero earned on the mound was a very welcomed addition to the efforts underway in Kansas (and elsewhere) during the era of the Chicano Movement. Torrez was then with the Oakland Athletics, who happened to be visiting the Kansas City Royals. Photograph courtesy of the Southwest Collection/Special Collections Library, Texas Tech University, Lubbock, Texas, Mike Torrez Scrapbook Collection, Binder 19036.

display. The barrio publication *Adelante* (Forward) noted the extensive preparations on the part of the barrios to celebrate Torrez's achievements, even though he was not scheduled to pitch. Topeka and Shawnee County commissioners declared July 3 "Mike Torrez Day," and festivities included a presentation of a commemorative plaque at city hall and an autograph session with neighborhood children. In addition, local Mexican American–owned businesses, such as Ortega's Tacos and Ramirez Dental Lab, helped sponsor a 44-passenger bus to take residents to Royals Stadium to cheer on the hometown hero.[32]

In an interview with Bob Hentze of the *Capital-Journal*, Mike Torrez provided his supporters with a sense of some of the shenanigans that were taking place inside the Oakland clubhouse as Finley worked to further gut his squad. Things had gotten so adversarial that the players took two votes to go on strike if the cantankerous owner did not play the newly reinstated Rudi, Fingers and Blue. "They are three outstanding major leaguers and we'd rather have them on our ballclub than playing against them. We were ready to take off.... We had to all stick together. We were being taken advantage of."[33] In addition to discussing the overall circumstances of the Athletics, Torrez also talked about his frustrations on the mound and indicated that he believed he would have a more successful second half of the campaign. "I started the season by pitching 13 outstanding games. I could have been 8–2 or 9–2. I feel I've got it going pretty good now. I've always been a pretty good second half pitcher, 29–6 the last three years."[34] This statement would prove very prophetic about the last part of the 1976 season for both Torrez and the Athletics.

Just before the All-Star break, on July 12, another major event took place for the Major Leagues: a tentative outline for the new Basic Agreement (it was signed a week later). Reporter and baseball historian Dan Epstein provides an effective overview of this accord in his book, *Stars and Strikes: Baseball and American in the Bicentennial Summer of '76*. In short, the contract called for a minimum salary of $19,000, to increase to $21,000 by the end of 1979. Most importantly for players such as Mike Torrez, however,

> the contract stipulated that all signed players would be eligible for free agency after six years of service with the same team and that all currently unsigned players who remained so through the end of the season would automatically become free agents in October. Clubs would not receive any financial compensation for losing players.... Thanks to the new Basic Agreement, the players would now have greater control over their own destinies than ever before; at the same time, there were enough provisions in place regarding the drafting and signing of free agents that the oft-repeated owners' nightmare of the wealthiest teams stockpiling all of the top-echelon talent seemed less likely to come true.[35]

While Torrez did not have six years with one team, given the turmoil in Oakland, he made it clear that he would not resign with the Athletics, and thus the team would lose him after the option year of 1977. Though he would have to bide his time, the new memorandum gave him a sense of hope that the substantial payday he had always dreamed off would finally come to pass, and almost surely in a locale other than Oakland, California. Now was the time to bear down even more and lay the groundwork for a contract that would make this happen. After the All-Star Game in Philadelphia on July 13, 1976, Torrez could not have picked a better time to go on the best streak of his professional career. During the last two months of the season, a pitcher who had a good ERA, but a losing record, would almost single-handedly lead his team into the American League playoffs, no matter what damage Charlie Finley had inflicted on the squad. By the start of 1977 Mike Torrez was a hot commodity, and he would make the most of this opportunity.

Although his first start of the second half on July 16 resulted in a no-decision, Torrez pitched effectively. He went eight shutout innings and allowed just five hits against the Detroit Tigers. Oakland eventually lost the game, 1–0, in ten innings, with Rollie Fingers taking the defeat. Another no-decision followed on July 28. In this game the Athletics suffered a 2–1 defeat and were no-hit by two Chicago pitchers. Torrez went only five innings and surrendered the White Sox's first run. Once the calendar turned to August, Torrez became the dominant pitcher in the American League. He lost his first start of the month, 3–0 to the Twins, and dropped his season mark to 8–10. Over the subsequent ten outings, he had six victories and four no-decisions. Three straight wins were complete-game shutouts. Another highlight of this stretch came on August 29, when he went toe-to-toe with the one-year sensation who swept the baseball nation in 1976: Mark "the Bird" Fidrych. This game went into extra innings with the Athletics defeating the Tigers, 2–1. Torrez pitched 11 innings and gave up only one run. Oakland finally pushed across the winning tally in the bottom of the 12th, with Rollie Fingers credited for the victory. Fidrych went the route and took the loss. After this classic pitchers' duel, Torrez proceeded to shut out the Angels, 3–0; the White Sox, 4–0; and the Rangers, 1–0. He did not surrender a run to the opposition in 37 consecutive innings, a team record.[36] Although the streak of goose eggs ended in his next start against Minnesota, he defeated the Twins, 5–2. By the end of this run, his record stood at 14–10.[37] In addition, Oakland began to make their move and inched ever closer to the division-leading Royals. Never one to miss an opportunity to gloat, Finley crowed, "'Kansas City is looking over their shoulders.... They can put it up on a big sign in their clubhouse: 'Finley Says Kansas City Is Going to Choke.'" For once, Torrez agreed with his owner, stating, "They [the Royals] could get an American Legion plague or something."[38]

While the Athletics made a dramatic charge, their attempt to overtake Kansas City fell short. Over the final four starts of 1976, Torrez suffered his final defeat on September 19, 9–1 against Texas. He did make his Topeka faithful happy, however, with a sterling, complete-game five-hitter against the Royals, 8–1, on the 23rd of September. His final two games were both 1–0 thrillers, another win against Kansas City, in which he surrendered only two hits, and a loss to California on October 3.[39] Given all of the tumult, Oakland overachieved in 1976, but failed to win their division for the first time since 1970. Players were disappointed at coming up short, and center fielder Billy North placed the blame squarely on the shoulders of Finley. Specifically, he argued, if Reggie Jackson had not been traded, things might have turned out differently. "We won five years in a row with Reggie and Ken Holtzman. And we didn't win the sixth without them."[40]

North cannot be blamed for complaining about the Jackson trade, though Mike Torrez certainly did his part to help the starting rotation. Although he won fewer games than in 1975, his ERA was more than one-half run better than during his time in Baltimore, and second only to Vida Blue's 2.35 mark. Further, Torrez pitched 266⅓ innings, again second only to Blue. As had occurred previously, *The Sporting News* had high praise for a hurler who finished fifth overall in ERA in the American League. Other key statistics included a dramatic decline in the number of walks issued (87 versus 133 the previous year), plus 39 starts (two more than Blue). Overall, beat writer Ron Bergman argued, "the A's failure to win a sixth straight division title can't be blamed on Mike Torrez. He did his part, and more, since coming over from the Orioles in a trade made one week before the start of the season."[41] Sensing his impending liberation from the Charlie Finley compound, the Kansan did not hold his tongue:

> "I think if Charlie would have signed the seven unsigned players, it would have been a different season. I know that from being around the clubhouse that a lot of players were aware of the 20 percent pay cut they had to take in their salaries.... I don't want to see this team broken up because it's a championship club. If Charlie would sign these guys, we would win it next year."[42]

Of course, Finley would do no such thing and consequently Torrez made it clear he would not re-sign with Oakland. The A's protected him in the expansion draft's first round anyway. Torrez was not alone in his sentiments about the circumstances surrounding the Athletics. After the final game of the 1976 campaign, North, Bando, Fingers and others shared champagne with teammates to commemorate the "liberation of the Oakland Seven." Joe Rudi noted what this would mean for the upcoming season of 1977. "I can't see Mike Torrez, Vida Blue, or Billy North being here next year because they're making too much money.... You are going to have a completely different ball club next year." If Torrez and Rudi expressed their frustrations, Vida Blue demonstrated utter contempt and hatred for Finley. "I hope the next breath Charlie Finley takes is his last. I hope he falls flat on his face and dies of polio." Thus the reign of the once mighty Oakland Athletics of the early 1970s ended with much acrimony and recriminations.[43]

The 1976 season was a surreal experience for Mike Torrez and his Oakland teammates (including flying commercial, not via charter, in order to save money), and the off-season was even more bizarre, portending a very, very poor 1977. Ron Bergman summarized succinctly the circumstances in a column that appeared in The Sporting News on November 27. The parsimonious organization/owner shed even more front office and managerial payroll starting right after players cleaned out their lockers. First, Finley traded manager Chuck Tanner to the Pirates for Manny Sanguillen and $100,000 in cash. Next, he dismissed the Athletics' first and third base coaches and pitching coach. The franchise also did not have in its employ at that moment a road secretary and farm director. Neither did they employ a general manager, for the owner served in that capacity as well. "What had been known ... as the closest thing to a one man operation ... became almost a solo act, literally ... the A's made sure they would once again avoid any offseason promoting that might put more fans in the Coliseum.... But think of the nickels saved."[44] Torrez knew that, given his substantial (in comparison with that of his teammates) salary of $83,000, he was likely not to return.[45]

Then, something quite extraordinary occurred. Danielle recounts that in November, Mike received his contract for the upcoming season. While the couple expected the worst (a 20 percent cut), they were astonished to find that Finley instead offered a 20 percent raise (to approximately $100,000). The Torrezes consulted with agent Gary Walker, who also expressed incredulity at the turn of events. "I don't know. I've covered every inch of it. I can't find a catch." Was Finley turning over a new leaf and actually interested in keeping Torrez? Shortly thereafter, Torrez received a call from his employer and the situation became clear. With little assistance in the front office, Finley had intended to cut Torrez's salary by the maximum permitted and instead increased it by the same percentage! "Let's treat this like gentlemen," he pleaded. "Let's tear up the contract." In exchange for saving himself $17,000, the proprietor offered Torrez a year's supply of his famous chili. He even went so far as to offer Danielle the recipe. Instead of taking the offer for the gastronomic delight, Torrez signed the contract. Now that he was a six-figure man, and had taken advantage of a Finley mistake, his time in Oakland was surely limited.[46]

Simultaneously, Jack McKeon agreed to become Chuck Tanner's replacement at the helm of the team's remnants. By the time the ink was dry on his agreement, five of the franchise's best players had already signed with other clubs as free agents. McKeon, who worked for the Braves organization as a minor-league manager in 1976, tried to put as positive a spin as possible on the circumstances. "One thing we do have is good pitching with people like Vida Blue, Mike Torrez and Paul Mitchell." Unfortunately for the new field general, the same article that covered his hiring also noted that "look for [Phil] Garner, Torrez and Mitchell to play out their options next year." So much for some decent defense and pitching for Oakland in 1978![47]

Given what he had accomplished over 1975 and 1976, Torrez would certainly be a much-sought-after commodity after the conclusion of the 1977 season. One franchise that expressed substantial interest even before the next spring training was Montreal. Not surprisingly, new manager Charlie Fox hoped to reverse the disastrous transaction of 1974 and bring back both Torrez and Ken Singleton, both married to French Canadian women and off-season denizens of Quebec. In addition, toward the end of 1976, Danielle was pregnant with the couple's first child, and she, understandably, wanted to be near family. It seemed there was a serious possibility that Torrez could once again find himself toiling north of the border. The dynamics of player-management relations had changed dramatically since he left Montreal, however. If the Expos and Athletics did swing a deal prior to the start of the 1977 regular season, it did not mean that Torrez would remain because, as he surmised:

> I can be a free agent though at the end of the season.... I wouldn't want to come to Montreal if I thought I could get a whole lot more with some other club. I'm one of the best in the business right now—my record shows that. I won when we didn't have a good team here [Montreal]. I know I can win again.[48]

The situation in Oakland deteriorated further over the remainder of the off-season. While Gene Tenace, Joe Rudi, Sal Bando and Rollie Fingers headed off to greener pastures, the cupboard was left nearly empty for those who wore the green and gold of the Athletics. Heading into Cactus League action, only four players had positions locked up: Sanguillen behind the plate (or as a designated hitter), Garner at second, Bill North in center field and Claudell Washington in right. While McKeon still felt comfortable with the three starters in place, "they may not be around because.... Finley is expected to deal during the spring to find bodies to fill the gaps."[49]

The bazaar reopened on March 15, and shrewd Finley showed that he could still pull a rabbit out of his hat. On that day, he traded Phil Garner to the Pirates for six players: Doc Medich, Dave Guisti, Tony Armas, Mitchell Page, Rick Langford and Doug Bair. As Green and Launius note in their work, the "deal seemed innocuous at the time but years later proved to be one of Finley's most profitable trades." Later, he shipped Claudell Washington to the Texas Rangers for two players and cash. While these transactions helped replenish the farm system, "the new economics of baseball and his dwindling personal wealth made his efforts to rebuild the A's even more difficult."[50] This was not the end of Finley's wheeling and dealing, and given Torrez's salary and trade value, it was only a matter of time before his name was included in one of these agreements.

As the calendar turned to April and the start of the regular season, Finley laid out an ultimatum to those who remained on his Opening Day roster: either sign or be traded. "I'm not going to sit back and let a player play out his option like last year." While several athletes were in a similar position, this assertion was addressed directly at Torrez. In an April 2, 1977, article in *The Sporting News*, the A's owner mentioned that he was not going to give in to what he considered the ridiculous salary demands of Torrez and agent Gary Walker. "Finley also disclosed the $2 million package requested by pitcher Mike Torrez—$1 million over five years, and another million spread over 20 years. The owner said 'That's the most idiotic thing I've ever heard.'"[51] With the two sides far apart in regard to salary, the rotation that Jack McKeon had hoped for would likely not last too long into the 1977 season. Torrez would start only four games this year for the A's before moving on to the Yankees.

Over his final starts for Oakland, Torrez showed why other teams were interested in acquiring his services. He won his first three starts, defeating the Twins on April 9, 7–4, and again on the 15th, 3–2. His final victory for the club was his best performance of the year for the Athletics; a complete-game six-hitter against the Brewers in a 4–2 triumph (which was his 100th Major League victory). His record now stood at 3–0. He donned the green and gold for the final time on April 24, and lasted just

1⅓ innings in a 12–5 loss to the White Sox. Overall, he finished his stint with a record of 3–1 and a 4.44 ERA. Only three days later, Finley consummated the deal with George Steinbrenner to send Torrez to the Yankees in exchange for Doc Ellis and two other players. Given how badly Finley had gutted his team (they finished 63–98), Torrez actually turned out to have the sixth-most victories on the squad that year in just one month of the season.[52]

Tom Weir, the Athletics' beat writer, provided an effective summary of these last tumultuous days in Oakland in an article published as Torrez moved on to New York. He noted that Torrez, usually a slow starter and excellent second-half pitcher, had instead charged out of the gate for 1977. Manager Jack McKeon agreed, stating that "this guy has quality and he knows how to close out a game. He gets stronger toward the end, every time." Torrez also had other matters on his mind besides a possible trade, and returned to Montreal often as the time for Danielle to give birth neared. The couple's son, Iannick, was born in early April, just as his dad headed from last-place Oakland to the defending American League champions.

By the end of April 1977, Mike Torrez was in his ninth full season in the Major Leagues. Since 1969, he had pitched for the Cardinals, Expos, Orioles, and Athletics, and was now heading to the Bronx to don Yankees pinstripes. He was a local celebrity in his native Topeka and hailed as a role model for Chicanos in his home state. He had just notched his 100th career victory in the big leagues and had become a father for the second time. Given the changes in his personal life, the numerous trades, and the revolutionary transformation regarding player-management relations in baseball, this was a period of great possibilities for this son of Mexican immigrants. Although he had had to deal with the cantankerous Charlie Finley in California, Torrez had signed a contract for $100,000 to play the 1977 season. This was a salary that Juan, Maria, and the rest of the Torrez clan could have never imagined as a possibility while toiling for the Santa Fe and making tortillas in the barrios of Kansas. Now, Torrez was not only an excellent pitcher in the highest level of baseball, he was heading to the very beating heart of the sport: Yankee Stadium. If he could do well there, he hoped not only to secure his family's economic wherewithal, but also to end the vagabond nature of his career. Shortly after the trade, he stated, "I'm tired of all this moving around. I'll be seeking security this time. I'd like to stay around here for five or six years." He now headed to the Big Apple to join the likes of Catfish Hunter, Reggie Jackson and Billy Martin in the Yankees clubhouse, and his life and career (and his ties to the Oakland barrio in Topeka) would never be the same.[53]

7

"I'm Curious to See What I'm Worth in the Open Market"

Torrez's Transformation from World Series Champion to Scapegoat, 1977–1978

When the Oakland Athletics and the New York Yankees finalized the trade of two discontented pitchers in late April of 1977, 30-year-old Mike Torrez went from the proverbial outhouse to the penthouse of Major League baseball (and Doc Ellis headed in the opposite direction). After being asked by the miserly Charlie Finley to give up $17,000 in salary in exchange for a year's supply of chili (no matter how good it might have been), the Kansan would now play for the organization that had led the charge into free agency by signing Jim "Catfish" Hunter to the then-staggering figure of $3.5 million over five years in 1974. George Steinbrenner might have been a difficult character in his own right, but he certainly spared little expense in order to improve the Yankees' roster. As Torrez noted in an interview with Bob Hentzen later in that season, the major difference between Oakland and New York was that "George Steinbrenner does almost everything first class. Charlie (Finley) would snake out of anything he could."[1] Whereas Torrez had had to take advantage of a mistake by his previous employer to receive a raise after a season in which he had an ERA of 2.50, if he generated similar results for the Bronx Bombers, he might finally achieve the financial rewards and stability he had long sought.

The relationship with his new ball club did not get off to a sterling start, however, for two specific reasons. First, as mentioned previously, Danielle gave birth to Iannick, about three weeks (April 8) before the Athletics and the Yankees consummated their trade, and subsequently suffered some serious medical issues.[2] Torrez had three days to report to the

Yankees, but had stopped in Montreal on the way from California to be with his ailing wife. The player, his agent, and the team had not connected in those pre-cellphone days, and fans and management in the Big Apple were concerned and frustrated. In an article by Vic Ziegel in the *New York Post* dated April 30, manager Billy Martin was described as having to scramble to find a replacement for Torrez to start the previous evening's game against the Seattle Mariners. The Bombers' skipper sent a hurler who had not started a game as a professional in over three years to the mound: Ron Guidry. The Yankees and their emergency pitcher managed to subdue the expansion squad, 3–0. "Guidry couldn't remember this much work in the same night since, oh, 1974, when he was struggling in the Eastern League."[3] This would not be the last time that the careers/paths of Torrez and Guidry would intersect.

Although all went well on the evening of April 29, by the following day Martin's consternation showed as rumors circulated that Torrez was not in Quebec with an ailing spouse but rather fishing and visiting with his agent, Gary Walker, to strategize about how to squeeze more money from his new club. "If it's his wife, then I have no qualms about his not being here. But if it's his contract, then I don't understand it because he is signed for the year." The Yankees did manage to speak with Walker's wife, who further complicated matters by stating that her husband was "on a fishing trip in northern Arizona." A columnist for *Newsday* supposedly confirmed that the pitcher was indeed visiting with his representative.[4]

Torrez had still not arrived in New York by the evening of the 30th, and the criticism intensified still more after he missed another start. The Yankees, this time behind Ed Figueroa, once again triumphed against the Mariners, 7–2. The main focus of an article by *Daily News* writer Jack Wilkinson the next day was not on the game, however. The local nine did not have much trouble with the club from the Pacific Northwest, but still had difficulty finding their new right-hander. Wilkinson expounded upon the search, stating that the Yankees were concerned that the issue with Danielle's health was a ruse.

> You remember Mike Torrez. He's the pitcher the Yankees acquired Wednesday from Oakland in exchange for Doc Ellis.... Torrez had been scheduled to pitch Friday night, but the Yankees said he had their permission to remain in Montreal with his wife.... At least that is where the Yankees said he was. But last night, a reporter called Torrez's home in Montreal and he wasn't there. Mike's brother said he wasn't anywhere in Montreal, either, but in Arizona, fishing with his agent.... What kind of fishing they're doing, however, is uncertain.... But when Walker was called at his Phoenix home yesterday, he answered and went silent when asked where Torrez was. End of conversation.[5]

Torrez, who indeed was with his wife, ultimately made it to the Bronx to take up his duties with the Yankees. Given the anxiety caused by this misunderstanding, he certainly did not make a good first impression on Martin, Steinbrenner, and his new teammates.

A second issue with Torrez joining the New Yorkers concerned his relationship with the team's star catcher, Thurman Munson. Two years prior, when Torrez was with Baltimore, the two had had a major dustup that led to fisticuffs. On the night of June 24, 1975, Torrez was the starter for the Orioles against Catfish Hunter. The Yankees ultimately won, 3–1, with both pitchers going the distance. The evening, however, was enlivened by a series of brushback offerings. First, Torrez hit Munson in the top of the second inning and the required counterpunch occurred when Hunter plunked catcher Elrod Hendricks in the bottom of the frame. Later, the New York backstop singled and scored on a hit by Graig Nettles in the top of the fourth. To show his displeasure, Torrez threw a brushback pitch to Munson in the sixth. Hunter followed this further provocation by hitting Bobby Grich in the home half of the seventh inning. The standoff culminated in the top of the eighth when, after being warned by home-plate umpire Nick Bremigan, Torrez instead blew kisses at Munson, rather than aiming for his head. The result was a bench-clearing "gathering" between the two squads. After Munson hit a groundout to Brooks Robinson, he charged the mound. Torrez stood his ground and his "choice of words aren't printable." After the game the two combatants continued to spar, this time in the local papers. Torrez summarized his encounter by saying, "I haven't been in this league that long, but apparently you try to pitch guys tight, they start hollering.... I can't change my pattern of pitching just because he's crying about it." In 1977, these two gladiators would have to work together instead of dueling in order to help the Yankees repeat as American League champions and, hopefully, win the team's first World Series title since 1962. Given the frayed nerves in the New York clubhouse, would this be possible?[6]

This chapter will examine the two most critical years of Mike Torrez's career in the Major Leagues. First, he would leave the relative obscurity of the Oakland Athletics' rotation and move on (with some bumps along the way) to become a mainstay in the Yankees' drive to another World Series. Second, Torrez's time in the Bronx Zoo featured more than just taking turns on the mound. Sources have noted that he was one of the more reasonable personages inside the zaniness that occurred regularly within the confines of New York's clubhouse. In particular, his ties to Reggie Jackson (they were friends and also both clients of agent Gary Walker) helped smooth out some of the slugger's hurt feelings after the June 18 Fenway Park incident with Billy Martin.[7] Even with all of these shenanigans, the talent on this team was extraordinary, and the Yankees claimed their first World Series in 15 years.

Third, Torrez's success on the mound made him an even greater hero than ever to the denizens of the barrios of Kansas (and elsewhere). After winning two games in the World Series, he was named "Kansan of the Year," an honor never before awarded to a person of Mexicano background. The praised heaped upon him was a source of great pride for the Latino community in the state, and in many ways, was viewed as a culmination of many of the efforts undertaken during the Chicano Movement era. The *Topeka Capital-Journal* even went so far as to call him "an accomplished American and a sports hero." Not a bad moniker for someone from the poor barrios of Topeka.[8]

Finally, the 1977 season set Torrez up to become a very wealthy man, certainly to an extent that family members trekking from Mexico to work for the Santa Fe in the Oakland barrio could have never imagined or foreseen. By jumping from the Yankees to Boston for 1978, Torrez earned a substantial increase in salary, but it would come at a great price, both personally and professionally. In the span of one year, from October to October, he would go from being a World Series champion who won two games in the fall classic, to being a player worthy of a chapter in a work entitled *Baseball's All-Time Goats: As Chosen by America's Top Sportswriters*, by Peter Weiss. Weiss rightly concluded that "Torrez pitched a decent game," on October 2, 1978, and that "there should never have been a playoff game in the first place." Still, it was not until "the Curse" finally ended in 2004 that New Englanders could let go of the hurt caused by the collapse of their team, and their new multi-millionaire pitcher, at the end of this particular season.[9]

After defeating the San Francisco Giants in the 1962 World Series, the New York Yankees' faithful endured what was, for them, an interminable length of time between post-season glories. After the futility of the later part of the 1960s and early 1970s, the Bronx Bombers finally made it again to the Fall Classic in 1976, but ran into the legendary buzzsaw of the Big Red Machine of Cincinnati, who unceremoniously swept the pinstripes with a squad that featured the likes of Johnny Bench, Tony Perez, Pete Rose, Joe Morgan, and other greats. Given this reminder of past success, it is not surprising that George Steinbrenner was even more aggressive in pursuing athletes to try to get his team back to (and win) the World Series in 1977. The leadership of Billy Martin, plus the addition of expensive talent such as Don Gullett and, most importantly, Reggie Jackson, demonstrated the "spare no expense" attitude of the franchise as it sought to reclaim its status among the elites of Major League baseball.

In addition to the on-field issues of the Yankees, the 1970s were a turbulent and demoralizing era for New York City as a whole. The year in question would feature both a devastating blackout as well as the manhunt for the dreaded Son of Sam killer. An excellent summary of this difficult and tumultuous epoch can be found in Jonathan Mahler's superb work, *Ladies and Gentlemen, the Bronx Is Burning: 1977, Baseball, Politics, and the Battle for the Soul of a City.*[10] To say that both the city and the baseball team endured an arduous and chaotic year would be a grave understatement.

As the various squads headed into spring training in 1977, many in the baseball world were appalled at how the Yankees, flush with Steinbrenner's cash and brash assertiveness, seemed to be in the process of purchasing a world championship. In two early examples of the rancor caused by this development, contributors to *The Sporting News*, Detroit-based scribe Joe Falls and Kansas City Royals beat writer Joe McGuff, made their feelings abundantly clear in the pages of the publication before the start of the regular season. Falls' essay decried the fact that the Yankees were not building their team in the "old fashioned way," through trades. Instead, he called out the newly minted millionaires, Don Gullett and Reggie Jackson, for being nothing more than mere "mercenaries peddling their flesh to the highest bidder ... they will be the Yankees and they will belong to these kids and it will be grand fun."[11] Likewise, McGuff argued that the Royals (who had lost to the Yankees in the American League playoffs the previous season) were, instead, going about constructing their squad in the "appropriate" manner. He cited the words of Kansas City star George Brett, who contrasted the two styles by saying:

> I think the Yankees are going to have trouble. I hear that (Thurman) Munson was at all the press conferences in New York when the signings were announced. He was supposed to have a verbal agreement that not one would get more than he does. When Jackson signed, he was laughing and saying, "I love you, Reggie." I think the Royals are smart in doing things the way they have. They didn't have to go out and buy a pennant.[12]

While other clubs and their writers may have decried the arrival of free agency, this was now the playing field upon which business was transacted, and the Yankees intended to use their clout to bring back the glory of bygone eras.

While financial resources were plentiful, so was the acrimony in the clubhouse, almost from the moment Grapefruit League action commenced in southern Florida. Yankees beat writer Phil Pepe made no bones about what was expected by the "Boss" and the rabid fan base. Indeed, he foresaw clearly much of what was to transpire in the clubhouse and the management offices of the team during 1977 in a late February article that deserves to be quoted at substantial length.

> Instead of enjoying their revival and looking ahead to bigger and better things, this seems to have been a winter of discontent for the Yankees ... [some on the team] grumble about the amount of money being spent on free agents. And writers, fans, foes and just plain pessimists predict problems ahead when Reggie Jackson gets all of the attention from the press next season.... Perhaps unrest is a better word, and the Yankees have their share of it.... As for Reggie and his new friends, that remains to be seen. Will he create hard feelings? Will there be dissention on the Yankees this year? Will Jackson cause jealously and resentment? It depends on just one thing, results. If the Yankees win, you won't hear a peep out of any of them. If they don't win, the explosion might rock the world.[13]

Going into the season the Yankees appeared set in all facets: they had speed, a plethora of outfielders (which could be used to pull off another trade or two, if necessary), a solid bullpen, the 1976 American League MVP, the previous year's home-run champion, and on the mound the "pitching seems fairly well set with a starting rotation of Catfish Hunter, Don Gullett, Ed Figueroa, Ken Holtzman, and Doc Ellis."[14] While scribes generated articles concerning the presence of big egos and other tensions in the ranks, Pepe summarized the team's time in Ft. Lauderdale as ultimately productive, a period in which nothing "was impaired, damaged, or in the slightest weakened under the Florida sun" heading into the 1977 regular campaign.[15]

On April 5, the Yankees pulled off one more deal that brought to fruition one of George Steinbrenner's visions for his team: fielding an All-Star in all ten positions for Opening Day (April 7). The addition of Bucky Dent from the Chicago White Sox (in exchange for Oscar Gamble and two minor league pitchers) made that dream a reality, and all appeared well when the Yankees defeated the Milwaukee Brewers, 3–0, on that occasion. Dent arrived in New York immediately and Martin had his new shortstop. The galaxy of luminaries was now complete and all would proceed according to a feel-good Broadway script. "They've got so many stars here, so many outstanding ballplayers, it's really a matter of them going out and playing and that other stuff will take care of itself. I'm just happy to be here."[16]

Then, just as quickly, the libretto turned decidedly sour and the squad of millionaires lost eight of their next nine outings. Most embarrassingly, they dropped to a 2–8 record after losing consecutively to expansion franchise Toronto, 5–1 and 8–3, at Yankee Stadium. It had been but 12 days from the first victory to a sense of, if not despair, certainly substantial consternation. Billy Martin even introduced the metaphor of a burning house into his dialogue with reporters. Not surprisingly, the heated discussion centered around the offerings of the "usual suspects" in this drama which generated "the inevitable predictions that Billy Martin was not long for his pin-striped world, that George Steinbrenner's patience was wearing thin, that the signing of Jackson was a mistake, and that Thurman Munson was feuding with Jackson."[17]

Circumstances were so frantic that Martin utilized an "out of the hat" lineup (selected by Reggie) for the April 20 game against the up-till-then insurmountable Blue Jays. This unorthodox order had Munson hitting second, Jackson third, and Chris Chambliss (who drove in 96 runs in 1976) batting eighth. No matter, as the cockamamie arrangement generated 14 hits and a 7–5 Yankees victory. The odd strategy helped right the ship, and New York finally pulled up to .500 (9–9) on April 27 with a 4–3 triumph over the Orioles, the very day they consummated the transaction for Mike Torrez with the Oakland Athletics.[18]

While there certainly was both behind-the-scenes and open haggling, one key issue troubling the squad did not involve verbal jousting. Shortly after the start of the season, Catfish Hunter went on the disabled list after a 1–2 start (he would finish the year 9–9, with a 4.71 ERA and only 22 starts) and was soon joined by Don Gullett after the prized free agent slipped on a wet pitching mound during a series in Baltimore (he would also be limited to only 22 starts in 1977). Suddenly, two of the vaunted, and high-priced, starters the Yankees counted on were not available, at least for a time. Also, another member of the rotation, Doc Ellis, was very unhappy, as he could not reach agreement with Steinbrenner and Gabe Paul on a new contract. He sought $500,000 over three years, but the team countered with an offer around $360,000. Thus, by the end of the first month of the season, the Yankees were certainly in the hunt for more starting pitching. Enter Mike Torrez.[19]

After sweeping the Mariners, the subsequent opponents to visit New York were the California Angels, a team Torrez was familiar with from his time in the American League West. Although there were issues getting him on the mound in the Bronx, Torrez provided hope for Yankees faithful as he pitched beautifully in his inaugural, surrendering only one hit over five innings and getting credit for an 8–1 victory. He followed that up with a 10–5 triumph over his old Oakland teammates, going the distance on

May 8. Overall, his record stood at a sterling 5–1 and the Yankees had moved to an overall mark of 16–10 after their less-than-auspicious start.[20] Suddenly, a rotation that had been shaky for a time appeared solidified. In addition to Torrez's positive contributions, Ed Figueroa, who had lost his first two games, pitched five consecutive complete games between late April and the end of May.[21] Figueroa would finish the year with a record of 16–11 and a 3.57 ERA, and would lead the team in starts with 32 (Torrez had 31). The biggest surprise of all was the ascendance of Ron "Gator" Guidry, who had filled in for several starts and was doing his part to merit joining the regular rotation (he finished the year 16–7 with an ERA of 2.82 and 25 starts).[22]

Subsequently, as had happened in previous seasons, Torrez went into a mid-season funk and appeared in danger of losing his spot in the rotation by the middle of June. After winning his first two turns, the next seven trips to the mound produced only mixed results. The best games during this stint were a no-decision (though he pitched well—going ten innings—in a game the Orioles won, 4–3, in 12 frames) on May 21; he then had two complete-game victories, one against Boston, 5–4, on the 30th, and another against the Brewers on June 8, 9–2. Sandwiched in between was probably his best outing during the stretch, a hard-luck, 1–0 loss to the Rangers on May 25. In his other three defeats, however, he did not pitch well; lasting less than 5⅓ innings against the Angels, the White Sox, and Kansas City. At this point in the season, his record stood at a pedestrian 7–5, and would bottom out at two games below .500 with an ERA of almost 5.00 by late July. The Yankees were doing better as a team, with a record of 36–27 going into Torrez's next start, which would take place on June 18 before a national television audience.[23] This turned out to be the turning point for the season.

As predicted before the start of 1977, the arrival of Reggie Jackson increased the talent level on the Yankees, but it also augmented the volatility within the clubhouse. According to Jackson's 2013 book, camaraderie between him and his teammates had improved somewhat by the end of May. "When you're winning, a lot of things, including animosity, disappear in the clubhouse.... Then that *Sport* magazine piece came out. Oh, my goodness!"[24] The June issue of *Sport* featured an article on Jackson by Robert Ward. In the essay, Jackson was quoted making controversial statements, the most famous/infamous being, "You know, this team … it all flows from me. I've got to keep it all going. I'm the straw that stirs the drink…. Maybe I should say me and Munson … but really he doesn't enter into it." Not only did this declaration raise the ire of the reigning AL MVP, it exacerbated tensions and divisions within the clubhouse. In *Becoming Mr. October*, Jackson noted that teammate Fran Healy presented him with a copy of the article, to which the outfielder expressed both shock and dismay, indicating that Ward had misquoted him. Healy passed that message along to Munson, who responded it was not possible to be misattributed "for three thousand f—-in' words." As recently as 2012, Ward asserted that, even though he did not tape the interview with Jackson in 1977, he "had a perfect memory and let people talk, then scribbled down what they said…. Obviously, you can't write as fast as someone talks, but I never missed a word."[25]

In addition to the tensions with the All Star backstop, Jackson believed that the article

> was an opportunity for Billy Martin to prove I was not a good fit. This gave him an opportunity to impress upon the team that he was in charge, rather than fix the situation. That he would embarrass me to get even. Billy was determined, regardless of the effect on the team, to prove I was a bad apple. He was so hell-bent to prove that I "wasn't a Yankee."[26]

The volatile relationship between Jackson and Martin came to a head during Torrez's start against the Red Sox. The three games in Boston in mid–June appeared disastrous for the New Yorkers. The two ancient rivals headed into the set with first place on the line, and fans expected a competitive series. The Yankees were unceremoniously swept by a combined score of 30–9. That, however, paled in comparison with what happened in the visitors' dugout on June 18. That incident led many to believe that the highly paid Yankees had indeed imploded, and right before the eyes of an NBC "Game of the Week" audience.

Torrez did not fare well in this start, and was shelled over his 5⅓ innings of work, giving up 13 hits and seven earned runs before being replaced by Sparky Lyle.[27] The last batter he faced, Jim Rice, hit a blooper into right field for a single. In his book on the 1978 Yankees, *October Men*, Roger Kahn indicated that "Jackson looked toward the infield, as though expecting…. Randolph to race down the looper. Then he broke slowly, picked up the ball on a few bounces, and soft-tossed it toward the pitcher's mound. Rice pulled into second base. The ball was not catchable." While most writers argue that the ball was destined to produce a hit, if Jackson had "broken smartly, he could have held Rice to a single. It was a poor play, the play of a ball player whose mind was out of focus."[28] Martin had seen enough, of both his pitcher and right fielder. As he went out to ask Torrez for the ball, Martin indicated that he was bringing in Sparky Lyle and also Paul Blair to replace Jackson. "He told Torrez, who had not asked,

'I'm pulling the son of a bitch for not hustling.' Munson nodded in agreement."[29] In Martin's view, he was pulling Jackson for loafing; in Jackson's perspective the manager was getting even for the *Sport* essay and other slights (perceived or otherwise). Later, Torrez advised Jackson to return to the team's hotel and "just keep away from Billy for a while."[30]

Phil Pepe's 1998 book, *Talking Baseball: An Oral History of Baseball in the 1970s*, supports many of these details. In the aftermath, Pepe indicated, in the hotel room that evening, trying to comfort and calm Jackson down was Mike Torrez, "there to console his friend."[31] In early 1979 Roger Kahn provided even more details about the evening of the 18th, and Torrez's role in helping soothe Jackson's hurt feelings.

> Aside from winning ballgames, his Yankee role was as a comforter of more fragile spirits…. Afterward, Jackson called Torrez … "All Reggie could think about was the game. The game and the humiliation. The more he talked, the more upset he got. So I said some things to him. He was a fine ballplayer. Baseball moves quickly. Things are forgotten. After a while, I got him feeling better."[32]

Jackson's account in his recent book supports Pepe, but adds a more ominous tone to what happened on the mound between Martin and Torrez. When the skipper went to replace his starter, "Mike said later, Billy told him, 'Watch this.' He also claimed that Mike asked Martin not to make the switch with Blair."[33] In interviews with this author, Torrez acknowledged Jackson's assertion, but he also was adamant that he too wanted Jackson out of the game due to a perceived "lack of hustle." Finally, Jackson argued that all of this was not based on a clash of personalities, but rather, racism. "It makes me cry the way they treat me on this team. I'm a big black man with an IQ of 160, making $700,000 a year, and they treat me like dirt. They've never had anyone like me on their team before."[34]

After the Yankees limped out of Boston, it appeared only a matter of time before Billy Martin would be fired. True, the team sported a 36–30 record and was in contention, but just two days after the incident, a column by a UPI reporter stated unequivocally that "Billy Martin is all finished with the Yankees. They'll make it official with a formal announcement in a day or so, at which time Yogi Berra will be named the new Yankees' manager."[35] This reporter jumped the gun, however, as Yankees management instead huddled with the beleaguered skipper and announced:

> "There will be no change in our organization regardless of what has been said. We don't feel there's a better manager than Billy Martin and we want the Yankees to have the best. There were some things that had to be straightened out. From the first pitch to the last out, there's no better manager in baseball than Billy, and he's the one we want."

Steinbrenner also visited with Jackson and told the disgruntled super-star that if he continued bringing up the race issue, he would beat his "head off." Finally, he brought in Munson to reaffirm his position/status on the club. "You are the captain. When I want Jackson to be captain, I'll tell him and you, too. You are the captain, now be the captain." The reaction was immediate, and "several Yankee players later told Steinbrenner the they thought his remarks would give the club a lift."[36]

The impact of all of this absurdity caused tension for Torrez both on the field and at home. After the Boston loss, his record stood at 7–6, a sharp drop-off after his positive start. The results of his next six outings, through July 22, were more of the same. He pitched one good game during this stint, against the Red Sox on June 25, resulting in a 5–1 victory. Then came four consecutive defeats in which he pitched beyond the 6th inning only once (going eight innings in a 4–3 loss to the Orioles and Mike Flanagan on July 11).[37] One particularly difficult outcome in this stretch occurred on July 16, when he lost to the Royals in Kansas City, 5–1. At that game, an old friend, John Martinez, sports editor for *North Platte Telegraph*, once again reminded the Mexican American community of the significance of having "one of their own" playing in the majors. While the results were not what both men wanted on the field at Royals Stadium, Martinez argued that Torrez was the personification of the "American dream" that so many other Chicanos/Latinos shared, putting on "a pin-stripe uniform and playing for the New York Yankees is something every kid dreams about." In that regard, a youth growing up on the barrio of Topeka was no different from most other "American" youths. Martinez also reminded readers of the ties between this Nebraska community, sport, and this Mexican America major leaguer who "helped the Topeka 7-Uppers win several championships at the North Platte Mexican Athletic Club basketball tournaments." This article, like others, helped to reinforce Torrez's ties to the broader Spanish-surnamed population of the Midwest.[38]

These poor outings dropped Torrez's record to 8–10 with an ERA of 4.90 almost 100 games into the season. The Yankees were doing well, with a mark of 51–44, just 3.5 games behind the Red Sox, but the emergence of the previously lightly-regarded Ron Guidry placed extra pressure on Torrez to keep his position in the starting rotation.[39]

Given his travels throughout the Major Leagues over previous seasons, the issues of security and money were ever-present. He now had the opportunity to pitch in New York, in the final year of his contract, in the early stages of free agency, and the season and opportunity for a substantial contract seemed to be slipping away. Circumstances at home were also not constructive. As Danielle noted during the late summer, "the pressure I'd seen building in Oakland was even more intense here. With George Steinbrenner around, Mike couldn't let up for a minute.... Mike's nervousness over this got the best of him, and ... we argued a lot."[40] The combination of difficulties at home and in the clubhouse echoed some of what Torrez endured after his trade from St. Louis to Montreal in 1970. Now, with successful players able to earn salaries previously unimaginable, the pressure was even more intense.

True to the work ethic he learned from family and friends in the Oakland barrio, and the pattern he established with other teams, Torrez sought to prove himself through more work and once again argued that the reason for his lack of success through late July was due to insufficient use. Billy Martin finally agreed to give his right-hander an opportunity to pitch every fourth day, and Torrez responded with another superb stretch similar to those produced with the Oilers, Cardinals, Expos and Athletics. Between July 28 and August 27, he pitched seven consecutive complete-game victories. During that period, the Yankees went from 55–45 to 78–52, a mark of 23 victories in 30 games.

For the same span, the Red Sox played well, fashioning a record of 19–11, but as the calendar reached the start of September, the Bronx Bombers had moved into first place, three games in front of their archrivals. In an article dated September 3, Phil Pepe discussed the turnaround in *The Sporting News.* "Once they agreed to go that way, the results have been amazing. In his first five starts under the new plan, Torrez had five wins, five complete games, allowed 25 hits, walked six, struck out 25, allowed seven earned runs for an ERA of 1.40 to raise his record to 13–10." Torrez would win two more games, with his best outing an 8–1 triumph over the Rangers. In that game he allowed only four hits and one earned run. Torrez summarized his success by making a plea to remain in the Big Apple. "I'd like to stay here, I really would. I've been on four teams in the last four years and I'd like to stay in one place, maybe finish out my career here."[41] Perhaps Torrez, after four trades in as many years, would finally find his Major League home within the kiln that was the 1977 Bronx Zoo. Before a new deal was finalized, however, the Yankees had a pennant to clinch, and Torrez would more than do his share to claim the AL East title, and beyond.

On September 1, the Yankees' record stood at 80–52. The Red Sox and Orioles trailed the division leaders with identical marks of 76–55 (3.5 games behind). Over the final month of the season, the New Yorkers continued their winning ways and finished 20–10 (including two games in

October). Boston and Baltimore also finished in good fashion with identical marks of 21–9. Though they managed to close the gap by one game, George Steinbrenner's troops had accomplished the first part of their mission; winning the division. Torrez contributed a mark of 17–13 with an ERA of 3.82. His best outing over the final weeks of the campaign came against the Blue Jays, a complete-game, 2–0 victory on September 9 in which he surrendered only three hits. Overall, he was second on the club in starts to Ed Figueroa, as well as in innings pitched (with 217 versus 239⅓), even though he did not start his first game in pinstripes until May 3.[42]

Now that they had clinched and moved on to play the Kansas City Royals in the AL playoffs, the sense among many in baseball was that the Yankees had "backed into" the title. After all, a team that started an all-star at every position on Opening Day should not have had a lick of trouble in winning its division, no? A review of the Yankees' season does support, in part, this argument as they did not have a winning mark against some of the better teams in their division. The team had a losing record against its two main division competitors, the Red Sox and the Orioles (both 7–8). They had the same outcome against the also-ran Milwaukee Brewers. Thus, the millionaires finished three games under .500 against these clubs (21–24). New York did win the season series against the Tigers and the expansion Blue Jays with identical 9–6 results, and they feasted against the Cleveland Indians, winning 12 of 15 contests to finish 30–15 against the remaining Eastern foes (for a mark of 51–39, a .567 winning percentage). Their best results, however, came against the Western rivals, which the Yankees dominated with a sterling record of 49–23 (a .681 winning percentage). The most lopsided split came against, not surprisingly, the undermanned Oakland Athletics squad that lost nine of 11 to New York. Torrez notched two of his victories, including one of his two shutouts, against his old team. As to the season results concerning their playoff opponents, the Yankees and Royals split the ten games played in 1977. Given the rivalry that began in the playoffs of the previous season, the ALCS was likely to come down to the wire yet again. In the eyes of many fans, this was a battle between a team that "did it the right way" versus one that "bought the pennant."

Of course, the Yankees players and management insisted that they had indeed earned their title, and given the constant turmoil within the locker room, that is not an unreasonable argument. As Billy Martin noted, "Have you ever had a 500-pound weight on your back? I feel like it just slipped off. I'm very happy. And I'm very proud of these guys." Reggie

Jackson agreed with his manager's assessment, but did harken back to some less pleasant days of the season. "This was a tough thing, psychologically and emotionally. It makes me sigh.... I subdued my personality and strengthened my character." Phil Pepe summarized the goings-on in the locker room by arguing that squad was "just like soldiers [that] grow closer together in war. They have been through something together and it was tough, but they had survived, triumphed."[43]

Not surprisingly, many on the club harkened back to the events of June 18, and the results do bear out how transformative Martin pulling Jackson out of right field at Fenway Park really was. In another column, Pepe laid out the numerical outcomes from a few weeks beyond that fateful day:

> From August 10 to September 28, with Reggie Jackson in the cleanup spot, the Yankees won 40 games out of 50. From August 10 to September 28, they went from five games out of first to a four game lead in the A.L. East.... Jackson was the cleanup hitter in 47 of those 50 games and, in those 47 games, he belted 13 home runs and drove in 48 runs to take over the club RBI lead.... Interestingly, the Yankees started winning when they stopped feuding. Or did they stop feuding when they started winning?[44]

To stress the point even more, after the 18th of June, the Yankees' record was 36–29, after that game, they went 64–33 for a final tally of 100–62 (a .617 winning percentage).

While Jackson, Munson and others certainly deserve credit for the pennant, Billy Martin provided a brief answer to Pepe when asked about the key element in the Bombers' turnaround. "Pitching. I always felt they'd come back. I always figured our pitching had got to come around and, when it did, we'd eventually do it."[45] If we use the same benchmark applied to the Yankees as a team and relate it to Mike Torrez's season, he finished the year with a 9–3 mark (from when he was 8–10 after a 6–3 defeat against the Brewers on June 22) and dropped his ERA from 4.90 to 3.82. Certainly, he had made a substantive case for not only remaining in pinstripes, but also for finally earning the "big money" he had sought since signing with the Cardinals right after graduating from Topeka High. Torrez would further bolster his case for a substantial raise over the next few weeks as he pitched against the Royals and the Los Angeles Dodgers in the American League Championship Series (ALCS) and World Series.

After several years of pitching well but playing for teams that came up short, such as the Oakland Athletics and their chase of the Royals in 1976, Mike Torrez finally had his first opportunity to experience (and benefit financially from) participation in playoff baseball. The 1973 Expos and the 1975 Orioles were also in contention almost to the end of those campaigns, but both failed to win division titles. He was a member of the 1967 Cardinals squad that reached the World Series, but since he was called up late in the year, he was not eligible to be on the fall roster. Now, it seemed, even with all of the tumult occurring in the Yankees clubhouse as well as in his private life, that 1977 would finally be his opportunity to play in the post-season and earn a dramatic increase in salary, as well as a championship ring. The fact that New York would (once again) face the Kansas City Royals in the American League playoffs was truly serendipitous for the Torrez clan. Here was a chance to root on their family member at the most significant time of the season, and they would not have to travel far to see him pitch.

While the Yankees and the Royals, playing in different divisions, clashed in only ten games during the regular season, there certainly was a rivalry between the clubs. The previous year, the New Yorkers had bested Kansas City in a scintillating five games that seesawed with great plays and emotions. The Yankees broke through first by winning, 4–1, in Royals Stadium on October 9, 1976. The Midwesterners won Game Two, 7–3, and then lost the next matchup of the series, 5–3, in Yankee Stadium. With New York ahead two games to one, the pinstripers sent out Catfish Hunter to finish off the ALCS on the night of October 13. Before a crowd of more than 56,000 rabid fans, the Royals showed great grit and hung the loss on Hunter, 7–4. The right to face the Reds in the 1976 World Series came down to a deciding contest the following evening. Just as previously, this final game went back and forth. The Royals, who trailed 6–3 going into the eighth inning, scored three tallies to forge a tie. Leading off the home half of the ninth, Chris Chambliss stroked a homer to give the Yankees a 7–6 victory and send New York to its first fall classic since 1964.[46]

This rematch featured competitors that won at least 100 games in 1977 (the Royals finished 102–60). Offensively, the West Division champion's roster featured all of the key elements: power, high averages, and speed on the basepaths. John Mayberry and Al Cowens led the club with 23 home runs each, while Cowens drove in 112 runs. Cowens and George Brett tied for the team lead in batting average at .312. Finally, with the terrific athleticism of Freddie Patek, Frank White, Amos Otis, and Hal McRae, the Royals swiped a total of 170 bases, finishing second in the American League. They scored 822 runs (fifth overall), finished fifth in hitting (.277), and led the circuit in doubles (299) and triples (77). On the mound, the Kansas City starters were impressive, finishing the campaign with the best ERA in the AL at 3.52. The rotation featured 20-game winner

Dennis Leonard (20–12, 3.04 ERA) as well as Jim Colborn (18–14, 3.62) and Paul Splittorff (16–6, 3.69).[47]

The Yankees matched up well, with similar numbers in runs scored (831, third in the league), more home runs than Kansas City (184 versus 146), and a slightly higher team batting average (.281). The principal difference between the combatants' offensive arsenal was in regard to stolen bases, with the Yankees totaling only 93. On the mound, there were many parallels. New York's overall team ERA was third in the AL, with a mark of 3.61. The teams allowed the exact same number of runs to opponents, 651, tied for the lowest in the league. In sum, the Royals and the Yankees were evenly paired going into the ALCS.[48] The personalities of the two organizations, however, could not have been more different. Whereas the Missourians were a franchise that was, as noted earlier, "built the right way" and which had few obvious internal fault lines, the Yankees were the "Bronx Zoo" and had suffered through numerous and intensive squabbles on their way to claiming the East. The stage was set for a classic encounter, and Mike Torrez played a key role in determining the ultimate outcome.

Once again, the ALCS went the distance, and to the chagrin of Kansas City fans, the result was just as in 1976: the Bronx Bombers emerged victorious. Even more frustrating, with the two-three format for the series (favoring the team with the better record), the last two Yankees triumphs occurred in Missouri, and Mike Torrez played a critical role in the deciding game. The series was tied after the first two games in Yankee Stadium, with the visitors winning first (versus Don Gullett), 7–2, and Ron Guidry leading his team to a 6–2 triumph the following night.

On the 7th of October, Mike Torrez realized a childhood dream, getting the opportunity to pitch a post-season start before a "home" crowd that featured family members, including his mother, siblings and nephews. Disappointingly, he did not have a good outing and lasted only 5⅔ innings, surrendering five earned runs. By the time he was replaced by Sparky Lyle in the sixth, the Yankees were down, 5–1, and would lose, 6–2. The Torrez clan was disappointed, but remained proud and hopeful. Mike's sister Yolanda and brother John recalled taking a bit of abuse from aficionados of the Royals, but still, "it is something to see your brother out there playing." Mary, who had her hair done at a local beauty shop for the occasion, was philosophical about the outcome. "How many mothers get to watch their son pitch in the playoffs? I think I was probably more excited this afternoon than he was." Even with all of the excitement surrounding the goings-on in the field, Mary noted that Mike would still return to his hometown and barrio to share in family traditions after the season. "No matter how these playoffs go, or even if the Yankees make it to the series, I'll still get to see him this fall for pheasant season."[49] While Mary and the rest of the family were happy to see Mike play on this grand stage, the Kansan hoped for an opportunity to redeem himself and show that the results generated toward the end of the regular campaign were not a fluke. After all, by this point in the season, Torrez was one only three Yankees who had not re-signed with the club for 1978. He would get his chance by replacing Ron Guidry on the mound in the rubber game of the Series.

After the first three games, the Royals had the AL pennant within their grasp, leading two victories to one, with the fourth, and if necessary deciding fifth tilt in their ballpark. On Saturday October 8, the Yankees sent Ed Figueroa to the mound to face Larry Gura (who started only six games that season, but did finish with a record of 8–5 and an ERA of 3.13). The use of a spot-starter by manager Whitey Herzog was not surprising; after all, he hoped that the Royals could close out the Yankees in this fourth game. Even if that did not occur, Herzog would have a member of his regular rotation to start a deciding fifth game. Unfortunately, Gura did not have a good start, and the New Yorkers led, 4–0, after their turn at bat in the third inning.[50] While the Royals managed to narrow the deficit to 5–4, the Yankees plated an insurance run in the top of the ninth to seal a 6–4 victory. Behind the sterling relief pitching of Sparky Lyle, who held Kansas City to two hits over the final 5⅓ innings, the Yankees lived to fight another day.[51] The ALCS was now knotted at two games each, and the home team faced the daunting task of challenging Ron Guidry as the New York starter the following evening. It was not be Guidry who starred in this contest, but rather Mike Torrez, who put together a sterling performance in relief before giving way to Lyle with two outs in the bottom of the eighth.

To say that the 1977 Yankees had a flair for the dramatic would be a serious understatement; the final game for the American League championship would be no different. Starter Guidry, who had come seemingly from nowhere to establish himself as one of the aces of the New York staff, did not have his usual excellent command, and right from the start the Royals had him in trouble. Before Guidry got out of the first inning, Kansas City tallied two runs on a McRae single, a Brett triple, and a hit by Otis. Just like that, the score was 2–0 and the 41,133 witnesses in the stands were euphoric. The Yankees did score one run on a Munson RBI single in the top of the third, but the Royals countered with another score in the bottom of the frame. At this point, with Guidry having pitched only 2⅓ innings, and with Al Cowens on first after singling home Hal McRae, that

Billy Martin called upon Torrez to stem the tide. Torrez responded with an excellent performance, promptly striking out Amos Otis and John Wathan to end the threat. Over 5⅓ innings, Torrez kept the Royals at bay, surrendering three singles and four walks. By the time he left the mound, New York still trailed, but no further damage had been done. With two outs in the bottom of the eighth, Lyle replaced Torrez, and struck out Cookie Rojas to close out the inning, leaving two men on base. Then, as in 1976, the final at-bat of the deciding game proved pivotal as New York used two hits, one walk, an error, and a sacrifice fly to manufacture three runs and take the lead, 5–3. The bottom of the frame was almost anti-climactic as Lyle surrendered one single, but induced Freddie Patek to hit into a Series-ending double play.[52]

Even with all that had transpired during the regular season, the Yankees were on their way to the World Series. While he did not get credit for the victory, Mike Torrez contributed mightily by holding the Royals scoreless and gave his team a chance to win. As Phil Pepe surmised, "there was no other way for the Yankees to win the American League championship…. No soap opera worth its Neilsen ratings would think of having anything but a dramatic and surprising ending that kept millions of TV viewers on the edge of their seats … and the Yankees of 1977 were baseball's soap opera."[53] Torrez had, once again, come through in the clutch. Now he was on his way to participate in every ballplayer's ultimate fantasy: playing in a World Series in Yankee Stadium. In addition to the possibility of becoming part of Yankees lore, Torrez's dream of security for his family was one step closer to reality if he pitched well in this grandest of sporting stages.

Once the Yankees dispatched the Royals in the ALCS, it was time to focus on their next foe: the Dodgers. Under the guidance of first-year manager Tommy Lasorda, Los Angeles won their division, toppling an aging Cincinnati Reds (who never got closer to the division leaders than 6½ games after April), and then took the NLCS from the Philadelphia Phillies, three games to one. The Dodgers were formidable, featuring the likes of Steve Garvey, Bill Russell, Dusty Baker, and Reggie Smith in their daily lineup. The squad from Chavez Ravine scored 769 runs (third in the senior circuit), led the league in home runs (191), and finished fifth with a team batting average of .266. As usual, however, they featured excellent pitching, finishing the season with an NL-best 3.22 team ERA. The rotation consisted of five hurlers who each started more than 30 games. The ace was Tommy John, who compiled a 20–7 mark (a .741 winning percentage) with a 2.78 ERA. All of the remaining member of the corps had at least a

.615 winning percentage. Don Sutton and Doug Rau were each 14–8 with ERAs of 3.18 and 3.43 respectively, Burt Hooton tallied a 12–7 record and an ERA of 2.62. The "least effective" member of the crew (by winning percentage), was Rick Rhoden, who ended 1977 with a 16–10 mark and an ERA of 3.74.[54]

Although Lasorda had a reputation for bravado and feistiness along the lines of Billy Martin's, the atmosphere in the Dodgers clubhouse from the start of spring training in Vero Beach, Florida, was radically different from the Yankees'. From the moment he took over the club, Lasorda preached unity and an expectation of winning. After the team clinched its division, various players noted the impact of the first-year skipper. For example, Don Sutton argued that Lasorda "is a master psychologist. Tommy preached from opening day that we could go all the way and he convinced us of it." Tommy John echoed, "we're all mirrors of the manager, and he made us cocky, confident, and convinced." Finally, and most tellingly, there seemed to be a greater amount of cohesion and team unity among the Dodgers going into the World Series. Bill Russell stated that Lasorda clearly articulated who would be in the starting lineup from February on, and stuck with his players through thick and thin. "Tommy got his eight regulars together the first day of spring training, and stayed with them. That lineup opened the first game of spring exhibitions, it opened the first game of the season, it opened the first game of the playoff, and it's the same one that will open the World Series." As Los Angeles headed to the Bronx, Lasorda continued to preach similar sermons. "If any manager thinks he's the reason a team got into the World Series, he's dead wrong. I haven't hit a ball or thrown one or stole [sic] a base or anything else.... Now, maybe I've helped in the area of spirit.... But nothing more. I'm the guy who needs them."[55]

Going into the fall classic, a principal question among insiders and fans throughout the nation was whether the Yankees' soap opera, going up against a united, potent, and excellent pitching team, would finally meet its match. Dodgers backstop Steve Yeager was not overconfident and believed that at this point in the season, the bickering and turmoil in the Yankees' clubhouse was not relevant. "You can't judge the Yankees by what they do off the field. Look at Oakland in 1972, '73, '74. They fought each other in the clubhouse all the time and beat everyone around."[56] While various players contributed to the Bombers' winning effort, Reggie Jackson certainly among them, Mike Torrez did his part and thereby cemented in the minds of many general managers the notion that this son and grandson of Santa Fe Railroad laborers from the barrio of Topeka, Kansas, was wor-

thy of having, finally, a permanent "home" in the majors and the opportunity to earn the "big money" and security he had long sought.

The Dodgers and Yankees began the 1977 World Series in Yankee
Stadium on October 11. The home team started one of its high-priced free
agents, Don Gullett, and the visitors countered with Don Sutton. Both
performed admirably, with Gullett going 8⅓ innings and surrendering
only five hits and three earned runs; Sutton lasted seven innings and gave
up three runs on eight hits. The Dodgers knotted the score in the top of
the ninth, and the game went into extra innings. In the bottom of the 12th,
Paul Blair, once again replacing Reggie Jackson in the outfield, was the
hero as he drove in Willie Randolph, who had led off the frame with a
double, for a 4–3 victory. The next evening, however, Dodgers pitching
came through as Burt Hooton hurled a complete-game five-hitter to defeat
Catfish Hunter (who lasted only 2⅓ innings), 6–1. Los Angeles supported
Hooton's effort with four home runs: a pair of two-run homers by Ron
Cey and Reggie Smith, and solo blasts by Steve Yeager and Steve Garvey.[57]

To no one's surprise, even at this point in the season, the Yankees did
not stop bickering. After Hunter's poor performance, Reggie Jackson noted
that Martin's decision to pitch his former Oakland teammate had been a
"stupid strategy." To this particularly ill-timed verbal gem, Martin replied
something along the lines of "Jackson could kiss my Italian posterior."
Jackson backed down a bit and noted, "I don't know how to handle a pitching staff—I don't know how to handle myself. The manager has brought
this club to a point where it's playing for the world championship." Not
one to be left out of a good Bronx Zoo locker-room exchange, Thurman
Munson famously chimed in that perhaps Martin should listen to Jackson
since, after all, "I guess that Billy doesn't realize that Reggie is Mr. October."
It was certainly good to see that not much had changed, even with the
pressure of competing in the World Series.[58] Heading back to Chavez
Ravine, the Dodgers had the next three games at home and a chance to
finish off the Yankees on their turf. The Yankees starter for the following
contest was Mike Torrez.

The third encounter of a best-of-seven series is usually critical, particularly if the team that hosted the first two games at home failed to
sweep. This was the situation the Yankees faced in Los Angeles on October
14, and they needed to win at least one contest in LA to assure themselves
of being able to return to their home field. After a stellar performance in
the final game of the ALCS five days previously, Billy Martin decided to
give Mike Torrez the ball. From the top of the first inning, the New Yorkers
jumped on 20-game winner Tommy John. After only five hitters had been

to the plate, the score was 3–0. John settled down after Lou Piniella drove in the final run of the inning, struck out Chris Chambliss and induced Graig Nettles to ground out to first. Torrez was not overpowering at the start and was in trouble in the first two innings, surrendering two walks, a double, and a single. Fortunately, he managed to get Steve Garvey to ground out to end the first, and then struck out his counterpart and got Davey Lopes to ground out to end the second.

While the Yankees led, Torrez's best pitches did not appear to be working effectively. In the third inning, the Dodgers broke through on singles by Reggie Smith and Steve Garvey, followed by a three-run home run by Dusty Baker. Suddenly, a substantial early lead by the Bombers had evaporated and Torrez appeared to be on the ropes. Given his performances over the last quarter of the season, however, Billy Martin did not come out to visit his right-hander. Torrez rebounded and stuck out Rick Monday to finish the inning. The pitch Baker hit, Torrez noted afterward, was a mistake. "I should have gone with my best pitch, the fast ball, but I threw him a slider and it stayed out over the plate." This was a critical moment in the game, if not the Series. Instead of getting rattled, Torrez bore down and dominated over the rest of the outing.

After his teammates tallied lone runs in the fourth and fifth to retake the lead, Torrez took charge and was in trouble just one more time: in the bottom of the fifth. Here, Martin did visit his starter and simply told him to "throw the damn thing as hard as I could and not worry about walking anyone." That did the trick, and Torrez mastered his opponents in the last innings. In the ninth, with the score still 5–3, he made short work of the Dodgers, inducing Yeager to ground out, and striking out pinch-hitter Manny Mota and second baseman Davey Lopes. All told, Torrez allowed only two more hits after Baker's homer, and retired the final 11 hitters he faced. Lasorda was very complimentary about the opposing pitcher during his post-game interview and stated, "I thought we had a chance to get him after we tied the score, but he got much stronger after the sixth inning and his breaking pitch gave him complete command of the game."[59] The Yankees went on to win Game 5 behind Ron Guidry, 4–2, but the Dodgers managed to stave off elimination by shelling Don Gullett and taking the final contest in their home park, 10–4.[60] The World Series now headed back to the Bronx for Game 6, scheduled for October 18.

Heading into the fall classic, Billy Martin had more than just the bickering in the clubhouse to deal with. One major issue was the physical condition of a substantial part of his starting rotation. As Lowell Reidenbaugh from *The Sporting News* noted, "Don Gullett had shoulder miseries, Cat-

Three quarters of the 1977 Yankees' starting rotation as Mike shares a moment with Ron Guidry and Ed Figueroa. Courtesy of Mike Torrez.

fish Hunter, suffering from a urinary infection, had not pitched since September 10. Ed Figueroa was suffering from tendinitis in his right index finger, Ken Holtzman had pitched so infrequently as to be of little value."[61] Note that the only two starters not mentioned were Ron Guidry and Mike Torrez. Thus, who would start Game 6? The young sensation had pitched and won Game 4, so he could not go. The decision to go with a less than healthy Catfish Hunter had not turned out well, so Martin scratched him. Figueroa was not completely healthy, so Martin passed him over. Finally, the skipper concluded that it was best to save Guidry for a decisive contest, and gave the starting assignment to Torrez.

The events of the night of October 18 are an indelible part of baseball and New York Yankees lore. Reggie Jackson proved he was worth every penny of his contract and had an evening for the ages, connecting on three home runs on three pitches in successive at bats (in the fourth, fifth and eighth innings). Overall, he scored four runs, drove in five, and was a perfect three-for-three (plus one walk) at the plate. Not surprisingly, Jackson was named Series MVP after the Yankees' 8–4 triumph claimed the franchise's 21st championship. While Jackson provided the offensive fireworks,

Torrez gets ready to pitch during Game 6 of the 1977 World Series. Torrez's two victories in that Classic helped catapult him to fortune (financial), and heartbreak with the Boston Red Sox. National Baseball Hall of Fame Library, Cooperstown, New York, 588–2005_Act_NBL.

Torrez pitched a game described as being "no masterpiece." Although overlooked amidst the hoopla of Jackson's evening, Torrez came out the winning pitcher of the final game of the 1977 season, and actually caught a pop-up bunt by Lee Lacy for the final out.

The Kansan's final statistics for the victory were two earned runs, nine hits surrendered, and six strikeouts. Lost amidst the merriment of the victory and the—not surprising—soap opera-like ending was Torrez's overall record for the Series: he won both starts, pitched two complete games, and finished with an ERA of 2.50. Back in Topeka it seemed that the entire Oakland barrio turned out at the Torrez home to celebrate Mike's success. Mary recalled "The people kept coming. It was about 12:30 or 1 o'clock when it finally ended." John, who was with his brother in New York on the evening of Game 6, echoed his younger sibling's statements as to what might be next for a pitcher who won two games in the World Series. "I know my mom would like to see him play for the Royals, but it's hard to say. I think he'll take the best offer, I know that his value went up."[62]

While Torrez did not take home the new car awarded to the MVP, he sought a larger reward: a long-term contract from an ecstatic George

Steinbrenner. Given Torrez' performance over the last quarter of the regular season, the ALCS, and the World Series, surely he was worth at least the approximately two million dollars given to Don Gullett by the Yankees after the 1976 season, no? This story would play out over the next few weeks and would result in Torrez becoming part of the new crop of baseball millionaires.[63]

Almost as quickly as the ink dried on stories surrounding the New Yorkers' triumph, a new round of hullabaloo commenced in regard to the composition of the team's roster for 1978. First, the club had to deal with the internal turmoil for, as shortly after the ticker-tape parade, various players commented on the difficulties of repeating, given the prevailing mayhem. "I can't go through another year like this. No way.... I'm tired. I don't know how I played the last few days," noted captain Thurman Munson. Lou Piniella echoed these sentiments when he argued:

> I don't think this club can take another year, another two weeks, another week of all of this. You don't have to be one big, happy family to concentrate on playing ball, but if everything isn't gonna be tranquil we might as well write off next year. You can believe this—that the players don't want any controversy. But I couldn't get it out of my mind during Sunday's game in Los Angeles.[64]

Second, the club, according to a report in *The Sporting News*, did make money in 1977 (an estimated $2 million on revenues of $16 million), but now more players wanted an increased cut of the pie, Mike Torrez among them. The Yankees spent approximately $3,500,000 in salaries, with about $1,500,000 of that divided among Jackson, Hunter and Gullett. Steinbrenner now had to determine what to do with his captain, who earned around $200,000, the seldom-used Ken Holtzman (who earned $165,000), Sparky Lyle (who made $140,000 and won the Cy Young Award for 1977), Bucky Dent (who cost $130,000), plus others. In the bottom rungs of the Yankees' payroll stood Torrez, who was earning the amount he had agreed to with Charlie Finley: $100,000. While the figure certainly appeared astronomical to the "average" American worker of 1977, it paled in comparison to what other pitchers were earning, men who did not have the stretch run that Mike Torrez generated. Now was the time to get paid. "My agent is going to meet with Mr. Steinbrenner and Mr. Paul ... but I'm still not sure where things stand. I'd like to be back here but I can't be sure of that."[65]

Before determining where he would continue his baseball career, be it in New York City or elsewhere, Torrez took time to enjoy some of the spoils of being a member of a World Series-winning team. Of course, there was a substantial payout of the winner's share: approximately $32,000.[66]

Next, Mike and Danielle (along with other Yankees players and their wives) were the guests of Don King and Caesar's Palace at the November 5 Norton vs. Young fight.[67] Even during such events, however, the ever-present Yankees turmoil lingered. Danielle, for example, believed that at the bout in Las Vegas, George Steinbrenner made sure that "Mike and I were sitting on the opposite side from the ring.... Mike was negotiating with other ball clubs ... [and Steinbrenner] would not publicly allow Mike to come anywhere near.... George treated Mike like a total outcast at this fight in Vegas."[68] This, in addition to how he had been treated previously, made it easier for Torrez to break his ties with New York.

A final, and welcomed, reward for Torrez's success came from both the city and state of his birth. In November the former youth from the Oakland barrio was named "Kansan of the Year" and given a parade down his hometown's main boulevard. In many ways, the designation was a culmination of much of what the Chicano Movement had sought for Mexican Americans in the Sunflower State: a chance to prove one's mettle and worth in the broader society. The city held "Mike Torrez Day" on November 19, and brought much of the flavor of the barrio to the broader community. As one paper noted, there were savory Mexican foods for sale, plus traditional dances. Further, Torrez's appearance was used to "kick off a special athletic fund to support sports at Our Lady of Guadalupe. The Mike Torrez Athletic Fund will be a worthwhile effort to back physical fitness and competitive sports for the parochial school that has come to be the community center for the Mexican American population of Topeka."[69] The "Kansan of the Year" article, which appeared in the *Topeka Daily Capital* on January 1, 1978, added to the community's sense of pride because "here was a Spanish-surnamed individual who was no longer from the 'wrong side of the tracks' but rather an 'accomplished American ... [having] reached the pinnacle millions of American men and boys have dreamed about.'"[70]

One other discussion surrounding Torrez's participation in the World Series and the Chicano Movement in Kansas merits consideration at this point. After Game 6, an unnamed UPI reporter asked Torrez to recall his childhood and the role of baseball in his life and neighborhood. Here, Torrez replied that his family had come from Mexico to Kansas in order to work for the railroad. He described Oakland in the following manner: "I guess you would call it a ghetto. It wasn't easy playing ball. We would play in the streets between cars and every so often a ball would go through one of the car windows and we'd all scat. I was hard to complete games back then."[71] He also noted that where he grew up "there were dirt roads and old barns ... outhouses ... cows, pigs and chickens.... It wasn't no Hollywood Hills."[72]

On the surface, this response seems quite innocuous and in line with the actual physical layout of where the Torrez clan lived, but given the changes that had taken place in Oakland, indeed in many barrios throughout the nation, this description was taken by some in the Kansas capital as an affront to the neighborhood—and in the national media, no less! Though this author found no specific evidence naming who reacted to this perceived "slight," it is evident that there was blowback because sportswriter Bob Hentzen had Torrez address the issue directly in a subsequent article in the *Daily Capital*. "I didn't mean it the way it was said. I want to apologize if I've hurt anybody's feelings." Clearly, the changes that had taken place in the 1970s, and the feeling of empowerment and greater opportunity these engendered made it imperative for locals to uphold the "honor" of their barrio. Torrez backtracked, and all was soon forgiven; after all, it was it big deal that a World Series hero hailed from your *comunidad*. "But I wasn't relating to the whole Oakland area, only a four or five block area. And that was twenty years ago. There have been a lot of changes. People have fixed up their houses and a lot of improvements have been made. It's a nice place to live." Lastly, Hentzen offered a final balm to any remaining frayed sentiments by stating:

> Ghetto is defined in my Webster's as "any section of a city in which many members of a minority group live." But since evidently some folks in Topeka were offended by Mike's description of his childhood surroundings, it's to his credit that he was big enough to call and explain. Big Mike ain't the type, no matter how big a baseball hero he becomes, to forget his ol' hometown.[73]

In short order, all actual or imagined offenses were pardoned and forgotten.

After entering the draft on November 4, and with the celebrations and parades in the Big Apple and Topeka fading into the background, it was time for Mike Torrez to head back to Montreal with Danielle and Iannick, and get down to the business at hand with Gary Walker and the various franchises. Danielle, not surprisingly, wanted her spouse to re-sign with her hometown Expos. The Torrez clan, on the other hand, would have loved it if he signed with the Royals, just a short drive on the interstate from Topeka. These two teams were possibilities, but as Torrez argued, "I believe that my value is more after the Series. I'm going to have to listen to all the bids. We want the money and we want security. We don't want to keep moving around.... I definitely would like to stay in the East." By the start of the bidding, the ante had increased for Torrez and potential employers as he turned down a long-term contract with the Yankees reported to be worth approximately $1.5 million just before the start of free agency.[74]

Torrez having spurned the Yankees and indicating that he would like to stay on the East Coast, another suitor soon entered the Torrez sweepstakes: the Red Sox. Boston, which had lost in the World Series to the Cincinnati Reds in 1975 in dramatic/tragic fashion, had an excellent hitting ball club, but lacked pitching. Though they finished 97–64 in 1977, a substantial improvement from their 83–79 mark in the bicentennial season, Boston could not catch their bitter rivals to win the American League East, finishing 2.5 games behind. After the death of owner Tom Yawkey in July of 1976, the franchise was in a state of transition, but by the end of the 1977 campaign, the executors of the estate had named the former vice-president for player personnel, Haywood Sullivan, as general manager. The new executive indicated that the Red Sox would be aggressive in their pursuit of free agents, particularly starting pitchers.

After visiting the city, Torrez admitted that he would not mind living in Massachusetts, and negotiations proceeded apace. On November 21, the *New York Times* headlined its sports section with the news that many Yankees fans found unfathomable: Mike Torrez was jumping to the hated Red Sox. A pitcher who had just won two games in the most recent World Series for the pinstripers was now going to do his best to defeat the Bombers and, hopefully, help end the "Curse of the Bambino" for New Englanders.[75] If fans were upset about Torrez's "betrayal," at least one local writer, Paul Zimmerman of the *New York Post*, felt that the Yankees had let a good pitcher and teammate get away.

> Torrez was a very solid Yankee last year. He didn't get much publicity as a peacemaker, but he was one of the few Yankees who didn't choose sides in the Munson-Jackson war. He logged many late-night hours with each of them to cool it enough to win the pennant. Friends of his say he was very upset that the Yanks never got back to him after their initial $1.5 million offer, that they really didn't seem to care if they lost him. There will probably be some negative innuendos coming out about Torrez in the next few weeks. I have already heard one Gabe Paul quote that "losing Torrez was no catastrophe." How quickly we forget.[76]

In this same article, Torrez went out of his way to put a positive spin on his relationship with New York. "Look, I don't want to leave with a sour taste.... Let's just say that I was very, very happy to be a part of the Yankees last year."[77] His tune would change dramatically in the not too distant future.

An article by Larry Whiteside provided extensive details regarding the negotiations between Walker and the club for Torrez's services. Red Sox's management spent around 30 hours working with the agent to hammer out the final agreement. The money, $2.5 million over seven years (with a no-trade clause over the first five seasons) was certainly part of the deal, but there were other factors at play. First, Torrez spoke with Red Sox first baseman George Scott, another Walker client, who indicated how great fans in Boston were. Next, the city was relatively near Montreal, where Danielle continued to work as a model and television personality. Also, Torrez was hurt by what he considered the original low-ball offer by the Yankees, and then a final proposal that did not match what the club provided for Don Gullett after 1976. Additionally, Torrez and Sullivan seemed to mesh on a personal level. "There was instant rapport.... I think the fact that Haywood had been an athlete helped. They spoke the same language." In a lot of ways, it seemed to be the perfect fit. Finally, as agent Walker summarized, "Mike wanted to do for the Red Sox what he had been able to do for the Yankees."[78]

Once ensconced in Massachusetts, however, Torrez pulled back the curtain a bit on some of the goings-on in the champions' locker room (and elsewhere) in early 1978. "Thurman Munson hates Reggie Jackson, and Graig Nettles hates Jackson, too. Reggie can handle the press, but not his teammates." He had some comments about Billy Martin as well, indicating that he held his skipper back on at least one occasion to avoid a fight in after-hours settings.[79] Torrez also made a prediction that by adding him to the starting rotation (which featured Luis Tiant, Bill Lee, and later, Dennis Eckersley), the Red Sox would surely win the AL East.[80] Lastly, Danielle got a shot in at George Steinbrenner who, she claimed, was not as magnanimous and generous in his dealings with players as rumored. "Two years ago, Steinbrenner promised that he would buy fur coats for all of the players' wives if we won the World Series.... This year he knew we'd win. He promised nothing."[81] In sum, if the rivalry between the two clubs was not sufficiently heated over previous seasons, it would certainly be even more rancorous for 1978. Torrez's new manager, Don Zimmer, believed that the Red Sox had made a good investment in the former Yankee, and that Torrez's best pitches would fit right in at Fenway Park. "A high ball pitcher might have trouble ... but I don't think Torrez should because he has good hard stuff and keeps it low."[82]

Going into spring training, many of the newly minted millionaires on the various Major League rosters faced a certain amount of razzing from fans troubled by the amounts of money being bandied about to athletes merely to "play a game." For Mike Torrez, the circumstances were a bit different. As noted in an earlier chapter, an article by Bill Liston of the *Boston Herald American* described at length some of the circumstances

that the new Red Sox hurler confronted during his childhood and inti-
mated that Torrez was different from other ballplayers. Not only had his
family come from Mexico and worked hard to forge a better life while
residing on the "wrong side of the tracks" in Topeka, Torrez had also been
subjected to a merciless merry-go-round while toiling at baseball's highest
level. He won everywhere he pitched, but instead of security his reward
had been to pack up and move four times since 1974; indeed, one scribe
even referred to him as an "unwanted child" though his record in the majors
included 114 victories.[83] Certainly if fans in Boston (and elsewhere) could
identify with an individual among baseball's nouveau riche it was Torrez,
the hard-working son of immigrants who had "made good" and was finally
getting his just recompense.

In addition to Liston, other writers chimed in to buttress this line of
reasoning. For example, Roger Kahn, after briefly describing life in the
Oakland barrio, noted that Torrez "is the first American of Mexican
extraction to have been a winning pitcher in the Series." Sports editor of
the *Miami Herald*, Edwin Pope, recounted Torrez's experience during high
school when the father of a date informed him that his daughter was not
permitted to date "Mexicans." Pope quoted Torrez, who sounded very
magnanimous by saying, "Geez, I don't even like to talk about it, because
he [the father] might remember and feel bad about what he said about
me. Besides, how could I be bitter, sitting where I am?" Thus, it seemed
that here was a "working class" hero who was worthy of support. Further,
for the long-suffering fans in New England, Torrez would, hopefully, bring
some of his 1977 magic and help the Red Sox win their first Series since
1918.[84] How could the baseball gods allow anything other than a happy
ending to this wonderful story?

As Opening Day 1978 approached, no less an authority than C. C.
Johnson Spink of *The Sporting News* prognosticated that, in addition to
their other moves, the presence of Mike Torrez in the Boston rotation
"ought to be enough to enable the Red Sox to overtake the Yankees, who
beat them by 2½ games last year."[85] Boston could certainly score, with the
likes of Fisk, Rice, Scott, Yastrzemski, and Lynn in the middle of their
lineup. In addition, Bill Campbell, the reliever of the year in 1977 (13 wins
and 31 saves) anchored the bullpen behind the starters. While Torrez did
not have a particularly good spring, with Red Sox beat writer Larry Whiteside summarizing his performance in Florida as "being shelled," no one
expressed much concern. While less than impressive, Zimmer tabbed his
new free agent right-hander as his Opening Day starter on April 7 against
the Chicago White Sox at Comiskey Park.[86]

Torrez did not pitch well in his first start; he lasted six innings and gave up ten hits and four earned runs in a no-decision (with Boston losing, 6–5), but quickly made up for this stumble. Between April 12 and May 13, he won five of six decisions (with one no-decision and the loss coming against the Brewers on April 26). His most impressive outing in this stretch came against the team that had spoiled his Red Sox debut, shutting out Chicago, 5–0, at Fenway on May 7.[87] By May 13, Boston sported a record of 21–11, two games ahead of New York (17–11). While Torrez got off to the same record in the previous season, he did not falter as he did with the Yankees (going from 5–1 to 8–10). Instead, after taking his second loss versus Detroit on May 19, he reeled off five consecutive wins through June 15.[88] More significantly, by that date, his team sported a mark of 43–19 versus the Yankees' 36–24, a six-game bulge over their rivals.

In his next start on June 20, against New York, Torrez had his poorest performance of their first half of the season, giving up seven runs in only 3⅓ innings. In this three-game set, the Yankees took two of three at Fenway, but still trailed Boston by eight games. Between the middle of June and the All-Star Game (on July 11), the Red Sox had pulled even further away from the Bombers, sporting a record of 57–26, an impressive 11½-game bulge. It seems that the change of scenery had done Torrez a world of good. He did not have an excellent last few games before the break, but still sported an 11–4 record. At this point, Red Sox starters were a combined 36–7. It seemed that 1978 might finally be "the year" after all! As if the rivalry was not heated sufficiently, Billy Martin, the AL skipper for the mid-summer classic, added fuel by not selecting Torrez, Tiant (7–1) or Eckersley (9–2) to his staff for the game.[89] Of course, things were about to get more interesting/heartbreaking than anyone could have imagined as the action resumed on July 13. Among the cast of characters in the incredible drama of the later stages of the 1978 season would be not only Mike Torrez, but also a "Spaceman," a "Gerbil," a "born liar," a "convicted liar," Billy Martin, and, of course, the man who would be forever remembered by Red Sox fans as Bucky "Bleeping" Dent.

After slogging through the emotional turmoil of a season in the "Bronx Zoo," Torrez was, hopefully, looking for a greater degree of tranquility in the Red Sox clubhouse. In part, he expected a better sense of camaraderie because several of the Boston players had "come up" in the organization and knew each other from their time in the minor leagues. The relationship among teammates was better than living in the middle of the Jackson-Munson-Martin circus, but there were important divisions. For example, in a December 2008 interview with "The Bleacher Report,"

Torrez brought up/confirmed the problems caused by the split between pitcher Bill "Spaceman" Lee and manager Don Zimmer.[90] These travails have been detailed extensively in Richard Bradley's *The Greatest Game: The Yankees, the Red Sox, and the Playoff of '78* and in Con Chapman's *The Year of the Gerbil: How the Yankees Won (and the Red Sox Lost) the Greatest Pennant Race Ever.*[91]

The crux of the matter came down to a difference in the expectations of a skipper from the "old generation" and the actions/behaviors of a group of "free spirits" of the 1960s and 1970s. Lee, who won 17 games for Boston in 1973, 1974 and 1975, never got along with Zimmer, who had been hired as a coach in 1974 and took over as manager in July 1976 (replacing Darrell Johnson). As Bradley recounts, Lee led a group of players nicknamed the "Buffalo Heads" who, as club member Bernie Carbo noted, "did run the streets hard. We chased women, we played hard, we drank hard, we did drugs, and played hard."[92] The "club's" name came from the members' belief that Zimmer resembled a buffalo. Later, possibly after more joints, cocaine, and booze, the analysis changed to likening the manager to a gerbil.

While Zimmer and other "old timers" were not averse to drinking and partying, as had occurred in the 1940s and 1950s, what seemed to bother the skipper most, especially about Lee, was that "infused in their behavior was a left-wing critique of American society and the management of baseball itself."[93] Among Lee's notable quotes/ideas were support for busing in Boston, the government in China, and open utilization of drugs. Eventually, Zimmer and Red Sox management traded Carbo and pitcher Jim Willoughby, and most detrimentally to the fortunes of the club, starter Ferguson Jenkins. By the middle of the 1978 season, then, Zimmer could focus his ire directly on "Spaceman." When things were going well, the antics were abrasive, but could be tolerated. As the Red Sox spiraled in both July (going 13–15) and September (14–15), in which they surrendered the better part of a 14-game lead to the Yankees, Zimmer was not as lenient and eventually took Lee out of the starting lineup. The Spaceman wound up the year 10–10, but with a more than acceptable 3.46 ERA (the team's mark for the season was 3.54). It is necessary to point out, however, that Lee's banishment was not due simply to ill will by his manager, as between May 26 and August 19, he went 3–9 and his ERA rose by a run. While there certainly was tension between the two men, the Spaceman also had not been pitching well.[94] The back and forth between the pitcher and manager was, in many ways, reminiscent of the Yankees of 1977. "I got shoved into the bullpen by a fat, ugly, bald man who doesn't know anything about pitching." To which Zimmer remarked that Lee was "right on three counts: I'm fat, ugly and bald."[95] This decision proved costly, particularly in the middle of the "Boston Massacre" which took place at Fenway September 7–10.[96]

On the Yankees' side of the equation, Billy Martin continued to feud with both George Steinbrenner and Reggie Jackson. An excellent source on this story is Roger Kahn's book, *October Men: Reggie Jackson, George Steinbrenner, Billy Martin, and the Yankees' Miraculous Finish in 1978.* The end of Martin's tumultuous tenure as skipper, and his replacement by Bob Lemon, came on July 24, one day after Martin let out one of the more famous/infamous quotes of the year, saying that his star player and employer "deserve each other.... One's a born liar, the other one is convicted."[97] In true New York fashion, however, just five days later, the team held a press conference to announce that Lemon had been signed to finish out 1978 and would return for the following season. Then, he would move to the front office as General Manager, to be replaced on the field by.... Billy Martin![98] On the day of the press conference to announce this "atypical" arrangement, the Red Sox's record stood at 64–37, while the Bombers were 56–45, eight games behind the division leaders.

In previous years, Torrez had always saved his best performances for the later stages of the campaign, sporting a 38–11 record after the All-Star Game over the previous four summers.[99] At first, it appeared that 1978 would be no different. He lost his first outing after the break, 4–3, to the Rangers on July 14, but came back with a complete-game victory over the Brewers, 8–2, on the 19th. This was followed by three wins, one loss, and two no-decisions over his next half-dozen trips to the mound. By August 18, his mark was 15–6. Included in this stretch was a dominant start against the Yankees in the Bronx, which the Red Sox won, 8–1, on August 3. On August 18, with about one-quarter of the season remaining, New York still trailed Boston by 7½ games (69–51 to 77–44, respectively).

Although one of the main cogs of the lineup, Rick Burleson, had been injured before the All-Star Game and missed 17 games, and the team went into a 1–9 slide starting on July 20, it appeared that Zimmer's troops had weathered the storm. There seemed no need to get flustered. As Con Chapman noted, "first, ... they were so far ahead.... The other reason the Sox appeared calm even as their fans began to experience a sense of foreboding was that the Yankees weren't gaining any ground on them."[100] Torrez was 4–2 since the hiatus, and Zimmer could not say enough good things about him. "He's done everything we've asked of him. And I don't see him doing much different now than he's always done. He's always been a good pitcher."[101] While the sense of trepidation was not yet palpable in the clubhouse, it soon would be, and an uncharacteristically poor late-season stint by Mike Torrez only added to the Red Sox's fall from their first-place perch.

A victory over the Athletics on August 18 would be Torrez's last for almost six weeks. This nightmarish period commenced on August 28 in a no-decision at the Kingdome against the second-year Mariners, where he lasted only 2⅔ innings and gave up four runs on seven hits in a game Seattle ultimately won, 10−9. After this shellacking, Torrez, uncharacteristically, criticized his manager by saying, "We've got to stop going for home runs and get back to bunts, hits-and-runs and the little things it takes to win ball games. You don't win pennants just with home runs." In a response reminiscent of Torrez's former Yankees teammates, Jim Rice chimed in, "We're losing because he's nibbling and giving up base hits to a bunch of Punch and Judy hitters. If he'd get out there and challenge somebody he'd get them out." Finally, Zimmer told Torrez that the job of strategizing for the club was his bailiwick, not that of a hurler. "There must be something in his contract that says he's not just a pitcher, but a player manager." This was followed by a loss to Oakland, 4−3, on September 2. Torrez had a more successful performance, going the distance, though he gave up 11 hits to his former team.[102] Next to visit Fenway were the New York Yankees, who had closed the gap to a mere four games behind (82–56 versus 86–52).

The four-game series known to fans in both cities as the "Boston Massacre" took place September 7–10. All of the games, save the last, were utter blowouts by the Yankees. Torrez was the first pitcher slaughtered by the Bombers. The game started out well, as Torrez struck out Mickey Rivers, but then the roof fell in. Randolph reached on an error by Butch Hobson, Munson and Jackson (driving in Randolph) followed with singles, and Chambliss hit a sacrifice fly to bring the Yankees captain home. Nettles grounded out to end the frame. The score stood 2−0. The onslaught continued in the second, with singles by Piniella, White, Dent (scoring Piniella) and Rivers (scoring White). Zimmer had seen enough and took Torrez out. His line for the game was brutal: one inning plus, five runs, three earned, and six hits permitted. The New Yorkers were no less effective against three relievers. The final score was 15−3, the most runs the Bombers scored in a game that season. The visitors knocked out 21 hits, with every starter contributing at least one, and Randolph, Munson and White three apiece. After the contest, reporters asked Chambliss whether the Yankees had a particular desire to show up their former teammate. The first baseman was fairly considerate in his response, indicating that the key issue was further whittling down the Red Sox lead. "I don't think there was any grudge at all. We would have gone out the same way no matter who was pitching, Bill Lee or anybody."[103] Later in the season, Reggie Jackson's and Graig Nettles' feelings about Torrez would not be as magnanimous.

Only the final game in the series, a 7–4 victory, was competitive. The offensive results were abysmal for the Fenway faithful: 42 runs and 67 hits for the visitors, to nine runs and 21 hits for the home team. The Red Sox even committed seven errors in the second game. What had once, on July 17, been a 14-game lead had vaporized. While the players were in shock, the Boston faithful had come to accept this horror as their lot in life. As Chapman noted, when a fan "making a belated return from a summer vacation beyond the reach of American news media ... muttered under his breath as he waited to collect his mail: 'I knew they'd blow it. I knew it.'"[104]

After the "Massacre," Torrez's torment continued for a while longer, as he lost his next two outings by identical 3–2 scores to the Orioles and Yankees on the 12th and 16th. After the Yankees left Boston, they went 5–3 in their next eight games, the Red Sox the reverse. Therefore, at the 150-game mark, the New Yorkers were now two games ahead, 91–59 to 89–61. A final assault on Torrez's professional pride occurred on September 20, when he lasted but four innings against Detroit in a 12–2 defeat. In a particularly cruel assessment of the pitcher's troubles after his outing versus the Tigers, a Fenway faithful argued, "he had won it for the Yankees in 1977 and he was doing it again in 1978."[105] Teammates and Zimmer were a bit more understanding. In the losses to the Orioles and Yankees, the manager stated, "you can't fault the way he pitched.... We didn't get him any runs." Carl Yastrzemski agreed. "He's a battler. Maybe he didn't win, but he kept us close. He's a great competitor." Torrez himself expressed his frustration at the slide noting, "I've never been through anything like this. Never in my career have I failed to finish strong.... I know I'm better than the record shows." The five-start losing streak finally ended with a no-decision against the Blue Jays on the 24th, a game the Red Sox eventually won, 7–6. After this matchup Boston remained one game behind the Yankees with six games to play.[106]

The Torrez start against Toronto, though not particularly effective, marked the second consecutive victory by the Red Sox; they would go on to win eight in a row, finally tying the New Yorkers on the last day of the season. After Torrez had not won since the middle of August, he produced a fine outing for his last regular-season start. On September 28, in a tremendous pitching duel, Boston nipped Detroit, 1–0, with each club generating only three hits. Although winning his 16th game of 1978, Torrez struggled with his control and surrendered seven walks in a complete game. Of particular note was the fact that he kept his pitches down, with only two Tigers making fly ball outs. Two double plays, one in the first inning and the other in the sixth, plus an excellent throw by Fred Lynn to Carlton Fisk to nab a runner at home plate preserved the shutout. The game's lone tally came from the bat of Jim Rice, with a leadoff home run in the bottom of the fourth inning.[107]

After 161 games, the tumultuous season of 1978 came down to the final day of the year on October 1. The Red Sox's record was 98–63, and the Yankees were 99–62. Both contenders were playing weak ball clubs in their final series: Boston played Toronto, and New York faced Cleveland. Pitching for the Red Sox was Luis Tiant, who over his career in Boston compiled a 26–12 mark in September. To no one's surprise, "Loo-ie" pitched beautifully against the Blue Jays, surrendering only two singles in a complete-game victory, 5–0. Now, Boston had to hope that the also-ran Indians would defeat Catfish Hunter in Yankee Stadium. The matchup did not look promising. Countering Hunter was Rick Waits, who had a 5.40 ERA in five starts against New York that season. The Bombers plated two runs in the first inning, but Hunter was not effective and Cleveland won, 9–2.[108]

This unexpected gift gave Boston one more chance to avoid a terrible fate. Not surprisingly, Billy Martin decided to send out Ron Guidry (24–3) for the playoff game at Fenway. Zimmer countered with Mike Torrez. For those looking for omens, there were plenty to be had. On the positive side for the Red Sox, as G. Richard McKelvey noted, the only "pitchers to have beaten Guidry that season were also named Mike—Caldwell, Flanagan, and Willis."[109] Further, since he had recently been their teammate, Torrez knew the Yankees hitters. While he may have been familiar with that lineup's proclivities, on the minus side of the equation, he went into the playoff with a 1–3 mark versus his old mates. Jackson, in particular, was chomping at the bit to get back at Torrez. As Jackson stated in his recent book, "I know a lot of guys on our team weren't too worried about that, because we usually hit him good."[110] Torrez was also anxious to prove his worth to his former employer and to make up for his poor streak during the season's second half. "It had to be written on a wall somewhere, and it couldn't be written any better. We've all been wishing and praying for a break like this, and now we've got it."[111] From a racial/ethnic group standpoint, Roger Kahn noted, "A tempered irony was at play in Fenway on this bright October day. The racist Red Sox, the franchise that had spurned both Jackie Robinson and Willie Mays, was now placing its hopes and dreams in the hands of a Mexican American. Were Robinson alive, he might have smiled."[112]

The first pitch was scheduled for 2:30 on October 2, 1978. The denizens of the Oakland barrio were surely all glued to their television screens. The script could not have been better.

Mike Torrez had already enjoyed the thrill of winning a World Series. He also had secured his family's financial future by signing a large free agent contract. He had pitched well during the first half of the season and helped stake Boston to a large, mid–July lead over their bitter rivals. After that point, things had gone terribly wrong. The 14-game lead disappeared and Torrez had suffered through the worst late-campaign streak in his career. Now, he had been granted another chance at redemption. Richard Bradley summarized Torrez's desire going into this game by stating that he hoped to "demonstrate that he'd made the right move in the off-season, that the Red Sox were a better team than the Yankees, and that the subtraction of him from one team and his addition to the other was, perhaps, the difference in the balance of power between the two."[113] For the first six innings of the game, all went according to script.

Boston scored single runs against Guidry in the second inning, on a Yastrzemski homer, and in the sixth on a Burleson double and Rice's RBI single. Meanwhile, Torrez was pitching a beautiful game. Going into the top of the seventh, he had thrown a paltry 66 pitches and given up only two hits (a double by Rivers in the third and a single by Piniella in the fourth). Nettles led off the seventh with a fly ball to right. One out. Chambliss singled to left, and White singled to center. For the first time in the game, it appeared that Torrez might be in trouble as the Yankees had two runners on base. Next, however, he got Jim Spencer (pinch-hitting) to fly out to left. Two outs. This brought up Bucky Dent, a .243 hitter with but four home runs during the season. The first pitch was a ball; the next Dent fouled off of the instep of his left foot. It was the most fateful moment of the entire season.

Mired in a slump during September, Dent had tried a few changes to improve his chances at the plate. One thing he did was to get rid of a shinguard he had worn since spring training in Florida. He had also considered using Roy White's bat, a 32-ounce model, lighter than his usual equipment, but had rejected the idea. After the foul ball, as Dent hobbled in pain, Mickey Rivers noticed that the Yankees shortstop was using a cracked bat and handed the batboy one of White's. "Give this to Bucky. Tell him there are lots of hits in it." There was at least one.[114]

While Dent struggled to get back in the box, Torrez waited, and waited, and waited. "I lost some of my concentration during the delay.... I thought slider on the next pitch. But Fisk and me were working so well together, I went along with his call of a fastball. When Dent hit it, I thought we were out of the inning.... I could see Yaz patting his glove."[115] But Yaz did not catch the ball. Instead, due to a shift in the wind, the ball carried and carried, all the way over the famed Green Monster. Suddenly, the score was 3–2 in favor of New York. As he had done in the first inning, Torrez then walked Mickey Rivers. The next batter was Munson, who had struck out three times. Torrez did not get a chance to face the Yankees' captain again. Zimmer replaced his starter with Bob Stanley. At this moment, Torrez had not yet become the scapegoat for the Boston collapse. As Bradley stated, "the crowd applauded Torrez's effort; through six and two-thirds innings, he had pitched brilliantly." It was only later that the more negative feelings surfaced. After Torrez disappeared into the dugout, Stanley promptly gave up a double to Munson, scoring Rivers. Piniella flied out to end the inning. Yankees 4, Red Sox 2.

Boston failed to score in the bottom of the seventh, and New York added its final tally in the top of the eighth, appropriately enough, on a solo home run by Reggie Jackson. There was still one final gasp left in the Red Sox, who tallied two runs in the bottom of the eighth on RBI singles by Yastrzemski and Lynn against Goose Gossage. After a quiet top of the ninth, Boston came up one last time. There was hope as, after a fly-out by Evans, Burleson walked and Remy singled. That meant that Rice and Yaz would have a chance to tie or win the game. It was not to be, however, as the two legends could not come through, flying out to right and popping out to third, respectively. Final score: Yankees 5, Red Sox 4.[116] The New Yorkers could not resist getting in one last shot at their former teammate as Graig Nettles crowed, "The thing that makes me happiest is that we did it by beating Torrez. He's been badmouthing us all year. If it wasn't for us he wouldn't be in the position to sign a 2.7 million dollar contract. Maybe this will teach him to keep his mouth shut."[117]

When Mike and Danielle returned home, they drank some scotch and watched the game on Betamax. "'Damn,' he said softly, the only word he could find."[118] While the players did not blame Torrez, and the Fenway Faithful initially did not, the sense of frustration eventually metastasized and caused fans to forget how well Torrez pitched on that fateful day. When he finally left Boston in 1983, feelings had indeed hardened to the point that, at his exit, he was considered "one of the most unpopular players ever to play for the Red Sox."[119]

Does Torrez, then, deserve the moniker of "scapegoat?" To answer that question, it is possible to return to Peter Weiss' work on players so designated. While Torrez did have a horrid spell in the second half of the year, losing a 14-game lead is not a one-player exploit. Indeed, Weiss has two chapters in his book on this topic, one on Torrez, the other on the entire 1978 team. His words are poignant:

> Torrez got a lot of the blame for this one—giving up the crucial home run to a non-power hitter—but there's no way you can pin 1978 on one guy ... blame the entire Red Sox team, and especially Don Zimmer, for the collapse.
>   Torrez pitched a decent game. Okay, so he forgot to stay loose during a delay and had the misfortune to pitch to Dent just as the wind shifted. This does not necessarily make him a goat.... There never should have been a playoff game in the first place.[120]

In the years since 1978, Torrez and Dent have done well for themselves, recreating and recounting the events of that momentous day. Even though he has benefited financially, Torrez, no doubt, still thinks about what might have been. As Bradley asserts, "when he talks about Bucky Dent's homerun his voice is tinged with a mixture of wistful acceptance, regret, frustration, and disappointment."[121] It was a long way from the Oakland barrio to the height of baseball glory in 1977. Then, just as quickly, even with a paycheck he never could have imagined, the collapse was terribly painful. Having completed the first year of a five-year, no-trade contract, Torrez and the Red Sox could only hope to forget 1978 and move forward. For Torrez, now was the time to return to Montreal, enjoy spending time with Iannick and Danielle, with a possible side-trip to Kansas for pheasant hunting, his mom's food, maybe some Mexican American basketball, and the camaraderie of *compadres* in the Oakland barrio. After all, by the middle of October, spring training for 1979 was a mere five months away.

8

No Ralph Branca or Fernando Valenzuela
Torrez's Final Years in Professional Baseball, 1979–1985

In an interesting coincidence, after retiring, both Mike Torrez and Ralph Branca moved to the Westchester, N.Y., area and lived just blocks apart. Torrez recalled that he and the former Brooklyn Dodger were occasionally paired as part of local golf events. When traveling to these, the neighbors often shared car service and had a chance to "talk baseball." Not surprisingly, Torrez's recollections of the excursions centered on the veterans' discussions of their infamous pitches from 1951 and 1978. While Torrez's offering did not end the playoff game, as did Branca's, it was just as excruciating. The more senior hurler believed he was the more fortunate of the two pitchers, for he managed to get off of the mound right after Thomson's round-tripper, as opposed to Mike and the Red Sox having to endure two more innings of torment. As true professionals, however, both moved on from these momentous events, completed good careers, were successful in their "civilian" endeavors, and made numerous appearances with their "adversaries" over subsequent decades, to a certain sense embracing and even glorying in their historical fates. After these unfortunate brushes with destiny, it is fair to say, the trajectory of both mound careers were not as positive as they had been previously.

Branca, for example, who had a 76–56 mark (.576 winning percentage) before Thomson's home run, was a mere .500 (12–12) in his final three seasons with Brooklyn, Detroit and the Yankees (for an 88–68 total). Torrez was 141–118 before his pitch to Bucky Dent (.544), and just 44–42 afterward (.515), finishing with a record of 185–160 (.536 overall). Torrez's record is a bit deceiving because, after enduring a disproportionate amount

174

of the blame for the Red Sox's 1978 collapse, he left New England and wound up pitching with a rebuilding Mets club over his final one season-plus in the majors (he finished 11–22 over 1983 and part of 1984).

While time, and three World Series titles, have eased (but not erased) the disappointment of 1978, it is interesting to note how Torrez was remembered as part of the 100th anniversary of Fenway Park. As will be evident in this chapter, though Torrez was not originally the sole individual "blamed" for the loss in the playoff game of October 2, the Red Sox faithful eventually did turn on him. After all, he had been granted a substantial contract, in part, to make it possible for Boston to overtake their ancient and hated rivals. This, unfortunately for Torrez, never happened during his tenure in Boston. By 2012, how-

Torrez at the tail end of this career pitching with a poor Mets team. The highlight of the 1983 season, in which he finished 10–17, was his victory over the great "El Torito," Fernando Valenzuela. National Baseball Hall of Fame Library, Cooperstown, New York, 2811-2000_act_Agustino_NBL.

ever, the passage of 34 years had made it possible for at least one anonymous author to present a more munificent assessment of the events of that day:

> It is widely held that Dent's homer beat the Red Sox in that 1978 playoff game and although I would not minimize its impact I will contend that there were more significant events which contributed to that loss ... today you simply need to know that Red Sox pitcher Mike Torrez, for lack of a better phrase, "wore the collar" for that loss for a long time. The goat horns were planted on his head by the media and there they stayed. The reality is, and you might think I'm crazy, Mike Torrez actually pitched at least as good of a game as Guidry that day.... I was there and not only that I've watched that game at least a half dozen times and I will stick to my guns.[1]

The rancor from the Fenway faithful was not Torrez's only travail, and over the final years of his career he was buffeted both on the mound and in his personal life. In addition to having to deal with a divorce from Danielle in 1980, he was also remembered for another pitch: one to up-

and-coming star Dickie Thon of the Houston Astros on April 8, 1984. Though not intentional, Torrez's beaning of Thon led to severe injuries and added another deleterious touchstone to Torrez's career, and earned him a place on the "most hated" list of a second franchise and city.[2]

An additional happenstance, perhaps more unkind, was to be overshadowed by another individual of Mexican heritage: Fernando Valenzuela. As noted earlier, Torrez had a career that in many ways was the equal of the legendary "El Torito." The winning percentages are quite similar (.536 to .531), as are the number of Major League victories (185 to 173). Further, both Torrez and Valenzuela helped lead legendary clubs to dramatic World Series titles, and were considered "role models" by many in the Chicano/Mexicano communities. One of Torrez's triumphs occurred when he pitched and defeated Valenzuela, 7–1, in a 1983 contest at Shea Stadium, one of the few highlights in a forgettable 10–17 campaign.

The two came from humble backgrounds and used their baseball acumen to create a better life for their families. Torrez, however, came along a bit earlier than did Valenzuela, and did not pitch in locales (except for his brief stint in Oakland) with substantial Mexican American populations. While Torrez was an important figure in his home state of Kansas and elsewhere in the Midwest, he never garnered a similar level of idolization as did the Mexican-born Valenzuela throughout the entire nation. Academic and popular studies on persons of Mexican background in the early 1980s still focused overwhelmingly on locales such as California and Texas; the story/history of Mexican Americans in the Midwest was barely on the radar. Finally, and perhaps most significantly, Valenzuela started out brilliantly (winning the Cy Young and Rookie of the Year awards in 1981) and was never saddled with the label "goat."

Although Torrez has dealt commendably with the events of October 2, 1978, there are still many who perceive it as the defining moment of his career.[3] It is a burden that he has handled with grace and aplomb, as well as a sense of humor. Among the many events that Bucky Dent and Mike Torrez have attended over the years, the strangest was the dedication of a miniature Fenway Park at the former Yankees shortstop's baseball academy in Delray Beach, Florida. As Bob McCoy indicated in his 1989 piece in *The Sporting News*, the president of the school argued that the reason for the recreation was simple: "Let's face it. That home run was his claim to fame." Torrez, of course, was invited to the occasion, but he argued good naturedly that "I'll only do it if they pay me enough money."[4] This chapter, then, will cover the final years of Mike Torrez's career in the majors, plus one highly forgettable season in the Florida State League with a misbegotten, non-affiliated, low-rent, but supersized-dreams franchise known as the Miami Marlins.

Beginning with 1979, the Red Sox and Torrez were determined to claim what had slipped through their fingers the previous autumn: the American League East title. It did not turn out that way as, much to their chagrin, Boston finished in third place. Nor did it happen in 1980 (fifth place), the strike-shortened year of 1981 (fifth place), or 1982 (third place). As the years passed, the acrimony over the "lost" pennant (and maybe more?) of 1978 grew and grew, eventually consuming Don Zimmer, Mike Torrez and other members of the Boston club. A further body-blow occurred when a player considered the "heart and soul" of that team, the great Luis Tiant, exited New England after 1978, to don the hated Yankees pinstripes.

By the end of the 1982 season Torrez's .500 mark (9–9, but with a 5.23 ERA), and disagreements with manager Ralph Houk over pitching every fourth day (similar to those he had with Gene Mauch in Montreal), made the one-time highly prized free agent expendable in Boston. His final turns on the mound at Fenway usually resulted in a chorus of boos cascading down and, as the season reached its terminus, Torrez turned uncharacteristically silent with the media. Joe Giuliotti, Red Sox beat writer for *The Sporting News*, noted that due to these circumstances, "If Mike Torrez is pitching for the Boston Red Sox next year, it won't be because he or the club wants it that way.... He still has a sound arm and he may be better off if he gets a chance to pitch away from Boston."[5]

After being a prominent "buyer" in the post–1977 season free agent market, the Red Sox took a more restrained approach after their late-season collapse, and by November of 1978 General Manager Haywood Sullivan was sounding a much more fastidious tone. "There isn't really a lot of talent in this year's crop.... In many cases, there isn't as much there as we've already got."[6] As further proof of the team's restraint, Sullivan was even willing to forgo re-signing a man whom Carl Yastrzemski described as "the heart of our pitching staff": Luis Tiant. The key issue in this parting of ways was that Boston was unwilling to guarantee the Cuban star a contract longer than one season; thus, the Yankees swooped in and snatched away a pitcher who had gone 121–74 over the previous seven years for their most bitter division foe.[7] Fenway fanatics were aghast. In addition, Sullivan followed Tiant's departure by signing Steve Renko (formerly of the Expos, A's, and other clubs), a man who arrived in Boston with an overall career mark of 89–107. All of the tumult led many in New

England to wonder whether the team's management was more interested in winning or simply making money.[8]

While there was much consternation about pitching (Bill Lee was also let go) over the off-season, the starting rotation for 1979 was still a potential area of strength. After all, 20-game winner Dennis Eckersley was still in uniform, as well as Mike Torrez (who did, it is easy to forget, win 16 games in his first year with the Red Sox). They would be joined in the rotation by Bob Stanley who, as a reliever, had gone 15–2 in 1978. Add to those three the possible return of Bill Campbell, a veteran like Renko, Dick Drago (replacing Stanley as closer) and some promising rookies (such as Bobby Sprowl), and Boston could field what Don Zimmer referred to as "the best collection of arms in the five years I've been here."[9] The manager had a similar appraisal of his second-year pitcher: "I'm not one bit concerned about Torrez … you don't become concerned about a man like that down here [in Florida], not until it means something." Torrez echoed his skipper's analysis, insisting that the past was past, and he was looking forward to moving beyond the events of the previous fall. "It won't ruin me. I never even think of it until one of you writers bring it up or someone else asks. It was just one of those things. He [Dent] may not get another hit off me for five years."[10]

All of this talent on the mound was in addition to a still-potent daily line up. This was a team that won 99 games in 1978; surely this would be "the year" to finally overtake New York, right? Well, yes and no. While the Red Sox did finish higher than the Yankees (who, among other issues, had to deal with the tragic death of Thurman Munson) in the standings, it was Baltimore (102–57) that won the AL East in 1979. The Orioles were dominant that season and left all contenders in their wake; even Milwaukee, which won 95 games, finished eight games behind the division champions. Again, Boston tallied more than 90 triumphs (91), but still came up short. The same can be said about Mike Torrez, who finished with an identical record as 1978, though his ERA increased from 3.96 to 4.49. His "failures" for the Red Sox were, once again, particularly evident against the Yankees.

Unlike his first year in Boston, Torrez did not get off to a good start in 1979 and failed to win his first game until almost three weeks into the season. Over his first three trips to the mound, he had one loss and two no decisions. His best performance took place in the defeat, 3–0 to Cleveland on April 7. Torrez went 7⅔ innings and give up only four hits (though he walked six). In the other two starts, he was hit hard, giving up eight earned runs in 4⅔ innings against the Brewers (a 12–10 loss) on April 12, and another poor showing against Milwaukee (a 6–5 defeat) on the 17th, where he surrendered five runs (four earned) over 7⅔ innings. His first victory did not come until the 22nd, when he blanked the Royals, 6–0, in Fenway. He closed out the season's first month with another no-decision against California (an 8–6 Boston defeat).[11]

Over the subsequent three starts, Torrez righted his performance and won each with a complete game. This set up the first opportunity to gain a measure of revenge against the Yankees, on May 18 in Fenway. While certainly not of the same magnitude as the game on October 2, Torrez was anxious for yet another occasion to pitch against his former team. Both squads downplayed the significance of an early-season series, but the Boston faithful knew better: the set attracted over 90,000 for the three games.[12] Unfortunately, things did not go well and the New Yorkers won, 10–0. Torrez pitched into the eighth inning and surrendered six earned runs and ten hits. To complete the miserable day, the final hitter he faced was Bucky Dent, who singled off of the beleaguered Red Sox starter. So much for the Yankee shortstop not getting another hit off of Mike for five years! At this point, Torrez's record stood at 4–2. To add further insult, the Bronx Bombers took two of three in Fenway, with both victories coming via shutouts.[13]

Between mid–May and the All-Star Game (played on July 17), Torrez went 5–3, with another three no-decisions. By the hiatus, he was 9–5 and the Red Sox were a more than respectable 56–32.[14] There still appeared to be a possibility for 20 wins for Torrez and at least an opportunity to finish ahead of the Yankees. The nightmare of 1978 was long past, right? Torrez looked forward to the last part of the campaign because "I've always been a strong finisher, except for last year. I feel good right now and it's nice to know the manager has the confidence to send me out there every fifth day. He believes in me and I appreciate that."[15]

The second half of the year did not start well as Torrez absorbed an embarrassing 8–0 loss to the third-year Mariners in Boston on July 20. After that poor outing, just like clockwork, followed another strong stretch of four consecutive victories. The most impressive outing during this run came against the Brewers at County Stadium. In a masterful complete game, Torrez surrendered only six hits and three walks in a 10–1 triumph on August 2. Then, just as suddenly, came three very poor weeks in which Torrez had no victories, four losses, and one no-decision. The only successful start came against the Royals, a 1–0 loss in Kansas City on August 25. Although he earned a victory on the last day of the month, 9–6 against Texas, Torrez still surrendered 11 hits and was relieved in the eighth inning when the Rangers scored a final three runs. As the calendar turned to September, Torrez's record stood at 14–9. Although maddeningly inconsistent, he still had an opportunity win more games than the previous season.

With the Orioles playing at a superb clip, the division title was out of reach and the final month of the Red Sox's 1979 campaign came down to two key goals: to finish ahead of the Yankees and see the great Carl Yastrzemski achieve his 3000th hit. Both objectives were realized. On September 12, appropriately enough against the Yankees, Yaz reached the plateau of hitting immortality. The next evening, Torrez had yet another opportunity to defeat the Bombers after having lost a second time to them on September 4, 3–2 at Yankee Stadium. The final chance for a measure of redemption against his nemesis evaporated quickly, as he failed to make it out of the fourth inning. Final score: Yankees 10, Red Sox 3. By the way, Bucky Dent drove in an unearned run in the fourth inning. Torrez's line for the game was a disappointing seven hits and seven runs allowed (though only two earned) over 3⅔ innings. The final, and anti-climactic starts of his season produced victories against the lowly Blue Jays (8–3 on the 18th) and Tigers (7–4 on the 28th) sandwiching a 3–2 loss to Detroit's Mexicano pitcher, Aurelio Lopez, at Fenway.[16]

Two seasons into a seven-year contract, Torrez's record for Boston stood at 32–26 (a .551 winning percentage). Not bad, but certainly not what he and the franchise had hoped for. In addition, while the Red Sox finished ahead of the Yankees in the standings in 1979, they played poorly against their rivals, finishing 5–8, with three of those defeats charged to Torrez. Although he had the same record as 1978, he gave up 121 walks—to lead the league in that undesirable category—over 252 innings, more than twice as many as the next Boston starter (Eckersley, with 59). His ERA ballooned by more than one-half run per game. There was still talk that Boston had three excellent starters, but the winter meetings in Toronto certainly produced a great deal of chatter about the team seeking more pitching help for 1980. If, after two winning seasons, Red Sox fans felt that Torrez had not been worth the investment of over $2.5 million, things were about to get much, much worse for both the pitcher and the team.[17]

After suffering several heartbreaking disappointments in the 1970s, Red Sox fans hoped that the new decade would bring better results. Though it seemed that there was sufficient talent on the squad, many in Boston had begun to grumble about the handling of the pitching staff, with Zimmer taking the brunt of the abuse. "How come I can't handle a pitching staff when we've been in the race three straight years…. When we start out, the pitching isn't good enough for them. Then when we won 97, 99, and 91 games, I didn't know how to run a pitching staff." Again, prognosticators believed that the team's fate rested on Eckersley, Torrez, and Stanley, but there was a sense that the back part of the rotation needed help.

Eventually, Zimmer and pitching coach Johnny Podres determined to go with a five-man rotation, adding second-year hurler Chuck Rainey and rookie Bruce Hurst as fourth and fifth starters. Even though he was injured and missed ten days of spring training, Torrez appeared healthy and primed, pitching 11 scoreless innings and permitting but nine hits over the last few games in Florida.[18] Though there were concerns expressed about the entire staff, it is clear that Mike Torrez, he of the large free agent contract, was under the most intense scrutiny. In an interview with this author, fellow starter Dennis Eckersley noted, "the frustration level was through the roof" in New England, given the events of the previous two seasons. While Torrez was still not being held up as the "goat," he seemed to have little wiggle room left with the faithful. Unfortunately for Torrez, those first two years Boston would seem downright positive by comparison.[19]

The baseball season is long and, especially at the start of the year, individual games are usually not of tremendous significance. The first two contests of 1980, however, were certainly an omen of the negative things to come. The Red Sox lost on opening day (April 10) in County Stadium to the Brewers, 9–5. Torrez was the starter for the next matchup on April 12. In one inning (and four batters faced in the second stanza), Torrez gave up six runs, five of them earned. The final score: Milwaukee 18, Boston 1. This was certainly not the result anticipated after Torrez's fairly solid spring training. Indeed, things got even worse, and Torrez had an 0–4 mark (with four no-decisions) before winning his first game against the Blue Jays, 11–2, on May 21. At this point, his ERA stood at 4.47. Later in the month, he absorbed another brutal beating by Milwaukee, 19–8, lasting only 2⅓ innings. At the time of the All-Star Game (played on July 8), he was 4–8 with an ERA up to 4.71. This was certainly not what the Fenway faithful anticipated when this highly prized former Yankee came north.[20]

By now, with the team doing poorly and the other starters Zimmer had counted on not performing well, memories drifted back to the bad taste created on October 2, 1978. A quick review of some of the articles penned by Joe Giuliotti (and others) reveal how awfully the starting pitching performed that year. In late May, the scribe wrote, "In their first twenty starts, the three combined for a 3–12 record, an earned-run average of 5.60 and only three complete games." One month later, Giuliotti had praise for the starters, but not the ones expected to help the club at the start of the year. "The big three has been Chuck Rainey (6–1), (Tom) Burgmeier (3–1 and nine saves), and Renko (3–0) [who have] carried the brunt of the workload while Eckersley, Stanley and Torrez tried to find a winning combination." Torrez even caused Zimmer to crack down on pitchers who were not staying in the ballpark after being pulled from a game. "After Mike Torrez was routed recently, he took a quick shower and left the park with the game still in progress. Zimmer hit the ceiling. 'There'll be no more duckouts. When I make a mistake, I have to stay here and face the music. From now on, they're going to have to face the music too.'"[21]

On September 13, Mike made his 32nd, and final, start of this nightmarish year. Previously, he had endured bad streaks but had been able to snap out of the doldrums and contributed, but 1980 was totally different. There was a modest three-game win streak between June 12 and 22, then back-to-back victories on August 3 and 7, but that was pretty much the extent of Torrez' support for the Red Sox cause. His ERA never went below 4.12, reached as high as 6.49 (after his fifth outing), and finished at 5.08. On September 13, coincidentally, he faced the Yankees. The first three innings went well, with three walks surrendered and three hits allowed. In the fourth, the roof caved in. Successive hits by Piniella, Cerone, and Dent, a sacrifice, and a single by Randolph plated three runs, and Zimmer pulled Torrez. When Randolph tallied the fourth run of the Yankees' at-bat, the action closed the book on Torrez as a starter. The defeat, by a final of 4–3, left his mark at 9–14.[22]

By this point, a chorus of boos would cascade as Torrez entered or left Fenway. Things got so bad that, as Dennis Eckersley indicated during our conversation, the rest of the starters wanted to spare Torrez the consternation of having to start home games. He certainly "became the punching bag," and the poor results of 1980 helped to plant firmly the "goat" image upon him.[23] The media chimed in as well. For example, Peter Gammons, in one of his "A.L. Beat" columns for *The Sporting News*, reminded fans, "Mike Torrez is 2–11 in September in a Boston uniform." Likewise, Stan Isle of the same publication reminded his readers, "Right-hander Mike Torrez, who signed a seven-year, $2.5 million contract with the Red Sox in 1977, has won only seven games in three years in which Boston scored fewer than five runs."[24]

After his poor showing against the Bombers, Zimmer removed Torrez from the rotation and used him out of the bullpen. While the two men had at least one run-in over the season, the manager was gracious enough to give his struggling pitcher his due. "I'll say this for Torrez. He understood. I told him the reason he was being taken out of the rotation was that he simply hadn't done the job." In his final four appearances, Torrez was not effective in a relief role and took two more losses. His ERA increased further, from 4.91 to 5.08. This year was very uncharacteristic in many ways. Not only did he wind up with a poor record of 9–16, but he also posted his highest ERA since 1971 (the staff ERA was 4.38, 11th in the American League). In addition, comparatively speaking, he did not pitch many innings, logging only 207⅓. The lone bright spot was a substantial reduction in walks, with only 75.[25] Just like after the Dent home run, Torrez did not shy away from the media and accepted his role in Boston's poor campaign. "I had two kinds of luck this year, bad and none at all. I have the talent and ability but, for whatever reason, I didn't get the job done.... I don't blame the fans for booing. They're good fans. I've been a disappointment to myself as well as them."[26]

Problems on the field were not the only concerns tormenting Mike Torrez. According to Danielle, the move to Boston created tensions in the marriage, and the pressure to earn the "big money" for his contract made him focus more and more on the game, and less on the family. In addition, she noted, Torrez continued to live up to his previous reputation as a regular visitor to area discos. By early that season, Danielle had determined that the marriage was irretrievably broken, and sought a divorce. "I'd been meeting with a ... lawyer for many weeks, and he devised a plan.... The papers would be handed to Mike while he was on the road."[27] The telegram from Danielle's lawyer reached Torrez while the team was in Chicago to play the White Sox in late April. The dissolution of their union was finalized early in 1981.

After completing the most difficult and ineffective season of his career, Torrez was more determined than ever to justify the Red Sox's investment and once again demonstrate his true abilities. During spring training of 1981, he discussed the impact of the divorce and how this season was going to be different. "Things are about settled now and they must remain personal. I've learned some things about myself. I found that baseball is not all there is to life.... I let a lot of personal things affect me. But now it's all over and I'm going on and doing my job. My arm is good, and I feel fine." In preparation for the upcoming campaign, he set a goal to be in the best shape of his career before going down to Winter Haven. "I was running five miles a day.... For the last two years I haven't really been Mike Torrez and the hitters knew it. This year things will be different because I'm going right after them." Another issue, this one on the field, was that former skipper Zimmer had gone to a five-man rotation. Once again, Torrez complained about not being able to pitch every fourth day. Finally, the now 34-year-old argued that in 1980 he had tried to become more of a "finesse" (breaking-ball) pitcher, whereas his strength had always been a dominant fastball. While new manager Ralph Houk still sought to operate with a five-man starting crew, he did advise Torrez to get back to utilizing his best offering on a more consistent basis.[28]

The conditioning and reduced pressure in his personal life made a difference right from the earliest stages of the new season. In his second start, on April 20, he pitched well against the Texas Rangers, going the distance and earning a 4–2 victory. He surrendered only seven hits and two walks. Although this was a good sign, many in the media were not yet convinced. Peter Gammons, for example, indicated to his readers that this win was "only the second time in two years (and fourth in three) that Torrez had won when the Red Sox scored fewer than six runs."[29] Two starts later, on May 2, Torrez had his poorest outing for all of 1981, lasting only ⅔ of an inning in an 11–2 loss to the Twins at Fenway. He surrendered four hits, two walks, and six earned runs. Was 1981 going to be a repeat of the previous, nightmare season?

As he had done in the past, Torrez stayed in touch with Bob Hentzen at his hometown newspaper to keep the folks in Topeka abreast of what was happening in his life and career. In an interview that took place shortly after the debacle against Minnesota, Torrez was in good spirits even though his record stood at 1–2 with an ERA of 6.50. Hentzen encouraged his readers by arguing that, although 1980 was difficult, this year was bound to be better. Torrez noted that against the Twins, "my luck was miserable, but I'm happy with the way I'm throwing the ball. I'm trying to get it back together piece by piece." In addition, he insisted that his new skipper, who hailed from nearby Stull, Kansas (between Lawrence and Topeka), had been a great help as he tried to rebound. "He's been super. He instills so much confidence in you. He's not a harsh type of person. He's an easy person to communicate with."[30]

By the middle of the year, it appeared that the change at the Red Sox helm had been a great benefit to Torrez. Over his next thirteen starts, which stretched from May 8 through September 14 (with the MLB strike in between), he won seven games and had six no-decisions. Most critically, his ERA dropped from 6.50 to 3.82. The key issue over this stretch was his improved control and an emphasis on his fastball. As Houk argued in a piece in *The Sporting News*, "When he gets behind hitters, he gets hurt. That's what was happening to him the last two years when he was trying to finesse with his slider. I told him to just rear back, fire the ball and let them hit it." The manager was not the only one who noticed the difference in Torrez. "He's looking like the Torrez who won 20 games for Baltimore back in 1975," observed Carl Yastrzemski. "He's doing what he should have been doing the last couple of years, just throwing the fastball and challenging guys to hit it."[31]

By the middle of September, Torrez's record stood at an impressive 8–2. Given the unusual arrangement set up for the division titles in 1981 because of the work stoppage, the Red Sox were still in the running for a playoff birth, competing against several teams: Milwaukee, Detroit and Baltimore (New York had "won" the "first half" crown, due to being in first place at the start of the strike), to win the "second half" championship. On September 19, Torrez's (and Boston's) nemesis came to Fenway again. Even though this had been an excellent year, Torrez had not faced his former club. The clash appeared to be heading toward yet another triumph for the Bombers, who were leading when Houk removed his right-hander. Torrez left two runners on base, Dave Winfield and Reggie Jackson (both on walks), and his replacement, John Tudor, promptly surrendered a single to Lou Piniella, driving in Winfield. The new Red Sox pitcher shut down the Yankees' threat by striking out Bob Watson and inducing Rick Cerone to pop out to second. At the end of eight stanzas, the New Yorkers led, 5–1, and that closed the line on the only start by Torrez against the Yankees in 1981. In seven innings plus, he surrendered eight hits, five runs (four earned), and two walks. Then something amazing happened. Boston struck back against two relievers to plate seven tallies in the bottom of the eighth to take an 8–5 lead, winning by that same margin. While he did not win, at least Torrez was able to exit a game against New York with a no-decision.[32]

Over the final three starts of the truncated season, Torrez went 2–1 and lowered his final ERA to 3.68. His "complete" record was 10–3, a .769 winning percentage. Although the Red Sox were unable to catch the Brewers to make the playoffs, they finished ten games over .500 (59–49), only 1.5 games behind Milwaukee. Overall, the final standings show, Boston ended the season in fifth place, but a scant 2.5 games out of first. If the team had had an opportunity to play the 54 games lost to the labor action, and with Torrez pitching as well as he did, who knows what might have happened.

Entering year five of his contract, it seemed that Torrez was on another upswing and there might be reason for optimism in New England for the summer of 1982.[33] It would not turn out that way, and that year would mark the end of the inconsistent and often disappointing and bitter relationship between Torrez and a club which had staked so much on the talent he demonstrated under the bright lights and glare of the 1977 World Series. Torrez got a sense of how the fans in Boston felt about him, even after his 10–3 season, during a Celtics game in the Garden that winter. During a time-out, "a member of the Celtics' public relations had paged him over the public address system to set off the boos, something Torrez suspects the guy did on purpose." As Torrez recalled, "There was no reason to page me, I was there to watch a basketball game. I got an apology from the Celtics."[34]

Heading into spring training for the 1982 season, there was renewed hope that the Red Sox would have sufficient pitching to remain competitive in the AL East if Torrez had a similar year to 1981, and if Dennis Eckersley (who finished 9–8), Tom Burgmeier (4–5), and Bill Campbell (1–1 and seven saves) could regain the form of previous campaigns. In addition, manager Houk expected continued good work by Mark Clear (8–3 plus nine saves), Bob Stanley (10–8), and Bob Ojeda (6–2 in only ten starts). Overall, the team's skipper reasoned that a talent such as Eckersley would bounce back, and the other members of the staff would help push the Red Sox back into contention.[35] Likewise, Mike Torrez surmised that he had turned the corner and would be "a workhorse for a pennant winner."

Ed Pope of the *Miami Herald* spent some time over spring training with Torrez in Winter Haven and presented a very hopeful scenario for the year to come. After Torrez got past his divorce and the 9–16 record of 1980 with a strong follow-up, Pope emphasized that Torrez was an effective starter in the majors by highlighting some of his accomplishments and argued that, "at 35, he is only 35 victories short of 200 and why he is one of only five active pitchers who have beaten every team in both leagues. The others are Gaylord Perry, Ferguson Jenkins, Doyle Alexander, and Tommy John." Not bad company, considering that many in Boston still held "the pitch" over Torrez's head. "They all came down on me after that—fans, writers, everybody. I still think it was a bum rap for a lucky pop." Clearly, he realized that even after a good season, he was still merely a bad stretch away from becoming, yet again, the object of fan derision at Fenway. Unfortunately, whatever positives were generated in the previous season soon evaporated as he struggled to get above .500 during 1982.[36]

Although there had been many boos directed at Torrez over previous seasons at Fenway, Houk selected his big right-hander to serve as the starter for the home opener on April 12. Torrez acquitted himself well in a potentially hostile environment, throwing an effective 6⅓ innings, giving up three runs (all earned), eight hits, and only three walks to the Chicago White Sox. Although he took the defeat, 3–2, it was a hopeful sign. Over his first four starts, Torrez was 2–1, with one no-decision. His best performance came on the last day of the month, a complete game, handcuffing the Texas Rangers on four hits in a 7–1 Red Sox triumph. At this point, his ERA was a more-than-respectable 3.33. At the end of April, Boston was 13–7.[37]

This early period would be as positive a stretch as Torrez would have for the season. While the team did well, finishing in third place at 89–73 (six games behind division-winning Milwaukee), Torrez's ERA would balloon as high as 6.65 by late May (overall, Boston's staff finished with a team ERA of 4.03—in ninth place in the American League). Additionally, unlike other years where he had reeled off one or two streaks of complete games and a substantial number of victories, he never generated more than two victories in consecutive starts for 1982. These came in late April (24 and 30), late July (21 and 25) and the middle of September (6 and 11). On the positive side of the equation, he did not suffer through an interminable losing stretch, either. His longest losing streak was two consecutive starts on June 27 and July 2. What did change from earlier years, however, was that he did not pitch anywhere near his usual number of innings. Even in 1980, he "ate up" more than 200 innings for the Red Sox. In 1982, he managed only 175⅔ over 31 starts; an average of less than six innings per start. Further, he surrendered 196 hits over the reduced number of innings.[38]

The only consistency was, again, his unpredictability, as well as a career-high ERA. In the middle of August, Joe Giuliotti's headline for an article in *The Sporting News* summarized the woes of Torrez's season: "'I'm Just Stupid,' Says Bosox' Torrez." In excruciating detail, the article covered the troughs and (minor) crests of the pitcher's year. After the positives of April, "suddenly ... it was the Torrez of old. He won only once in his next six starts, and couldn't finish the fourth inning in three of those games.... Torrez picked up a paper and found himself last in the American League in earned-run-average [6.80]. 'I was embarrassed.'" About the only highlight was a 5–0 victory over the Twins on July 25. But, "just as fast as Torrez appeared to turn it around, he collapsed." Out of frustration, Torrez ultimately blamed himself for a lack of concentration that ruined his rhythm on the mound. "I know I should pitch the same way all the time, but I don't. I'm just stupid but I have to start being a smart pitcher again and stay that way."[39]

Three more games can be cited to encapsulate further Torrez's travails over 1982. First, in a contest against another former team, the Orioles, Torrez was, according to Joe Giuliotti, "pitching one of his better games" before being hit on the head by a line drive in the fourth inning. The smash, coincidentally, came off of the bat of his good friend and former Montreal and Baltimore teammate, Ken Singleton. Torrez did not go down after being struck, and actually completed the inning, inducing the next hitter, Eddie Murray, to bounce into an inning-ending double play. During the mid-stanza change, however, Torrez complained about having a headache, and Houk insisted that he go to the hospital. Bob Stanley came in to relieve, and when Boston scored eight runs in the bottom of the seventh, he came away with the victory. Given how difficult things had been, Torrez could only jest about the events. "I really didn't experience the pain I thought maybe I would. In fact, when I talked to [Ken] Singleton [who hit the ball], I told him he must be getting weak."[40]

As was only fitting, the last two starts of Torrez's career on behalf of the Red Sox came against the Yankees, resulting in no-decisions (even though Boston won both, 5–2 and 3–2). The first game, played on September 26 in Fenway, was a good performance, with Torrez allowing six hits, striking out six, and giving up two earned runs over 5⅔ innings. Unfortunately, he committed a costly error in trying to pick off Willie Randolph at second base and the Yankees second baseman eventually scored. Torrez was unable to shut down the rally and gave up a double to Dave Winfield and a single to Oscar Gamble that brought in a second Yankees tally. Houk had seen enough and replaced his starter with Stanley, who got out of the inning and pitched the final 3⅓ frames to earn the win.[41]

A final chance to defeat the Bombers came on the first of three games to wrap up the season at Yankee Stadium. Torrez took the hill for the final time in Boston colors and acquitted himself well, shutting out New York over six innings, leaving with a 1–0 lead. The chance for victory evaporated in the bottom of the eighth, as Tom Burgmeier surrendered an unearned run. The game went into extra innings, with Boston finally winning in 12 frames. The Red Sox swept the Yankees in that meaningless series and finished ten games ahead of their rivals in the AL East standings.[42]

While certainly not content about his overall performance for the 1982 season, Torrez pitched better toward the end of the year; lowering his ERA by 0.79 over the final 11 starts (from 6.02 to 5.23). However, it was apparent that Red Sox management had determined to move in a different direction, even shopping the pitcher before the Cardinals' victory over the Brewers in the Fall Classic. "There is some interest in Mike because he goes to the post." If that was not enough of a clue, Haywood Sullivan followed that statement with "He's always pitched well his first year with a new team. Maybe a change of scenery will help him." The relationship with fellow Kansan Houk also seemed to have deteriorated, as Torrez was upset with what he considered to be "early hooks" and the use of a five-man rotation by his skipper. Finally, the heckling by fans and dustups with writers clearly got on his nerves over the last months of the year. Indeed, Torrez even snapped at one scribe when he "listed Torrez's statistics and mentioned that the Sox scored over six runs a game for him [and] was accused of 'stabbing me in the back.'"

The writing was clearly on the wall, and the move to another franchise happened in relatively short order.[43] Unlike some of his previous trades in the "early" days of collective bargaining and pre–free agency, Torrez had an option as to whether he would accept a transfer (given that he was a 10/5—ten years in the majors and five years with one club—player). As Peter Gammons noted in a January 1983 article in *The Sporting News*, "Torrez feels that he's earned certain rights by being one of the few to last long enough to qualify for 10/5. He wants to be duly compensated."[44]

While the desire to be remunerated based on his tenure was significant, the ties with Boston, as far as Torrez was concerned, were irretrievably broken. The treatment given him by Red Sox fans became more and more difficult to bear, and a final article on the relationship by Joe Giuliotti summarized the story effectively:

> Torrez did not want to pitch for Manager Ralph Houk and the fans didn't want him pitching for Houk, either. Torrez started becoming one of the most unpopular players ever to play for the Red Sox after he served up the three-run homer to Bucky Dent that helped the New York Yankees defeat the Red Sox in the playoff game for the American League East Division title in 1978.... [Houk said] "I think he found it very difficult pitching in Boston the way he was treated by the fans. I've never knocked the man.... I wish him well. He was a competitor. I know he did not like coming out of games, but what competitor does?" Torrez, who never had an ache or pain that caused him to miss a start, would have preferred to pitch every fourth day, but that wasn't Houk's way.[45]

In discussing the end of his career in Boston, it is crucial to address the question of whether Mike Torrez "deserved" the mantle thrust upon him by writers and Red Sox fans (even to this day). As noted previously, Peter Weiss, in his book on "all-time goats," argued that the "lost" pennant of 1978 was a team-wide endeavor, and not just the fault of one player. After all, it is quite a tall order to lose a 14-game lead from the middle of July. While Torrez endured one of his difficult stretches, he was not the only pitcher who struggled over the final months. Likewise, Richard Bradley, in his book on "that game," does not "blame" the defeat on Torrez. His career, the author correctly argues, is more than just one pitch to Bucky Dent. "But to this day, Mike Torrez is a competitive man, frustrated that he is only remembered for one thing and not his many years of pitching, not the 100 games he won between 1974 and 1979, the two World Series games he won for the Yankees in 1977."[46]

In addition to examining what writers have to say, it is important to include the voices of two individuals who were there: Bucky Dent and Dennis Eckersley. In conversations with the two former players, their recollections and analysis of October 2, 1978, and Torrez's career overall, tells them that he does not warrant the moniker. Dent's recollection of rounding the bases at Fenway on that fateful day was of the total, utter silence in the ballpark. Once Torrez came out, he does recall applause by Boston fans and the overall effort on the part of both teams. Dennis Eckersley supports this recollection. "Mike was a horse, and he always gave his best. He was old school, and could be wild, but on this day, he was not to blame, and he is not a goat." Given Eckersley's offering to Kirk Gibson a few years later in the World Series between the Athletics and the Dodgers, it seems that his analysis carries more weight than that of other athletes. Such events "hurt and stay with you, but eventually you have to accept what happened and move on." As noted by Bradley, Torrez has been able to benefit from this happenstance. "When he talks about Bucky Dent's home run his voice is tinged with a mixture of wistful acceptance, regret, frustration and disappointment. 'I'm not going to complain, I've made some money off it—sometimes bad does turn into good.'"[47]

On the personal front, things did improve for Torrez during 1982, as he met and married his current wife, Teresa Wilson, whom he met on a blind date arranged by former New England Patriots end Jim Boudreaux and his wife, who was, like the new Mrs. Torrez, a flight attendant with American Airlines. The couple married on October 6, 1982, in Portsmouth, New Hampshire. Dennis Eckersley and his wife Nancy served as best man and maid of honor. Now that he was remarried, it was time to look forward to a new start in his professional life as well.

Given that by 1983, Mike Torrez was entering the tail end of his career, it would seem he would be traded to teams fitting one of the following two scenarios: either to a pennant contender looking for a veteran who might add depth to the back of a rotation; or to a team with a lot of young arms that might benefit from sage advice from an older, wiser pitcher. The rebuilding New York Mets quickly emerged as the most likely candidate

A wedding day picture of Mike and Teresa, along with best man Dennis Eckersley and his wife, Nancy. Courtesy Mike Torrez.

for a transaction, for several key reasons. First, the team had pretty much hit rock bottom over the previous two seasons. In 1981, they finished 41–62 (.398 winning percentage) under manager (and past teammate of Torrez) Joe Torre, and the following year they improved just a bit to a 65–97 (.401) mark under George Bamberger. The Mets' new manager for 1982 was a key element in bringing Torrez back to the Big Apple. Bamberger had been Torrez's pitching coach at Baltimore in 1975, when he had his best year (in terms of victories), finishing 20–9. Second, the general manager of the Mets was another individual familiar with Torrez's value and qualities. Frank Cashen had been responsible for bringing Torrez to Charm City when he held the same post with the Orioles. The combination of these two men, who had been involved in the best year of his career, was definitely an enticement. Finally, the situation was also quite positive in that, as Cashen noted, "Mike will take some of the pressure off our young pitchers, given them more time to develop."[48] Unlike Boston, where the large free-agent contract placed a tremendous amount of pressure to win big and immediately, the Mets' state of affairs required Torrez to serve as a mentor to the likes of Ed Lynch, Walt Terrell, Jesse Orosco, Tom Gorman, Ron Darling, and later, Dwight Gooden. A further benefit was that Torrez would not be the only veteran brought in to serve as a guru for the youngsters; Cashen also brought back Mets legend Tom Seaver from Cincinnati.

Even with all of these inducements, Torrez felt that he was due his fair compensation. Given the poor years of 1980 and 1982, he did not expect to see an increase in pay. He did, however, want to maintain the same salary he was due from Boston. Cashen and Sullivan actually agreed to the transaction during the winter meetings in Hawaii, but initially, Torrez invoked the 10/5 clause to prevent the swap. As the Mets' beat reporter for *The Sporting News*, Jack Lang, indicated in early 1983, he did not get an increase, but did get a two-year contract laden with incentives. "I didn't want to risk the chance of him having a big year for us and then demanding a trade…. If he has a good year, the incentive clauses will reward him." Given this arrangement, there were good feelings all around, and the Mets finalized the deal by sending third baseman Mike Davis to the Red Sox. It seemed that, given the consternation he endured at Fenway, Torrez was walking into an ideal situation in New York. "In my mind, there isn't a better pitching coach in baseball than Bambi," he argued. The feeling was mutual. "Mike knows how to win. He is a leader who will take the ball very fifth day and go out and do the job consistently. He told me he is still throwing the ball 90 miles an hour and that's good enough for me."[49]

Prognosticators were not very upbeat about the chances of New York's National League entry for 1983. Still, George Bamberger indicated in no uncertain terms that two years of playing roughly .400 level-baseball would no longer be tolerated. Young arms or not, the "future is now" was to be a rallying cry at Shea Stadium. Not quite as upbeat as "You Gotta Believe" from a decade earlier, but it was a start for a franchise that had hit a nadir. "It's time … for the Mets to stop talking about getting better and start getting better." The influence of Torrez and Seaver, it was hoped would move this process along. A youth movement was certainly in full swing, as the team jettisoned five pitchers who combined to start 105 games in 1982. "Bamberger says he is confident the Mets pitching will be better this year than it was last season, when their 3.88 earned run average placed 11th in the National League." Although he hoped for better results on the mound, Bamberger was also cognizant of the pressure placed on his hurlers, adding, "we're not going to score many runs so these guys have got to keep us in games."[50]

It would not be a very successful year, as the Mets wound up 68–94, though the ERA for the staff did improve to eighth in the NL at 3.68. Torrez was a good mentor to some of the younger pitchers but struggled, finishing 10–17 with an ERA of 4.37. He led the league in defeats and, once again, in bases on balls (113 over 222⅓ innings pitched). On the offensive side of the ledger, the New Yorkers did not have much punch, ending up

11th in the league with a .241 team average.[51] This turned out to be the last full year for Mike Torrez in the Majors, and some of the issues he confronted in Boston followed him to Shea Stadium. For example, George Bamberger, who had helped him so much during 1975, quit as manager after a wretched 16–30 start (by early June) and was replaced by Frank Howard. As the team sank further in the NL East standings, the fans at the ballpark turned on Torrez, just as they had done in Fenway. Still, there were a few bright spots, and none more so than defeating the "other" Mexican star in the National League, Fernando Valenzuela.

A great deal has been written in regard to the phenomenon known as "Fernandomania" by both popular and academic authors. For example, historian Samuel O. Regalado, in his impressive work, *Viva Baseball: Latin Major Leaguers and Their Special Hunger*, argued that the sport for the Spanish-surnamed "was a competition that carried social and economic implications ... [and] was a path out of poverty ... and it provided a sliver of hope to many younger Latins who might otherwise have envisioned a dim future." In many ways, the career of Mike Torrez demonstrated such possibilities for Mexican Americans in Topeka and elsewhere in the Midwest. Further, Regalado's research on various players provides parallels to the story of this tall pitcher from the barrios of the Kansas capital. Although he was not overtly political, Torrez's success on the mound (and in other athletic pursuits dating back to his youth) was part of a *movimiento* in his hometown that used sports and other political, economic, and religious endeavors from the 1950s through the 1970s which "campaigned for recognition within the mainstream, struggled to maintain their identity, battled to overcome stereotypes and adapted to white institutions."[52]

It is fair to argue that Torrez and other Mexican and Mexican American major leaguers who came before Valenzuela helped lay the groundwork for what became the phenomenon of "Fernandomania." By the time that "El Torito" burst on the scene in 1980 and 1981, various "Mexicano" pitchers (from both sides of the border) had plied their trade on baseball's biggest stage. For example, the previously mentioned Aurelio Lopez finished his career with a mark of 62–36 and pitched from 1974–1987. Brothers Vicente (1968–1982) and Enrique Romo (1977–1982) combined to win 76 games over their careers. Mexican American hurlers had been successful at the Major League level as well. Mike Garcia (142–97 from 1948–1961) had an excellent career, mostly with the Cleveland Indians. Finally, Hank Aguirre (75–72 from 1955–1970) was not only successful on the mound, mostly with the Detroit Tigers, but also after his retirement as an entrepreneur.

By the time that Torrez's career was winding down in the early 1980s, the demographic, political and economic landscape for the Spanish-surnamed population in the United States had indeed changed dramatically. Regalado, for example, noted that in 1979, "Raul Yzaguirre, editor of the Hispanic journal *Agenda* pronounced that the next ten years would be the 'Decade of the Hispanic.' Convinced that a 'golden age' was near, he envisioned in the United States an era of unprecedented Hispanic accomplishments, increased awareness, explosive creativity, and greater Latin influence."[53] Still, there were critical issues and gaps in Latino life:

> Despite the optimism, Hispanics had no universal event or figure to rally around as they entered the eighties. Few of the leaders of the sixties remained prominent; major community organizations held only nominal appeal. Furthermore the political spearheads of the past were handicapped by a largely apolitical constituency. And cultural heroes appeared all but absent. As early as 1974, one Latin YMCA leader in New York complained that "there are black heroes, black films, black music and black movements. [However] Spanish-speaking kids don't have an established image to look up to.... Indeed, America's 'forgotten people' remained well outside the limelight." In April of 1981, this changed.[54]

The time was ripe for an iconic figure, no matter in what field, to take center stage as the "hero" of the Latinos: enter Fernando Valenzuela.

The young pitcher blazed onto the national consciousness for a variety of reasons. First, he was in the "right" market. The Dodgers had worked to cultivate the Mexicano/Mexican American constituency since their arrival in Los Angeles. Games were broadcast in Spanish from the time the team moved West. Second, by the end of the 1970s, the Spanish-language media had grown not only in Southern California, but throughout the nation as well. Finally, the organization, though it had attempted to promote "Mexican" players in the past, had not met with great success in this endeavor. True, they had brought up various Latino players, such as Manny Mota, but a "true Mexicano" star had not yet donned Dodger blue. By 1977, Roberto "Bobby" Castillo was the next in a succession of hoped-for *estrellas* that the Dodgers and their Spanish-surnamed fans had yearned for. It turned out that Castillo did not achieve his greatest success on the field (an overall 38–40 career mark), but as a mentor: the man who taught Valenzuela to throw the screwball.

Using this vicious pitch, Fernando arrived in Los Angeles after a stint in the AA Texas League with San Antonio that featured no earned runs surrendered over his final 35 frames. His appearances in 1980 for the Dodgers were just as impressive, with 17⅔ innings completed, a 2–0 record, and an ERA of 0.00. Finally, he started the following year with shutouts over Houston (2–0 and 1–0) and San Diego (2–0) before finally being nicked for one run by the Giants in a 7–1 victory. The fans in Chavez Ravine went wild, particularly those of Mexicano descent. As noted in an contemporary article on the prodigy in *Sports Illustrated*:

> According to the 1980 census, there are 2,065,724 people of Spanish origin in Los Angeles County, and the number is increasing rapidly. Until recently, though, the Dodgers drew poorly from the Hispanic community. "We never said we wouldn't go to games," says Valenzuela's agent, Antonio De Marco, a Mexican immigrant, "but we did tell the Dodgers they should get some Mexican players, and they were slow to do it." Although Valenzuela appeals to fans of all backgrounds, he's especially popular among his countrymen. "I've never seen anything like it," say KTNQ radio's Jaime Jarrin, who has broadcast games in Spanish since the Dodgers moved West in 1958.[55]

The 1981 Major League campaign is remembered mostly for the strike that stopped play for 50+ games per team. In regard to Latino history (sport or otherwise), however, the season is remembered mostly for the entrance onto the larger national sporting spotlight of a portly young man from Etchohuaquila, Sonora, who came to signify more than just athletic success. Given where he pitched, and the other changes that had taken place since the start of the Chicano Movement in the mid–1960s, Fernando Valenzuela was the apparatus that "catapulted [Mexican American] … identity into the national limelight as never before and in a manner that captured the essence of their culture. 'He makes me feel proud,' claimed one fan of Mexican heritage. 'When he looks good we all look good.'"[56] Mike Torrez would have two opportunities to pitch against Fernando Valenzuela, and though he had a lackluster season in 1983, he acquitted himself well against the sensational Dodgers pitcher.

The two matchups versus Valenzuela were certainly among the best performances of the season by Mike Torrez. In the first contest, on June 2 at Dodger Stadium, the two hurlers had very similar results. Valenzuela gave up ten hits, four earned runs, and five walks over a full eight innings. Torrez pitched the same length but surrendered only six hits, three walks, with only three of the four runs the Dodgers scored earned. The two left well before the climax of the contest. Los Angeles eventually prevailed, 5–4, in 12 frames, with Jesse Orosco taking the loss for the Mets.[57] The rematch took place on the other coast on August 31. Here, Torrez was masterful, going the distance and allowing only eight hits with but two free passes and six strikeouts as part of a 7–1 Mets triumph. He even managed to get a hit off of his counterpart, drove in a run, and scored in a five-tally fourth inning for the New Yorkers. This victory improved his record to 9–14 and dropped his ERA to a more than respectable 3.94.[58]

As the season entered its final month, there was a sense among many in the National League that the Mets were beginning to turn things around. Though they still occupied last place in the East, local scribe Jack Lang noted that knowledgeable individuals around the senior circuit, "Pittsburgh Manager Chuck Tanner among them, see the Mets as the more improved team [in the division].... They also were 4–3 on a California tour, the first time in six years they managed to have a winning trip to the West Coast." A great deal of credit for the upturn in the Mets' fortunes was laid at the feet of the veteran starters. The team's pitching had improved as "Tom Seaver and Mike Torrez manage to keep the Mets in most games for six, seven or eight innings until Howard can go to his bullpen, which is his strong suit."[59] It seems that the "greybeards" were providing both stability and insight on pitching at this level for the younger members of the staff, just as Cashen had envisioned prior to the start of the year.

After his victory against Valenzuela, Torrez hit another one of his recurring bad stretches. Over his final six trips to the mound in 1983, he won one, lost three, and had two no-decisions. The low point in this period came in a start against the Cubs on September 24, where he lasted but ⅓ of an inning and gave up five earned runs and two walks in the game that the Mets still managed to win, 7–6. As had occurred many times over his career, his next start produced the opposite result, with Torrez pitching eight strong innings and giving up three runs in a 4–3 victory over the Pirates. Overall, he led the circuit in both defeats and walks, but wound up tied for second on the clubs in victories. His final ERA for the year was 4.37.

Although finishing in the cellar, there was reason for optimism for 1984. Ron Darling had five starts and a 1–3 record, but his ERA was 2.50. Walt Terrell finished at 8–8, but had an ERA of 3.57, with four complete games and two shutouts. In addition to what occurred with the Major League club, there was a prized youngster named Dwight Gooden waiting in the wings (although he pitched only at the A level in 1983) as a possible addition to bolster the starting rotation in the near future. The current relief corps looked solid with Jessie Orosco finishing 13–7 with 17 saves and an ERA of 1.47 and Doug Sisk completing the year with a mark of 5–4, 11 saves and an ERA of 2.24. With the pitching seemingly on the right track, there was a need to improve the offensive production, as the most glaring statistic for this season was that New York finished dead last in the National League with but 575 runs scored (just 3.55 tallies per game).[60]

Going into 1984, the Mets' management decided to go with Davey Johnson as manager. Over spring training, the new skipper discussed some of the important considerations for the upcoming season. To the shock of Mets fans, the great Tom Seaver was gone (claimed off of waivers by the Chicago White Sox), and that left Mike Torrez and Walt Terrell as the only confirmed starters. Ed Lynch was another possibility, but Johnson indicated that he was willing to take an extended look at "some of the young arms." Included in this group were Darling, Sid Fernandez, and possibly Dwight Gooden. By the time the Mets broke camp and headed to the Big Apple, the new field general had made some very bold decisions. First, given his experience, Torrez was named as the number one starter. Behind him were Terrell, Darling, and Lynch. The biggest surprise was the decision to keep Gooden as part of the rotation. As Johnson noted, "can you really open with a pitching staff that has four kids as starters? With the prediction that we're going to finish last, I guess I can." The young hurler from Tampa was ecstatic. "I was expecting to start the season at Tidewater (AAA) and would not have been disappointed if I did. I didn't think I was ready yet, but they do."[61]

The first game of the new season had the Mets playing the Cincinnati Reds at Riverfront Stadium on April 2. Mike Torrez was the starter for New York, but did not last very long, pitching just 1⅓ innings. He was quite ineffective, giving up three runs in the first inning and being responsible for another three in the second. Overall, it was a very inauspicious start for his campaign, in contrast with the team's early results. After splitting a two-game set with the Reds, the Mets traveled to the Astrodome to play Houston. They won the first two games of that series, 8–1 and 3–2, before Torrez's next start, on April 8. It was during this contest that a pitch that got away from Torrez would provide a second negative hallmark to his career.

In what can only be considered an enigmatic happenstance, *The Sporting News* presented a story on the Astros' Dickie Thon in the April 16, 1984, issue. The title of the piece, "Sky Is the Limit for All-Star Thon," by Harry Shattuck, highlighted what many in the majors saw as the bright future that lay ahead of this 25-year-old shortstop. His teammates were effusive in their praise of this budding Puerto Rican star. "He's already the best shortstop in the league," indicated Craig Reynolds, the man he had replaced in the starting lineup. Third baseman Phil Garner crowed, "He's already an excellent ballplayer, but he'll get even better." His double-play partner, Billy Doran, insisted, "I'd be afraid to predict how great Dickie Thon can become. I know I'd love to play second base for Houston for the next 20 years and have Dickie by my side." Finally, the team's general manager, Al Rosen, made the boldest assertion of all, stating, "when I see Dickie Thon, I see a future Hall of Famer."[62]

Unfortunately, in the same article, Shattuck noted an event that had taken place about one week earlier: a fastball by Mike Torrez struck Thon "square in the face" and changed dramatically the trajectory of his, until then, blossoming career. In a conversation with this author, Dickie Thon noted that it was quite difficult to pick up pitches in the Astrodome. "I also liked to stand as much over the plate as I possibly could." A recent article on the incident by Greg Hanlon tells what happened:

> He assumed his normal coiled stance, leaning in, his front foot nearly touching home plate…. His lightning quick wrists meant that he was entitled to that space just like he was entitled to his burgeoning greatness. Thon remembers what happened next as another dull Astrodome thud. The ball ran up and in, and up an in—home plate umpire Doug Harvey said it moved 10 inches—and hit Thon's earflap and then socked him on the orbital bone above the left eye, fracturing it…. With that, Thon went from being a potential Hall of Famer to a hard luck journeyman.[63]

While the event had a very negative impact on his career, Thon indicated that he had "no hard feelings" toward Torrez, who called him two days after the dreadful event. In many ways, as Hanlon indicates in his essay, there are parallels between the physical injuries of Thon and the psychic ones endured by Torrez because of this pitch and the one to Bucky Dent six years earlier. "A devout Catholic, Thon says his life has had 'many blessings,' and he sees his injury as a stroke of bad luck in a life otherwise defined by good luck: 'I've had a lot of good things happen to me. I try to think about it that way,' he says." Likewise, Torrez summarized his brush with such events in 1989 to Terry Scott for a Quebec-based magazine on the Expos. While focusing specifically on Dent, the same can be said about the accident with Thon. "Hey, I didn't win 185 games to let one game ruin everything for me. You just do the best you can for as long as you can. Life is way too short to worry about something like that."[64]

Though he continued to pitch for the Mets, time was running out on Torrez's Major League career. There were young hurlers on their way up the team's farm system, and an aging veteran who was being pummeled on a regular basis, while collecting roughly one-quarter of a million dollars in salary, would not hang on for much longer. After the incident in Houston, Torrez made only seven more appearances (with six starts) for New York. Again, there was much inconsistency. In his next trip to the mound, he lasted but one frame against the Phillies (a 12–2 loss) on April 21. The next four starts resulted in three defeats and one no-decision. Of these, his best performance came against the team that originally signed him out of high school: the Cardinals. On June 3, he pitched eight strong innings, gave up ten hits, but only one earned run (and three walks) in a 1–0 loss to St. Louis. At this point, his record dropped to 0–5, and the Shea Stadium fans were only too happy to show their displeasure with his performance. Still, he continued to work and help his team win. At least some of his teammates noted and appreciated his efforts:

> Shea Stadium fans start booing Mets righthander Mike Torrez when he begins warming up in the bullpen. "It hurts.... I hear the boos, too. Anybody who says they done hear them is lying." Torrez may not be pitching effectively, but he's credited with helping some of New York's young pitchers. "He helps out all of the young guys," said first baseman Keith Hernandez, "and that's the sign of unselfishness. But you never hear about that."[65]

Torrez tried to be philosophical about his situation, comparing it to how far he and his family had come from toiling for the Santa Fe. In an interview with Maury Allen, he noted that the Torrez family had endured difficulties during his youth in Oakland. "I guess I learned how to deal with hard times as a kid.... A lot of Mexicans started working in the railroad and just followed the tracks north.... I've had tough times before. I'll still help this club."[66] He was not to have that opportunity, however.

There were other issues that helped make Torrez expendable. For example, some of the young guns were off to great starts, and this made it possible to jettison "older" hurlers such as Dick Tidrow and Craig Swan. The team was so eager to move up talent from their farm system that they willingly absorbed the final year of Swan's contract for a salary of approximately $600,000. Thus, the handwriting was on the wall for a 37-year-old pitcher who had an ERA of 4.40, even after a positive performance in his last outing.[67]

Torrez's final two turns for the Mets must have generated some nostalgic rumination for him. On June 9, he started against the Expos in Olympic Stadium in Montreal. He did not have a particularly good outing, but did manage to complete six innings, allowing seven hits and five earned runs. On that day, the New Yorkers managed to plate six runs and won, 6–5. Three days later, he came in as a reliever for the ninth frame against the team against which he threw his first pitches in the Major Leagues back in 1967—the Pittsburgh Pirates. He was not effective, as he gave up two singles, a walk, and a home run. This final performance lifted his ERA for the season to 5.02. He was released shortly thereafter and claimed by the Oakland Athletics.[68]

This second trip to the Bay Area took a slight detour to Tacoma for a couple of outings with the A's Pacific Coast League-based AAA farm team. He took the hill for the first time in this stint in Oakland on July 23. The Athletics' mound situation was quite desperate by the time of Torrez's signing. As *The Sporting News'* beat writer for the club, Kit Stier, noted in an essay published on July 16, "The Oakland A's are desperately hoping at least a couple of young pitchers will settle down and become consistent. Meantime, they are searching just about everywhere except the local want ads for established pitchers." This is why his former club reached out to Torrez. Although he arrived with a 1–5 record, once again, Torrez argued that, with consistent work, he would contribute to the club. "I hadn't really gotten the ball in New York. I was getting the ball only every seventh, eighth or ninth day." With the team a few games below the break-even mark (44–49 on the day this article appeared), Oakland management still felt the A's had a chance for the playoffs. "If you look at our staff," said Sandy Alderson, vice-president of baseball operations, "you only have three or four guys you will feel comfortable with in the stretch." Hence, this seemed like a good opportunity for Mike Torrez to hang on in the Major Leagues.[69]

The experiment proved to be very, very short-lived. Torrez made two appearances for Oakland, both in relief and quite ineffective. On July 23, he entered the game in the bottom of the seventh against Minnesota. In ⅔ of an inning, he surrendered five earned runs. The final score was 14–4 in favor of the Twins. In his next outing, against Seattle, he did better, giving up only two runs and two walks over 1⅓ frames in a 12–2 A's defeat. After two relief efforts, his ERA was an astronomical 27.00 (down from 67.50 after the earlier game). The Athletics waived him shortly thereafter.[70] These would be his final appearances as an active Major Leaguer.

Often at the end of a career at the highest levels of professional sport, it is the individual athlete who is last to accept the finality of the situation. For Mike Torrez, the passion and desire to compete were still there after he was let go by the Athletics in August of 1984, but subsequently no Major League franchise was willing to take a chance on the veteran hurler. He went back to the Dominican Republic and pitched for Licey, helping that squad win the Caribbean Series.[71] He noted that he was still throwing around 90 miles per hour and had perfected a new pitch over the winter: the forkball. His goal was to achieve the 200-victory mark at the Major League level. With no calls coming from the top tier, he settled eventually for an opportunity to pitch with an organization about as far removed from the big leagues as was possible in the mid–1980s: the Miami Marlins, an unaffiliated, shoestring squad playing in the dilapidated and cavernous (10,000 seats) Miami Stadium, located in one of the roughest parts of the city. "I'm going to give it a couple of months…. I'm swallowing a little of my pride, but everyone does at some point…. I can help someone." Torrez was not alone in his belief. His first manager with the Marlins, Tom Burgess, stated emphatically, "Oh, he won't be with us long. The scouts will come. They'll see him pitch."[72]

These are not the current Miami Marlins (though some of their moves over recent years do have a circus-like quality similar to that of this A-level franchise). Neither were these the AAA Miami Marlins of the International League, who played between 1956 and 1960 and drew, in their final season, over 109,000 fans (topping out at almost 289,000 in their first year).[73] No, this was a team described in an article in *Baseball America* as "perennial doormats of the Florida State League."[74] In order to attract fans to their games, General Manager Mal Fichman, along with owners Joe Ryan and Rob Fine, worked to develop a "shtick" by recruiting former major leaguers who sought one more chance to go back up the career ladder. Hopefully, by bringing in familiar names, they surmised, the fans would come, and so would an improved level of play on the field. Fichman first approached Vida Blue and Greg Luzinski. No deal. The first fish to take the bait (pardon the pun) was Mike Torrez (who would also serve as a coach). There was a slight dropoff in pay for Torrez from what he earned with the Mets. His monthly salary in the Florida State League would be $1,500. Still, his signing led other former MLB players to ink contracts with the Marlins, including Jim Essian, Eric Rasmussen, Hipolito Pena, Will McEnaney, and Juan Eichelberger.[75]

As the Marlins ended training to begin their regular season, Fichman had a wonderful idea for an opening night promotion. The Marlins' opponents that evening would be the Ft. Lauderdale Yankees, managed by none other than Bucky Dent. The first game of the season was billed as "Torrez-Dent II," and management hoped for a large turnout of at least 4,000. As usual during a South Florida spring, it rained most of the day and the turnout was a paltry 800 fans. After the game, Dent was asked about Torrez and his chances of making it back to the majors. "It's tough.... I understand what Mike is trying to do. He wants to get back, and he's got to pitch somewhere.... Even, if it takes coming to a place like this to find out."[76]

Things would only get worse for the Marlins over the remainder of the campaign. By the time that the *Baseball America* article appeared in mid–July, average attendance for Marlins home games had dwindled to around 300 aficionados per contest. The team drew a paltry 32,000 fans for the season (an average of 461 per game) and finished dead last in their division (58–83) with the second worst record in the FSL. Torrez was effective, finishing with a mark of 7–8 with an ERA of 2.80. Though the numbers were solid, the competition was just not of sufficient quality to entice MLB organizations to bring him in for a look. The end was finally here. Within a few months, Mike Torrez would be moving on and commencing his post-baseball (as a player) life.

The last few years of Mike Torrez's career were filled with some good moments both on the field and in his personal life. He met and married Teresa, and together they had a son, Michael, and later another, Wesley. He also had a daughter, Christiann, and son, Yannick, with his previous spouses. He had an excellent season in 1981 and defeated the great Valenzuela in his last full season in the majors. There were also some troughs on and off the field: his divorce, the 1980 and 1982 seasons with the Red Sox, how he was branded as a goat by fans in Boston, and the incident with Dickie Thon. Still, he had made a decent living over the years in professional baseball, and a move into sales with Contract Furnishing Systems in New York City made it possible for him to be a "regular" husband and father.

As Torrez noted to the Expos' magazine in 1989, he enjoyed the chance to "return home each night and to have weekends free to spend with ... family." Still, the competitive fire burned, and this would eventually lead to success as an entrepreneur and also to a stint in coaching and working as a general manager for a minor league team. As late as 1989, however, Torrez still fantasized about putting on the uniform and pitching. At that interview, he noted to writer Terry Scott that there was talk about investors starting a senior league for retired major leaguers. At an autograph signing session with Luis Tiant, he told his old Red Sox teammate that he might be interested only if "I could fly down after work on Friday and pitch a game—you know, be their weekend warrior—and be back in time to go to work on Monday morning."[77] Indeed, by 1986, Mike Torrez was ready to move on with the rest of his life. However, the game and the business of baseball would still pull him back in over the subsequent years.

9

Unloading the Poltergeist
Torrez's Post-MLB Life, His Career and Its Significance, 1986–2016

Mike Torrez had more than just a passing interest in the 1986 World Series between the Red Sox and the Mets. After all, he had played for (and been booed by the fans of) both squads. Since he now worked in and lived near the New York City area, he was in attendance the evening of October 25, the night of Game 6. As Red Sox fans everywhere remember in excruciating detail, a grounder by Mookie Wilson squirted below the glove of first baseman Bill Buckner and permitted the winning run to score in the bottom of the tenth inning, producing an improbable 6–5 victory for the New Yorkers. Of course, as fate would have it, Boston then lost the Series in Game 7, and New Englanders waited another 18 years before exorcising "the curse" in 2004. In a column for *The Atlantic* in 2013, Andrew Cohen sought to encapsulate for younger members of Red Sox Nation how crushing such events had been to previous generations of Fenway Faithful.

> If you are 18 years old today and a Red Sox fan it means you have spent half your life—*half your life*—basking in a series of team accomplishments of which your parents, and your grandparents, and maybe even your great grandparents could only dream…. In this worldview, the Sox almost always come through with clutch hits, or timely defense, or lights-out pitching. In this worldview, there is almost always a walk-off or an otherwise happy ending. So good, so good, indeed.[1]

If the pain was piercing for fans, imagine what it was like to have lived with being one of the players (supposed goats?) involved in one of the too-numerous-to-mention, tragic and disappointing moments in Boston baseball history. For players who were Red Sox lifers, the feeling had to create great angst, though they retained their loyalty to the franchise. For a player like Mike Torrez, who played for numerous clubs and was basically run out of town and blamed overly for one such event, the sentiments were different.

Given the bad feelings in the years leading up to his 1983 trade to the Mets, it is not surprising that Torrez celebrated along with others in the Big Apple when Ray Knight motored home with the winning tally that October night. In an article that appeared just after the end of the Fall Classic, Peter Gammons noted that colleague Clark Booth went and found Torrez on the 25th to gage his reaction to the events that had played out at Shea Stadium. While certainly mindful of what Buckner endured (and would experience in subsequent years), Torrez could not help but express joy that, with this occurrence, he was now "off the hook." Gammons added, "when Booth's TV camera turned off the light, Torrez unloaded the poltergeist that he had carried for eight years by yelling, '----- Boston!'"[2]

Not too long beyond the autumn of 1986, Torrez confronted the marking of the ten-year anniversary of his pitch to Bucky Dent. Not surprisingly, commemorative stories appeared in numerous outlets. An article by Randy Schultz in *The Sporting News* was almost clinical in its analysis of the event, going over key moments in the 1978 season, and focused mostly on the Yankees shortstop's perspective of the game and at-bat.[3] The *Boston Globe* marked the occasion by contacting both players and provided Torrez with an extended opportunity to reminisce about the game, his time with the Red Sox, and his career. He was measured in his response, and it was evident that the hard feelings expressed two years earlier had mellowed somewhat, though they were not totally forgotten. "I honestly thought the two best teams [played].... We really played great baseball to force that playoff.... I took the brunt of it. Boston's the type of town that they have to blame somebody, and I was the guy. I was on top of the world in '77 and in '78 I hit the bottom of the world." Torrez also reached out to Bill Buckner by noting, "I had a feeling for him because I knew what he was going to be dealing with. Life is ... there are ups and downs. You've just got to learn to take the good with the bad."[4] The pattern begun in 1988 has continued in subsequent decades, with similar stories appearing in 1998 and 2008.[5] Time, as is said, does heal all wounds, and by 2005 Torrez sounded a much more conciliatory tone after the Red Sox's victory in 2004. "I was happy for them and they deserve it. They played great coming back from three games to none and showed character. It was just their year. Everything fell into place for them and everything went right for them."[6]

This concluding chapter will focus on the post-playing career and life of Mike Torrez, and place him in historical context both as an individual athlete and as a symbol of the importance of athletics among the Mexican American population. The first part will provide a brief summary of his career in business. Next will be an overview of his endeavors in coaching and management in minor league baseball with the Newark Bears of the Atlantic League and the Canadian American League (class A unaffiliated). The final section will discuss the historical and socially significant role of sport in the lives of many *comunidades* in the Midwest (and elsewhere) and how Torrez's story can be utilized as a model to study this important topic.

When Mike Torrez retired from playing baseball, he and Teresa initially remained in Florida and lived briefly in the St. Petersburg area. After spending some time fishing and enjoying the warm climate, the couple moved back to New York State, where Torrez commenced a career in sales with a furniture company based out of New York City.[7] Over time, as he developed contacts in the commercial sector, he eventually moved on to work with a group that specialized in promotional premiums. By the early 1990s, he established his own firm in this area of endeavor, MAT Premiums, which has now been in operation for over two decades. The company sells all matter of hats, t-shirts and other items embossed with their customers' corporate logos. It has been a profitable venture, and the business continues to operate in the White Plains area. Torrez goes back to the Empire State on a regular basis to meet with his associates in this enterprise. Meanwhile, as Teresa hails from Ohio, the couple moved to Illinois to remain close to both families.

Much of the Torrez clan still lives in the Topeka area. Oldest brother John, who is now retired from the Santa Fe, and sisters Ernestine, Mickey and Yolanda still reside in the Kansas capital. John was active in the Mexican softball scene in the Midwest until the early 2000s, and is considered to be one of the "legends" of the sport. A recent paper presented by University of Kansas scholar Ben Chapell at an American Studies conference had one of his interviewees, Gil Solis, remark, "You have to understand, when I was younger, my heroes weren't Mickey Mantle or one of those major leaguers. My heroes were 'Johnny Boy' Torrez, Rocket Rocha, and Blanco Gomez."[8] The efforts that familias like the Torrezes began back in the 1920s continue to bear fruit, and although not in the same format (such as being "exclusively" Mexican American), the leagues and tournaments (softball and basketball) continue to be an important part of Mexican American life in the Midwest. Recent work by Chapell, Gene Chavez and other researchers is now beginning to provide an overview of the social and historical significance of this overlooked aspect of Latino life in this region.[9] The youngest brother in the Torrez clan, Richard, is the owner of a plumbing business in Topeka, sister Evelyn lives in the Kansas City, Missouri, area, and Stella resides in the vicinity of Silver Lake/Harrison in New York State.

Both Juan and Mary have passed away. Juan died in 1996, and Mary succumbed in 2014. Until the day she died, she continued to live in the family's domicile at 208 North Lake Street. Uncle Louis retired from working at the Veterans Administration Hospital and still lives a couple of blocks away, just steps away from his beloved Our Lady of Guadalupe parish on Banner Street. Louis is still very active in the church's annual fiesta celebration, which is now a bigger and broader community event than ever before.

As noted in the previous chapter, part of Torrez's responsibilities with the woebegone Marlins in Miami was to serve as a kind of unofficial

coach to the younger pitchers on the staff. This experience, in addition to mentoring some of the young hurlers with the Mets in 1983 and 1984, proved enjoyable and gave him a sense that this might be a way to continue to work in baseball. Eventually, with his business doing well, he felt it was possible to serve in this capacity starting at the lower levels of the minor leagues. When the opportunity arose to take up this task with the 2009 Newark Bears, Torrez jumped at the prospect. It was a decision he came to regret.

Torrez sporting the home whites of the hapless 1985 Miami Marlins. Even with the infusion of talent of former-Major Leaguers, the stands at the team's ballpark were usually almost as empty during games. Mike, however, did benefit from mentoring other pitchers on this squad, and eventually moved into coaching and management at the minor league level. Courtesy Mike Torrez.

The attempt to revive the glorious tradition of the Bears' franchise in New Jersey's largest city began in the late 1990s with the efforts of native son, and former Yankees backstop, Rick Cerone. As documented in Bob Golon's book, *No Minor Accomplishment: The Revival of New*

Jersey Professional Baseball, the former Major Leaguer and Essex County officials believed that, after an absence of more than 50 years, the time was right to re-establish a fabled club.[10] As Golon noted, the demographics looked appealing: the city had almost 300,000 in population and was surrounded by numerous highly populated communities such as Elizabeth and East Orange. Unfortunately, the club was beset by problems from the start. First, the facility, Newark Bears and Eagles Riverfront Stadium, "was supposed to be the lynchpin in the revitalization of the city's downtown area." This program did not develop as foreseen in the late 1990s, however. Even with the club signing many former MLB players (like the Marlins tried to do in the mid–1980s), such as Ozzie and José Canseco and Rickey Henderson, the Bears never attracted a substantial number of fans to what many still perceived as a "rough" part of town.[11]

The unaffiliated organization did not field very competitive teams initially, but did qualify for the playoffs in 2001, losing in the title round to the Somerset Patriots. A winning record did not mean that the turnstiles counted more paying customers, and "Cerone found the business of running the Newark Bears more troublesome and challenging than he ever imagined." By 2003, Cerone sold controlling interests to auto dealership owner Steve Kalafer. The two ran the club until the former Yankee ceded his remaining percentage to real estate developer Marc Berson. By 2006, Kalafer moved into the background and Berson assumed full control of day-to-day operations. The team continued to lose money. Berson eventually brought in John Brandt as general manager of the struggling organization. There was some success, at least on the field, as the Bears won the Atlantic League title in 2007.[12]

By 2008 the Bears were roughly a .500 team on the field (finishing 72–68, last in their division), but still had difficulties attracting fans. By October the team was in much debt and appeared on the verge of extinction. Berson noted to a local reporter, "this is not a philanthropy ... this was good for Newark and good for the city ... but there are limits. We're doing everything we can to find a solution here." Even though the squad was competitive, there were two key issues that proved intractable: the perception that the stadium was in a "dangerous" setting and the demographic changes in the area. For example, articles in local media noted that this section of Newark was now more heavily African American (who have, over the past decades, lost interest in baseball), and Hispanic (from countries where soccer is the most popular sport, not baseball), and that made it difficult to attract a sufficient number of customers.[13]

Just when the franchise's demise appeared imminent, a conglomerate called Bases Loaded Group came through and saved the Bears, paying a reported $100,000 for the team, plus assuming about $1 million in debt. The face of this association, James Wankmiller, and new general manager Mark Skeels convinced another former Yankee, Tim Raines, to take over the managerial duties for 2009. Skeels brought in former White Sox Ron Karkovice to serve as hitting coach, and Mike Torrez to handle the pitchers. With this new on-field leadership, Newark charged into its tenth season in the Atlantic League. Under the tutelage of Raines and his cohorts, the Bears gave their minuscule number of aficionados an exciting season. The team finished 74–66, second in their division, and lost to Somerset again in the league championship round. Torrez's charges finished the year with an overall team ERA of 5.36.[14]

Even with the Bears reaching the title round, finances remained problematic. Yet another ownership group was unable to make a go of the endeavor of Newark baseball, and Atlantic League's founder Frank Boulton took control of the Bears for 2010. After claiming a championship, the team slumped badly to 53–86 and eventually yet another new owner, Thomas Cetnar, took over. The latest entrepreneur declared that he would move the organization out of its current association and into the Canadian-American League (Can-Am). The notion was that with a shorter schedule, 94 games instead of 140, expenses would decrease and the hemorrhaging would be reduced. By October, the proposal became reality and the Bears joined a natural rival, the New Jersey Jackals (based in Montclair), in the association. Cetnar also made another decision; he named Mike Torrez to be his general manager. Eventually, there were three former Yankees—Torrez, Raines and later, recently acquitted of manslaughter charges in Florida, Jim Leyritz (to serve as hitting coach)—running the front office and on-field fortunes of the Bears.[15] This arrangement would not last long and would mark the end of Torrez's association with the organization.

Given the tumult that had surrounded the franchise almost since its inception, events in July of 2011 were merely par for the course. Still another ownership team, Dr. Doug Spiel and his fiancée, Danielle Dronet, took over the team from Cetnar after further legal wrangling. The couple hoped to pump new life into the franchise with aggressive promotions, including even a possible TV reality show. Torrez did not want to go along with this arrangement, and was promptly fired.

In an extensive article by Amy Brittain for the *Newark Star-Ledger*, the reporter noted that Torrez was very disappointed about this turn of events, saying "I always tried to do the best I could." Torrez also indicated that he was still owed around $60,000, the balance of his pay for the season. Spiel and Dronet countered that they fired Torrez because "he wasn't on my team." "As Spiel tells it," Brittain added, "he didn't have a choice ... because Torrez had told the players not to trust Spiel. Torrez said he never bad-mouthed Spiel to the players, but only cautioned them about TV-release forms." The issue has not yet been settled. In an interview with this author, Brittain recounted that Torrez was very upset and felt that this situation had done a great deal of damage to his reputation in baseball.[16]

While this was the end of Torrez's ties to this franchise, he has continued his interest in the Atlantic League, though now it is through the career of his second son with Teresa, Wesley, who as of 2015 pitched for another independent team, the Camden Riversharks.[17] The sad saga of the "new" version of the Bears culminated in April of 2014. Tim Raines left his managerial post after 2011 and was replaced as skipper by another ex-big leaguer, Ken Oberkfell. The 2012 Bears finished a horrid 35–65. The final season took place in 2013 as Garry Templeton led a Newark squad that improved only slightly, to 37–63. Dan Barry, in an article for the *New York Times*, recounted the funeral pyre that was the last season of Newark baseball, stating, "last year, the fat lady sang all season long…. The team claimed to draw 500 fans a game—a generous estimate—when at least 2000 were needed to keep things sane. In late September, burglars stole computer equipment, memorabilia and several flat-screen televisions still in boxes. And in November, the Can-Am League dropped Newark." The few remaining assets were finally sold off to the highest bidders.[18]

So, how to summarize the career of Michael Augustine Torrez? He won almost 200 games in the majors, something that not many individuals have achieved. In regard to the number of victories, he fares very well in regard to other Mexican Americans who have pitched at the highest level of baseball. He made a total of 458 big league starts and struck out 3,044 hitters. He also won more than 14 games in a season on seven occasions.[19] In a review of hurlers designated as "Mexican American" in the majors, one encounters over 40 names. Some of these individuals stayed in "the show" for just a brief time, while others had significant careers. Ranking among the highest in winning percentage is the great Mike Garcia, an excellent hurler for the Cleveland Indians from 1948 through 1959, who pitched a final two seasons with the White Sox (1960) and Senators (1961). His overall mark was 142–97 (.594 winning percentage). Other important pitchers of this background are the aforementioned Hank Aguirre, and some of more recent vintage such as the legendary Jesse Orosco, and still-active major leaguers such as Matt Garza (currently with the Brewers) and Yovani Gallardo (currently with the Rangers).[20]

Depending on how one defines the term "Mexican American," it can be argued that Mike Torrez is the individual of this ethnic background with the most wins ever in the Majors. Of the pitchers in the list noted above, only the great Lefty Gomez (189–102, a winning percentage of .649) has more victories to his credit. Here is where the definition comes into play. In a recent biography of Lefty Gomez, his daughter Vernona Gomez and co-author Lawrence Goldstone delineated the family's lineage. Gomez was the descendant of a Spanish sea captain who wound up in California after his ship was torched by a Confederate privateer in 1862. Juan Gomez and his Portuguese wife, Rita, were the parents of Lefty's father, Francisco. Francisco was nicknamed "Coyote" by the cowhands with whom he worked around the Pinole Valley. Eventually, the young man struck out and worked in the cattle industry in both Nevada and Texas. Francisco ultimately returned to El Sobrante, the family ranch, and married Lizzie Herring in 1893. The last offspring of this marital union was Vernon Luis Gomez, born in November of 1908.[21]

So the question becomes, does this make Lefty Gomez a "Mexican?" The recent biography provides a direct response by the Yankees immortal himself who, after the 1931 season, participated in a barnstorming tour that worked its way to Juarez. It was there that Gomez, in no uncertain terms, self-identified as being something "other" than a Mexicano to an audience at a post-game gala, much to the chagrin of his thirsty and hungry teammates.

> After the last game in Juarez, we went to a Mexican restaurant where everything was on the house. The owner and city dignitaries honored us with a toast…. Right after the toast, the owner leaned over to me and said, "Mr. Gomez, where exactly were you born in Mexico?" I looked up in surprise. "I'm not Mexican, I'm Spanish." Two seconds of stunned silence, then boom, bang. The party was off…. After we're out the door, my teammates jumped me, shouting, "Son of a bitch, Gomez. You could have been a Mexican for another two hours."[22]

Given Gomez's own words, then, it is fair to argue that Mike Torrez is the "Mexican American" with the most victories ever in the Major Leagues.

Though he earned a substantial number of triumphs, and defeated every team then in existence (his record against the Yankees was only 1–10 in 18 starts, however), Mike Torrez has never, at least in the eyes of some, lived down the pitch to Bucky Dent.[23] Several years after his retirement, in 1989, Moss Klein, in his "A.L Beat" column in *The Sporting News*, noted that even with his victories, his World Series performance, and his contract with the Red Sox, "he's remembered for that one pitch." Later that year, Torrez's name was listed among those considered as first-year candidates for Hall of Fame balloting. The reaction by one fan indicated how much antipathy remained. Larry Sullivan from Bellwood, Illinois (a bitter Red Sox fan, perhaps—hope he lived to see 2004!) castigated the few writers who voted for Torrez's induction into Cooperstown. "First, make the writers' ballots a matter of public record so we can see which morons voted for Jim Bibby, Mike Torrez ... and other undeserving players." The point here is not to argue that Torrez deserves induction, but rather to make note of the amount of vitriol that remained in the consciousness of at least some baseball aficionados more than a decade beyond October 2, 1978.[24]

By the early 2000s, there was a greater sense of the significance of Torrez's accomplishments, even among some Red Sox fans. In an article that appeared in February of 2004, John Napolitano ranked Torrez as number 95 among the 100 "Top Red Sox" in the long history of the franchise. It is reasonable to assume that a large number of Fenway faithful must have been flabbergasted. In an even-handed analysis, Napolitano argued that "his successes always seemed to come with a price, for he is often remembered more for his bouts of wildness ... more than being a twenty game and World Series winner." A fair assessment, and one substantiated by the research presented in this work. Napolitano goes on to finish his essay with a "tip of the cap" to a competitor who suffered mightily at the hands of New England's baseball fanatics.

> Mike Torrez played longer than the average player and won more games than the average pitcher, but there was nothing average about his career. A hero in New York and a goat in Boston, he handled the highs and lows of professional baseball with dignity, as few have experienced more ups and downs in one career.[25]

One locale where Torrez has never had to apologize for his career and achievements has been with the folks back in Topeka. While many in the media were focusing on the coming tenth anniversary of his pitch to Bucky Dent in October of 1988, his barrio friends and neighbors instead granted him the significant honor of serving as grand marshal of the Fiesta Mexicana parade on July 9 of that year. The events of a decade prior in Fenway Park were not on the minds of locals that day, and Torrez was presented to the broader community as the epitome of many of the goals of the Chicano Movement era. Deborah Ortega, the chair of the fiesta noted:

> "We are proud of him. He has proved that anyone can be successful and go on to realize their dreams. Mike is someone who has made it, (who) has been successful

and still comes back (to the community). Mike is part of Oakland and part of our fiesta." He also serves as a role model for the young people of the community showing that "if you dream big dreams, those dreams can be realized if you really want them," Ortega said.[26]

The events for this fiesta culminated with the park where Torrez played his Pony League baseball being renamed in his honor.

Another article on Torrez coincided with the upcoming 20th anniversary of the event, and sheds even more light upon how the *comunidad* perceives its native son. Again in town for the fiesta, Torrez was once again in the middle of the annual events. "I love it when I come home. I've been walking around the Fiesta the last couple of nights and I see a lot of the guys I grew up with, and that's been great…. It's a great place to bring up a family and my feelings are here. This is home."[27] A final, and more recent, honor for Torrez occurred in 2011, when he was named the greatest athlete in the history of Shawnee County, beating out luminaries such as wrestling legend Melvin Douglas and basketball player and coach Lon Kruger.[28]

In the story announcing his status among the elites of his hometown's athletes, Torrez brought up some interesting points about how the game has changed. First, he mentioned the modifications that have taken place in regard to training, and decried the amount of pressure placed on hurlers at a tender age, the damage that it often does to their arms. "And I swear

Mike Torrez (left) and his brother John, in front of the entrance to the Mike Torrez Baseball Complex in the Oakland neighborhood of Topeka, Kansas (photograph by the author).

to God, I think the pitchers today from the time they were in Little League and in college, a lot of coaches have overpitched kids. They come up lame in the big leagues. They come up lame because they pitched them a lot."

Later in the article, Torrez gave credit to his former Cardinals teammate, Curt Flood, for helping to change the business of baseball and for making it possible for players to achieve previously undreamed of financial success. Noting the difference between the start of his career and signing with the Red Sox, Torrez recalled that after his 10–4 season with St. Louis in 1969, "They gave me a $2,500 raise. I thought, 'wow, by winning all these games I'll have a $15,000 raise by the end of my career.' It was big business. They tried to pay you with as less as they could. You had no other choice. Eat or go home, they said." As a result of Flood's heroic stance, Torrez benefited greatly, and he shared some of his bounty with his former teammate. Shortly after signing with Boston:

> Torrez sent a gift to Flood, one of the first Cardinals to befriend him when he was a rookie in St. Louis. In a recent HBO documentary about Flood and his case, Torrez was cited as one contemporary player ... who rewarded Flood for his courage. "I had to give him something, because he was down and out and I had to help him. I was happy and proud when I saw that documentary about him. Baseball basically blackballed him. But you know what, once a friend always a friend. I was always on his side as a player.... In fact, I think we should nominate him for the Hall of Fame for what he did for baseball, for the players. He changed the game, not only for the players now, but for ourselves when we became free agents."[29]

The story of Mike Torrez is significant because of what he accomplished, the personages he interacted with, and also as a way to examine the role of the sport in Mexican American life. It is a story of overcoming obstacles both before and after achieving athletic success. It also provides a model for studying the significance of sport in the lives of the burgeoning Latino/a population throughout the United States.

The role of athletics in the lives of Mexican Americans and Latinos in general is only now coming to light in both academic and popular literature. Given the demographic changes currently taking place, in the Midwest and elsewhere, it is an important element of this community's historical and present experiences that deserves extensive coverage. There have been several stories that have dealt with the growing presence of Latino/a athletes in this region over the past few years.[30] As other writers have noted, the surge of this population into smaller communities has, in many way, helped to save such towns. As the children of this wave of Latinos make their way into local schools, they will be the ones who bear the names of community teams throughout their regions.[31] By gaining a greater understanding of the role of sport in the history of Mexican Americans and other Latinos, it is possible to comprehend how athletics has been used in the past to hold on to a group's ethnic pride and identity, as well as how it has been used to break down barriers between Spanish-speakers and the majority population. The story of Mike Torrez is an example of how this worked in the recent past and given the changes now taking place in our nation, it is to be expected that there will be more individuals like him in the future. As noted in a recent book on the history of Latino/a participation in sport in the United States, at

> all levels of sport, Latinos are breaking barriers, forging friendships, and demonstrating in a very effective way that they are just as spirited and dedicated as the rest of the American populace ... recent immigrants are using sport in order to hold on to important parts of their cultural heritage as they fight to establish themselves in new territory. Hopefully, in the future, the stories of even more of these athletes ... will find their way into the broader literature of American sport history.[32]

The story of this great Mexican American pitcher, the offspring of families seeking to escape the turmoil of the Mexican Revolution and live the "American Dream," will hopefully serve as a further introduction to this topic and stimulate even more research and discussion among academicians and fans of all sports in general.

Chapter Notes

Introduction

1. For the most recent treatments on this story, please see: Joshua Prager, *The Echoing Green: The Untold Story of Bobby Thomson, Ralph Branca and the Shot Heard Round the World* (New York: Knopf/Doubleday, 2008) and Ralph Branca, *A Moment in Time: An American Story of Baseball, Heartbreak and Grace* (New York: Scribner, 2011). For an overview of "scapegoats" in baseball lore (which includes a chapter on Mike Torrez), please also see: Christopher Bell, *Scapegoats: Baseballers Whose Careers Are Marked by One Fateful Play* (Jefferson, NC: McFarland, 2002): 62–87.

2. The term Latino will be used throughout this work, as it is the most widely accepted nomenclature used for the persons of Spanish-speaking descent in the United States. Please see: Jorge Iber, Samuel O. Regalado, José A. Alamillo, and Arnoldo De Leon, *Latinos in U.S. Sport: A History of Isolation, Cultural Identity, and Acceptance* (Champaign, IL: Human Kinetics, 2011), 6–8 for a discussion on the use of this term in regard to sports history.

3. William Tasker, "Mike Torrez and His Unique Yankee History," June 25, 2013. See: http://itsaboutthemoney.net/archives/2013/06/25/mike-torrez-and-his-unique-yankees-history. There are various videos that feature the two men discussing the home run. A recent one from Steiner Sports Memorabilia can be accessed here: www.youtube.com/watch?v=IVEMu_Az8QA.

4. Nick C. Wilson, *Early Latino Ballplayers in the United States: Major, Minor and Negro Leagues, 1901–1949* (Jefferson, NC: McFarland, 2005); Noe Torres, *Baseball's First Mexican American Star: The Amazing Story of Leo* (Llumina Press); Tim Wendel, *The New Face of Baseball: The One Hundred Year Rise and Triumph of Latinos in Amer-ica's Favorite Sport* (New York: Harper-Collins, 2003); Mark Kurlansky, *The Eastern Stars: How Baseball Changed the Dominican Town of San Pedro de Macoris* (New York City: Penguin Group, 2010); and Rafael Hermoso, *Speak English! The Rise of Latinos in Baseball* (Kent, Ohio: Black Squirrel Books, 2013). This list is by no means exhaustive.

5. David Maraniss, *Clemente: The Passion and Grace of Baseball's Last Hero* (New York City: Simon & Schuster, 2006).

6. Samuel O. Regalado, *Viva Baseball!: Latin Major Leaguers and Their Special Hunger* (Champaign: University of Illinois Press, 2008); Adrian Burgos, *Playing America's Game: Baseball, Latinos and the Color Line* (Berkeley: University of California Press, 2007); Richard Santillan, et al., *Mexican American Baseball in the Central Coast* (Charleston, SC: Arcadia Press, 2013); and Roberto Gonzalez Echevarria, *The Pride of Havana: A History of Cuban Baseball* (New York: Oxford University Press, 2001). As with the works written by non-academics, this list is by no means exhaustive.

7. Louise Ann Fisch, *All Rise: Reynaldo G. Garza, the First Mexican American Federal Judge* (College Station: Texas A&M University Press, 1996); Felix Almaraz, *Knight Without Armor: Carlos Eduardo Castaneda, 1896–1958* (College Station: Texas A&M University Press, 1999); Ignacio M. Garcia, *Hector P. Garcia: In Relentless Pursuit of Justice* (Houston: Arte Publico Press, 2002); and Mario T. Garcia, *The Making of a Mexican American Mayor: Raymond L. Telles of El Paso* (El Paso: Texas Western Press, 1998).

8. See the following: Henry J. Avila, "Immigration and Integration: The Mexican American Community in Garden City, Kansas, 1900–1950," *Kansas History*, 20, no. 1 (Spring 1997): 22–37; Michael J. Broadway, "Meatpacking and Its Social and Economic Consequences for Garden City, Kansas, in

the 1980s," *Urban Anthropology* 19, no. 4 (1990): 321–344; Arthur Campa, "Immigrant Latinos and Resident Mexican Americans in Garden City, KS: Ethnicity and Ethnic Relations," *Urban Anthropology* 19, no. 4 (1990): 345–360; Donald Stull, "'I Come to the Garden': Changing Ethnic Relations in Garden City, KS," *Urban Anthropology* 19, no. 4 (1990): 303–320; Donald D. Stull and Michael Broadway, "Meatpacking and Mexicans on the High Plains: From Minority to Majority in Garden City, Kansas," in Richard C. Jones, ed., *Immigrants Outside of the Megalopolis: Ethnic Transformation in the Heartland* (Lanham, MD: Rowan and Littlefield, 2008): 115–133; Valdes, D.N., "Settlers, Sojourners and Proletarians: Social Formation in the Great Plains Sugar Beet Industry, 1890–1940," *Journal of the Great Plains Quarterly* 10, no. 2 (Spring 1990): 110–123; Tomas R. Jimenez, *Replenished Ethnicity: Mexican Americans, Immigration and Identity,*" (Berkeley: University of California Press, 2011); Daniel E. Aguilar, "Mexican Immigrants in Meatpacking Areas of Kansas: Transition and Acquisition of Cultural Capital," Doctoral Dissertation, Kansas State University, 2008; Russell Wayne Graves, "Garden City: The Development of an Agricultural Community on the Great Plains," Doctoral Dissertation, University of Wisconsin-Madison, 2004; Kathie Hinnen, "Mexican Immigrants to Hutchinson, Kansas, 1905–1940: How a Temporary Haven Became Home," Master's Thesis, Southwest Missouri State University, 1998; and Domingo Ricart, "Just Across the Tracks: A Survey of Five Mexican Communities in the State of Kansas (Emporia, Florence, Newton, Wichita, Hutchinson), Report, University of Kansas, 1950 (among others).

9. Rita G. Napier, "Rethinking the Past, Reimagining the Future," *Kansas History* 24, no. 3 (Autumn 2001): 218–247. Quote from page 247. A similar argument is presented in James N. Leiker, "Race Relations in the Sunflower State," 25, no. 3 (Autumn 2002): 214–236.

10. This list is by no means exhaustive, but demonstrates the plethora of articles on other racial and ethnic groups and sport by academics. By comparison, the research on Latinos and Latinas and their role in American athletics is scant. Gerald R. Gems, *Sport and the Shaping of Italian American Identity* (Syracuse, NY: Syracuse University Press, 2013); Peter Levine, *From Ellis Island to Ebbets Field: Sport and the American Jewish Experience* (New York: Oxford University Press, 1993); Lane Demas, *Integrating the Gridiron: Black Civil Rights and American College Football* (New Brunswick, NJ: Rutgers University Press, 2011); Kathleen S. Yep, *Outside the Paint: When Basketball Ruled at the Chinese Playground* (Philadelphia: Temple University Press, 2009); John Bloom *To Show What an Indian Can Do: Sports at Native American Boarding Schools* (Minneapolis: University of Minnesota Press, 2005); Kurt Edward Kemper, "The Smell of Roses and the Color of the Players: College Football and the Expansion of the Civil Rights Movement in the West," *Journal of Sport History* 31, no. 3 (Fall 2004): 317–339; Raymond Schmidt, "Lords of the Prairie: Haskell Indian School Football, 1919–1930," *Journal of Sport History* 28, no. 3 (Fall 2001): 403–426; Jennifer H. Lansbury, "'The Tuskegee Flash' and 'the Slender Harlem Stroker': Black Women Athletes on the Margin," *Journal of Sports History* 28, no. 1 (Summer 2001): 233–252; and Roberta J. Park, "Sport and Recreation Among Chinese American Communities of the Pacific Coast From the Time of Arrival to the 'Quiet Decade' of the 1950s," *Journal of Sport History* 27, no. 3 (Fall 2000): 445–480.

11. Larry Gerlach, "Ernie Quigley: An Official for All Seasons," *Kansas History: A Journal of the Great Plains* 33 (Winter 2010–2011): 218–239; Aram Goudsouzian, "'Can Basketball Survive Wilt Chamberlain?': The Kansas Years of Wilt the Stilt," *Kansas History: A Journal of the Great Plains* 28 (Autumn 2005): 150–173; Christopher H. Lee, "Adaptation on the Plains: The Development of Six Man and Eight Man Football in Kansas," *Kansas History* 12 (Winter 1989–1990): 192–201; Jason Pendelton, "Jim Crow Strikes Out: Interracial Baseball in Wichita, Kansas, 1920–1935," *Kansas History* 20 (Summer 1997): 86–101; Keith J. Sculle, "'The New Carlisle of the West': Haskell Institute and Big-Time Sports, 1920–1932," *Kansas History* 17 (Autumn 1994): 192–208; and Kim Warren, "All Indian Trails Lead to Lawrence, October 27 to 30, 1926: American Identity and the Dedication of Haskell Institute's Football Stadium," *Kansas History: A Journal of the Great Plains* 30 (Spring 2007): 2–19.

12. Jorge Iber, "Prologue: The Perils and Possibilities of 'Quarterbacking While Mexican': A Brief Introduction to the Participation of Latino/a Athletes in U.S. Sports History," *International Journal for the History of Sport* 26, no 7 (June 2009): 881–888; Fernando Delgado, "Golden But Not Brown: Oscar De La Hoya and the Complications of Culture, Manhood and Boxing," *International Journal for the History of Sport* 22, no.

1 (March 2005): 196–211; Alan Klein, "Latinizing the 'National Pastime.'" 24, no. 2 (February 2007): 296–310; Hilary A. Braysmith, "Constructing Athletic Agents in the Chicano/a Culture of Los Angeles," 22, no. 2 (March 2005): 177–195; José M. Alamillo, "Richard 'Pancho' Gonzalez, Race and the Print Media in Postwar Tennis America," *International Journal for the History of Sport* 26, no. 7 (June 2009): 947–965; Benita Heiskanen, "The *Latinization* of Boxing: A Texas Case Study," *Journal of Sport History* 32, no. 1 (Spring 2005): 45–66; and Enver M. Casimir, "Contours of Transnational Contact: Kid Chocolate, Cuba and the United States in the 1920s and 1930s," *International Journal for the History of Sport* 39, no. 3 (Fall 2012): 487–506.

13. Gilberto Garcia, "Louis 'Count Castro': The Story of a Forgotten Latino Major Leaguer," *Nine: A Journal of Baseball History and Culture* 16: 2 (Spring 2008): 35–51; Kevin A. Johnson and Joseph W. Anderson, "Rhetorical Constructions of Anger Management, Emotions, and Public Argument in Baseball Culture: The Case of Carlos Zambrano," *Nine: A Journal of Baseball History and Culture* 21: 2 (Spring 2013), 56–76; Roberta Newman, "'Let's Just Say It Works for Me': Rafael Palmeiro, Major League Baseball and the Marketing of Viagra," *Nine: A Journal of Baseball History and Culture* 14:2 (Spring 2006): 1–14; and Larry R. Gerlach, "Crime and Punishment: The Marichal-Roseboro Incident," *Nine: A Journal of Baseball History and Culture* 12:2 (Spring 2004): 1–28.

14. John N. Ingham, "Managing Integration: Clemente, Willis, 'Harry the Hat,' and the Pittsburgh Pirates' 1967 Season of Discontent," *Nine: A Journal of Baseball History and Culture* 21:1 (Fall 2012): 69–102; and Samuel O. Regalado, "Hey Chico!: The Latin Identity in Major League Baseball," *Nine: A Journal of Baseball History and Culture* 11:1 (Fall 2002): 16–24.

15. See for example: Sam Quinones, *Antonio's Gun and Delfino's Dream: True Tales of Mexican Migration* (Albuquerque: University of New Mexico Press, 2007): 219–279.

16. Mark A. Grey, "Sport and Immigrant, Minority and Anglo Relations in Garden City (Kansas) High School," *Sociology of Sport Journal* 9 (1992): 255–270.

17. *Ibid.*, 256.

18. *Ibid.*, 259 and 262, in particular.

19. *Ibid.*, 266.

20. *Ibid.*, 268.

21. Sam Quinones, *Antonio's Gun and Delfino's Dream: True Tales of Mexican Migration* (Albuquerque: University of New Mexico Press, 2007): 219–279.

22. *Ibid.*, 220. A review of the 2012 season roster for the Buffaloes reveals that 24 of the 55 members (44 percent) of the football team is Hispanic surnamed. Obviously, it is not possible to tell from the roster if these are children of recent immigrants, or from the more "established" *familias.*

23. *Ibid.*, 222 and 239.

24. *Ibid.*, 227 and 241.

25. *Ibid.*, 244 and 245.

26. *Ibid.*, 278 and 279.

27. See the following for an example of this trend: Wayne Drehs, "Cultures are Teammates at Iowa High School," October 11, 2006. www.sports.espn.go.com/espn/hispa nichistory/news/story?id=2618295.

Chapter 1

1. Howard Bryant, *Shut Out: A Story of Race and Baseball in Boston* (New York: Routledge, 2002). For information on Bill Russell's experiences with the Celtics, please see: Bill Russell and Alan Steinberg, *Red and Me: My Coach, My Lifelong Friend* (New York: HarperCollins, 2009); Bill Russell and Taylor Branch, *Second Wind: The Memoirs of an Opinionated Man* (New York: Random House, 1979); and Aram Goudsouzian, *King of the Court: Bill Russell and the Basketball Revolution* (Berkeley: University of California Press, 2010).

2. *Ibid.*, 154. The story of Tommy Harper's dealings with the Red Sox are noted in Chapter 12 of this work, pages 147–155.

3. *Ibid.*, 127.

4. *Ibid.*, 130. For a discussion of the racial climate in Boston during this time, and the impact of sports upon such issues, please see: Michael Connelly, *Rebound: Basketball, Busing, Larry Bird and the Rebirth of Boston* (Minneapolis: Voyageur Press, 2008).

5. All relevant statistical materials concerning the Red Sox and other teams noted in this book were gleaned from either www.baseball-reference.com or www.baseball-almanac.com.

6. Bill Liston, "Mike Torrez: He Had to Shoot for His Supper," *Boston Herald American,* 1978, 51 and 53.

7. The Oakland barrio of Topeka dates from 1909 and is an area of concentration for Mexicans/Mexican Americans in the capital of Kansas. The first section, known as "little Mexico" was in the same general vicinity (near the Santa Fe tracks), but was eliminated in 1939. Please see: Roy Bird, "An Ethnic History of Shawnee County, Kansas," (Metropolitan Planning Commission, 1974):

67, 68 and 72; and Richard Santillan, "Mexican Social History in the Mid-West United States: A Study of Four Generations, 1915–1995," unpublished manuscript (copy in author's possession); and Karleen Wende, *Generations United* (Topeka: Kansas Humanities Council, 1994), particularly, Chapter 1.

8. For one example of this type of discrimination, please see the following interview: Antonio "Tony" Tabares, April 10, 2006. Oral History Project, Veterans Services. http://www.kansashistory.org/item/211484/text.

9. James N. Leiker, "Race Relations in the Sunflower State," *Kansas History* 25 (Autumn 2002): 214–236. See specifically, pg. 235.

10. Lorena Lopez, "Mexican Immigration in Topeka and [the] Santa Fe," in Karleen Wende, *Generations United*: 11–21, quote on p. 18.

11. James N. Leiker, "Race Relations in the Sunflower State," 229–231 and 233–235. The 1928 article is part of the Richard A. Santillan Midwest Latino Collection, "Kansas," Box 3, News-articles, Hispanics in Topeka, KS (1928–1987), Indiana University Northwest.

12. Cynthia Mines, *Riding the Rails to Kansas: The Mexican Immigrants*, N.p.: National Endowment for the Humanities, 1980.

13. *Ibid.*, 1 and 4.

14. *Ibid.*, 28, 31 and 40. Mexicans comprised roughly 12 percent of all foreign-born in the state, trailing only the Germans, who made up roughly 21 percent of this total population.

15. Lorena Lopez, "Social Mobility and Discrimination," in Karleen Wende, *Generations United*: 21–30, quote on p. 24.

16. Richard Santillan, "Mexican Social History in the MidWest United States: A Study of Four Generations, 1915–1995," unpublished manuscript (copy in author's possession), 37.

17. *Ibid.*, 44, 48, 57, 75 and 77. The specific information on the Torrez family is gleaned from oral history interviews with Mike and John Torrez in August of 2012. Copies of these interviews are in the author's possession.

18. *Ibid.*, 57.

19. *Ibid.*, 55–58. For information on how this impacted Mexicans in the western part of Kansas, please see: Henry Avila, "Immigration and Integration: The Mexican American Community in Garden City, Kansas, 1900–1950," *Kansas History* 20 (Spring 1997): 22–37; and Pamela Riney-Kehrberg, "Hard Times, Hungry Years: Failure of Poor Relief in Southwestern Kansas, 1930–1933," *Kansas History* 15 (Autumn 1992): 154–167.

20. Richard Santillan, "Mexican Social History in the MidWest United States: A Study of Four Generations, 1915–1995," 143.

21. Robert Oppenheimer, "Acculturation or Assimilation: Mexican Immigrants in Kansas, 1900 to World War II," *Western Historical Quarterly* 16, no. 4 (October 1985): 429–448. Quote on page 446.

22. *Ibid.*, 437.

23. *Ibid.*, 438 and 440.

24. Lorena Lopez, "Social Mobility and Discrimination," in Karleen Wende, *Generations United*, 26.

25. Richard Santillan, "Mexican Social History in the MidWest United States: A Study of Four Generations, 1915–1995," 80.

26. Robert Oppenheimer, "Acculturation or Assimilation: Mexican Immigrants in Kansas, 1900 to World War II," 441.

27. Richard Santillan, "Mexican Social History in the MidWest United States: A Study of Four Generations, 1915–1995," 49.

28. *Ibid.*, 77.

29. For more information on the community in and around Kansas City and the newspaper published there, please see: Michael M. Smith, "The Mexican Immigrant Press Beyond the Borderlands: The Case of *El Cosmopolita*, 1914–1919," *Great Plains Quarterly* 10 (Spring 1990): 71–85; and Michael M. Smith, "Mexicans in Kansas City: The First Generation, 1900–1920," *Perspectives in Mexican American Studies* 2 (1989): 29–57.

30. Michael M. Smith, "Mexicans in Kansas City," 37.

31. Michael M. Smith, "The Mexican Immigrant Press Beyond the Borderlands," 77–80.

32. Richard Santillan, "Mexican Social History in the MidWest United States: A Study of Four Generations, 1915–1995," 78 and 79.

33. *Ibid.*, 85. See also: Roy Bird, "An Ethnic History of Shawnee County, Kansas," (Metropolitan Planning Commission, 1974): 71 and 72. Information on the Diamante Club is also presented in José M. Garcia, "History of the Mexicans in Topeka, 1906–1966," 1973, 21. Copy of document in author's possession.

34. *Ibid.*, 73 and 74. See also: Helen Wallau, "Our Lady of Guadalupe Church," in Karleen Wende, *Generations United*, 31–37.

35. Helen Wallau, "Our Lady of Guadalupe Church," in Karleen Wende, *Generations United*, 32–34, 63 and 64.

36. Kevin Groenhagen, "Torrez, Church Prepare for Fiesta Mexicana," *Kaw Valley Senior Monthly*, 9, no. 1, July 2009, 1 and 3.

37. José M. Garcia, "History of the Mexicans in Topeka, 1906–1966," 1973, 14–19. Copy of this document in author's possession.

38. Dionicio Valdez, *Barrios Nortenos: St. Paul and Midwestern Mexican Communities in the Twentieth Century* (Austin: University of Texas Press, 2000), 130.

39. For an extensive discussion on this topic, please see: Jorge Iber and Arnoldo De Leon, *Hispanics in the American West* (Santa Barbara, CA: ABC-Clio, 2006), 233–244 and 260–261.

40. Hector Franco, "The Mexican People in the State of Kansas," doctoral dissertation (University of Wichita, 1950), 85, 87, 91.

41. *Ibid.*, 92, 115.

42. Anonymous, "Three Sons in Service," *Topeka State Journal*, December 6, 1942. Material is part of the Richard A. Santillan Midwest Latino Collection, "Kansas," Box 3, News-articles, Hispanics in Topeka, KS (1928–1987).

43. Richard Santillan, "Mexican Social History in the MidWest United States: A Study of Four Generations, 1915–1995," 178.

44. Materials are part of the Richard A. Santillan Midwest Latino Collection, "Kansas," Box 3, News-articles, Hispanics in Topeka, KS (1928–1987). None of these articles featured a by-line: "Sack that Carried Flour to Belgium, Returns," November 22, 1942; "Y Senoritas Hold Fellowship Banquet," November 21, 1942; and "Y Senoritas Club to Entertain for Mexican Soldiers," January 21, 1943.

45. Santillan Collection: Mrs. Tom McDade, "Justice and Fair Play," April 26, 1943. Another article that provides further examples of Mrs. McDade's activism among Topeka's Mexican Americans can be found in the *Topeka Journal* of May 7, 1948, by Joan Skipsey, "Making New Citizens Her Vital Work."

46. Richard Santillan, "Mexican Social History in the MidWest United States: A Study of Four Generations, 1915–1995," 193.

47. *Ibid.*, 194.

48. *Ibid.*, 187, 188, 190 and 191.

49. Jorge Iber, Samuel O. Regalado, José M. Alamillo and Arnoldo De Leon, *Latinos in U.S. Sport: A History of Isolation, Cultural Identity, and Acceptance* (Champaign, IL: Human Kinetics, 2011), 158–163. See also: Jorge Iber and Arnoldo De Leon, *Hispanics in the American West*, 244–251.

50. *Ibid.*, 170–173.

51. Richard Santillan, "Mexican Social History in the MidWest United States: A Study of Four Generations, 1915–1995," 242.

52. *Ibid.*, 95. Another article that examines this topic is by José A. Alamillo, "Peloteros in Paradise: Mexican American Baseball and Oppositional Politics in Southern California,

1930–1950," *Western Historical Quarterly*, 34, n. 2 (Summer 2003): 191–211.

Chapter 2

1. Bob Hartzell, "Prep Parade," *Topeka Capital Journal* October 19, 1967, 38. Binder 5018, Mike Torrez Scrapbook Collection, Southwest Collection, Texas Tech University.

2. Cited in Jorge Iber, Samuel O. Regalado, José M. Alamillo, and Arnoldo De Leon, *Latinos in U.S. Sport: A History of Isolation, Cultural Identity and Acceptance* (Champaign, IL: Human Kinetics, 2011), 74.

3. *Ibid.*, 75.

4. Ignacio M. Garcia, *When Mexicans Could Play Ball: Basketball, Race and Identity in San Antonio, 1928–1945* (Austin: University of Texas Press, 2013), 219.

5. For many more examples, please see: Jorge Iber, et al., *Latinos in U.S. Sports.*

6. "Football in Mexico," *Dallas Morning News*, December 7, 1896, 6; and "Football in Mexico," *Los Angeles Times*, January 11, 1897, 3.

7. For an overview of the rise and history of high school football in Texas, please see: Mike Bynum, ed., *King Football: Greatest Moments in Texas High School Football History* (Birmingham, AL: Epic Sports Classics, 2003). Specifically, see: David Barron, "The Birth of Texas Schoolboy Football," 26–39.

8. Jorge Iber, et al., *Latinos in U.S. Sports*, 90–94.

9. See the following: "Mississippi Eleven In Mexico City for Clash with Mexicans," *Dallas Morning News*, November 20, 1929, 21; "Mexican Gridders Badly Beaten by Louisiana College," *Dallas Morning News*, October 5, 1930, 3; "Santone Eleven Drubs Mexicans," *Dallas Morning News*, November 16, 1930, 5; "Tulsa U. Smothers Mexican Gridders," *Dallas Morning News*, November 8, 1931, 12; "Jeff Defeats Mexicans," *Dallas Morning News*, December 17, 1933, 4; and "San Antonio Tech Wins Over Mexican Eleven," *Dallas Morning News*, November 23, 1935, 3.

10. William Berlin Goolsby, "Native Mexican Sports," *Dallas Morning News*, March 20, 1938, 4.

11. Quoted in Jorge Iber, "On-Field Foes and Racial Misconceptions: The 1961 Donna Redskins and Their Drive to the Texas State Football Championship," in Jorge Iber and Samuel O. Regalado, eds., *Mexican Americans and Sport: A Reader on Athletics and Barrio Life* (College Station: Texas A&M University Press, 2007): 121–144. Quote on page 123.

12. Jorge Iber, et al., *Latinos in U.S. Sports*,

126–131. See also: Jorge Iber, "Mexican Americans of South Texas Football: The Athletic and Coaching Careers of E.C. Lerma and Bobby Cavazos, 1932–1965," *Southwestern Historical Quarterly*, 55, n. 4 (April 2002): 617–633; "Bobby Cavazos: A Vaquero in the Backfield," *College Football Historical Society*, 14, no. 4 (August 2001): 1–5; and Mario Longoria, *Athletes Remembered: Mexicano/ Latino Professional Football Players, 1929– 1970* (Tempe, AZ: Bilingual Press, 1997): 3– 5 and 141–143.

13. William Berlin Goolsby, "Native Mexican Sports," *Dallas Morning News*, March 20, 1938, 4.

14. José M. Alamillo, *"Peloteros* in Paradise: Mexican American Baseball and Oppositional Politics in Southern California, 1930–1950," *Western Historical Quarterly* 34, no. 2 (Summer 2003): 191–211, quote on page 192. See also: Jorge Iber, et al., *Latinos in U.S. Sports*, 122–124.

15. José M. Alamillo, "Playing Across Borders: Transnational Sports and Identities in Southern California and Mexico, 1930– 1945," *Pacific Historical Review*, 79, no. 3 (August 2010): 360–392.

16. For more information on this North Dakota team, please see: Tom Dunkel, *Color Blind: The Forgotten Team that Broke Baseball's Color Line* (New York: Atlantic Monthly Press, 2013).

17. Alan Klein, *Baseball on the Border: A Tale of Two Laredos* (Princeton, NJ: Princeton University Press, 1997), 50–61.

18. Alexander Wolff, "The Barrio Boys," *Sports Illustrated* June 27, 2011. http://cnnsi. printthis.clickability.com/pt/cpt?expire=& title=IN+1949+...trated.cnn.com%2Fvault%2 Farticle%2Fmagazine%2FMAG1187581%2Fi ndex.htm. Accessed on March 17, 2014. For more information on Mexicans/Mexican Americans and baseball during this era, please also see: Richard A. Santillan, et. al., *Mexican Baseball in the Central Coast* (Charleston, SC: Arcadia Publishing, 2013). Professor Santillan has published a series of these picture books, with the item noted being but the most recent.

19. Jorge Iber, et al., *Latinos in U.S. Sports*, 97–100 and 136–138.

20. *Ibid.*, 102–103, 139–140, and 177–180. See also: Troy Rondinone, *Friday Night Fighter: Gaspar "Indio" Ortega and the Golden Age of Television Boxing* (Champaign: University of Illinois Press, 2013); and Tom I. Romero II, "Wearning the Red, Which, and Blue Trunks of Aztlan: Rodolfo 'Corky' Gonzales and the Convergence of American and Chicano Nationalism," in Jorge Iber and

Samuel O. Regalado, eds., *Mexican Americans and Sports: A Reader on Athletics and Barrio Life* (College Station, TX: Texas A&M University Press, 2006): 89–120.

21. Gilbert Rogin, "Capital of the World," *Sports Illustrated*, September 8, 1958. http:// sportsillustrated.cnn.com/vault/article/mag azine/MAG1002791/index.htm. Accessed on March 24, 2014.

22. James Murray, "The Little World of Bantams Gets a New Champ," July 20, 1959. http://sportsillustrated.cnn.com/vault/ article/magazine/MAG1070797/index.htm. Accessed on March 24, 2014.

23. Richard Santillan, "Mexican Social History in the Midwest, 1915–1995," unpublished manuscript, copy in author's possession, 104.

24. Domingo Ricart, "Just Across the Tracks: Report on a Survey of Five Mexican Communities in the State of Kansas," University of Kansas, 1950, 42.

25. Richard Santillan, "Mexican Baseball Teams in the Midwest, 1916–1965: The Politics of Cultural Survival and Civil Rights," *Perspectives in Mexican American Studies* vol. 7 (2000): 131–151.

26. *Ibid.*

27. Paula Jasso-Wedel, "A Tribute to the Newton Holy Name Softball Tournaments: Looking Back 40 Years," July 1988. Unpublished manuscript. Copy in author's possession.

28. Richard Santillan, "Mexican Social History in the Midwest, 1915–1995," unpublished manuscript, copy in author's possession, 239.

29. All of the following stories are from the *Garden City Telegram* and are just some of the items that note the presence of Latinos on scholastic and other basketball teams in the region prior to World War II. "Tri-Motors Entered the Victory Column Last Night," October 17, 1939, 6; "Liberal Wins vs. Copeland in OT," December 13, 1939, 6; "Larkin has no Trouble Defeating Deerfield," December 16, 1939, 6; "Copeland 41, Plains 21," January 13, 1940, 4; "Larkin Rebounds from Loss," February 3, 1940, 4; and "Larkin High School Wins Game vs. Johnson High," January 4, 1941, 4. Richard Santillan, "Mexican Social History in the Midwest, 1915–1995," unpublished manuscript, copy in author's possession, 111 and 112.

30. For information on the Omaha tournament, please see: "'Golden Anniversary,' Omaha Mexican Basketball Tournaments, 1954–2004" program. See also: Allen Quakenbush, *Topeka Capital Journal*, "Hispanic Hoops," January 8, 1991, 7-C and program

for the "Topeka Mexican Basketball Tournament, January 20th and 21st, 1973." Copies of the various items are in author's possession.

31. See the following, all from the *Garden City Telegram*: "Fighters to Wichita," March 8, 1941, 4; "Around Town," August 16, 1941, 1; Brett Marshall, "Local Leaders Trace Sport's History," in "Star Power" supplement, September 15, 2011, 2 and 10 and Ortiz Has Made it to Top of Boxing World with Hard Work," 6 and 8; Jordan Wickstrom, "Rios Says He Can't Wait for Return to the Ring," 4 and 5. See also: Richard Santillan, "Mexican Social History in the Midwest, 1915–1995," unpublished manuscript, copy in author's possession, 110 and 110 and 251 and 252; Chris Mannix, "Fight of His Life," http://sportsillustrated.cnn.com/vault/article/magazine/MAG1190469/index.htm. Accessed on March 31, 2014; and "Ex-Champ Victor Ortiz Ready to Put Mayweather Episode Behind Him," http://sportsillustrated.cnn.com/2012/writers/chris_mannix/01/27/ortizberto/index.html. Accessed on March 31, 2014.

Chapter 3

1. See: Bob Hurt, "Capitalizing on Sports," February 21, 1968, *Topeka Capital Journal*; Neal Russo, "Rookie Torrez Ducks Disaster in First Victory," *The Sporting News*, May 4, 1968, 13.

2. There is a plethora of materials that cover the arrival and work history of Mexicans in various parts of the American West and Midwest. A good, basic textbook with which to commence a reading of this literature would be Jorge Iber and Arnoldo De Leon, *Hispanics in the American West*, Santa Barbara, CA: ABC-Clio, 2006.

3. These materials come from a family genealogy provided by John Torrez. A copy of these materials is in the author's possession.

4. Interview with members of the Torrez family, August 2012. Family members included: Mike Torrez, John Torrez, Louis Torrez, Maria Torrez, and others. Copies of interviews are in the author's possession.

5. *Ibid.*

6. *Ibid.*

7. Robert Oppenheimer, "Acculturation or Assimilation: Mexican Immigrants in Kansas, 1900 to World War II," *Western Historical Quarterly* 16, no. 4 (October 1985): 429–448.

8. *Ibid.*, 432.

9. Interview with members of the Torrez family, August 2012.

10. Jorge Iber, Samuel O. Regalado, José M. Alamillo, and Arnoldo De Leon, *Latinos in U.S. Sport: A History of Isolation, Cultural Identity, and Acceptance*, 158–161.

11. Santillan, "Mexican Social History in the Mid-West United States: A Study of Four Generations, 1915–1995," 242.

12. Maury Allen, "Mets' Torrez Weathering Latest Strom," *New York Post*, May 17, 1983, Binder 18044, Mike Torrez Collection, Southwest Collection Archive, Texas Tech University.

13. Interview with John Torrez, August 2012. Copy in author's possession.

14. *Ibid.* See also: "Golden Anniversary Omaha Mexican Basketball Tournaments: 1954–2004," sponsored by the Mexican American Athletic Club, Omaha, Nebraska. Copy of this document is in author's possession.

15. "9th Annual Topeka Mexican Basketball Tournament" brochure. Copy of this document is in author's possession.

16. Interviews with John and Mike Torrez, August 2012. See also: "9th Annual Topeka Mexican Basketball Tournament," brochure. A copy of this item is in the author's possession. For a discussion on a similar topic, please see: Allen Quakenbush, "Hispanic Hoops," *Topeka Capital Journal* January 8, 1991, 7-C.

17. Neal Russo, "Torrez Left Benson with Stinging Hand," *St. Louis Post-Dispatch*, April 23, 1968, C1.

18. Interview with John and Mike Torrez, August 2012.

19. *Ibid.*

20. Interview with members of the Torrez family, August 2012.

21. Richard Santillan, "Mexican Social History in the MidWest United States," unpublished manuscript, 1995, 254.

22. Interview with John and Mike Torrez, August 2012.

23. *Ibid.*

24. *Ibid.*

25. *Ibid.*

26. Matt Walsh, "1977 Kansan of the Year: Mike Torrez," *Topeka Capital Journal*, January 1, 1978, 19–20.

27. John Grow, "Torrez Wants to Leave His Mark," *St. Louis Post Dispatch*, July 2, 1978, 4F. For a discussion on a similar situation in regard to Latino athletes and dating, please see: Jorge Iber, "On Field Foes and Racial Misperceptions: The 1961 Donna Redskins and Their Drive to the Texas State Football Championship," in Jorge Iber and

Samuel O. Regalado, eds., *Mexican Americans and Sport: A Reader on Athletics and Barrio Life* (College Station: Texas A&M University Press, 2007): 121–144.

28. Bob Hartzell, "Prep Parade," *Topeka Capital Journal,* October 19, 1967, 38, Binder 5018. Mike Torrez Scrapbook Collection, Southwest Collection, Texas Tech University.

29. "Torrez *Started* as 'Skinny' Cager," *St. Louis Globe Democrat*, November 7, 1977, 14B.

30. Neal Russo, "Torrez Left Benson with Stinging Hand."

31. Neal Russo, "Spirit of St. Louis Starts with Swinger Orlando," *The Sporting News*, May 25, 1968, 3 and 4. For a different perspective on the integration of whites, Latinos and African Americans on a Major League ball club during this era, please see: John Ingham, "Managing Integration: Clemente, Wills, 'Harry the Hat,' and the Pittsburgh Pirates' 1967 Season of Discontent," *Nine: A Journal of Baseball History and Culture* 21, no. 1, Fall 2012, 69–102.

32. For a discussion on the perceived limitations of Latinos/Mexican Americans as athletes, please see: Jorge Iber, Samuel O. Regalado, José M. Alamillo, and Arnoldo De Leon, *Latinos in U.S. Sport: A History of Isolation, Cultural Identity, and Acceptance* (Champaign, IL: Human Kinetics, 2011): 71–76 and 116–118. See also: Robert E. Copley, *The Tall Mexican: The Life of Hank Aguirre: All Star Pitcher, Businessman, Humanitarian* (Houston: Piñata Books, 2000).

33. Interview with John and Mike Torrez, August 2012.

34. Jen Clark, "When We Were Young: History Examined Through Kids' Perspective," *Topeka Capital Journal*, November 12, 2011, 1A and 14A.

35. Kevin Haskin, "Finally Four: No. 1 Torrez Armed for Success," *Topeka Capital Journal*, August 28, 2011, 1D and 10D.

36. Neal Russo, "Torrez Left Benson with Stinging Hand."

Chapter 4

1. Bill Connors, *Tulsa World,* "Sports of the World," 1968, Binder 7015, Mike Torrez Scrapbook Collection, Southwest Collection, Texas Tech University.

2. *Ibid.*

3. Bob Broeg, "Cards Pitching Depth Reminds Devine of '41," *The Sporting News*, April 20, 1968, 14.

4. *Ibid.*

5. Dick Kaegel, "Who Are Blue-Ribbon Greenies of '68?" *The Sporting News,* April 27, 1968, 11.

6. For an overview of the integration of this classification of professional baseball in the South, please see: Bruce Adelson, *Brushing Back Jim Crow: The Integration of Minor League Baseball in the American South* (Charlottesville: University of Virginia Press, 2007).

7. Samuel O. Regalado, "The Minor League Experience of Latin American Baseball Players in Western Communities, 1950–1970," *Journal of the West*, 26, no. 1 (January 1987): 65–70.

8. *Ibid.*

9. The roster of the 1965 Raleigh Cardinals can be accessed at: http://www.baseball-reference.com/minors/team.cgi?id=3b43bae6. There were two other Spanish-surnamed athletes on this 1965 Raleigh team, Victor Torres and José Villar, but their places of birth were not indicated on the team roster. Neither player reached the majors.

10. Bob Wills, "First Victory 'G-R-E-A-T' Sings Torrez," Binder 21004, Mike Torrez Scrapbook Collection, Southwest Collection, Texas Tech University.

11. Bruce Phillips, "Mike Torrez Proves Plenty Tough on Sox," and Joe Tiede, "R-Cards Win Again at Expense of W-S," Binders 21003 and 21006, Mike Torrez Scrapbook Collection, Southwest Collection, Texas Tech University.

12. Lloyd Johnson and Miles Wolff, *The Encyclopedia of Minor League Baseball: The Official Records of Minor League Baseball* (Durham, NC: Baseball America, 1993), 316. The hitting and pitching statistics for the Raleigh Cardinals squad of 1965 are drawn from: http://www.baseball-reference.com/minors/team.cgi?id=3b43bae6.

13. Ken Wynn, "Cards, Torrez Sweep Astros," Binder 7018, Mike Torrez Scrapbook Collection, Southwest Collection, Texas Tech University.

14. Lloyd Johnson and Miles Wolff, *The Encyclopedia of Minor League Baseball: The Official Records of Minor League Baseball*, 317. The statistics for Mike Torrez and the Rock Hill Cardinals squad of 1966 are drawn from: http://www.baseball-reference.com/minors/team.cgi?id=bb2464e8. Copy of the letter from Western Carolinas League President, John H. Moss to Mike Torrez, dated July 5, 1966. Copy in author's possession.

15. Jim Bailey, "Torrez Prevails, 5–2, Travelers Tie Sonics," *Little Rock Gazette*, July 18, 1966, Binder 7017, Mike Torrez Scrapbook Collection, Southwest Collection, Texas Tech University.

16. Bob Howell, "Sun Kings Finally Defeat Travelers," *Arkansas Democrat*, Binder 21008, Mike Torrez Scrapbook Collection, Southwest Collection, Texas Tech University.

17. Bob Howell, *Arkansas Democrat*, "Unearned Runs Whip Torrez, Travelers," Binder 21005, Mike Torrez Scrapbook Collection, Southwest Collection, Texas Tech University.

18. The individual statistics for Mike Torrez's minor league career are also available at: www.baseball-reference.com/minors/player.cgi?id=torrez001mic.

19. Bill Connors, *Tulsa World*, "Sports of the World," Binder 7015, Mike Torrez Scrapbook Collection, Southwest Collection, Texas Tech University.

20. Bob Hentzen, "Sports Journal," Binders 21014 and 21020, Mike Torrez Scrapbook Collection, Southwest Collection, Texas Tech University.

21. Season statistics for the 1967 Cardinals found at www.baseball-reference.com/teams/STL/1967.shtml.

22. Bob Eger, "Giants in 4-Game Sweep Over Tulsa," and *Tulsa World*, "Phoenix Edges Oilers, 3 to 2, in 11th Inning," Binders 7002 and 7014, Mike Torrez Scrapbook Collection, Southwest Collection, Texas Tech University.

23. Dick Suagee, "Spahn Likes His 'Winning Lineup,'" *Tulsa Tribune*, Binder 7005, Mike Torrez Scrapbook Collection, Southwest Collection, Texas Tech University.

24. Dick Suagee, "Cosman, Hot Oilers Bid For 5th in Row Tonight," *Tulsa Tribune*, Binder 7004, Mike Torrez Scrapbook Collection, Southwest Collection, Texas Tech University.

25. Dick Suagee, "Makeshift Crew Quiets Oilers," *Tulsa Tribune*, Binder 7010, Mike Torrez Scrapbook Collection, Southwest Collection, Texas Tech University.

26. *Tulsa Tribune*, "Padres Cash 5 Hits To Beat Oilers, 7–3," Binder 7012, Mike Torrez Scrapbook Collection, Southwest Collection, Texas Tech University.

27. John Ferguson, "Think ... and Serve Up Strikes—It's Paying Off for Tulsa's Torrez," *The Sporting News*, September 2, 1967, 37.

28. *Tulsa Tribune*, "Blister or Not, Torrez Finishes What He Starts," Binder 7020, Mike Torrez Scrapbook Collection, Southwest Collection, Texas Tech University.

29. John Ferguson, "Think ... and Serve Up Strikes—It's Paying Off for Tulsa's Torrez," *The Sporting News*, September 2, 1967, 37.

30. Dick Suagee, "Oilers Streak To Latin Beat-Cha-Cha-Cha," Binder 7011, Mike Torrez Scrapbook Collection, Southwest Collec-tion, Texas Tech University. It should be noted that the 1967 Oilers also featured one Venezuelan and two Puerto Ricans on their roster. See: http://www.baseball-reference.com/minors/team.cgi?id=fb3a44dd.

31. William Leggett, "Some Hot Rookies for a New Season," *Sports Illustrated*, March 11, 1968. Accessed at: http://sportsillustrated.cnn.com/vault/article/magazine/MAG1080929/index.htm

32. Neal Russo, "Bucs, Buck Card Tide, Glimpse Hot Torrez," *St. Louis Post Dispatch*, September 11, 1967, 4C.

33. William Leggett, "Some Hot Rookies for a New Season," *Sports Illustrated*, March 11, 1968. Accessed at: http://sportsillustrated.cnn.com/vault/article/magazine/MAG1080929/index.htm. See also: Doug Feldmann, *El Birdos: The 1967 and 1968 St. Louis Cardinals* (Jefferson, NC: McFarland, 2007), 148.

34. Bob Hartzell, "Prep Parade," *Topeka Capital Journal*, October 19, 1967, 38, Binder 5018, Mike Torrez Scrapbook Collection, Southwest Collection, Texas Tech University.

35. Fernando Vicioso, "Hot Bat Carries Carty Into Top Spot at .376," *The Sporting News*, January 6, 1968, 53.

36. Bob Hurt, "Capitalizing on Sports," *Topeka Capital Journal*, February 21, 1968, 11, Binder 5010, Mike Torrez Scrapbook Collection, Southwest Collection, Texas Tech University.

37. Bob Hartzell, "Prep Parade," *Topeka Capital Journal*, October 19, 1967, 38, Binder 5018, Mike Torrez Scrapbook Collection, Southwest Collection, Texas Tech University.

38. Dave Grote, "N.L. Teams Ready to Reap Big Crop of Talented Frosh," *The Sporting News*, March 2, 1968, 16.

39. William Leggett, "Some Hot Rookies for a New Season," *Sports Illustrated*, March 11, 1968. Accessed at: http://sportsillustrated.cnn.com/vault/article/magazine/MAG1080929/index.htm.

40. Neal Russo, "Rookie Torrez Ducks Disaster in First Victory," *The Sporting News*, May 4, 1968, pg. 13. See also: Doug Feldmann, *El Birdos: The 1967 and 1968 St. Louis Cardinals*, 239. The statistical information for this game was gleaned from Retrosheet. The information used here was obtained free of charge from and is copyrighted by Retrosheet. Interested parties may contact Retrosheet at: www.retrosheet.org.

41. Larry Harnly, "Cards' Torrez Needs to Pitch," *Springfield Journal-Register*, May 31, 1968, 24.

42. "Pacific Coast League," *The Sporting News*, June 15, 1968, 32.

43. Dick Suagee, "Torrez Eyes Fast Return to Redbirds," *Tulsa Tribune*, June 1, 1968. See also: Jesse Owens, "Hutto, Hicks Belt Homers as Torrez Halts Spokane," *Tulsa World*, June 1, 1968.

44. John Ferguson, "Torrez Gigs 89ers as 7,892 Roar," *Tulsa World*, June, Binder 11006, Mike Torrez Scrapbook Collection, Southwest Collection, Texas Tech University.

45. Bob Broeg, "Red Takes Rosy View If Torrez is Torrid," *The Sporting News*, March 8, 1969, 28.

46. The statistical information for this season comes from: www.baseball-reference.com/minors/player.cgi?id=torrez001mic. See also: John Ferguson, "Oilers Blend Defense, Pitching and Swatting Into Rocket Fuel," *The Sporting News*, September 28, 1968, 31–32 and "Spahn on His Way Back?" *Topeka Daily Capital*, August 1, 1968, 42.

47. Bill Connors, "Sports of the World," *Tulsa World*, Binder 7015, Mike Torrez Scrapbook Collection, Southwest Collection, Texas Tech University.

48. Neal Russo, "Cards Taking 4 Former Redbirds on Japan Trip," *The Sporting News*, November 2, 1968.

49. Mike Berger, "Redbirds Hold No Terror For Polished Nippon Club," *The Sporting News*, November 16, 1968, 37.

50. "Torrez Posts 5–3 Victory for Cards," *Topeka State Journal*, November 12, 1968, 13.

51. Kent Nixon, "Happy Days for Torrez," Binders 6013 and 9006, Mike Torrez Scrapbook Collection, Southwest Collection, Texas Tech University.

52. *Ibid.* See also: Neal Russo, "If Rugged Redbirds Have One Worry, It's on Mound Staff," *The Sporting News*, March 1, 1969; Mike Berger, "Redbirds Hold No Terror For Polished Nippon Club," *The Sporting News*, November 16, 1968, 37; and "Redhead Says Japan Teams Overwork Hurlers," *The Sporting News*, December 7, 1968, 36.

53. Benjamin G. Rader, *Baseball: A History of America's Game*, 2nd edition (Urbana: University of Illinois Press, 2002), 205.

54. *Ibid.*, 206.

55. Neal Russo, "If Rugged Redbirds Have One Worry, It's on Mound Staff," *The Sporting News*, March 1, 1968, 10. See also: Bob Broeg, "Redbirds Twitter Over Rookie Pair Of Hague and Day," *The Sporting News*, March 22, 1969.

56. Bob Broeg, "Red Takes Rosy View if Torrez Is Torrid," *The Sporting News*, March 8, 1969, 28.

57. Bob Broeg, "Vada Buffs Already Shiny Card Picture," *The Sporting News*, March 29, 1969, 12; Bob Hentzen, "Baseball Returns."

58. Robert H. Boyle, "The Latins Storm Las Grandes Ligas," August 9, 1965. http://www.si.com/vault/1965/08/09/606430/the-latins-storm-las-grandes-ligas.

59. *Ibid.*

60. John N. Ingham, "Managing Integration: Clemente, Wills, 'Harry the Hat,' and the Pittsburgh Pirates' 1967 Season of Discontent," *Nine: A Journal of Baseball History and Culture*, 21, no. 1 (Fall 2012): 69–102.

61. *Ibid.*

62. Neal Russo, "Spirit of St. Louis Starts with Swinger Orlando," *The Sporting News*, May 25, 1968, 3.

63. "'El Birdos' Will Fly Again: 1968 Cardinals May Eclipse Glory of 1934 'Gas House Gang,'" *Ebony*, 143–145. For more background on this party, please see: Doug Feldmann, *El Birdos: The 1967 and 1968 St. Louis Cardinals*, 178–179.

64. "Cards Payroll Gives Insight," *The State Journal*, April 2, 1969, 16.

65. Doug Feldmann, *El Birdos: The 1967 and 1968 St. Louis Cardinals*, 363.

66. Manuel G. Gonzalez, *Mexicanos: A History of Mexicans in the United States*, 2nd Edition (Bloomington: Indiana University Press, 2009), and Jorge Iber and Arnoldo De Leon, *Hispanics in the American West* (Santa Barbara, CA: ABC-Clio, 2006).

67. Santillan, 281, 284, 287, and 295.

68. Thomas Rodriguez, *Americano: My Journey to the Dream* (Topeka: Amigos Publishing, 2004).

69. *Ibid.*, 276 , 278 and 279.

70. Jorge Iber, Samuel O. Regalado, José M. Alamillo, and Arnoldo De Leon, *Latinos in U.S. Sport: A History of Isolation, Cultural Identity, and Acceptance* (Champaign, IL: Human Kinetics, 2011).

71. *Ibid.*, 209–210.

72. Rick Peterson, "Recalling Another Era," *Topeka Capital-Journal*, July 19, 1998, 3-G.

Chapter 5

1. Neal Russo, "One Mistake Foils Torrez No-Hit Bid," *St. Louis Post-Dispatch* April 16, 1970, 1.

2. Bob Broeg, "Red Takes Rosy View if Torrez is Torrid," *The Sporting News,* March 8, 1969, 28.

3. Bob Broeg, "Vida Buffs Already Shiny Card Picture," *The Sporting News*, March 29, 1969, 12.

4. *Ibid.*

5. Bob Hentzen, "Baseball Returns to KC," *Topeka Daily Capital,* April 5, 1969, 15;

and "Torrez' Pitching, Double Edge KC," *Topeka Daily Capital,* Binders 9014 and 9015, Mike Torrez Scrapbook Collection, Southwest Collection, Texas Tech University.

6. Statistical information from Retrosheet for games on April 16, 20, and May 2, 1969.

7. Statistical information from Retrosheet for games on May 9–10, 1969. See also: *The Sporting News,* May 24, 1969, 4 and 29.

8. Statistical information from Retrosheet for games on May 24, 31, June 5 and 11, 1969.

9. Statistical information from Retrosheet for games on June 22, 28 and 29, 1969. See also, Neal Russo, "Chuck Taylor, as Chucker, Suits Redbirds to a T," *The Sporting News,* July 26, 1969, 24.

10. Bob Hentzen, "Torrez Eyes 1964 Repeat," *Topeka Daily Capital,* July 24, 1969.

11. *Ibid.*

12. For a discussion of the significance of an ethnic community "claiming" a professional athlete, please see: Nicolas P. Ciotola, "Spignesi, Sinatra, and the Pittsburgh Steelers: Franco's Italian Army as an Expression of Ethnic Identity, 1972–1977," *Journal of Sport History* 27 (Summer 2000): 271–289.

13. Statistical information from Retrosheet for games on July 27, August 7, and September 19, 1969.

14. Neal Russo, "Torrez and Torre Leading Torrid Tempo by El Birdos," *The Sporting News,* August 16, 1969, 7.

15. Neil Russo, "Cards Flout Laws of Nature, Rise in West and Set in East," *The Sporting News,* August 30, 1969, 4.

16. Neil Russo, "The Demise of the Ailing Redbirds—Now It's Official," *The Sporting News,* October 4, 1969, 21.

17. Curt Flood and Richard Carter, *The Way It Is* (New York City: Trident Press, 1971).

18. Doug Feldmann, *Gibson's Last Stand: The Rise, Fall and Near Misses of the St. Louis Cardinals, 1969–1975* (Columbia: University of Missouri Press, 2011), 38–40.

19. *Ibid.,* 36.

20. *Ibid.,* 74.

21. Fernando Vicioso, "Licey Carts Off Dominican Season, Playoff Laurels," *The Sporting News,* February 14, 1970, 47.

22. Neal Russo, "Winter Ball Adds Sheen to Torrez' Mound Feats," *The Sporting News,* February 7, 1970, 43.

23. See: Neal Russo, "Swift Cardenal to Roam CF for Cards," *The Sporting News,* November 22, 1969, 35; Fernando Vicioso, "Licey Comes Alive, Takes League Lead," *The*

Sporting News, December 27, 1969, 47; and "Baseball Briefs," *The Sporting News,* January 17, 1970, 6.

24. Neal Russo, "Cards Counting on Latins to Ward Off Calendar Hoodoo," *The Sporting News,* January 10, 1970, 47.

25. Statistical information from Retrosheet for games on April 9, 15, 22, 28, and May 4 and 10, 1970.

26. Neal Russo, "No Easy Rest of N.L. Hurlers with Simmons Awake," *The Sporting News,* June 27, 1970, 23; and "Readhead Lay It on the Line and Cards Snap to Attention," *The Sporting News,* July 4, 1970, 12.

27. Statistical information from Retrosheet for games on June 20, 22, and July 2, 1970.

28. "Pitching Averages," *The Sporting News,* August 8, 1970, 26.

29. See the following: Statistical information from Retrosheet for games on July 7, 12, 19, 24, 29, August 3, 25, 31, September 4, 7, 13, 18, and 24, 1970. Neal Russo, "Gibson Last Forlorn Hope of Cardinals' Sinking Ship," *The Sporting News,* July 25, 1970, 18; "Gibson Signs for 150 Grand," *The Sporting News,* October 17, 1970, 24; and "Cards See Shaw as Bullpen Sleeper," *The Sporting News,* January 16, 1971, 57.

30. Doug Feldmann, *Gibson's Last Stand,* 102–109. Quote is from page 109.

31. Bob Broeg, "Southpaw Steve Could Be Redbirds' Secret Weapon," *The Sporting News,* April 3, 1971, 28.

32. Neal Russo, "Redhead Sees Blue Beyond Storm Clouds Over Birds' Nest," *The Sporting News,* April 17, 1971, 16.

33. Bob Hentzen, "Streamlined Torrez Eyes Comeback," *Topeka Capital Journal,* Binder 16017, Mike Torrez Scrapbook Collection, Southwest Collection, Texas Tech University.

34. Statistical information from Retrosheet for games on April 13, 18, 23, 28, May 9, 21, 24, June 7 and 12, 1971.

35. Neal Russo, "Satorini, Reynolds Bolster Cards Hill Staff," *The Sporting News,* July 3, 1971, 10.

36. See: http://www.baseball-reference.com/players/t/torrmi01.shtml.

37. Ian MacDonald, "Expos Stymied, Seeking 4th Starter," *The Sporting News,* July 3, 1971, 13.

38. See the following: "Winnipeg Entertains Two Sellout Crowds," and "How They Stand," *The Sporting News,* July 10, 1971, 37; and http://www.baseball-reference.com/minors/league.cgi?id=2fdac6bc.

39. See the following: "Mike Torrez Wins," *The Sporting News,* July 10, 1971, 38; "Inter-

national Index for Saturday, June 26th, 1971," *The Sporting News*, July 17, 1971, 57; "Major Flashes, New Tune by Mauch," *The Sporting News*, September 4, 1971, 34; Ian MacDonald, "Day and Staub Boost Their Swatting Marks," *The Sporting News*, September 11, 1971, 8 and 24; and "Major Flashes, Torrez Trims Down," *The Sporting News*, October 9, 1971, 27.

40. Ian MacDonald, "Starter Role with Expos? Sounds Good to Lemaster," *The Sporting News*, October 30, 1971, 23; and "Expos Get Taylor to Mend Bullpen," *The Sporting News*, November 6, 1971, 48. See also: Eduardo Moncada, "Tovar Swinging Torrid Bat in Venezuela," *The Sporting News*, December 4, 1971, 55.

41. Bob Hartzell, "Torrez Looks to Next Year," *Topeka Capital Journal*, Binder 19019, Mike Torrez Scrapbook Collection, Southwest Archive, Texas Tech University.

42. Ian MacDonald, "Trim Torrez Balloons Expo Win Total," *The Sporting News*, May 20, 1972, 20.

43. Statistical information from Retrosheet for games on April 23, 29, May 3, 9, 14, 18, 22, 27, June 2, 7, 13, 18, 23, and 27, 1972.

44. Doug Feldmann, *Gibson's Last Stand*, 156.

45. Statistical information from Retrosheet for game on July 23, 1972.

46. Ian MacDonald, "Torrez' Blazer Signals Shot at 20-Win Season," *The Sporting News*, July 1, 1972, 11 and 26.

47. "Major Flashes—Torrez Masters Slider," *The Sporting News*, July 8, 1972, 30.

48. See: http://www.baseball-reference.com/teams/MON/1972.shtml.

49. Ian MacDonald, "Expos Rest Hopes on Making Big Deal," *The Sporting News*, December 16, 1972, 50.

50. Ian MacDonald, "Mauch to Take Aim at 'Too Many Parachutes,'" *The Sporting News*, February 17, 1973, 44.

51. Ian MacDonald, "23 Victories Is Torrez' Goal," *The Sporting News*, January 13, 1973, 49.

52. Ian MacDonald, "Mike Torrez Sees Early Signing with Expos as Eagleson Takes Hand in Contract Talks," *The Gazette*, February 14, 1973.

53. Statistical information from Retrosheet for games of April 6, 10, and 15, 1973.

54. Statistical information from Retrosheet for game of April 19 and 24, 1973.

55. Statistical information from Retrosheet for game of July 20, 1973.

56. Statistical information from Retrosheet for game of July 28 and August 1, 1973.

57. Statistical information from Retrosheet for games of August 5, 9, 13, 15, 20, 25, 29, and September 2, 1973.

58. Statistical information from Retrosheet for games of September 7, 15, 19, and 23, 1973.

59. Ian MacDonald, "Expos Chances Hurt Again by 'One Black Week,'" *The Sporting News*, October 6, 1973. See also: http://www.baseball-reference.com/teams/MON/1973.shtml.

60. Author interview with Jacques Doucet, April 28, 2012.

61. Statistical information from Retrosheet for games of July 1, 6, 10, 15, 20, and 28, 1973.

62. Author interview with Ken Singleton, April 24, 2012.

63. Danielle Gagnon Torrez and Ken Lizotte, *High Inside: Memoirs of a Baseball Wife* (New York: G.P. Putnam's Sons, 1983).

64. Bob Dunn, "Rogers Brightest Hope on Expo Mound," *The Sporting News*, March 9, 1974, 31.

65. Statistical information from Retrosheet for games of April 13, 18 and 23, 1974. See also: Bob Dunn, "Renko Puzzled by His Failures in Early Outings," *The Sporting News*, May 18, 1974, 29.

66. Statistical information from Retrosheet for games of April 28, May 5 and 16, 1974.

67. Statistical information from Retrosheet for games of May 20, 25, 30, June 5, 9, 15, 19, 24, 28, July 2, 6, 14 and 19, 1974.

68. Bob Dunn, "Rogers Stat Pick Reflects Rise of Expo Hurlers," *The Sporting News*, August 3, 1974, 19.

69. Author interview with Ken Singleton, April 24, 2012.

70. Bob Dunn, "Rogers, Singleton Branded Expo '74 Flops," *The Sporting News*, September 14, 1974, 13.

71. Statistical information from Retrosheet for games of September 1, 3, 7, 12, 16, 22, 27, and October 1, 1974.

72. See: http://www.baseball-reference.com/teams/MON/1974.shtml.

73. Bob Dunn, "Hunt's Exit Seen as Beginning of Expo Shakeup," *The Sporting News*, September 21, 1974, 20.

74. Bob Dunn, "Torrez and Mauch Bury Hatchet, Discuss '75 Plans," *The Sporting News*, October 19, 1974, 31.

75. *Ibid.*

76. "Major Deals," *The Sporting News*, December 21, 1974, 44.

77. Bob Dunn, "Expos Get Southpaw, But Was Price Too Steep?," *The Sporting News*,

December 21, 1974, 54. Author interview with Jacques Doucet, April 28, 2012.

78. Bob Dunn, "Expos Get Southpaw, But Was Price Too Steep?," *The Sporting News*, December 21, 1974, 54. See also: Danielle Gagnon Torrez and Ken Lizotte, *High Inside: Memoirs of a Baseball Wife*, 62.

79. Thomas Rodriguez, *Americano: My Journey to the Dream* (Topeka, KS: Amigos Publishing, 2004). See pages: 241–295. Quote is from page 293.

80. See the following: Paula Jasso-Wedel, "A Tribute to the Newton Holy Name Softball Tournaments: Looking Back–40 Years," (1988), copy in author's possession; "Topeka Mexican Basketball Tournament" brochure, copy in author's possession; Allen Quakenbush, "Hispanic Hoops," *Topeka Capital Journal*, January 8, 1991, 7-C; and Karleen Wende, et. al., "Generations United," (Topeka, KS: Our Lady of Guadalupe School, 1994), copy in author's possession.

81. Karleen Wende, et al., "Generations United," 46.

82. Thomas Rodriguez, *Americano: My Journey to the Dream*, 120.

83. Fiesta 1974 brochure. Copy in author's possession.

84. Fiesta 1973 brochure. Copy in author's possession.

85. Doug Brown, "Orioles Called 'Tough to Beat' Because of Deals," *The Sporting News*, January 11, 1975, 32.

86. Ken Leiker, "Torrez Eyes 20 Again," *Topeka Daily Capital*, April 1, 1976, 25.

Chapter 6

1. Ron Bergman, "A's Hold Their Noses Over 'Crabcake' Deal," *The Sporting News*, April 17, 1976, 16.

2. Ron Bergman, "Lady Luck Blind-Sides Vida In Year of Big Gold Strike," *The Sporting News,* October 2, 1976, 8.

3. Ron Bergman, "Torrez Red-Hot Hurler in A's Futile Drive for A.L. West Title," *The Sporting News*, October 16, 1976, 19.

4. Bob Hentzen, "Torrez Lauds Orioles' Support," *Topeka Capital Journal*, April 23, 1975, 11.

5. *Ibid.*

6. Jim Henneman, "Orioles' Answer to 'The Cat'—It's Healthy Palmer," *The Sporting News*, April 12, 1975, 19; and "Shuffling of Rosters Confuses Orioles' Players," *The Sporting News*, April 26, 1975, 7.

7. Jim Henneman, "Orioles Free Fall Sets Eight-Year Mark," *The Sporting News*, June 14, 1975, 18.

8. Statistical information from Retrosheet for games of April 13, 26, May 4, 14, and 18, 1975.

9. "A Day to Be Remembered," Binder, 10001, Mike Torrez Scrapbook Collection, Southwest Collection, Texas Tech University.

10. "Michael Torrez, Pride of Topeka Chicanos," Binders 10002, 10029 and 15053, Mike Torrez Scrapbook Collection, Southwest Collection, Texas Tech University.

11. Statistical information from Retrosheet for game of May 24, 1975.

12. Jim Henneman, "Fans Puzzled as Orioles Remove For-Sale Sign," *The Sporting News*, June 28, 1975, 16.

13. Statistical information from Retrosheet for game of July 11, 1975.

14. Jim Henneman, "May's HR Spree Sparks Oriole Talk of Fast Finish," *The Sporting News*, August 9, 1975, 7.

15. Statistical information from Retrosheet for games of July 17, 21, 25, 29, August 2, 6, 10, 15, 18, 22, 27, September 4, 8, 12, 17, 21, and 27, 1975. See also: http://www.baseball-reference.com/teams/BAL/1975.shtml.

16. Jim Henneman, "Orioles Chirp in Double Time Over Mike and Ken," *The Sporting News*, October 11, 1975, 9.

17. Jim Henneman, "Johnson Strikes Sour Note in Oriole Sonata," *The Sporting News*, April 10, 1976, 21.

18. Jim Henneman, "Visions of Jackson Are Dancing in Oriole Heads," *The Sporting News*, January 10, 1976, 34.

19. Tom Clark, *Champagne and Baloney: The Rise and Fall of Finley's A's* (New York: Harper and Row, 1976); and G. Michael Green and Roger D. Launius, *Charlie Finley: The Outrageous Story of Baseball's Super Showman* (New York: Walker, 2010).

20. G. Michael Green and Roger D. Launius, *Charlie Finley: The Outrageous Story of Baseball's Super Showman*, 207–218; quote from pages 217 and 218.

21. *Ibid.*, 221.

22. *Ibid.*, 239–257.

23. *Ibid.*, 244.

24. Ron Bergman, "A's Hold Their Noses Over 'Crabcake' Deal."

25. Jim Henneman, "Orioles Dream of Flag Pole With Reggie Leading Band," *The Sporting News,* April 17, 1976, 16.

26. Danielle Gagnon Torrez and Ken Lizotte, *High Inside: Memoirs of a Baseball Wife* (New York: G. P. Putnam's Sons, 1983), 102.

27. Dan Epstein, *Stars and Strikes: Baseball and American in the Bicentennial Summer of '76* (New York: Thomas Dunne Books, 2014), 101–102.

28. Statistical information from Retrosheet for game on April 30, 1976.

29. G. Michael Green and Roger D. Launius, *Charlie Finley: The Outrageous Story of Baseball's Super Showman*, 245.

30. *Ibid.*, 246–255. See also: Ron Bergman, "Diary of Defeat—A's Were Losers Even in the Bus League," *The Sporting News*, June 12, 1976, 10.

31. Statistical information from Retrosheet for games on June 30, July 5, and July 9, 1976.

32. "Mike Torrez Day," *Adelante*, 5, no. 1, June 20, 1976.

33. Bob Hentzen, "Royals Nervous 7–5 Winners," *Topeka Capital-Journal*, July 4, 1976.

34. *Ibid.*

35. Dan Epstein, *Stars and Strikes: Baseball and American in the Bicentennial Summer of '76*, 211–212.

36. Tom Weir, "Rumors of Trade Fail to Faze Torrez," *The Sporting News*, May 7, 1977, 16.

37. Statistical information from Retrosheet for games on July 16, 28, August 2, 7, 11, 15, 20, 24, 29, September 3, 7, 11 and 15, 1976.

38. Dan Epstein, *Stars and Strikes: Baseball and American in the Bicentennial Summer of '76*, 260–261.

39. Statistical information from Retrosheet for games on September 19, 23, 28 and October 3, 1976.

40. Ron Bergman, "'We Were Traded Out of a Pennant,' A's Moan," *The Sporting News*, October 30, 1976, 21.

41. Ron Bergman, "Torrez Red-Hot Hurler in A's Futile Drive for A.L. West Title," *The Sporting News*, October 16, 1976, 19. See also: "1976 Oakland Athletics," http://www.baseball-reference.com/teams/OAK/1976.shtml.

42. *Ibid.*

43. Ron Bergman, "Liberated A's Give Champagne Party," *The Sporting News*, October 23, 1976, 22.

44. Ron Bergman, "A's Three-Ring Circus, With Charlie in Charge," *The Sporting News*, November 27, 1976, 48.

45. Danielle Gagnon Torrez and Ken Lizotte, *High Inside*, 127.

46. *Ibid.*, 128–129.

47. Ron Bergman, "McKeon Talks Bravely About A's Job," *The Sporting News*, December 11, 1976, 52.

48. Ian MacDonald, "Expos Anxious to Reverse a Bad Deal," *The Sporting News*, January 22, 1977, 40.

49. Ron Bergman, "Only the Ex-A's Grin as They Leave the Bay Area," and "Name Almost Anything, McKeon Can Use It," *The Sporting News*, March 5, 1977, 30.

50. G. Michael Green and Roger D. Launius, *Charlie Finley: The Outrageous Story of Baseball's Super Showman*, 270.

51. Tom Weir, "Either Sign or Be Seated, Charlie Informs Balky A's," *The Sporting News*, April 2, 1977, 8.

52. Statistical information from Retrosheet for games on April 9, 15, 20, and 24, 1977. See also: http://www.baseball-reference.com/teams/OAK/1977.shtml.

53. A.L. Flashes, "Torrez Wants Security," *The Sporting News*, May 28, 1977, 23.

Chapter 7

1. Mike Torrez Collection, Southwest Collection Archive, Texas Tech University, Folder #4048.

2. Danielle Gagnon Torrez and Ken Lizotte, *High Inside: Memoirs of a Baseball Wife* (New York: G. P. Putnam's Sons, 1983), 131.

3. Vic Ziegel, "Torrez Doesn't Show Up," *New York Post*, April 30, 1977, 54.

4. Mike Torrez Collection, Southwest Collection Archive, Texas Tech University, Folder #19035.

5. Jack Wilkinson, "Yanks Roll, 7–2 … Where's Torrez?" *Daily News*, May 1, 1977, C32.

6. Phil Hersh, "Munson and Torrez Played a Little Duet," *Baltimore Evening Sun*, June 25, 1975, 6D; and Jim Henneman, "Yanks Outbrawl Orioles: Torrez, Munson Bout Sealed with a Kiss," *Baltimore News American*, June 25, 1975, 8B. See also: Retrosheet box score for game played on June 24, 1975.

7. In his recent book, Reggie Jackson mentions Mike Torrez specifically and calls him one of his few friends on the 1977 team. See: Reggie Jackson and Kevin Baker, *Becoming Mr. October* (New York: Doubleday, 2013), 67 and 101.

8. Matt Walsh, "Mike Torrez: 1977 Kansan of the Year," *Topeka Capital-Journal*, January 1, 1978, 19 and 20.

9. Peter Weiss, *Baseball's All-Time Goats: As Chosen by America's Top Sportswriters* (Holbrook, MA: Bob Adams, Inc., 1992), 168–171. Quote from page 171.

10. Jonathan Mahler, *Ladies and Gentlemen, the Bronx Is Burning: 1977, Baseball, Politics, and the Battle for the Soul of a City* (New York: Farrar, Straus and Giroux, 2005).

11. Joe Falls, "Sad to See Decline in Deals," *The Sporting News*, January 1, 1977, 18.

12. Joe McGuff, "Brett Cools His Pay

Pitch, Calls Royals Fair," *The Sporting News*, February 19, 1977, 53.

13. Phil Pepe, "Yanks Have Unrest, All They Need Is Results," *The Sporting News*, February 26, 1977, 39.

14. Phil Pepe, "Yankees to Improve on a Champion," *The Sporting News*, March 5, 1977, 26.

15. Phil Pepe, "If Yanks Have a Weakness, It May be Their Lack of Depth," *The Sporting News*, April 9, 1977, 14.

16. Phil Pepe. "Deal for Dent Gives Yanks An All-Star at Every Spot," *The Sporting News*, April 23, 1977, 5.

17. Phil Pepe, "Sagging Yankees Turn Tongues to Wagging," *The Sporting News*, May 7, 1977, 5.

18. Retrosheet box score for game played on April 20, 1977. See also: Phil Pepe, Chambliss' "Bat Revived by Yankee Hat Trick," *The Sporting News*, May 14, 1977, 17; and, 1977 New York Yankee schedule: http://www.baseball-almanac.com/teamstats/schedule.php?y=1977&t=NYA.

19. Phil Pepe, "Chambliss' Bat Revived by Yankee Hat Trick," *The Sporting News*, May 14, 1977, 17; and Tom Weir, "Trader Finley Swaps Headaches, Torrez for Ellis," *The Sporting News*, May 14, 1977, 17.

20. Retrosheet box score for games played on May 3 and 8, 1977.

21. Phil Pepe, "Figueroa Makes Pitch for Super-Star Class," *The Sporting News*, June 4, 1977, 12.

22. Phil Pepe, "Yankees' Elite Make Way for Guidry," *The Sporting News*, June 11, 1977, 8. See also: http://www.baseball-reference.com/teams/NYY1977.shtml.

23. Retrosheet box scores for games played May 15, 21, 25, 30, June 3, 8, and 13, 1977. See also: Phil Pepe, "Torrez' Plea for Work Pays Off for Yankees," *The Sporting News*, September 3, 1977, 9; and 1977 New York Yankee schedule: http://www.baseball-almanac.com/teamstats/schedule.php?y=1977&t=NYA.

24. Reggie Jackson and Kevin Baker, *Becoming Mr. October*, 82.

25. Robert Ward, "Reggie Jackson in No-Man's Land," by Alex Beth in "Bronx Banter," April 30, 2012. See: http://www.bronxbanterblog.com/2012/04/30/reggie-jackson-in-no-mans-land/.

26. *Ibid*. See also: Reggie Jackson and Kevin Baker, *Becoming Mr. October*, 89.

27. Retrosheet box score for game played on June 18, 1977.

28. Roger Kahn, *October Men: Reggie Jackson, George Steinbrenner, Billy Martin, and the Yankees' Miraculous Finish in 1978* (New York: Harcourt, 2003), 151 and 152.

29. *Ibid.*, 152.

30. *Ibid.*, 153.

31. Phil Pepe, *Talking Baseball: An Oral History of Baseball in the 1970s* (New York: Ballantine Books, 1998), 287–289.

32. Roger Kahn, "Torrez Ends an Odyssey," *New York Times*, April 9, 1979.

33. Reggie Jackson and Kevin Baker, *Becoming Mr. October*, 98.

34. Phil Pepe, *Talking Baseball: An Oral History of Baseball in the 1970s*, 290.

35. Quoted in Phil Pepe, "Peace Pipe or Exit Sign for Yanks' Martin?" *The Sporting News*, July 2, 1977, 13.

36. Phil Pepe, "'Shape Up,' Steinbrenner Tells Martin, Yanks," *The Sporting News*, July 9, 1977, 11.

37. Retrosheet box scores for games played on June 25, July 1, 5, 11, 16, and 22, 1977.

38. John Martinez, "Playing for N.Y. Yankees is Great, but set Pitching Rotation Wanted," and "From the Sidelines," both from *North Platte Telegraph*, July 20, 1977, 9.

39. Baseball Almanac schedules for both the Red Sox and the Yankees for 1977. See also: http://www.baseball-almanac.com/teamstats/schedule.php?y=1977&t=BOS; http://www.baseball-almanac.com/teamstats/schedule.php?y=1977&t=NYA and Phil Pepe, "Torrez' Plea for Work Pays Off for Yankees," *The Sporting News*, September 3, 1977, 9.

40. Danielle Gagnon Torrez and Ken Lizotte, *High Inside: Memoirs of a Baseball Wife*, 141.

41. Phil Pepe, "Torrez' Plea for Work Pays Off for Yankees," *The Sporting News*, September 3, 1977, 9.

42. Baseball Almanac schedules for both the Red Sox and the Yankees for 1977. See also: http://www.baseball-almanac.com/teamstats/schedule.php?y=1977&t=BOS; http://www.baseball-almanac.com/teamstats/schedule.php?y=1977&t=NYA. See also: http://www.baseball-reference.com/teams/NYY/1977.shtml.

43. Phil Pepe, "'Backed into Pennant?' No Way, Roar Yankees," *The Sporting News*, October 15, 1977, 7.

44. Phil Pepe, "Boston Blowup 'Made' Yanks, Billy Believes," *The Sporting News*, October 22, 1977, 3.

45. *Ibid.*

46. See: www.baseball-reference.com/postseason/1976_ALCS.shtml.

47. See: www.baseball-reference.com/teams/KCR/1977.shtml.

48. *Ibid.* See also: www.baseball-reference.com/teams/NYY/1977.shtml.

49. Mike Torrez Collection, Southwest

Collection Archive, Texas Tech University, Folder #3022.

50. See: www.baseball-reference.com/post season/1977_ALCS.shtml and www.baseball-reference.com/teams/KCR/1977.shtml

51. Phil Pepe, "Yanks Put Last-Ditch Trademark on A.L. Title," *The Sporting News*, October 22, 1977, 16.

52. Retrosheet box score for game played on October 9, 1977.

53. Phil Pepe, "Yanks Put Last-Ditch Trademark on A.L. Title," *The Sporting News*, October 22, 1977, 16.

54. Gordon Verrell, "Consistency Was Keystone to Dodger Conquest," *The Sporting News*, October 22, 1977, 3. See also: http://www.baseball-reference.com/teams/LAD/1977.shtml.

55. *Ibid.*

56. "Game Three Slants," *The Sporting News*, October 29, 1977, 8.

57. Lowell Reidenbaugh, "Yanks' Extra-Inning Heroics Subdue Dodgers," *The Sporting News*, October 29, 1977, 5; and "Hooton's Baffling Knuckler Masters Yankee Swingers," *The Sporting News*, October 29, 1977, 6. See also: "Yankees Win Opener on Blair's Single"; and "Hooton, Homers Help Dodgers Even Series," *The Sporting News*, November 5, 1977, 6.

58. Dick Kaegel, "Yankee Stadium or Zoo? The Routine Rivals Soap Opera," *The Sporting News*, October 29, 1977, 18 and Lowell Reidenbaugh, "Yankees Stow Brass Knucks and Take Bows," *The Sporting News*, November 5, 1977, 3.

59. Lowell Reidenbuagh, "Torrez in Charge—L.A. Bats Wilt as Yanks Log 2nd Win," *The Sporting News*, October 29, 1977, 8. See also: Retrosheet boxscore for game of October 14, 1977; "Turnaround by Torrez," *The Sporting News*, November 5, 1977, 6; and Bill Shirley, "Yankees Put Childish Things Aside, Beat Dodgers," *Los Angeles Times*, October 15, 1977.

60. Lowell Reidenbaugh, "Guidry, Yanks' Mr. Cool, Chills Dodger Bats," and "Pride Spurs Dodgers to Bounce Off Deck," *The Sporting News*, October 29, 1977, 9 and 11.

61. Lowell Reidenbaugh, "Yankees Stow Brass Knucks and Take Bows," *The Sporting News*, November 5, 1977, 3.

62. Pete Goering, "Hero Son Absent, but Torrez Family Enjoys Celebration," *Topeka Daily Capital*, October 20, 1977, 21.

63. *Ibid.* Also, see the following: Retrosheet for game played on October 18, 1977; "No Masterpiece but Torrez Happy," Mike Torrez Collection, Southwest Collection Archive, Texas Tech University, Folder #3054;

64. Herschel Nissenson, "Yankees Still Not Happy," *Topeka Daily Journal*, October 20, 1977, 22.

65. Joseph Durso, "The Yanks: Great Gamble with Greater Payoff," *The Sporting News*, November 19, 1977, 45 and "No Masterpiece but Torrez Happy," Mike Torrez Collection, Southwest Collection Archive, Texas Tech University, Folder #3054.

66. Bob Hentzen, "Yanks' Only Certainty is Uncertainty," *Topeka Daily Capital* October 20, 1977, 21.

67. Phil Pepe, "Yanks Look to 'Goose' for Another Golden Egg," *The Sporting News*, November 26, 1977, 51.

68. Danielle Gagnon Torrez and Ken Lizotte, *High Inside: Memoirs of a Baseball Wife*, 183.

69. Mike Torrez Collection, Southwest Collection Archive, Texas Tech University, Folder #8012.

70. Quoted in Jorge Iber, "The Early Life and Career of Topeka's Mike Torrez, 1946–1978: Sport as Means for Studying Latino/a Life in Kansas," *Kansas History: A Journal of the Central Plains* 37, no. 3, Autumn 2014: 164–179. Quote from page 179. See also: Matt Walsh, "Mike Torrez: 1977 Kansan of the Year," *Topeka Daily Capital*, January 1, 1978, 19 and 20.

71. "Torrez Win a Struggle," *Topeka Daily Capital*, October 19, 1977, 25 and 26.

72. Bob Hentzen, "Aw, Oakland Natives, Don't Be Mad at Mike," *Topeka Daily Capital*, October 21, 1977, 23.

73. *Ibid.* See also: Jorge Iber, "The Early Life and Career of Topeka's Mike Torrez, 1946–1978: Sport as Means for Studying Latino/a Life in Kansas," 179.

74. Ian MacDonald, "Mike Going Where Money Is," *Montreal Gazette*, October 24, 1977, 34. See also: Jack Lang, "Torrez Sweepstakes: Angels, Expos Likely Top Bidders," *New York Daily News*, November 4, 1977, 72; and "Torrez, Hisle, Gamble Top Royals Draft Picks," *Topeka Capital Journal*, November 5, 1977, 23.

75. Larry Whiteside, "Sullivan Named New G.M. of Red Sox," *The Sporting News*, November 5, 1977, 20; "Bosox Gunning for Free-Agent Hurlers," *The Sporting News*, November 26, 1977, 50; and "Red Sox Land Torrez with $2 Million Pact," *The Sporting News*, December 3, 1977, 71. See also: Murray Chass, "Torrez Near to Signing 7-Year Pact

with Red Sox," *The New York Times*, November 21, 1977.

76. Paul Zimmerman, "Yankees Give Their Series Ticket to the Red Sox," *New York Post*, November 25, 1977.

77. *Ibid.*

78. Larry Whiteside, "Bosox Beef Up Staff with Series Hero Torrez," *The Sporting News*, December 10, 1977, 57.

79. "Oil on Yankee Fires: Torrez—More Like '77," *Binghamton Press*, January 24, 1978.

80. "Torrez: Sox Better Than Yankees," *Syracuse Post-Standard*, November 25, 1977, 25.

81. Alan Richman, "The Travels of Torrez," *The Boston Globe*, January 6, 1978, 4–6. Quote on page 6.

82. Larry Whiteside, "Bosox Beef Up Staff with Series Hero Torrez," *The Sporting News*, December 10, 1977, 57.

83. Karl Gulbronsen, "Mike Torrez: Traveling Man Finding Security in Boston." *Palm Beach Post*, April 3, 1978, D1.

84. Roger Kahn, "Torrez Ends an Odyssey," *New York Times*, April 9, 1979. See also: Edwin Pope, "A Home Sweet Home for Mike Torrez," *Miami Herald*, May 16, 1978, 1D.

85. C. C. Johnson Spink, "We Believe," *The Sporting News*, April 8, 1978, 18.

86. Randy Harvey, "Red Sox Will Mean Plenty of Trouble," *Sun Times*, April 6, 1978; and Larry Whiteside, "No Question Bosox Good, But Questions Do Exist," *The Sporting News*, April 8, 1978.

87. Retrosheet for games played on April 7, 12, 17, 21, 26, May 1, 7 and 13, 1978. All of the figures for team records mentioned are drawn from the Baseball Almanac. See: http://www.baseball-almanac.com/teamstats/schedule.php?=1978&t=BOS and http://www.baseball-almanac.com/teamstats/schedule.php?=1978&t=NYA.

88. Retrosheet for games played on May 19, 24, 29, June 3, 10 and 15, 1978.

89. Retrosheet for games played on June 20, 25, July 1 and 7, 1978. See also: Larry Whiteside, "Eck's Heater Still Missing but He's Hot Red Sox Item," *The Sporting News*, July 15, 1978, 18; and "Red Sox Hot—Lynn Is Torrid," *The Sporting News*, July 22, 1978, 8.

90. Jimmy Scott, "Mike Torrez, Retired MLB Player & "The Club," http://bleacherreport.com/articles/91406-mike-torrez-retired-mlb-player-the-club.

91. Richard Bradley, *The Greatest Game: The Yankees, the Red Sox, and the Playoff of '78* (New York: Free Press, 2008); and Con Chapman, *The Year of the Gerbil: How the Yankees Won (and the Red Sox Lost) the*

Greatest Pennant Race Ever (Danbury, CT: Rutledge Books, 1998), especially 123–132.

92. Richard Bradley, *The Greatest Game: The Yankees, the Red Sox, and the Playoff of '78*, 52.

93. *Ibid.*

94. Con Chapman, *The Year of the Gerbil: How the Yankees Won (and the Red Sox Lost) the Greatest Pennant Race Ever*, 202.

95. Richard Bradley, *The Greatest Game: The Yankees, the Red Sox, and the Playoff of '78*, 68–69.

96. *Ibid.*, 53. See also: http://www.baseball-reference.com/players/l/leebi03.shtml.

97. Roger Kahn, *October Men: Reggie Jackson, George Steinbrenner, Billy Martin, and the Yankees' Miraculous Finish in 1978*, 302. See also: G. Richard McKelvey, *Fisk's Home, Willie's Catch and the Shot Heard Round the World* (Jefferson, NC: McFarland, 1998), 132.

98. Phil Pepe, "Yankees Give Billy a Second Chance—in 1980," *The Sporting News*, August 12, 1978, 13.

99. Con Chapman, *The Year of the Gerbil: How the Yankees Won (and the Red Sox Lost) the Greatest Pennant Race Ever*, 219.

100. *Ibid.*, 136–140, quote on pages 139–140.

101. Larry Whiteside, "Busiest Bosox Starter, Torrez Loves Work," *The Sporting News*, August 26, 1978, 12.

102. Ray Fitzgerald, "...and, Now, Another Problem: Mike Torrez Is Making Grumbles," *Boston Globe*, Mike Torrez Collection, Southwest Collection Archive, Texas Tech University, Folder #2042. See also: Retrosheet for game played on August 28, 1978.

103. Con Chapman, *The Year of the Gerbil: How the Yankees Won (and the Red Sox Lost) the Greatest Pennant Race Ever*, 208. See also: Retrosheet for game played on September 7, 1978.

104. *Ibid.*, 211–212.

105. *Ibid.*, 219.

106. Larry Whiteside, "Sox Didn't Quit on Torrez," *The Sporting News*, October 7, 1978, 36. See also: Retrosheet for games played on September 12, 16, 20 and 24, 1978. Con Chapman, *The Year of the Gerbil: How the Yankees Won (and the Red Sox Lost) the Greatest Pennant Race Ever*, 223.

107. Con Chapman, *The Year of the Gerbil: How the Yankees Won (and the Red Sox Lost) the Greatest Pennant Race Ever*, 225–226. See also: Retrosheet for game played on September 28, 1978.

108. *Ibid.*, 245–246.

109. G. Richard McKelvey, *Fisk's Homer,*

Willie's Catch and the Shot Heard Round the World, 135.

110. Reggie Jackson and Kevin Baker, *Becoming Mr. October*, 264.

111. Kevin Dupont, *Boston Herald American*, "At Last: It's Sox-Yanks!" October 2, 1978, 1 and 4.

112. Roger Kahn, *October Men: Reggie Jackson, George Steinbrenner, Billy Martin, and the Yankees' Miraculous Finish in 1978*, 339.

113. Richard Bradley, *The Greatest Game: The Yankees, the Red Sox, and the Playoff of '78*, 151.

114. *Ibid.*, 216–218. See also: G. Richard McKelvey, *Fisk's Homer, Willie's Catch and the Shot Heard Round the World*, 135.

115. Jonathan Schwartz, *A Day of Light and Shadows* (Pleasantville, NY: Akadine Press, 2000), 35.

116. Retrosheet for game played on October 2, 1978.

117. Quoted in: Bill Reynolds, *'78: The Boston Red Sox, A Historic Game, and a Divided City* (New York City: New American Library, 2009), 271.

118. Danielle Gagnon Torrez and Ken Lizotte, *High Inside: Memoirs of a Baseball Wife* (New York: G. P. Putnam's Sons, 1983), 218–219.

119. Joe Giuliotti, "Stigma of '78 Homer Stays with Torrez," *The Sporting News*, January 24, 1983, 47.

120. Peter Weiss, *Baseball's All-Time Goats: As Chosen by America's Top Sportswriters* (Holbrook, MA: Bob Adams, 1992), 27 and 171.

121. Richard Bradley, *The Greatest Game: The Yankees, the Red Sox, and the Playoff of '78*, 255.

Chapter 8

1. Anonymous, "The Steamer, The Dodger of History's Bullets...," May 15, 2012. See: http://fenway100.org/page/20/?app-download=nokia. Accessed on April 27, 2015.

2. See: http://www.chron.com/sports/rockets/slideshow/The-most-hated-sports-figures-in-Houston-history-70106/photo-5180468.php.

3. See: http://bleacherreport.com/articles/1329359-baseballs-15-biggest-pennant-chase-goats-of-all-time/page/14. This article ranks Mike Torrez as the third biggest "pennant chase goat" in history.

4. Bob McCoy, "Keeping Score," *The Sporting News*, January 23, 1989, 10.

5. Joe Giuliotti, "Frustrated Torrez Asks to Be Traded," *The Sporting News*, November 1, 1982, 30.

6. Larry Whiteside, "Bosox Wary of Free-Agent Market," *The Sporting News*, November 4, 1978, 54.

7. Larry Whiteside, "Loss of Tiant 'Tears Out Heart' of Red Sox," *The Sporting News*, December 2, 1978, 51.

8. See: Jack Craig, "Do Bosox Owners Want Profits or Pennant?" and Larry Whiteside, "Renko Fills Boston Need for Extra Starter," both in *The Sporting News*, February 3, 1979, 33.

9. Larry Whiteside, "Bosox Expect Prime Kids to Replace Lee and Tiant," *The Sporting News*, March 3, 1979, 25; and "Pitching Could Make Red Sox Even Rosier," *The Sporting News*, April 7, 1979, 31.

10. "Torrez Not Thinking About Past," *The State Journal*, March 28, 1979, 21. Binder 4049, Mike Torrez Scrapbook Collection, Southwest Collection, Texas Tech University.

11. Retrosheet for games played on April 7, 12, 17, 22 and 27, 1979.

12. Larry Whiteside, "Red Sox Refuse to Worry After Yank Blanks," *The Sporting News*, June 2, 1979, 19.

13. Retrosheet for games played on May 2, 7, 12 and 18, 1979.

14. Retrosheet for games played on May 24, 30, June 4, 9, 15, 20, 24, 29, July 4, 9 and 14, 1979. See also: "1979 Boston Red Sox Schedule," http://www.baseball-almanac.com/teamstats/schedule.php?y=1979&t=BOS.

15. Larry Whiteside, "Torrez Turns Torrid by Being Less Fine," *The Sporting News*, July 21, 1979, 13.

16. Retrosheet for games played on July 20, 25, 29, August 2, 7, 11, 15, 20, 25, 31, September 4, 9, 13, 18, 23, and 28, 1979.

17. Joe Giuliotti, "Red Sox Whiff in Trade Mart—Fans Irked," *The Sporting News*, December 22, 1979, 60. See also: http://www.baseball-reference.com/teams/BOS/1979.shtml.

18. See: Joe Giuliotti, "Fisk's Arm No. 1 Red Sox Question Mark," *The Sporting News*, January 19, 1980, 41; "Red Sox' Stanley Excited Over His New Change-Up," *The Sporting News*, February 9, 1980, 39; "Red Sox' Fate? It's Up to Fisk," *The Sporting News*, March 8, 1980, 21; "Ifs Plague Red Sox," *The Sporting News*, April 12, 1980, 42; and "Rader Bosox' New Fisk Insurance," *The Sporting News*, April 19, 1980, 30.

19. Dennis Eckersley, interview with author, April 30, 2015.

20. Retrosheet for games played on April 12, 17, 22, 27, May 2, 7, 12, 17, 21, 26, 31, June 7, 12, 17, 22, 28, and July 4, 1980.

21. Joe Giuliotti, "Struggling Starters Send Red Sox into Deep Swoon," *The Sporting News*, May 31, 1980, 27; "Burgmeier Rescue Ace of Fading Bosox," *The Sporting News*, June 7, 1980, 13; and "Willing Renko: Start or Stop," *The Sporting News*, June 28, 1980, 25. See also: "Major League Flashes—Zimmer Wants Company," *The Sporting News*, August 9, 1980, 12.
22. Retrosheet for game played September 13, 1980.
23. Dennis Eckersley, interview with author, April 30, 2015.
24. Peter Gammons, "Umpire Quality Is Sinking—Bad Calls and Poor Attitudes," *The Sporting News*, September 20, 1980, 15 and Stan Isle, "Notebook," *The Sporting News*, October 11, 1980, 18.
25. "1980 Boston Red Sox," http://www.baseball-reference.com/teams/BOS/1980.shtml.
26. Joe Giuliotti, "Torrez' Misery Is Almost Over," *The Sporting News*, October 4, 1980, 21.
27. Danielle Gagnon-Torrez and Ken Lizotte, *High Inside: Memoirs of a Baseball Wife* (New York: G. P. Putnam's Sons, 1983), 233.
28. Joe Giuliotti, "'The Old Torrez is Back,' Red Sox Assured," *The Sporting News*, March 14, 1981, 44; Peter Gammons, "Fisk Will Help Chisox," *The Sporting News*, April 4, 1981, 47; and Larry Whiteside, "A New Torrez?," *Boston Globe*, February 24, 1981, 50.
29. Peter Gammons, "Bill Weaves Patches to Perfection," *The Sporting News*, May 9, 1981, 13. See also: Retrosheet for game played on April 20, 1981.
30. Bob Hentzen, "Torrez Rebounds After Tough Year," *Topeka Capital Journal*. Binder 4046, Mike Torrez Scrapbook Collection, Southwest Collection, Texas Tech University.
31. Joe Giuliotti, "Torrez Sets a Torrid Pace with Return of His Fastball," *The Sporting News*, June 27, 1981, 38.
32. Retrosheet for game played on September 19, 1981.
33. Retrosheet, "The 1981 Season Final Standings." See also: "1981 Boston Red Sox," http://www.baseball-reference.com/teams/BOS/1981.shtml.
34. Stephen Borelli, "Torrez Can Relate to Clemens," http://www.usatoday30.usatoday.com/sports/baseball/comment/Borelli/2000-10-26-borelli.htm.
35. Joe Giuliotti, "Eckersley Primed for Big Comeback," *The Sporting News*, February 6, 1982, 38. See also: http://www.baseball-reference.com/teams/BOS/1981.shtml.
36. Edwin Pope, "Coping: At 35, Torrez

Still Hanging Tough," *Philadelphia Enquirer*, March 21, 1982.
37. Retrosheet for games of April 12, 18, 24, and 30, 1982. See also: http://www.baseball-almanac.com/teamstats/schedule.php?y=1982&t=BOS.
38. See: http://www.baseball-reference.com/teams/BOS/1982.shtml.
39. Joe Giuliotti, "'I'm Just Stupid,' Says Bosox' Torrez," *The Sporting News*, August 16, 1982, 17.
40. Retrosheet for game played on August 15, 1982. See also: Joe Giuliotti, "Sox Blast Orioles, 8–0," *Boston Herald American*, August 16, 1982, and "Chipper Torrez Starts Tomorrow," *Boston Globe*, August 19, 1982.
41. Retrosheet for game played on September 26, 1982.
42. Retrosheet for game played on October 1, 1982.
43. Joe Giuliotti, "Frustrated Torrez Asks to Be Traded," *The Sporting News*, November 1, 1982, 30.
44. Peter Gammons, "Steinbrenner Rapped as Inflation Culprit," *The Sporting News*, January 3, 1983, 38.
45. Joe Giuliotti, "Stigma of '78 Homer Stays with Torrez," *The Sporting News*, January 24, 1983, 47.
46. Richard Bradley, *The Greatest Game: The Yankees, the Red Sox and the Playoff of '78* (New York: Free Press, 2008), 255.
47. *Ibid*. Interview with Dennis Eckersley, April 30, 2015. Interview with Bucky Dent, April 30, 2015.
48. Jack Lang, "Mets Lure Torrez with 2-Year Deal," *The Sporting News*, January 24, 1983, 42.
49. *Ibid*.
50. Jack Lang, "Future Is Now, Bambi Tells Hurlers," *The Sporting News*, February 7, 1983, 40; and "Mets Expect Big Pickup in Pitching," *The Sporting News*, March 21, 1984, 31.
51. Statistics drawn from "1983 New York Mets," see: http://www.baseball-reference.com/teams/NYM/1983.shtml.
52. Samuel O. Regalado, *Viva Baseball: Latin Major Leaguers and Their Special Hunger* (Urbana and Chicago: University of Illinois Press, 1998), xiv.
53. Samuel O. Regalado, *Viva Baseball: Latin Major Leaguers and Their Special Hunger*, 170.
54. *Ibid.*, 171.
55. Jim Kaplan, "Epidemic of Fernando Fever: Los Angeles is Delirious Over Dazzling Rookie Lefthander Fernando Valenzuela." See: http://www.si.com/vault/1981/05/04/825589/epidemic-of-fernando-fever-

los-angeles-is-delirious-over-dazzling-rookie-lefthander-fernando-valenzuela.

56. Samuel O. Regalado, *Viva Baseball: Latin Major Leaguers and Their Special Hunger*, 189.

57. Retrosheet for game played on June 2, 1983.

58. Retrosheet for game played on August 31, 1983.

59. Jack Lang, "Howard's Mets Ooze Confidence," *The Sporting News*, September 5, 1983, 51.

60. Statistics drawn from "1983 New York Mets," see: http://www.baseball-reference.com/teams/NYM/1983.shtml.

61. Jack Lang, "Keystone Combo Is Mets' Top Concern," *The Sporting News*, March 4, 1984, 19 and "Rookies Earn Way Into Mets Rotation," *The Sporting News*, April 9, 1984, 23.

62. Harry Shattuck, "Sky is the Limit For All-Star Thon," *The Sporting News*, April 16, 1984, 20.

63. Greg Hanlon, "Lost Greatness, Scar Tissue, and Survival: The Life of Baseball's Brief Superstar, Dickie Thon" May 7, 2015. See: http://sports.vice.com/en_us/article/lost-greatness-scar-tissue-and-survival-the-life-of-baseballs-brief-superstar-dickie-thon.

64. *Ibid.* Interview with Dickie Thon, April 30, 2015. See also: Terry Scott, "Back in Time with Mike Torrez," *Expos: Quebec's Baseball Magazine*, Vol. 3, Number 5, 1989, 106–111.

65. Stan Isle, "Caught on the Fly—Shea Fans Rough on Torrez," *The Sporting News*, June 18, 1984, 32.

66. Maury Allen, "Torrez Coping with Hard Times," *New York Post*, May 17, 1983.

67. Jack Lang, "Mets' Start: It's Amazin'," *The Sporting News*, April 23, 1984, and "Out with the Old: Tidrow, Swan Cut," *The Sporting News*, May 21, 1984, 20. See also: Retrosheet for games played on April 21, May 13, 20, 27, and June 3, 1983.

68. Retrosheet for games played on June 9 and 12, 1983.

69. Kit Stier, "A's Dredge Every Source for Hurling," *The Sporting News*, July 16, 1984, 30; and "Will Rainey, Torrez Fulfill Caudill?" *The Sporting News*, July 30, 1984, 20.

70. Retrosheet for games played on July 23 and 27, 1984.

71. Nick Moschella, "Miami's Grande Experiment," *Baseball America*, July 10–24, 1985, 3 and 19.

72. Harvey Araton, "Dent-Torrez Again, But It's in the Bushes," *Daily News*, April 14, 1985, 66.

73. For information on the 1956–1960 Marlins, see: Sam Zygner, *The Forgotten Marlins: A Tribute to the 1956–1960 Original Miami Marlins* (Lanham, MD: 2013). Attendance figures drawn from Lloyd Johnson and Miles Wolff, *The Encyclopedia of Minor League Baseball* (Durham, NC: Baseball America, Inc., 1997), 442, 448, 454, 459, and 464.

74. Nick Moschella, "Miami's Grande Experiment," 3.

75. *Ibid.* See also: http://www.baseball-reference.com/minors/team.cgi?id=1623615e.

76. Harvey Araton, "Dent-Torrez Again, But It's in the Bushes," 66.

77. Terry Scott, "Back in Time with Mike Torrez," *Expos: Quebec's Baseball Magazine* 3, no. 5, 1989, 106–111.

Chapter 9

1. Andrew Cohen, "A Divided Red Sox Nation," *The Atlantic*, October 30, 2013. See: http://www.theatlantic.com/entertainment/archive/2013/10/a-divided-red-sox-nation/281011/. Accessed on April 27, 2015.

2. Peter Gammons, "Living and Dying with the Woe Sox," *Sports Illustrated*, November 3, 1986. See: http://sportsillustrated.cnn.com/vault/article/magazine/MAG1065413/index.htm. Accessed on February 24, 2012.

3. Randy Schultz, "Bucky's Feat Was Indelible Dent," *The Sporting News*, October 17, 1988, 18–19.

4. Anthony Rieber, "...When It Was Bucky at the Bat," *The Boston Globe*, July 31, 1988, 53 and 61.

5. See, for example: David Lennon, "HR Links Dent, Torrez Forever," *Newsday*, October 18, 1998, A41 and A51 and Hal Habib, "One Swing Made Bucky Dent a New York Legend and a Boston Pariah," *Palm Beach Post*, October 1, 2008. See: http://www.palmbeachpost.com/sports/content/sportss/epaper/2008/10/01/a1c_d Accessed on April 20, 2012.

6. John Goode, "Torrez Played Both Sides," Boston.com, May 10, 2005. See: http://www.boston.com/sports/baseball/redsox/articles/2005/05/10/torrez_played_both_sides/.

7. Alan Eskew, "Torrez Dons Uniform Again for Old-Timers Game," *Topeka Capital-Journal*, August 1, 1987, 23.

8. Ben Chapell, "Ballplayers in Barrio Life," paper presented at the American Studies Association Meeting, November 6, 2014, Los Angeles, California. Cited with permission of the author.

9. For more information on this research, please visit this YouTube link: https://m.you tube.com/watch?v=eSyPlY_KhZM. See also: Gene T. Chavez, "Pitch'm Fast Pauly.... The Mexican American Fast-Pitch Softball Leagues," *Historical Journal of Wyandotte County*, 3, no. 12, Winter 2015: 412–414. Finally, for an overview of the type of work being done on Mexican Americans and baseball in other parts of the country, please see: Francisco Balderrama and Richard Santillan, *Mexican American Baseball in Los Angeles* (Charleston, SC: Arcadia, 2011).

10. Bob Golon, *No Minor Accomplishment: The Revival of New Jersey Professional Baseball* (New Brunswick, NJ: Rivergate Books, 2008). See specifically, Chapter 7, pages 105–122. For a glimpse of the history of the most glorious times of Newark baseball, see: Ronald A. Mayer, *The 1937 Newark Bears: A Baseball Legend* (New Brunswick, NJ: Rutgers University Press, 1994).

11. Bob Golon, *No Minor Accomplishment: The Revival of New Jersey Professional Baseball*, 110–115. See also: Steve Politi, "Newark Bears Baseball Team on the Verge of Folding," *Newark Star-Ledger*, October 26, 2008. Blog.nj.com/ledgerupdates_impact/ print.html?entry=/2008/10/Newark_bears_ baseball_team_on.html. Accessed on March 26, 2013.

12. *Ibid.*, 115–119.

13. Harvey Araton, "Did Newark Bet on the Wrong Sport?," *New York Times*, August 21, 2011. See: www.nytimes.com/2011/08/ 22/sports/baseball.did-newark-bet-on-the-wrong-sport.html?pagewanted=all&_r= 0&pagewanted=print. Accessed on April 11, 2013.

14. Phillip Read, "Despite Economy, Newark Bears Owners Envision Big Season," *Newark Star-Ledger*, January 8, 2009. See: blog.nj.com/ledgerupdates_impact/print. html?entry=/2009/01/despite_economy_ newark_bears_o.html; Steve Polity, "Newark Bears' New Ownership Group Determined to Make Baseball in Newark Work," *Newark Star-Ledger*, May 2, 2009. See: blog.nj.com/ ledgerupdates_impact/print.html?entry=/ 2009/05/Newark_bears_new_ownership_ gro.html. Accessed on March 26, 2013. See also: http://www.baseball-reference.com/ minors/team.cgi?id=294a9243.

15. Kevin Reichard, "It's Official: Bears to Can-Am Association," October 6, 2010. See: http://baseballparkdigest.com/2010100 63169/independent-baseball/news/its-official-bears-to-can-am-association. Accessed on May 22, 2015. See also: Tom Wright, "Under New Ownership, Newark Bears Hope

to Switch Leagues," *Newark Star-Ledger*, October 1, 2010. See: blog.nj.com/ledgerupda tes_impact/print.html?entry=/2010/10/ under_new_ownership_newark_bea.html. Accessed on March 26, 2013. Press release by Newark Bears: "Mike Torrez Returns to Newark Bears as General Manager," http:// www.newarkbears.com/news0010.html Accessed on February 16, 2012.

16. Amy Brittain, "Newark Bears: A Tale of a Sidetracked Baseball Franchise," *Newark Star-Ledger*, July 17, 2011. See:http://www.nj. com/news/index.ssf/2011/07/how_court_ battles_unpaid_bills/html. Accessed on March 26, 2013. Interview with Amy Brittain, April 11, 2013.

17. See: http://www.baseball-reference. com/minors/player.cgi?id=torrez000wes.

18. Dan Barry, "Newark Bears' Items Going, Going...," *New York Times*, April 24, 2014. See: http://www.nytimes.com/2014/ 04/25/sports/baseball/newark-bears-are-holding-a-liquidation-auction.html?_r=0. Accessed on May 21, 2015. See also: Mark Di Ionno, "Game Over: Newark Bears Officially Out of Business, as Baseball Fades From City Again," *Newark Star-Ledger*, April 26, 2014. See: http://www.nj.com/essex/index.ssf/2014/ 04/newark_bears_officially_out_of_busi ness_as_baseball_fades_from_city_again. html. Accessed on May 21, 2015.

19. Chuck Carree, "No Regrets for Red Sox's Mike Torrez," Starnewsonline.com, January 8, 2009. See: http://www.starnews online.com/article/20090108/ARTICLES/ 901080281?template-=print. Accessed on April 27, 2015.

20. See the following: http://top-topics. thefullwiki.org/Mexican_American_Major_ League_Baseball_players and http://en.wiki pedia.org/wiki/List_of_Mexican_Ameri cans#Baseball.

21. Vernona Gomez and Lawrence Goldstone, *Lefty: An American Odyssey* (New York: Ballantine Books, 2012), 4–8.

22. *Ibid.*, 141.

23. "Milestones," *The Sporting News*, June 26, 1989, 34. See also: "Mike Torrez and His Unique Yankees History," June 25, 2013. See: http://itsaboutthemoney.net/archives/2013/ 06/25/mike-torrez-and-his-unique-yankees-history/.

24. Larry Sullivan, "Fair Voting," in "Voice of the Fan," *The Sporting News*, February 19, 1990, 3.

25. John Napolitano, "Top 100 Red Sox: #95, Mike Torrez," February 29, 2004. See: http://redsox.scout.com/story/238246-top-100-red-sox-95-mike-torrez. Accessed on October 31, 2014.

26. Ray Nolting, "Former Topekan to Lead Fiesta Parade," *Topeka Capital-Journal*, July 1988.

27. Rick Peterson, "Recalling Another Era," *Topeka Capital Journal*, July 19, 1988, 3-G.

28. Kevin Haskin, "Finally Four: No. 1 Torrez Armed for Success," *Topeka Capital Journal*, August 28, 2011, 1D and 10D.

29. *Ibid.*

30. See for example: A. G. Sulzberger, "Hispanics Reviving Faded Towns on the Plains," *New York Times*, November 14, 2011, A1. For academic work on this topic, though it is not specifically focused on sports, please see: Robert Wuthnow, *Remaking the Heartland: Middle American Since the 1950s* (Princeton, NJ: Princeton University Press, 2011), particularly chapter six, "The Changing Face of Agribusiness"; Ann V. Millard and Jorge Chapa, *Apple Pie and Enchiladas: Latino Newcomers in the Rural Midwest* (Austin: University of Texas Press, 2001); and Tomas R. Jimenez, *Replenished Identity: Mexican Americans, Immigration and Identity* (Berkeley, CA: University of California Press, 2010).

31. Jorge Iber, Samuel O. Regalado, José M. Alamillo, and Arnoldo De Leon, *Latinos in U.S. Sport: A History of Isolation, Cultural Identity, and Acceptance* (Champaign, IL: Human Kinetics, 2011). See, particularly, 228–230.

32. *Ibid.*, 278.

Bibliography

Books

Adelson, Bruce. *Brushing Back Jim Crow: The Integration of Minor League Baseball in the American South.* Charlottesville: University of Virginia Press, 2007.

Alamillo, José. *Making Lemonade Out of Lemons: Mexican American Labor and Leisure in a California Town.* Champaign and Urbana: University of Illinois Press, 2006.

Almaraz, Felix. *Knight Without Armor: Carlos Eduardo Castaneda, 1896–1958.* College Station: Texas A&M University Press, 1999.

Arreola, Daniel D. *Tejano South Texas: A Mexican American Cultural Province.* Austin: University of Texas Press, 2002.

Balderrama, Francisco E., and Richard A. Santillan. *Mexican American Baseball in Los Angeles* Charleston, SC: Arcadia, 2011.

Bell, Christopher. *Scapegoats: Baseballers Whose Careers Are Marked by One Fateful Play.* Jefferson, NC: McFarland, 2002.

Bergad, Laird W., and Herbert S. Klein. *Hispanics in the United States: A Demographic, Social and Economic History, 1980–2005.* New York: Cambridge University Press, 2010.

Bloom, John. *To Show What an Indian Can Do: Sports at Native American Boarding Schools.* Minneapolis: University of Minnesota Press, 2005.

Bradley, Glenn D. *The Story of the Santa Fe.* Boston: Gorham Press, 1920.

Bradley, Richard. *The Greatest Game: The Yankees, the Red Sox, and the Playoff of '78.* New York: Free Press, 2008.

Branca, Ralph. *A Moment in Time: An American Story of Baseball, Heartbreak and Grace.* New York: Scribner, 2011.

Bryant, Howard. *Shut Out: A Story of Race and Baseball in Boston.* New York: Routledge, 2002.

Bryant, Keith L., Jr. *History of the Atchison, Topeka and Santa Fe Railway.* New York: Macmillan, 1974.

Burgos, Adrian. *Playing America's Game: Baseball, Latinos and the Color Line.* Berkeley: University of California Press, 2007.

Bynum, Mike, ed. *King Football: Greatest Moments in Texas High School Football History.* Birmingham, AL: Epic Sports Classics, 2003.

Chapman, Con. *The Year of the Gerbil: How the Yankees Won (And the Red Sox Lost) the Greatest Pennant Race Ever.* Danbury, CT: Rutledge, 1998.

Clark, Tom. *Champagne and Baloney: The Rise and Fall of Finley's A's.* New York: Harper and Row, 1976.

Connelly, Michael. *Rebound: Basketball, Busing, Larry Bird and the Rebirth of Boston.* Minneapolis: Voyageur Press, 2008.

Copley, Robert E. *The Tall Mexican: The Life of Hank Aguirre: All-Star Pitcher, Businessman, Humanitarian.* Houston: Piñata Books, 2000.

Demas, Lane. *Integrating the Gridiron: Black Civil Rights and American College Football.* New Brunswick, NJ: Rutgers University Press, 2011.

Dunkel, Tim. *Color Blind: The Forgotten Team That Broke Baseball's Color Line.* New York: Atlantic Monthly Press, 2013.

Epstein, Dan. *Stars and Stripes: Baseball and America in the Bicentennial Summer of '76.* New York: Thomas Dunne Books, 2014.

Feldmann, Doug. *El Birdos: The 1967 and 1968 St. Louis Cardinals.* Jefferson, NC: McFarland, 2007.

_____. *Gibson's Last Stand: The Rise, Fall and Near Misses of the St. Louis Cardinals, 1969–1975.* Columbia: University of Missouri Press, 2011.

Fisch, Louise Ann. *All Rise: Reynaldo G. Garza, the First Mexican American Fed-*

eral Judge. College Station: Texas A&M University Press, 1996.

Flood, Curt, and Richard Carter. *The Way It Is.* New York: Trident Press, 1971.

Gagnon-Torrez, Danielle, and Ken Lizotte. *High Inside: Memoirs of a Baseball Wife.* New York: G. P. Putnam's Sons, 1983.

Garcia, Ignacio M. *Hector P. Garcia: In Relentless Pursuit of Justice.* Houston: Arte Publico Press, 2002.

_____. *When Mexicans Could Play Ball: Basketball, Race and Identity in San Antonio, 1928–1945.* Austin: University of Texas Press, 2013.

Garcia, José M. *History of the Mexicans in Topeka: 1906–1966.* Topeka, KS: self-published, 1973.

Garcia, Mario T. *The Making of a Mexican American Mayor: Raymond L. Telles of El Paso.* El Paso: Texas Western Press, 1998.

_____. *Memories of Chicano History: The Life and Narrative of Bert Corona.* Berkeley: University of California Press, 1994.

Gems, Gerald R. *For Pride, Profit and Patriarchy: Football and the Incorporation of American Cultural Values.* Lanham, MD: Scarecrow, 2000.

_____. *Sport and the Shaping of Italian American Identity.* Syracuse, NY: Syracuse University Press, 2013.

Golon, Bob. *No Minor Accomplishment: The Revival of New Jersey Professional Baseball.* New Brunswick, NJ: Rivergate, 2008.

Gomez, Vernona, and Lawrence Goldstone. *Lefty: An American Odyssey.* New York: Ballantine, 2012.

Gonzalez, Juan. *Harvest of Empire: A History of Latinos in America.* New York: Penguin Books, 2000.

Gonzalez, Manuel G. *Mexicanos: A History of Mexicans in the United States, 2d Ed.* Bloomington: Indiana University Press, 2009.

Gonzalez-Echevarria, Roberto. *The Pride of Havana: A History of Cuban Baseball.* New York: Oxford University Press, 2001.

Goudsouzian, Aram. *King of the Court: Bill Russell and the Basketball Revolution.* Berkeley: University of California Press, 2010.

Green, G. Michael, and Roger D. Launius. *Charlie Finley: The Outrageous Story of Baseball's Super Showman.* New York: Walker, 2010.

Gutierrez, David G. *The Columbia History of Latinos in the United States Since 1960.* New York: Columbia University Press, 2004.

Hamilton, Nigel. *How to Do Biography: A Primer.* Cambridge: Harvard University Press, 2008.

Hermoso, Rafael. *Speak English! The Rise of Latinos in Baseball.* Kent, OH: Black Squirrel Books, 2013.

Hernandez, Norma. *Variables Affecting Achievement of Middle School Mexican American Students.* El Paso: University of Texas, El Paso, Reprint Series.

Hope, Holly. *Garden City: Dreams in a Kansas Town.* Norman: University of Oklahoma Press, 1988.

Iber, Jorge, and Samuel O. Regalado. *Mexican Americans and Sport: A Reader on Athletics and Barrio Life.* College Station: Texas A&M University Press, 2007.

Iber, Jorge, Samuel O. Regalado, José Alamillo, and Arnoldo De Leon. *Latinos in U.S. Sport: A History of Isolation, Cultural Identity, and Acceptance.* Champaign, IL: Human Kinetics, 2011.

Jackson, Reggie, and Kevin Baker. *Becoming Mr. October.* New York: Doubleday, 2013.

Jimenez, Tomas R. *Replenished Ethnicity: Mexican Americans, Immigration and Identity.* Berkeley: University of California Press, 2011.

Johnson, Lloyd, and Miles Wolff. *The Encyclopedia of Minor League Baseball: The Official Records of Minor League Baseball.* Durham, NC: Baseball America, 1993.

Kahn, Roger. *October Men: Reggie Jackson, George Steinbrenner, Billy Martin, and the Yankees' Miraculous Finish in 1978.* New York: Harcourt, 2003.

Kline, Alan. *Baseball on the Border: A Tale of Two Laredos.* Princeton, NJ: Princeton University Press, 1997.

Kreneck, Thomas A. *Mexican American Odyssey: Felix Tijerina, Entrepreneur and Civic Leader, 1905–1965.* College Station: Texas A&M University Press, 2001.

Kurlansky, Mark. *The Eastern Stars: How Baseball Changed the Dominican Town of San Pedro De Macoris.* New York: Penguin Group, 2010.

Lamphere, Louise, ed. *Structuring Diversity: Ethnographic Perspectives on the New Immigration.* Chicago: University of Chicago Press, 1992.

Lane, James B., and Edward J. Escobar. *Forging a Community: The Latino Experience in Northwest Indiana, 1919–1975.* Chicago: Cattails Press, 1987.

Levine, Peter. *From Ellis Island to Ebbets Field: Sport and the American Jewish Experience.* New York: Oxford University Press, 1993.

Lopez, D.A. *The Latino Experience in Omaha:*

A Visual Essay. Lewiston, NY: Edwin Mellen Press, 2001.

Mahler, Jonathan. *Ladies and Gentlemen, the Bronx Is Burning: 1977, Baseball, Politics, and the Battle for the Soul of a City.* New York: Farrar, Straus and Giroux, 2005.

Manuel, H. T. *The Education of Mexican and Spanish-Speaking Children in Texas.* Austin: Fund for Research in the Social Sciences, 1930.

_____. *Spanish-Speaking Children of the Southwest: Their Education and the Public Welfare.* Austin: University of Texas Press, 1965.

Maraniss, David. *Clemente: The Passion and Grace of Baseball's Last Hero.* New York: Simon & Schuster, 2006.

Mayer, Ronald A. *The 1937 Newark Bears: A Baseball Legend.* New Brunswick, NJ: Rutgers University Press, 1994.

McKelvey, G. Richard. *Fisk's Homer, Willie's Catch and the Shot Heard Round the World.* Jefferson, NC: McFarland, 1998.

Millard, Ann V., and Jorge Chapa. *Apple Pie and Enchiladas: Latino Newcomers in the Rural Midwest.* Austin: University of Texas Press, 2001.

Miner, Craig. *Kansas: The History of the Sunflower State, 1854–2002.* Lawrence: University of Kansas Press, 2002.

_____. *Next Year Country: Dust to Dust in Western Kansas, 1890–1940.* Lawrence: University of Kansas Press, 2006.

Monroy, Douglas. *Rebirth: Mexican Los Angeles from the Great Migration to the Great Depression.* Berkeley: University of California Press, 1999.

Padilla, Genaro M. *My History, Not Yours: The Formation of Mexican American Autobiography.* Madison: University of Wisconsin Press, 1993.

Pepe, Phil. *Talking Baseball: An Oral History of Baseball in the 1970s.* New York: Ballantine, 1998.

Perez, Louis A., Jr. *On Becoming Cuban: Identity, Nationality & Culture.* New York: HarperCollins, 1999.

Prager, Joshua. *The Echoing Green: The Untold Story of Bobby Thomson, Ralph Branca and the Shot Heard Round the World.* New York: Knopf/Doubleday, 2008.

Quinonez, Sam. *Antonio's Gun and Delfino's Dream: True Tales of Mexican Migration.* Albuquerque: University of New Mexico Press, 2007.

Quiroz, Anthony. *Claiming Citizenship: Mexican Americans in Victoria, Texas.* College Station: Texas A&M University Press, 2005.

Rader, Benjamin G. *Baseball: A History of America's Game,* 2d ed. Urbana: University of Illinois Press, 2002.

Regalado, Samuel O. *Viva Baseball: Latin Major Leaguers and Their Special Hunger.* Champaign: University of Illinois Press, 2008.

Reynolds, Bill. *'78: The Boston Red Sox, a Historic Game, and a Divided City.* New York: New American Library, 2009.

Richardson, Chad. *Batos, Bolillos, Pochos, and Pelados: Class and Culture on the South Texas Border.* Austin: University of Texas Press, 1999.

Rodriguez, Thomas. *Americano: My Journey to the Dream.* Topeka, KS: Amigos Publishing, 2004.

Rondinone, Troy. *Friday Night Fighter: Gaspar "Indio" Ortega and the Golden Age of Television Boxing.* Champaign: University of Illinois Press, 2013.

Russell, Bill, and Alan Steinberg. *Red and Me: My Coach, My Lifelong Friend.* New York: HarperCollins, 2009.

Russell, Bill, and Taylor Branch. *Second Wind: The Memoirs of an Opinionated Man.* New York: Random House, 1979.

San Miguel, Guadalupe, Jr. *"Let Them All Take Heed": Mexican Americans and the Campaign for Educational Equality in Texas, 1910–1981.* Austin: University of Texas Press, 1987.

_____. *Brown, Not White: School Integration and the Chicano Movement in Houston.* College Station: Texas A&M University Press, 2001.

Sanchez, George I. *First Regional Conference on the Education of Spanish-Speaking People in the Southwest: A Report.* Austin: University of Texas Press, 1946.

_____. *Concerning the Segregation of Spanish-Speaking Children in the Public Schools.* Austin: University of Texas Press, 1951.

Sanchez, George J. *Becoming Mexican American: Ethnicity, Culture and Identity in Chicano Los Angeles, 1900–1945.* New York: Oxford University Press, 1993.

Sandoval, Moises. *Our Legacy: The First Fifty Years.* Washington, D.C.: League of United Latin American Citizens, 1979.

Santillan, Richard, et al. *Mexican American Baseball in the Central Coast.* Charleston, SC: Arcadia, 2013.

Schwartz, Jonathan. *A Day of Light and Shadows.* Pleasantville, NY: Akadine Press, 2000.

Stavans, Ilan. *The Hispanic Condition: Reflections on Culture and Identity in America.* New York: HarperCollins, 1995.

Stull, Donald D., and Michael J. Broadway. *Slaughterhouse Blues: The Meat and Poul-*

try Industry in North America. Belmont, CA: Thompson-Wadsworth, 2003.

Stull, Donald D., Michael J. Broadway, and David Griffith. *Any Way You Cut It: Meat Processing and Small-Town America.* Lawrence: University Press of Kansas, 1995.

Suro, Roberto. *Strangers Among Us: Latino Lives in a Changing America.* New York: Vintage Books, 1999.

Torres, Noe. *Baseball's First Mexican American Star: The Amazing Story of Leo "Najo" Torres.* Plantation, FL: Llumina Press, 2006.

Valdez, Dionicio. *Barrios Nortenos: St. Paul and Midwestern Mexican Communities in the Twentieth Century.* Austin: University of Texas Press, 2000.

Verma, Gagendra K., and Douglas S. Darby. *Winners and Losers: Ethnic Minorities in Sport and Recreation.* London: Falmer Press, 1994.

Weiss, Peter. *Baseball's All-Time Goats: As Chosen by America's Top Sportswriters.* Holbrook, MA: Bob Adams, 1992.

Wendel, Tim. *The New Face of Baseball: The One Hundred Year Rise and Triumph of Latinos in America's Favorite Sport.* New York: HarperCollins, 2003.

Wilson, Nick C. *Early Latino Ballplayers in the United States: Major, Minor and Negro Leagues, 1901–1949.* Jefferson, NC: McFarland, 2005.

Wood, David, and P. Louise Johnson. *Sporting Cultures: Hispanic Perspectives on Sport, Text and the Body.* London: Routledge, 2008.

Wuthnow, Robert. *Remaking the Land: Middle America Since the 1950s.* Princeton, NJ: Princeton University Press, 2011.

Yep, Kathleen S. *Outside the Paint: When Basketball Ruled at the Chinese Playground.* Philadelphia: Temple University Press, 2009.

Zygner, Sam. *The Forgotten Marlins: A Tribute to the 1956–1960 Original Miami Marlins.* Lanham, MD: Scarecrow, 2013.

Theses, Dissertations, Undergraduate Papers, Unpublished Papers and Reports

Abreo, Rosa Maria. "A History of Rio Grande City, Texas High School." Doctoral Dissertation, University of Texas, 2001.

Aguilar, Daniel E. "Mexican Immigrants in Meatpacking Areas of Kansas: Transition and Acquisition of Cultural Capital." Doctoral Dissertation, Kansas State University, 2008.

Barrientos, David. "Roma Basketball: An Analysis of the Social and Community Impact of Mexican American Sports Involvement in the Rio Grande Valley of Texas." Undergraduate paper, Texas Tech University, 2005.

Bird, Roy. "An Ethnic History of Shawnee County, Kansas (Metropolitan Planning Commission, 1974).

Bolton, Debra J. "Social Capital in Rural Southwest Kansas." Doctoral Dissertation, Kansas State University, 2011.

Braun, Marian Frances. "A Survey of the American-Mexicans in Topeka, Kansas." Master's Thesis, Kansas State Teachers College, Emporia, 1970.

Bridge, Jim. "A Historical Review of High School Wrestling in the United States." Master's Thesis, University of Wyoming, 1964.

Chacón Avila, MonaLisa. "Mexican American Adolescent Girls: The Relationship Between Sports Participation and Self-Esteem, Grade Point Average, Sexual Activity, and Acculturation from a Relational Perspective." Doctoral Dissertation, Alliant International University-Fresno Campus, 2005.

Cleary, Robert Martin. "The Education of Mexican Americans in Kansas City, Kansas, 1916–1951." Master's Thesis, University of Missouri–Kansas City, 2002.

Cummings, Van E. "The Effect of Interscholastic Participation on the Academic Achievement (G.P.A.) of Mexican American High School Students." Master's Thesis, Central Washington University, 1987.

Davidson, Galen Floyd. "The Growth and Development of Public Education in Dodge City, Kansas." Master's Thesis, Kansas State Teachers College of Emporia, 1953.

DesBaillets, Molly. "Cultural Pluralism and Social Capital in Garden City, Kansas." Master's Thesis, University of Kansas, 2008.

Dow-Anaya, Ricardo. "An Historical Prospective of Influence Sport Had on Sport Legends of New Mexico, 1925–1975." Doctoral Dissertation, University of New Mexico, 1997.

Duda, Joan L. "A Cross-Cultural Analysis of Achievement Motivation in Sport and in the Classroom." Doctoral Dissertation, University of Illinois at Urbana-Champaign, 1981.

English, Earl Haywood. "The Recreational Preferences of the Male Students of the Vocational and Technical School of San

Antonio, Texas." Master's Thesis, University of Texas, 1936.

Fahrbach, Carl G. "The Growth and Development of Public Education in Newton, KS." Master's Thesis, Kansas State Teachers' College of Emporia, 1950.

Franco, Hector. "The Mexican People in the State of Kansas." Master's Thesis, University of Wichita, 1950.

Fry, Richard. "Latino Settlement in the New Century." Washington, D.C.: Pew Hispanic Center, October 23, 2008.

Fuhlhage, Michael. "From the Margins to the Majority: Portrayal of Hispanic Immigrants in the *Garden City (Kansas) Telegram,* 1980–2000." Master's Thesis, University of Missouri–Columbia, 2007.

Garabedian, Charles A. "The Wildcats Vs. the Mustangs: The Consolidation of the San Felipe and Del Rio School Districts." Master's Thesis, Sul Ross State University, 1994.

Graves, Russell Wayne. "Garden City: The Development of an Agricultural Community on the Great Plains." Doctoral Dissertation, University of Wisconsin–Madison, 2004.

Hartmann, Douglas. "High School Sports Participation and Educational Attainment: Recognizing, Assessing, and Utilizing the Relationship." Report to the LA84 Foundation, 2008.

Hernandez, Mike Angel. "A Comparative Study of Attitudes Toward Athletics as Expressed by Mexican American and Non-Mexican American High School Boys." Doctoral Dissertation, University of Utah, 1975.

Hinnen, Kathie. "Mexican Immigrants to Hutchinson, Kansas, 1905–1940: How a Temporary Haven Became a Home." Master's Thesis, Southwest Missouri State University, 1998.

Howard, Russell C. "Perceptions of Athletic Directors Concerning the Decline of Division 1 Wrestling Programs in the National Collegiate Athletic Association." Applied Dissertation Project, United States Sports Academy, 2002.

Huerta, Joel. "Red, Brown, and Blue: A History and Cultural Poetics of High School Football in Mexican America." Doctoral Dissertation, University of Texas, 2005.

JacAngelo, Nick Paul. "The Relation of Sports Participation to Academic Performance of High School Students." Master's Thesis, Florida International University, 2003.

Jasso-Wedel, Paula. "A Tribute to the Newton Holy Name Softball Tournaments." Newton, KS: self-published, 1988.

Johnson, Kenneth F., John J. Hartman and James W. McKenney. "Wichita's Hispanics: Tensions, Concerns, and the Migrant Stream." Wichita State University, 1986.

Kaliss, Gregory John. "Everyone's All Americans: Race, Men's College Athletics, and the Ideal of Equal Opportunity." Doctoral Dissertation, University of North Carolina, 2008.

Kral, Karla. "You Get What You Pay For: Landlords and Latino-Immigrant Tenants in Garden City, Kansas." Master's Thesis, University of Kansas, 1997.

Laird, Judith Ann Fincher. "Argentine, KS: The Evolution of a Mexican American Community, 1905–1940." Doctoral Dissertation, University of Kansas, 1975.

Lazos, Sylvia R., and Stephen C. Jeanetta. "Cambio De Colores: Immigration of Latinos to Missouri." Columbia, MO: MU Extension, 2002.

Leissner-Raven, Lillian. "Comparative Study of Sociometric Status and Athletic Ability of Anglo-American and Latin-American Sixth-Grade Boys." Master's Thesis, University of Texas, 1951.

Lowry, Sarah Jean. "A Comparison of Certain Physical Abilities of Anglo and Latin American Fifth and Sixth Grade Girls." Master's Thesis, University of Texas, 1952.

Martinez, Camilo. "School Walkout in Edcouch-Elsa, 1968." Graduate paper, University of Texas, Pan American, 1981.

Mendoza, Valerie Marie. "The Creation of a Mexican Immigrant Community in Kansas City, 1890–1930." Doctoral Dissertation, University of California, Berkeley, 1997.

Mines, Cynthia. "Riding the Rails to Kansas: The Mexican Immigrants." National Endowment for the Humanities, 1980.

Myers, Dowell, and John Pitkin. "Assimilation Tomorrow: How America's Immigrants Will Integrate by 2030." Center for American Progress, 2011.

Ortega, Frank. "Scholar Athletes: Education, Sports, and Coming of Age in Los Angeles, 1940-Present." Unpublished paper, copy in author's possession, 2009.

Ortiz, Mary Jane. "The Experiences of Some Mexican American Students in the Pharr San Juan-Alamo Schools During the 1920s, 1930s and 1940s." Graduate paper, University of Texas, Pan American, 1985.

Paino, Troy D. "The End of Nostalgia: A Cultural History of Indiana High School Basketball During the Progressive Era." Doctoral Dissertation, Michigan State University, 1997.

Paulseen, Jan S. "An Analysis of Newspaper and Photographic Coverage of Kansas High School Boys and Girls Basketball."

Doctoral Dissertation, University of Kansas, 2000.

Pew Hispanic Center. "Between Two Worlds: How Young Latinos Come of Age in America," Washington, D.C. December 11, 2009.

_____. "When Labels Don't Fit: Hispanics and Their Views of Identity," Washington, D.C. April 4, 2012.

Pilling, Michael. "Boys in the Background: The Impact of Sports on Males Growing Up in a Small Town." Master's Thesis, University of Lethbridge, 2003.

Porter, Charles Jesse. "Recreational Interests and Activities of High School Boys of the Lower Rio Grande Valley of Texas." Master's Thesis, University of Texas, 1940.

Ramirez, Socorro. "A Survey of the Mexicans in Emporia, Kansas." Master's Thesis, Kansas State Teachers College of Emporia, 1942.

Randall-Hale, Jesse. "Significance of a High School Athletic Program to School Culture, Community Development, and School-Community Relations in Rural Settings." Doctor of Education, Vanderbilt University, 1999.

Ricart, Domingo. "Just Across the Tracks: Report on a Survey of Five Mexican Communities in the State of Kansas (Emporia, Florence, Newton, Wichita, Hutchinson)." Report, University of Kansas, 1950.

Rutter, Larry G. "Mexican Americans in Kansas: A Survey and Social Mobility Study, 1900–1970." Master's Thesis, Kansas State University, 1972.

Santillan, Richard. "Mexican Social History in the Mid West United States: A Study of Four Generations, 1915–1995," unpublished manuscript.

Shaw, Jennifer L. "Boundaries, Barriers, and Benefits: The Struggle for Immigrant Children's Health Care in Garden City, Kansas." Master's Thesis, University of Kansas, 1999.

Springer-Schwatken, Shellaine Lynn. "Selected Impacts of a Freshman Academy on Student Grade-Level Transition: A Study of One Large Kansas High." Doctoral Dissertation, Kansas State University, 2004.

Stull, Donald D., et al. "Changing Relations: Newcomers and Established Residents in Garden City, Kansas." Final Report, Institute for Public Policy and Business Research, University of Kansas, 1990.

Suarez-Montero, Natalia "The Expression of Latinidad at Soccer Games in Kansas City." Master's Thesis, University of Kansas, 2010.

_____. "El Medioeste De Estados Unidos Como Una Opcion Novedosa Para La Imigracion Mexicana: Los Casos De Kansas Y Missouri." Master's Thesis, Universidad de las Americas, Puebla, Mexico, 2006.

Tabares, Arthur J, "A Study of Hispanic, Black and Anglo Students' Perceptions as a Measure of Their Middle School Experiences." Doctoral Dissertation, Kansas State University, 1989.

Torrico, Cesar. "The Effects of Sports Participation on the Chicano Athlete." Master's Thesis, San Jose State University, 1999.

Volk, Michael. "Demographic Change and White Flight in Rural America: Exploiting Minority Labor and Segregating Public Schools in Garden City, Ks." Doctoral Dissertation, Arizona State University, 2011.

Walsh-Shaw, Bruce. "Sociometric Status and Athletic Ability of Anglo-American and Latin-American Boys in a San Antonio Junior High School." Master's Thesis, University of Texas, 1951.

Wende, Karleen, Lorena Lopez and Helen Wallau. "Generations United," Topeka, KS: Our Lady of Guadalupe School and Kansas Humanities Council, 1994.

Yep, Kathleen Susan. "They Got Game: The Racial and Gender Politics of Basketball in San Francisco's Chinatown, 1932–1949." Doctoral Dissertation, University of California, Berkeley, 2002.

Journal Articles and Articles in Collections

Acosta, R. Vivian. "Minorities in Sport: Educational Opportunities Affect Representation." *Journal of Physical Education, Recreation and Dance* 57 (March 1986): 52–55.

Alamillo, José M. "Peloteros in Paradise: Mexican American Baseball and Oppositional Politics in Southern California, 1930–1950." *Western Historical Quarterly* 34, no. 2 (Summer 2003): 191–211.

_____. "Playing Across Borders: Transnational Sports and Identities in Southern California and Mexico, 1930–1945." *Pacific Historical Review* 79, no. 3 (August 2010): 360–392.

_____. "Richard 'Pancho' Gonzalez, Race and the Print Media in Postwar Tennis America." *International Journal for the History of Sport* 26, no. 7 (June 2009): 947–965.

Altimore, Michael. "'Gentleman Athlete': Joe DiMaggio and the Celebration and Submergence of Ethnicity." *International Review for the Sociology of Sport* 34, no. 4 (1999): 359–367.

Anderson, Mark C. "'What's to Be Done with 'Em': Images of Mexican Cultural Backwardness, Racial Limitations, and Moral Decrepitude in the United States Press, 1913–1915." *Mexican Studies/Estudios Mexicanos* 14, no. 1 (Winter 1998): 23–70.

Anderson, William B. "Does the Cheerleading Ever Stop? Major League Baseball and Sports Journalism." *Journalism and Mass Communication Quarterly* 78, no. 2 (Summer 2001): 355–382.

_____. "Sports Page Boosterism: Atlanta and Its Newspapers Accomplish the Unprecedented." *American Journalism* 17, no. 3 (Summer 2000): 89–107.

Avila, Henry J. "Immigration and Integration: The Mexican American Community in Garden City, Kansas, 1900–1950." *Kansas History* 20, no. 1 (Spring 1997): 22–37.

Benson, Janet E. "'Good Neighbors': Ethnic Relations in Garden City Trailer Courts." *Urban Anthropology* 19, no. 4 (1990): 361–386.

_____. "Staying Alive: Economic Strategies Among Hispanic Immigrant Packing Plant Workers in Three Southwest Kansas Communities." *Kansas Quarterly* 25, no. 2 (1994): 107–120.

Berrigan, David, et al. "Physical Activity and Acculturation Among Adult Hispanics in the United States." *Research Quarterly for Exercise and Sport* 77, no. 2. (June 2006): 147–157.

Blanton, Carlos Kevin. "'They Cannot Master Abstractions, but They Can Often Be Made Efficient Workers': Race and Class in the Intelligence Testing of Mexican Americans and African Americans in Texas During the 1920s." *Social Science Quarterly* 81, no. 4 (December 2000): 1014–1026.

Braysmith, Hilary A. "Constructing Athletic Agents in Chicano/A Culture of Los Angeles." *International Journal for the History of Sport* 22, no. 2 (March 2005): 177–195.

Briley, Ron "Dick Young: Not So 'Young Ideas' on the Barricades in 1968." *Nine* 15, no. 1 (Fall 2006): 45–53.

Britz, Kevin. "Of Football and Frontiers: The Meaning of Bronko Nagurski." *Journal of Sport History* 20, no. 2 (Summer 1993): 101–126.

Broadway, Michael J. "Meatpacking and Its Social and Economic Consequences for Garden City, KS in the 1980s." *Urban Anthropology* 19, no. 4 (1990): 321–344.

Brown, Tony N., et al. "'There Is No Race on the Playing Field': Perceptions of Racial Discrimination Among White and Black Athletes." *Journal of Sport and Social Issues* 27, no. 2 (May 2003): 162–183.

Butterworth, Michael L. "'The Race': Mark McGwire, Sammy Sosa, and Heroic Con-

structions of Whiteness." *Critical Studies in Media Communication* 24, no. 3 (August 2007): 228–244.

Cahn, Susan K. "Sports Talk: Oral History and Its Uses, Problems, and Possibilities for Sports History." *Journal of American History* 81, no. 2 (September 1994): 594–609.

Campa, Arthur. "Immigrant Latinos and Resident Mexican Americans in Garden City, KS: Ethnicity and Ethnic Relations." *Urban Anthropology* 19, no. 4 (1990): 345–360.

Chavez, Gene T. "Pitch'm Fast Pauly ... The Mexican American Fast-Pitch Softball Leagues." *Historical Journal of Wyandotte County* 3, no. 12 (Winter 2015): 412–414.

Ciotola, Nicolas P. "Spignesi, Sinatra, and the Pittsburgh Steelers: Franco's Italian Army as an Expression of Ethnic Identity, 1972–1977." *Journal of Sport History* 27 (Summer 2000): 271–289.

Courturier, Lynn E. "The Influence of the Eugenics Movement on Physical Education in the United States." *Sports History Review* 36 (2005): 21–42.

Davis, Roger P. "Latinos Along the Platte: The Hispanic Experience in Central Nebraska." *Journal of Rural Studies* 12, no. 1 (May 2002): 27–50.

De Leon, Arnoldo. "Whither Tejano History: Origins, Development, and Status." *Southwestern Historical Quarterly* 51, no. 3 (January 2003): 348–364.

Delgado, Fernando. "Golden but Not Brown: Oscar De La Hoya and the Complications of Culture, Manhood and Boxing." *International Journal for the History of Sport* 22, no. 1 (March 2005): 196–211.

Donato, Ruben. "Hispano Education and the Implications of Autonomy: Four School Systems in Southern Colorado, 1920–1963." *Harvard Educational Review* 69, no. 2 (Summer 1999): 117–149.

Driever, Steven L. "Latinos in Polynucleated Kansas City." in Daniel D. Arreola, editor, *Hispanic Spaces, Latino Places: Community and Cultural Diversity in Contemporary America* (Austin: University of Texas Press, 2004): 207–224.

Duda, Joan L. "Goals and Achievement Orientations of Anglo and Mexican American Adolescents in Sports and in the Classroom." *International Review for the Sociology of Sport* 18, no. 4 (1983): 63–80.

Dyreson, Mark. "Marketing Weismuller to the World: Hollywood's Olympics and Federal Schemes for Americanization Through Sport." *International Journal of the History of Sport* 25, no. 2 (2008): 284–306.

Erkut, Sumru, and Allison J. Tracy. "Predicting Adolescent Self-Esteem from Participation in School Sports Among Latino Subgroups." *Hispanic Journal of Behavioral Sciences* 24, no. 4 (November 2002): 409–429.

Fabrizio-Pelak, Cynthia. "Athletes as Agents of Change: An Examination of Shifting Race Relations Within Women's Netball in Post-Apartheid South Africa." *Sociology of Sports Journal* 21 (2005): 59–77.

Fair, John. "Mr. America: Idealism or Racism: Color Consciousness and the AAU Mr. American Contest, 1939–1982." *Iron Game History* (June/July 2003): 9–30.

Fejgin, Naomi. "Participation in High School Competitive Sports: A Subversion of School Mission or Contribution to Academic Goals?" *Sociology of Sport Journal* 11 (1994): 211–230.

Fernandez, Lilia. "Of Immigrants and Migrants: Mexican and Puerto Rican Labor Migration in Comparative Perspective." *Journal of American Ethnic History* 29, no. 3 (Spring 2010): 6–39.

Floyd, Myron, et al. "Research on Race and Ethnicity in Leisure Studies: A Review of Five Major Journals." *Journal of Leisure Research* 40, no. 1 (2008): 1–22.

Floyd, Myron F., and James H. Gramann. "Effects of Acculturation and Structural Assimilation in Resource-Based Recreation: The Case of Mexican Americans." *Journal of Leisure Research* 25, no. 1 (1993): 6–21.

Foley, Douglas E. "The Great American Football Ritual: Reproducing Race, Class, and Gender Inequality." *Sociology of Sport Journal* 7 (1990): 111–135.

Franks, Joel. "Pacific Islanders in American Football." *International Journal for the History of Sport* 26, no. 16 (2009): 2397–2411.

Garcia, Gilberto. "Louis 'Count' Castro: The Story of a Forgotten Major Leaguer." *Nine: A Journal of Baseball History and Culture* 16, no. 2 (Spring 2008): 35–51.

Gems, Gerald R. "The Construction, Negotiation, and Transformation of Racial Identity in American Football: A Study of Native and African Americans." *American Indian Culture and Research Journal* 22, no. 2 (1998): 131–150.

_____. "The Prep Bowl: Football and Religious Acculturation in Chicago, 1927–1963." *Journal of Sport History* 23, no. 3 (Fall 1996): 284–302.

_____. "Puerto Rico: Sport and the Restoration of National Pride." *The International Journal of Regional and Local Studies* 1, no. 1 (Spring 2005): 107–120.

Gerlach, Larry. "Crime and Punishment: The Marichal-Roseboro Incident." *Nine: A Journal of Baseball History and Culture* 12, no. 2 (Spring 2004): 1–28.

_____. "Ernie Quigley: An Official for All Seasons." *Kansas History: A Journal of the Great Plains* 33 (Winter 2010–2011): 218–239.

Glover, Troy D., and John L. Hemingway. "Locating Leisure in the Social Capital Literature." *Journal of Leisure Research* 37, no. 4 (2005): 387–401.

Goldsmith, Pat Antonio. "Race Relations and Racial Patterns in School Sports Participation." *Sociology of Sport Journal* 20 (2003): 147–171.

Goudsouzian, Aram. "'Can Basketball Survive Wilt Chamberlin': The Kansas Years of Wilt the Stilt." *Kansas History: A Journal of the Great Plains* 28 (Autumn 2005): 150–173.

Grey, Mark A. "Sports and Immigrants, Minority and Anglo Relations in Garden City (Kansas) High School." *Sociology of Sport Journal* 9 (1992): 255–270.

Haverluk, Terrence W. "Hispanization of Hereford, Texas." In *Hispanic Spaces, Latino Places: Community and Cultural Diversity in Contemporary America*, edited by Daniel D. Arreola. Austin: University of Texas Press, 2004: 277–292.

Hazucha, Andrew. "Leo Durocher's Last Stand: Anti-Semitism, Racism, and the Cubs Player Rebellion of 1971." *Nine* 15, no. 1 (Fall 2006): 1–12.

Heiskanen, Benita. "The *Latinization* of Boxing: A Texas Case Study." *Journal of Sports History* 32, no. 1 (Spring 2005): 45–66.

Henderson, Simon. "Crossing the Lines: Sports and the Limit of Civil Rights Protest." *International Journal for the History of Sport* 26, no. 1 (2009): 101–121.

Iber, Jorge. "Bobby Cavazos: A Vaquero in the Backfield." *College Football Historical Society* 14, no. 4 (August 2001): 1–5.

_____. "The Early Life and Career of Topeka's Mike Torrez, 1946–1978: Sport as Means for Studying Latino/A Life in Kansas." *Kansas History: A Journal of the Central Plains* 37 (Autumn 2014): 164–179.

_____. "Mexican Americans of South Texas Football: The Athletic and Coaching Careers of E. C. Lerma and Bobby Cavazos, 1932–1965." *Southwestern Historical Quarterly* 55, no. 4 (April 2002): 616–633.

_____. "On Field Foes and Racial Misperceptions: The 1961 Donna Redskins and Their Drive to the Texas State Football Championship." *International Journal for the History of Sport* 21, no. 2 (March 2004): 75–94.

_____. "Prologue: The Perils and Possibilities of 'Quarterbacking While Mexican': A Brief Introduction to the Participation of Latino/A Athletes in US Sport History." *International Journal for the History of Sport* 26, no. 7 (June 2009): 881–888.

Ingham, John N. "Managing Integration: Clemente, Willis, 'Harry the Hat,' and the Pittsburgh Pirates' 1967 Season of Discontent." *Nine: A Journal of Baseball History and Culture* 21, no. 1 (Fall 2012): 69–102.

Jaimeson, Katherine. "Reading Nancy Lopez: Decoding Representations of Race, Class, and Sexuality." *Sociology of Sport Journal* 15 (1998): 343–358.

Johnson, Kevin A., and Joseph W. Anderson. "Rhetorical Constructions of Anger Management, Emotions, and Public Argument in Baseball Culture: The Case of Carlos Zambrano." *Nine: A Journal of Baseball History and Culture*, 21, no. 2 (Spring 2013): 56–76.

Kemper, Kurt Edward. "The Smell of Roses and the Color of the Players: Football and the Expansion of the Civil Rights Movement in the West." *Journal of Sport History* 31, no. 3 (Fall 2004): 317–339.

King-White, Ryan. "Danny Almonte: Discursive Construction(S) of (Im)Migrant Citizenship in Neoliberal America." *Sociology of Sport Journal* 27 (2010): 178–199.

Kline, Alan. "Latinizing the 'National Pastime.'" *International Journal for the History of Sport* 24, no. 2 (February 2007): 296–310.

Knowlton, David. "Kansas." In *Latino America: A State by State Encyclopedia, Vol 1.*, edited by Mark Overmeyer-Velazques. Westport, CT: Greenwood Press, 2008, 311–333.

Koerber, Duncan. "Constructing the Sports Community: Canadian Sport Columnists, Identity and the Business of Sport in the 1940s." *Sport History Review* 40 (2009): 126–142.

Lansbury, Jennifer H. "'The Tuskegee Flash' and 'The Harlem Stroker': Black Women Athletes on the Margin." *Journal of Sport History* 28, no. 1 (Summer 2001): 233–252.

Lasley-Barajas Heidi, and Jennifer L. Pierce. "The Significance of Race and Gender in School Success Among Latinas and Latinos in College." *Gender & Society* 15, no. 6 (December 2001): 859–878.

Lee, Christopher H. "Adaptation on the Plains: The Development of Six Man and Eight Man Football in Kansas." *Kansas History* 12, no. 4 (Winter 1989–1990): 192–201.

Leiker, James N. "Race Relations in the Sunflower State." *Kansas History* 25, no. 3 (Autumn 2002): 214–236.

MacClancy, Jeremy. "Sport, Identity, and Ethnicity." In *Sports, Identity and Ethnicity*, edited by Jeremy MacClancy. Oxford: Berg, 1996, 1–20.

MacClean, Malcolm. "Ambiguity Within a Boundary: Re-Reading C.L.R. James's *Beyond a Boundary*." *Journal of Sport History* 37, no. 1 (2010): 99–118.

Makin, Robert Sean, and Carol S. Walther. "Race, Sport and Social Mobility: Horatio Alger in Short Pants?" *International Journal for the Sociology of Sport*, published online on 22 December 2011. http://irs.sagepub.com/content/early/2011/12/22/1012690211429212.

Marcello, Ronald E. "The Integration of Intercollegiate Athletics in Texas: North Texas State College as a Test Case, 1956." *Journal of Sport History* 14, no. 3 (Winter 1987): 286–316.

Martin, Charles H. "Integrating New Year's Day: The Racial Politics of College Bowl Games in the American South." *Journal of Sport History* 24, no. 3 (Fall 1997): 358–377.

McClendon, McKee J., and D. Stanley Eitzen. "Interracial Contact on Collegiate Basketball Teams: A Test of Sherif's Theory of Superordinate Goals." *Social Science Quarterly* 55, no. 4 (March 1975): 926–947.

McDonald, Victoria-Maria. "Historiographic Essay: Hispanic, Latino, Chicano, or 'Other': Deconstructing the Relationship Between Historians and Hispanic-American Educational History." *History of Education Quarterly* 41, no. 3 (Fall 2001): 365–413.

McHale, Susan M., Kimberly A. Updegraff, Ji-Yeon Kim, and Emily Cansler. "Cultural Orientations, Daily Activities, and Adjustment in Mexican American Youth." *Journal of Youth Adolescence* 38 (2009): 627–641.

McMillen, Jay B. "The Social Organization of Leisure Among Mexican Americans." *Journal of Leisure Research* (Second Quarter 1983): 164–173.

Melnick, Merrill J., and Donald Sabo. "Sport and Social Mobility Among African American and Hispanic Athletes." In *Ethnicity and Sport in North American History and Culture*, edited by George Eisen and David K. Wiggins. Westport, CT: Greenwood Press, 1994: 221–241.

Melnick, Merrill J., Donald Sabo, and Beth Vanfossen. "Effects of Interscholastic Athletic Participation on the Social, Educational and Career Mobility of Hispanic Girls and Boys." *International Review for the Sociology of Sport* 27, no. 1 (1992): 57–73.

Mendoza, Valerie M. "They Came to Kansas

Searching for a Better Life." *Kansas Quarterly* 25, no. 2 (1994): 97–106.

Monroy, Douglas. "'Our Children Get So Different Here': Film, Fashion, Popular Culture, and the Process of Cultural Syncretization in Mexican Los Angeles, 1900–1935." *Aztlan* 19, no. 1 (Spring 1988–1990): 79–108.

Moody, James. "Race, School Integration, and Friendship Segregation in America." *The American Journal of Sociology* 107, no. 3 (November 2001): 679–716.

Munoz, Ed A., and Suzanne T. Ortega. "Regional Socioeconomic and Sociocultural Differences Among Us Latinos; the Effects of Historical and Contemporary Latino Immigration/Migration Streams." *Great Plains Research* 7, no. 2 (Fall 1997): 289–314.

Murrell, Audrey J., and Samuel L. Gaertner. "Cohesion and Sport Team Effectiveness: The Benefit of a Common Group Identity." *Journal of Sport and Social Issues* 16, no. 1 (1992): 1–14.

Napier, Rita G. "Rethinking the Past, Reimagining the Future." *Kansas History* 24, no. 3 (Autumn 2001): 218–247.

Newman, Roberta. "Driven: Branding Derek Jeter, Redefining Race." *Nine: A Journal of Baseball History and Culture* 17, no. 2 (Spring 2009): 70–79.

_____. "'Let's Just Say It Works for Me': Rafael Palmeiro, Major League Baseball, and the Marketing of Viagra." *Nine: A Journal of Baseball History and Culture* 14, no. 2 (Spring 2006): 1–14.

Oppenheimer, Robert. "Acculturation or Assimilation: Mexican Immigrants in Kansas, 1900 to World War I." *Western Historical Quarterly* 16, no. 4 (October 1985): 429–448.

Ortiz, Leonard David. "'La Voz de la Gente': Chicano Activist Publications in the Kansas City Area, 1968–1969." *Kansas History: A Journal of the Central Plains* 22, no. 3 (Autumn 1999): 229–244.

Palmer, Susan L. "The Community-Building Experiences of Mexicans in Aurora, Illinois, 1915–1935." *Journal of the Illinois State Historical Society* 98, no. 3 (Autumn 2005): 125–143.

Park, Roberta J. "Boys Clubs Are Better than Policeman's Clubs." *International Journal for the History of Sport* 24, no. 6 (2007): 749–775.

_____. "Sport and Recreation Among Chinese American Communities of the Pacific Coast from the Time of Arrival to the 'Quiet Decade' of the 1950s." *Journal of Sports History* 27, no. 3 (Fall 2000): 445–480.

Pendelton, Jason. "Jim Crow Strikes Out: Interracial Baseball in Wichita, Kansas, 1920–1935." *Kansas History* 20, no. 2 (Summer 1997): 86–101.

Pope, Steven W. "Negotiating the 'Folk Highway' of the Nation: Sport, Public Culture and American Identity, 1870–1940." *Journal of Social History* 27, no. 2 (Winter 1993): 327–340.

Price, Marie, and Courtney Whitworth. "Soccer and Latino Cultural Space: Metropolitan Washington *Fútbol* Leagues." In *Hispanic Spaces, Latino Places: Community and Cultural Diversity in Contemporary America,* edited by Daniel D. Arreola. Austin: University of Texas Press, 2004: 167–186.

Primm, Eric, Summer DuBois and Robert Regoli. "Every Picture Tells a Story: Racial Representation on *Sports Illustrated* Covers." *The Journal of American Culture* 30, no. 2 (June 2007): 222–231.

Regalado, Samuel O. "'Hey Chico!': The Latin Identity in Major League Baseball." *Nine: A Journal of Baseball History and Culture* 11, no. 1 (Fall 2002): 16–24.

_____. "'Image Is Everything': Latin Ballplayers and the United States Press." *Studies in Latin American Popular Culture* 13 (1994): 101–114.

_____. "The Minor League Experience of Latin American Baseball Players in Western Communities, 1950–1970." *Journal of the West* 26, no. 1 (January 1987): 65–70.

_____. "Roberto Clemente: Images, Identity and Legacy." *International Journal for the History of Sport* 25, no. 6 (2008): 678–690.

_____. "Sport and Community in California's Japanese American 'Yamato Colony,' 1930–1945." *Journal of Sport History* 19, no. 2 (Summer 1992): 131–143.

Riney-Kehrberg, Pamela. "Hard Times, Hungry Years: Failure of the Poor Relief in Southwestern Kansas, 1930–1933." *Kansas History: A Journal of the Central Plains* 15, no. 3 (Autumn 1992): 154–167.

Rodriguez, Roberto. "Dispelling the Myths of Latinos in Sports." *Black Issues in Higher Education* 10, no. 20 (December 2, 1993): 30–31.

Ryska, Todd A. "The Impact of Acculturation on Sports Motivation Among Mexican American Adolescent Athletes." *The Psychological Record* 51 (2001): 533–547.

Santillan, Richard. "Mexican Baseball Teams in the Midwest, 1916–1965: The Politics of Cultural Survival and Civil Rights." *Perspectives in Mexican American Studies* 7 (2000): 131–151.

Satterlee, Thom. "Making Soccer a 'Kick in

the Grass': The Media's Role in Promoting a Marginal Sport, 1975–1977." *International Review for the Sociology of Sport* 36, no. 3 (2001): 305–317.

Schmidt, Raymond. "Lords of the Prairie: Haskell Indian School Football, 1919–1930." *Journal of Sport History* 28, no. 3 (Fall 2001): 403–426.

Sculle, Keith J. "'The New Carlisle of the West': Haskell Institute and Big-Time Sports, 1920–1932." *Kansas History* 17, no. 3 (Autumn 1994): 192–208.

Seifred, Chad S., and Matthew Katz. "The Creation of Domestic and International Bowl Games from 1942 to 1964: The United States Military and Football as Conjoined Twins." *Sports History Review* 42 (2011): 153–175.

Shakib, Sohalia, Phillip Veliz, Michele D. Dunbar, and Don Sabo. "Athletics as a Source for Social Status Among Youth: Examining Variation by Gender, Race/Ethnicity, and Socioeconomic Status." *Sociology of Sport Journal* 28 (2011): 303–328.

Simons, William M. "The Athlete as Jewish Standard Bearer: Media Images of Hank Greenberg." *Jewish Social Studies* 44 (Spring 1982): 95–112.

Smith, Michael M., "The Mexican Immigrant Press Beyond the Borderlands: The Case of *El Cosmopolita*, 1914–1919." *Journal of the Great Plains Quarterly* 10 (Spring 1990): 71–85.

_____. "The Mexican Revolution in Kansas City: Jack Danciger Versus the Colonia Elite." *Kansas History* 14 (Fall 1991): 206–218.

_____. "Mexicans in Kansas City: The First Generation, 1900–1920." *Perspectives in Mexican American Studies* 2 (1989): 29–57.

Snyder, Eldon E., and Elmer Spreitzer. "High School Athletic Participation as Related to College Attendance Among Black, Hispanic and White Males." *Youth and Society: A Quarterly Journal* 21, no. 3 (March 1990): 390–398.

Stull, Donald D. "'I Come to the Garden': Changing Ethnic Relations in Garden City, Kansas." *Urban Anthropology* 19, no. 4 (1990): 303–320.

Stull, Donald D., and Michael Broadway. "Meatpacking and Mexicans on the High Plains: From Minority to Majority in Garden City, Kansas." In *Immigrants Outside the Megalopolis: Ethnic Transformation in the Heartland,* edited by Richard C. Jones. Lanham, MD: Rowan & Littlefield, 2008: 115–133.

Ten Kate, Nancy. "Hispanics Hit the Hoops." *American Demographics* 15, no. 6 (June 1993): 22.

Thompson, Merrell T., and Claude Dove. "A Comparison of Physical Achievement of Anglo and Spanish American Boys in Junior High School." *The Research Quarterly of the American Association for Health, Physical Education and Recreation* 13, no. 3 (October 1942): 41–46.

Valdes, D.N. "Settlers, Sojourners and Proletarians: Social Formation in the Great Plains Sugar Beet Industry, 1890–1940." *Journal of the Great Plains Quarterly* 10, no. 2 (Spring 1990): 110–123.

Warren, Kim. "All Indian Trials Lead to Lawrence, October 27 to 30, 1926: American Identity and the Dedication of the Haskell Institute's Football Stadium." *Kansas History: A Journal of the Great Plains* 30 (Spring 2007): 2–19.

Williams, Susan, Sandra A. Alvarez and Kevin S. Andrade Hauck. "'My Name Is Not Maria': Young Latinas Seeking Home in the Heartland." *Social Problems* 49, no. 4 (November 2002): 563–584.

Winters, Jet C. "A Report on the Health and Nutrition of Mexicans Living in Texas." July 15, 1931, no. 3127. Austin: The University of Texas Bulletin, Bureau of Research in Social Sciences.

Wunder, John R. "The Last Season: Crisis Times in Modern Plains Agricultural Communities and the End of Six-Man Football." Charles L. Wood Agricultural History Lecture, Texas Tech University, February 2003.

Yoseloff, Anthony A. "From Ethnic Hero to National Icon: The Americanization of Joe DiMaggio." *International Journal of the History of Sport* 16, no. 3 (September 1999): 1–20.

Newspapers Articles, Magazine Articles, and Websites

Allen, Maury. "Torrez Coping with Hard Times." *New York Post,* May 17, 1983.

Araton, Harvey. "Dent-Torrez Again, but It's in the Bushes." *Daily News,* April 14, 1985.

_____. "Did Newark Bet on the Wrong Sport?" *New York Times,* August 21, 2011. See: www.nytimes.com/2011/08/22/sports/baseball.did-newark-bet-on-the-wrong-sport.html?pagewanted=all&_r=0&pagewanted=print.

Armour, Basil. "Problems in the Education of the Mexican Child." *The Texas Outlook* 16 (December 1932): 29–31.

Arrieta, Victor. "Belen Jesuit's Rodriguez Plays for His Father." http://espn.go.com/

blog/high-school/baseball/post/_/id/1500/belen-jesuits-rodriguez.... Accessed on 4/6/12.

Barry, Dan. "Newark Bears' Items Going, Going...." *New York Times*, April 24, 2014. See: http://www.nytimes.com/2014/04/25/sports/baseball/newark-bears-are-holding-a-liquidation-auction.html?_r=0.

"Baseball Briefs." *The Sporting News*, January 17, 1970.

"Baseball's 15 Biggest Pennant Chase Goats of All Time." See: http://bleacherreport.com/articles/1329359-baseballs-15-biggest-pennant-chase-goats-of-all-time/page/14.

Berger, Mike. "Redbirds Hold No Terror for Polished Nippon Club." *The Sporting News*, November 16, 1968.

_____. "Redhead Says Japan Teams Overwork Hurlers." *The Sporting News*, December 7, 1968.

Bergman, Ron. "A's Hold Their Noses Over 'Crabcake' Deal." *The Sporting News*, April 17, 1976.

_____. "Diary of Defeat—A's Were Losers Even in the Bus League." *The Sporting News*, June 12, 1976.

_____. "Lady Luck Blind-Sides Vida in Year of Big Gold Strike." *The Sporting News*, October 2, 1976.

_____. "Liberated A's Give Champagne Party." *The Sporting News*, October 23, 1976.

_____. "McKeon Talks Bravely About A's Job." *The Sporting News*, December 11, 1976.

_____. "Name Almost Anything, McKeon Can Use It." *The Sporting News*, March 5, 1977.

_____. "Only the Ex-A's Grin as They Leave the Bay Area." *The Sporting News*, March 5, 1977.

_____. "Three Ring Circus, with Charlie in Charge." *The Sporting News*, November 27, 1976.

_____. "Torrez Red-Hot Hurler in A's Futile Drive for A.L. West Title." *The Sporting News*, October 16, 1976.

_____. "We Were Traded Out of a Pennant." *The Sporting News*, October 30, 1976.

Blount, Roy, Jr. "Pan Am Finds the Going Great." *Sports Illustrated*, February 17, 1975: 46–47.

Borrelli, Stephen. "Torrez Can Relate to Clemens." See: http://www.usatoday30.usatoday.com/sports/baseball/comment/Borrelli/2000–10-26-borelli.htm.

Bowers, Gladine. "Mexican Education in East Donna." *The Texas Outlook* 15 (March 1931): 29–30.

Boyle, Robert H. "The Latins Storm Las Grandes Ligas." *Sports Illustrated*, August 9, 1965. See: http://www.si.com/vault.19 65/08/09/606430/the-latins-storm-las-grandes-ligas.

Brittain, Amy. "Newark Bears: A Tale of a Sidetracked Baseball Franchise." *Newark Star-Ledger*, July 17, 2011. See: http://www.nj.com/news/index.ssf/2011/o7/how_court_battles_unpaid_bills/html.

Broeg, Bob. "Cards Pitching Depth Reminds Devine of '41." *The Sporting News*, April 20, 1968.

_____. "Red Takes Rosy View If Torrez Is Torrid." *The Sporting News*, March 8, 1969.

_____. "Redbirds Twitter Over Rookie Pair of Hague and Day." *The Sporting News*, March 22, 1969.

_____. "Southpaw Steve Could Be Redbirds' Secret Weapon." *The Sporting News*, April 3, 1971.

_____. "Vada Buffs Already Shiny Card Picture." *The Sporting News*, March 29, 1969.

Brown, Doug. "Orioles Called 'Tough to Beat' Because of Deals" *The Sporting News*, January 11, 1975.

Burkhart, J. Austin "I Teach in a Border Town." *The Texas Outlook* 23 (December 1939): 34.

Callcott, Frank. "The Mexican Peon in Texas." *The Survey* June 26, 1920.

"Cards Payroll Gives Insight." *The State Journal*, April 2, 1969.

Carree, Chuck. "No Regrets for Red Sox's Mike Torrez." Starnewsonline.com, January 8, 2009. See: http://www.starnewsonline.com/article/20090108/ARTICLES/901080281?template=print.

Carter, Andrew. "Why Don't Hispanics Play?" *Orlando Sentinel* May 20, 2007. Accessed on 9/18/2007. http://www.orlandosentinel.com/sports/local/orl-hispanics2007may20,0,220998,print.story.

Chass, Murray. "Torrez Near to Signing 7-Year Pact with Red Sox." *New York Times*, November 21, 1977.

Clark, Jen. "When We Were Young: History Examined Through Kids' Perspective." *Topeka Capital-Journal*, November 12, 2011.

Cohen, Andrew. "A Divided Red Sox Nation." *The Atlantic*, October 30, 2013. See: http://www.theatlantic.com/entertainment/archive/2013/10/a-divided-red-sox-nation/281011.

Craig, Jack. "Do Bosox Owners Want Profits or Pennant?" *The Sporting News*, February 3, 1979.

Di Ionno, Mark. "Game Over: Newark Bears Officially Out of Business, as Baseball Fades from City Again." *Newark Star-Ledger*, April 26, 2014. See: http://www.nj.com/essex/index.ssf/2014/04/newark_bears_offi

cially_out_of_business_as_baseball_fades_from_city_again.html.

Dodd, E. C. "The Lower Rio Grande Valley Elementary Principals Association." *The Texas Outlook* 12 (June 1928): 30–31.

Drehs, Wayne. "Cultures Are Teammates at Iowa High School." October 11, 2006. See: http://sports.espn.go.com/espn/print?id=2618295&type=story. Accessed on 9/18/2007.

Dunn, Bob. "Expos Get Southpaw, but Was Price Too Steep?" *The Sporting News*, December 21, 1974.

_____. "Hunt's Exit Seen as Beginning of Expo Shakeup." *The Sporting News*, September 21, 1974.

_____. "Renko Puzzled by His Failures in Early Outings." *The Sporting News*, May 18, 1974.

_____. "Rogers Brightest Hope on Expo Mound." *The Sporting News*, March 9, 1974.

_____. "Rogers, Singleton Branded Expo '74 Flops." *The Sporting News*, September 14, 1974.

_____. "Rogers Stat Pick Reflect Rise of Expo Hurlers." *The Sporting News*, August 3, 1974.

_____. "Torrez and Mauch Bury Hatchet, Discuss '75 Plans." *The Sporting News*, October 19, 1974.

Dupont, Kevin. "At Last: It's Sox-Yanks!" *Boston Herald American*, October 2, 1978.

Durso, Joseph. "The Yanks: Great Gamble with Greater Payoff." *The Sporting News*, November 19, 1977.

El-Nasser, Haya. "Minority Kids Grow to a Majority." *USA Today*, June 17, 2009, 1.

Eskew, Alan. "Torrez Dons Uniform Again for Old-Timers Game." *Topeka Capital-Journal*, August 1, 1987.

Falls, Joe. "Sad to See Decline in Deals." *The Sporting News*, January 1, 1977.

Ferguson, John. "Oilers Blend Defense, Pitching and Swatting into Rocket Fuel." *The Sporting News*, September 28, 1968.

_____. "Think ... And Serve Up Strikes—It's Paying Off for Tulsa's Torrez." *The Sporting News*, September 2, 1967.

"Game Three Slants." *The Sporting News*, October 29, 1977.

Gammons, Peter. "Bill Weaves Patches to Perfection." *The Sporting News*, May 9, 1981.

_____. "Fisk Will Help Chisox." *The Sporting News*, April 4, 1981.

_____. "Living and Dying with the Woe Sox." *Sports Illustrated*, November 3, 1986. See: http://sportsillustrated.cnn.com/vault/article/magazine/MAG1065413/index.htm.

_____. "Steinbrenner Rapped as Inflation Culprit." *The Sporting News*, January 3, 1983.

_____. "Umpire Quality Is Sinking—Bad Calls and Poor Attitudes." *The Sporting News*, September 20, 1980.

Giuliotti, Joe. "Burgmeier Rescue Ace of Fading Bosox." *The Sporting News*, June 7, 1980.

_____. "Chipper Torrez Starts Tomorrow." *Boston Globe*, August 19, 1982.

_____. "Eckersley Primed for Big Comeback." *The Sporting News*, February 6, 1982.

_____. "Fisk's Arm No. 1 Red Sox Question Mark." *The Sporting News*, January 19, 1980.

_____. "Frustrated Torrez Asks to Be Traded." *The Sporting News*, November 1, 1982.

_____. "Ifs Plague Red Sox." *The Sporting News*, April 12, 1980.

_____. "'I'm Just Stupid,' Says Bosox' Torrez." *The Sporting News*, August 16, 1982.

_____. "'The Old Torrez Is Back,' Red Sox Assured." *The Sporting News*, March 14, 1981.

_____. "Rader Bosox' New Fisk Insurance." *The Sporting News*, April 19, 1980.

_____. "Red Sox' Fate? It's Up to Fisk." *The Sporting News*, March 8, 1980.

_____. "Red Sox' Stanley Excited Over His New Change-Up." *The Sporting News*, February 9, 1980.

_____. "Red Sox Whiff in Trade Mart—Fans Irked." *The Sporting News*, December 22, 1979.

_____. "Sox Blast Orioles, 8–0." *Boston Herald American*, August 16, 1982.

_____. "Stigma of '78 Homer Stays with Torrez." *The Sporting News*, January 24, 1983.

_____. "Struggling Starters Send Red Sox into Deep Swoon." *The Sporting News*, May 31, 1980.

_____. "Torrez' Misery Is Almost Over." *The Sporting News*, October 4, 1980.

_____. "Torrez Sets Torrid Pace with Return of His Fastball." *The Sporting News*, June 27, 1981.

_____. "Willing Renko: Start or Stop." *The Sporting News*, June 28, 1980.

Goering, Pete. "Hero Son Absent, but Torrez Family Enjoys Celebration." *Topeka Daily Capital*, October 20, 1977.

Goode, John. "Torrez Played Both Sides." Boston.com, May 10, 2005. See: http://www.boston.com/sports/baseball/redsox/articles/2005/05/10/torrez_played_both_sides/.

Groenhagen, Kevin. "Torrez, Church Prepare for Fiesta Mexicana." *Kaw Valley Senior Monthly* 9, no. 1 (July 2009).

Grote, Dave. "N.L. Teams Ready to Reap Big Crop of Talented Frosh." *The Sporting News*, March 2, 1968.

Grow, John. "Torrez Wants to Leave His Mark." *St. Louis Post-Dispatch*, July 2, 1978.

Gulbronsen, Karl. "Mike Torrez: Traveling Man Finding Security in Boston." *Palm Beach Post*, April 3, 1978.

Habib, Hal. "One Swing Made Bucky Dent a New York Legend and a Boston Pariah." *Palm Beach Post,* October 1, 2008. See: http://www.palmbeachpost.com/sports/content/sportss/epaper/2008/10/01/a1c_d.

Hanlon, Greg. "Lost Greatness, Scar Tissue, and Survival: The Life of Baseball's Brief Superstar, Dickie Thon." May 7, 2015. See: http://sports.vice.com/en_us/article/lost-greatness-scar-tissue-and-survival-the-life-of-baseballs-brief-superstar-dickie-thon.

Harnly, Larry. "Cards' Torrez Needs to Pitch." *Springfield Journal-Register,* May 31, 1968.

Harvey, Randy. "Red Sox Will Mean Plenty of Trouble." *Sun Times,* April 6, 1978.

Haskin, Kevin. "Finally Four: No. 1 Torrez Armed for Success." *Topeka Capital-Journal,* August 28, 2011.

Henneman, Jim. "Fans Puzzled as Orioles Remove For-Sale Sign." *The Sporting News,* June 28, 1975.

_____. "Johnson Strikes Sour Note in Oriole Sonata." *The Sporting News,* April 10, 1976.

_____. "May's HR Spree Sparks Oriole Talk of Fast Finish." *The Sporting News,* August 9, 1975.

_____. "Orioles' Answer to 'The Cat'—It's Healthy Palmer." *The Sporting News,* April 12, 1975.

_____. "Orioles Chirp in Double Time Over Mike and Ken." *The Sporting News,* October 11, 1975.

_____. "Orioles Dream of Flag Pole with Reggie Leading the Band." *The Sporting News,* April 17, 1976.

_____. "Orioles' Free Fall Sets Eight-Year Mark." *The Sporting News,* June 14, 1975.

_____. "Shuffling of Rosters Confuses Orioles' Players." *The Sporting News,* April 26, 1975.

_____. "Visions of Jackson Are Dancing in Oriole Heads." *The Sporting News,* January 10, 1976.

_____. "Yanks Outbrawl Orioles: Torrez, Munson Bout Sealed with a Kiss." *Baltimore News American,* June 25, 1975.

Hentzen, Bob. "Aw, Oakland Natives, Don't Be Mad at Mike." *Topeka Daily Capital,* October 21, 1977.

_____. "Royals Nervous 7–5 Winners." *Topeka Capital Journal,* July 4, 1976.

_____. "Torrez Eyes 1964 Repeat." *Topeka Daily Capital,* July 24, 1969.

_____. "Torrez Lauds Orioles' Support." *Topeka Capital Journal,* April 23, 1975.

_____. "Yanks' Only Certainty Is Uncertainty." *Topeka Capital Journal,* October 20, 1977.

Hersh, Phil. "Munson and Torrez Played a Little Duet." *Baltimore Evening Sun,* June 25, 1975.

Hurt, Bob. "Capitalizing on Sports." *Topeka Capital-Journal,* February 21, 1968.

"International Index for Saturday, June 26, 1971." *The Sporting News,* July 17, 1971.

Isle, Stan. "Caught on the Fly—Shea Fans Rough on Torrez." *The Sporting News,* June 18, 1984.

_____. "Notebook." *The Sporting News,* October 11, 1980.

Kaegel, Dick. "Who Are Blue-Ribbon Greenies of '68?" *The Sporting News,* April 27, 1968.

_____. "Yankee Stadium or Zoo? The Routine Rivals Soap Opera." *The Sporting News,* October 29, 1977.

Kahn, Roger. "Torrez Ends an Odyssey." *New York Times,* April 9, 1979.

Kaplan, Jim. "Epidemic of Fernando Fever: Los Angeles Is Delirious Over Dazzling Rookie Lefthander Fernando Valenzuela." See: http://www.si.com/vault/1981/05/04/825589/epidemic-of-fernando-fever-los-angeles-is-delirious-over-dazzling-rookie-lefthander-fernando-valenzuela.

Kress, Dorothy. "The Spanish-Speaking Child in Texas." *The Texas Outlook* 18 (December 1934): 24.

Lang, Jack. "Future Is Now, Bambi Tells Hurlers." *The Sporting News,* February 7, 1983.

_____. "Howard's Mets Ooze Confidence." *The Sporting News,* September 5, 1983.

_____. "Keystone Combo Is Mets' Top Concern." *The Sporting News,* March 4, 1984.

_____. "Mets Expect Big Pickup in Pitching." *The Sporting News,* March 21, 1983.

_____. "Mets Lure Torrez with 2-Year Deal." *The Sporting News,* January 24, 1983.

_____. "Mets' Start: It's Amazin." *The Sporting News,* April 23, 1984.

_____. "Out with the Old: Tidrow, Swan Cut." *The Sporting News,* May 21, 1984.

_____. "Rookies Earn Way into Mets Rotation." *The Sporting News,* April 9, 1984.

_____. "Torrez Sweepstakes: Angels, KC, Expos Likely Top Bidders." *New York Daily News,* November 4, 1977.

Leggett, William. "Some Hot Rookies for a New Season." *Sports Illustrated,* March 11, 1968. See: http://sportsillustrated.cnn.com/vault/article/magazine/MAG1080929/index.htm.

Lennon, David. "HR Links Dent, Torrez Forever." *Newsday,* October 18, 1998.

Lieker, Ken. "Torrez Eyes 20 Again." *Topeka Daily Capital,* April 1, 1976.

Lopez, Goyo. "They Had Game, Too: Básquetbol in the 1930s." *Laredo Sports Journal* 3, no. 1 (January 10, 1999).

MacDonald, Ian. "Day and Staub Boost Their Swatting Marks." *The Sporting News,* September 11, 1971.

_____. "Expos Anxious to Reverse Bad Deal." *The Sporting News*, January 22, 1977.

_____. "Expos' Chances Hurt Again by 'One Black Week.'" *The Sporting News*, October 6, 1973.

_____. "Expos Get Taylor to Mend Bullpen." *The Sporting News*, November 6, 1971.

_____. "Expos Rest Hopes on Making Big Deal." *The Sporting News*, December 16, 1972.

_____. "Expos Stymied, Seeking 4th Starter." *The Sporting News*, July 3, 1971.

_____. "Mauch to Take Aim at 'Too Many Parachutes.'" *The Sporting News*, February 17, 1973.

_____. "Mike Going Where the Money Is." *Montreal Gazette*, October 24, 1977.

_____. "Mike Torrez Sees Early Signing with Expos as Eagleson Takes Hand in Contract Talks." *The Sporting News*, February 13, 1973.

_____. "Starter Role with Expos? Sounds Good to Lemaster." *The Sporting News*, October 30, 1971.

_____. "Torrez Blazer Signals Shot at 20-Win Season." *The Sporting News*, July 1, 1972.

_____. "Trim Torrez Balloons Expo Win Total." *The Sporting News*, May 20, 1972.

_____. "23 Victories Is Torrez' Goal." *The Sporting News*, January 13, 1973.

"Major Deals." *The Sporting News*, December 21, 1974.

"Major Flashes, New Tune by Mauch." *The Sporting News*, September 4, 1971.

"Major Flashes, Torrez Trims Down." *The Sporting News*, October 9, 1971.

"Major Flashes-Torrez Masters Slider." *The Sporting News*, July 8, 1972.

"Major Flashes—Zimmer Wants Company." *The Sporting News*, August 9, 1980.

Mannix, Chris. "Fight of His Life." *Sports Illustrated*. See: http://sportsillustrated.cnn.com/vault/article/magazine/MAG1190469/index.htm.

Martinez, John. "Playing for N.Y. Yankees Is Great, but Set Pitching Rotation Wanted" and "From the Sidelines." *North Platte Telegraph*, July 20, 1977.

Mavreles, Todd. "The Town Built on Basketball." *McAllen Monitor*, January 27, 2002.

McCoy, Bob. "Keeping Score." *The Sporting News*, January 23, 1989.

McGuff, Joe. "Brett Cools His Pay Pitch, Calls Royals Fair." *The Sporting News*, February 19, 1977.

Merrill, Elizabeth. "Changing the Games for Hispanic Girls." Accessed on 3/27/2009. http://sports.espn.go.com/espn/print?id=4012596&type=story.

"Mike Torrez and His Unique Yankee History." June 25, 2013. See: http://itsaboutthemoney.net/archives/2013/06/25/mike-torrez-and-his-unique-yankees-history/

"Mike Torrez Wins." *The Sporting News*, July 10, 1971.

"Milestones." *The Sporting News*, June 26, 1989.

Millea, John. "The Spanish Voice of Minnesota Sports." Accessed on 9/18/2007. http://juantornoe.blogs.com/hispanictrending/2007/07/the-spanish-voice.html.

Moncada, Eduardo. "Tovar Swinging Torrid Bat in Venezuela." *The Sporting News*, December 4, 1971.

Moschella, Nick. "Miami's Grande Experiment." *Baseball America*, July 10–24, 1985.

"The Most Hated Sports Figures in Houston History." See: http://www.chron.com/sports/rockets/slideshow/The-most-hated-sports-figures-in-Houston-history-70106/photo-5180468.php.

Murray, James. "The Little World of Bantams Gets a New Champ." *Sports Illustrated*, July 20, 1959. See: http://sportsillustrated.cnn.com/vault/article/magazine/MAG1070797/index.htm.

Napolitano, John. "Top 100 Red Sox: #95, Mike Torrez." February 29, 2004. See: http://redsox.scout.com/story/23846-top-100-red-sox-95-mike-torrez.

Nissenson, Herschel. "Yankees Still Not Happy." *Topeka Daily Journal*, October 20, 1977.

Nolting, Ray. "Former Topekan to Lead Fiesta Parade." *Topeka Capital-Journal*, July 1988.

"Oil on Yankees Fires: Torrez—More Like 1977." *Binghamton Press*, January 24, 1978.

Owens, Jesse. "Hutto, Hicks Belt Homers as Torrez Halts Spokane." *Tulsa World*, June 1, 1968.

Pace, Eli. "Latinos Wrestle with Low Participation." *Greeley Tribune* July 24, 2005. Accessed on 9/18/2007. http://www.greeleytribune.com/apps/pbcs.dll/article?AID=/20050724/SPORTS/10724006.

"Pacific Coast League." *The Sporting News*, June 15, 1968.

Pepe, Phil. "'Backed into Pennant?': No Way; Roar Yankees." *The Sporting News*, October 15, 1977.

_____. "Boston Blowup 'Made' Yanks, Billy Believes." *The Sporting News*, October 22, 1977.

_____. "Chambliss' Bat Revived by Yankee Hat Trick." *The Sporting News*, May 14, 1977.

_____. "Deal for Dent Gives Yanks an All-Star at Every Spot." *The Sporting News*, April 23, 1977.

_____. "Figueroa Makes Pitch for Super-Star Class." *The Sporting News*, June 4, 1977.

_____. "If Yankees Have a Weakness, It May

Be Their Lack of Depth." *The Sporting News,* April 9, 1977.

_____. "Peace Pipe or Exit Sign for Yanks' Martin?" *The Sporting News,* July 2, 1977.

_____. "Sagging Yanks Turn Tongues to Wagging." *The Sporting News,* May 7, 1977.

_____. "'Shape Up,' Steinbrenner Tells Martin, Yanks." *The Sporting News,* July 9, 1977.

_____. "Torrez' Plea for Work Pays Off for Yankees." *The Sporting News,* September 3, 1977.

_____. "Yankees' Elite Make Way for Guidry." *The Sporting News,* June 11, 1977.

_____. "Yankees Give Billy a Second Chance— In 1980." *The Sporting News,* August 12, 1978.

_____. "Yankees Have Unrest, All They Need Is Results." *The Sporting News,* February 26, 1977.

_____. "Yankees Improve on a Champion." *The Sporting News,* March 5, 1977.

_____. "Yanks Look to 'Goose' for Another Golden Egg." *The Sporting News,* November 26, 1977.

_____. "Yanks Put Last-Ditch Trademark on A.L. Title." *The Sporting News,* October 22, 1977.

Peterson, Rick. "Recalling Another Era." *Topeka Capital-Journal,* July 19, 1988.

"Pitching Averages." *The Sporting News,* August 8, 1970.

Politi, Steve. "Newark Bears Baseball Team on the Verge of Folding." *Newark Star-Ledger,* October 26, 2008. See: http://blog.nj.com/ledgerupdates_impact/print.html?entry=/2008/10/Newark_bears_baseball_team_on.html.

_____. "Newark Bears' New Ownership Group Determined to Make Baseball in Newark Work." *Newark Star-Ledger,* May 2, 2009. See: http://blog.nj.com/ledgerupdates_impact/print.html?entry=/2009/05/Newark_bears_new_ownership_gro.html.

Pope, Edwin. "Coping: At 35, Torrez Still Hanging Tough." *Philadelphia Enquirer,* March 21, 1982.

_____. "A Home Sweet Home for Mike Torrez." *Miami Herald,* May 16, 1978.

"Press Release: Mike Torrez Returns to Newark Bears as General Manager." See: http://www.newarkbears.com/news0010.html.

Quakenbush, Allen. "Hispanic Hoops." *Topeka Capital-Journal,* January 8, 1991.

Read, Phillip. "Despite Economy, Newark Bears Owners Envision Big Season." *Newark Star-Ledger,* January 8, 2009. See: http://blog.nj.com/ledgerupdates_impact/print.html?entry=/2009/01/despite_economy_newark_bears_o.html.

Reichard, Kevin. "It's Official: Bears to Can-Am Association." October 6, 2010. See: http://baseballparkdigest.com/201010063169/independent-baseball/news/its-official-bears-to-can-am-association.

Reidenbaugh, Lowell. "Guidry, Yanks' Mr. Cool, Chills Dodger Bats." *The Sporting News,* October 29, 1977.

_____. "Hooton, Homers Help Dodgers Even Series." *The Sporting News,* November 5, 1977.

_____. "Hooton's Baffling Knuckler Masters Yankee Swingers," *The Sporting News,* October 29, 1977.

_____. "Pride Spurs Dodgers to Bounce Off Deck." *The Sporting News,* October 29, 1977.

_____. "Reggie Reigns Supreme, and So Do Yankees." *The Sporting News,* November 5, 1977.

_____. "Torrez Takes Charge—LA Bats Wilt as Yankees Log 2nd Win," *The Sporting News,* October 29, 1977.

_____. "Turnaround by Torrez," *The Sporting News.* November 5, 1977.

_____. "Yankees Stow Brass Knuckles and Take Bows." *The Sporting News,* November 5, 1977.

_____. "Yankees Win Opener on Blair's Single." *The Sporting News,* November 5, 1977.

_____. "Yanks; Extra-Inning Heroics Subdue Dodgers." *The Sporting News,* October 29, 1977.

Richman, Alan. "The Travels of Torrez." *The Boston Globe,* January 6, 1978.

Rieber, Anthony. "...When It Was Bucky at the Bat." *Boston Globe,* July 31, 1988.

Rogin, Gilbert. "Capital of the World." *Sports Illustrated,* September 8, 1958. See: http://sportsillustrated.cnn.com/vault/article/magazine/MAG1002791/index.htm.

Russell, Joel. "More Than Just a Game: Basketball Can Be a Real Motivator to Keep Hispanic Athletes in School." *Hispanic Business* 12, no. 1 (January 1990): 30.

Russo, Neal. "Bucs Buck Card Tide, Glimpse Hot Torrez." *St. Louis Post-Dispatch,* September 11, 1967.

_____. "Cards Counting on Latins to Ward Off Calendar Hoodoo." *The Sporting News,* January 10, 1970.

_____. "Cards Flout Laws of Nature, Rise in West and Set in East." *The Sporting News,* August 30, 1969.

_____. "Cards See Shaw as Bullpen Sleeper." *The Sporting News,* January 16, 1971.

_____. "Cards Taking 4 Former Redbirds on Japan Trip." *The Sporting News,* November 2, 1968.

_____. "Chuck Taylor, as Chucker, Suits Redbirds to a T." *The Sporting News,* July 26, 1969.

_____. "The Demise of the Ailing Redbirds—Now It's Official." *The Sporting News,* October 4, 1969.

_____. "Gibson Last Forlorn Hope of Cardinals' Sinking Ship." *The Sporting News,* July 25, 1970.

_____. "Gibson Signs for 150 Grand." *The Sporting News,* October 17, 1970.

_____. "If Rugged Redbirds Have One Worry, It's on Mound Staff." *The Sporting News,* March 1, 1969.

_____. "No Easy Rest of N.L. Hurlers with Simmons Awake." *The Sporting News,* June 27, 1970.

_____. "One Mistake Foils Torrez No-Hit Bid." *St. Louis Post-Dispatch,* April 16, 1970.

_____. "Redhead Lay It on the Line and Cards Snap to Attention." *The Sporting News,* July 4, 1970.

_____. "Redhead Sees Blue Beyond Storm Clouds Over Birds' Nest." *The Sporting News,* April 17, 1971.

_____. "Rookie Torrez Ducks Disaster in First Victory." *The Sporting News,* May 4, 1968.

_____. "Satorini, Reynolds Bolster Cards' Hill Staff." *The Sporting News,* July 3, 1971.

_____. "Spirit of St. Louis Starts with Swinger Orlando." *The Sporting News,* May 25, 1968.

_____. "Swift Cardenal to Roam CF for Cards." *The Sporting News,* November 22, 1969.

_____. "Torrez and Torre Leading Torrid Tempo by El Birdos," *The Sporting News,* August 16, 1969.

_____. "Torrez Left Benson with Stinging Hand." *St. Louis Post-Dispatch,* April 23, 1968.

_____. "Winter Ball Adds Sheen to Torrez' Mound Feats." *The Sporting News,* February 7, 1970.

Saenz, J. Luz. "Has Time Come?" *The Texas Outlook* 26 (April 1942): 44.

_____. "Racial Discrimination: A Number One Problem of Texas Schools." *The Texas Outlook* 30 (December 1946): 12 and 40.

Schultz, Randy. "Bucky's Feat Was Indelible Dent." *The Sporting News,* October 17, 1988.

Scott, Jimmy. "Mike Torrez, Retired MLB Player & 'The Club.'" See: http://bleacherreport.com/articles/91406-mike-torrez-retired-mlb-player-the-club.

Segura, Melissa. "The Latino Athlete Now." *Sports Illustrated* October 6, 2008, 52–55.

Shattuck, Harry. "Sky Is the Limit for All-Star Thon." *The Sporting News,* April 16, 1984.

Shirley, Bill. "Yankees Put Childish Things Aside, Beat Dodgers." *Los Angeles Times,* October 15, 1977.

"Spahn on His Way Back?" *Topeka Daily-Capital,* August 1, 1968.

Spink, C. C. Johnson. "We Believe." *The Sporting News,* April 8, 1978.

"The Steamer, the Dodgers and History's Bullets...." May 15, 2012. See: http://fenway100.org/page/20/?app-download=nokia.

Stephenson, Madge. "Education Will Make Good Neighbors." *The Texas Outlook* 27 (March 1943): 26.

Stier, Kit. "A's Dredge Every Source for Hurling." *The Sporting News,* July 16, 1984.

_____. "Will Rainey, Torrez Fulfill Caudill?" *The Sporting News,* July 30, 1984.

Strickland, Virgil E., and George I. Sanchez. "Spanish Name Spells Discrimination." *The Nation's School* 41, no. 1 (January 1948): 22–24.

Suagee, Dick. "Torrez Eyes Fast Return to Redbirds." *Tulsa Tribune,* June 1, 1968.

Sullivan, Larry. "Fair Voting" in "Voice of the Fan." *The Sporting News,* February 19, 1990.

Sulzberger, A.G. "Hispanics Reviving Faded Towns on the Plains." *New York Times,* November 14, 2011.

Tasker, William. "Mike Torrez and His Unique Yankee History." June 25, 2013. http://itsaboutthemoney.net/archives/2013/06/25/mike-torrez-and-his-unique-yankees-history.

Taylor, Mrs. J. T. "The Americanization of Harlingen's Mexican School Population." *The Texas Outlook* 18 (September 1934).

"Torrez Posts 5–3 Victory for Cards." *Topeka State Journal,* November 12, 1968.

"Torrez Sox Better than Yankees." *Syracuse Post-Standard,* November 25, 1977.

"Torrez Started as Skinny Cager." *St. Louis Globe-Democrat,* November 7, 1977.

"Torrez Wants Security." *The Sporting News,* May 28, 1977.

"Torrez Wins a Struggle." *Topeka Daily Capital,* October 19, 1977.

Trillin, Calvin. "U.S. Journal: Crystal City, Texas-New Cheerleaders." *The New Yorker,* April 7, 1971.

Tudor, Dan. "Why Are Minorities Hard to Recruit for College Baseball and Softball?" Accessed on 2/22/2008. http://www.dantudor.com/2007/07/post_52.htm.

Verrell, Gordon. "Consistency Was Keystone to Dodger Conquest." *The Sporting News,* October 22, 1977.

Vicioso, Fernando. "Hot Bat Carries Carty into Top Spot at .376." *The Sporting News,* January 6, 1968.

_____. "Licey Carts Off Dominican Season, Playoff Laurels." *The Sporting News,* February 14, 1970.

_____. "Licey Comes Alive, Takes League Lead." *The Sporting News,* December 27, 1969.

Walsh, Matt. "1977 Kansan of the Year: Mike Torrez." *Topeka Capital-Journal*, January 1, 1978, 19–20.

Ward, Robert. "Reggie Jackson in No-Man's Land," by Alex Beth in "Bronx Banter." April 30, 2012. See: http://www.bronxban terblog.com/2012/04/30/reggie-jackson-in-no-mans-land/.

Weir, Tom. "Either Sign or Be Seated, Charlie Informs Balky A's." *The Sporting News*, April 2, 1977.

_____. "Rumors of Trade Fail to Faze Torrez." *The Sporting News*, May 7, 1977.

_____. "Trader Finley Swaps Headaches, Torrez for Ellis." *The Sporting News*, May 14, 1977.

Whiteside, Larry. "Bosox Beef Up Staff with Series Hero Torrez." *The Sporting News*, December 10, 1977.

_____. "Bosox Expect Prime Kids to Replace Lee and Tiant." *The Sporting News*, March 3, 1979.

_____. "Bosox Gunning for Free-Agent Hurlers." *The Sporting News*, November 26, 1977.

_____. "Bosox Wary of Free-Agent Market." *The Sporting News*, November 4, 1978.

_____. "Busiest Bosox Starter, Torrez Loves Work." *The Sporting News*, August 26, 1978.

_____. "Eck's Heater Still Missing but He's Hot Red Sox Item." *The Sporting News*, July 15, 1978.

_____. "Loss of Tiant 'Tears Out Heart' of Red Sox." *The Sporting News*, December 2, 1978.

_____. "A New Torrez?" *Boston Globe*, February 24, 1981.

_____. "No Question Bosox Good, but Questions Do Exist." *The Sporting News*, April 8, 1978.

_____. "Pitching Could Make Red Sox Even Better." *The Sporting News*, April 7, 1979.

_____. "Red Sox Hot—Lynn Is Torrid." *The Sporting News*, July 22, 1978.

_____. "Red Sox Land Torrez with $2 Million Pact." *The Sporting News*, December 3, 1977.

_____. "Red Sox Refuse to Worry After Yank Blanks." *The Sporting News*, June 2, 1979.

_____. "Renko Fills Boston Need for Extra Starter." *The Sporting News*, February 3, 1979.

_____. "Sox Didn't Quit on Torrez." *The Sporting News*, October 7, 1978.

_____. "Sullivan Named New G.M. of Red Sox." *The Sporting News*, November 5, 1977.

_____. "Torrez Turns Torrid by Being Less Fine." *The Sporting News*, July 21, 1979.

Wilkinson, Jack. "Yankees Roll ... Where's Torrez?" *Daily News*, May 1, 1977.

"Winnipeg Entertains Two Sellout Crowds" and "How They Stand." *The Sporting News*, July 10, 1971.

Wolff, Alexander. "The Barrio Boys." *Sports Illustrated*, June 27, 2011. See: http://cnnsi. printthis.clickability.co/pt/cpt?expire=&ti tle=IN+1949+...trated.cnn.com%Fvault%2 zfarticle%2Fmagazine%2FMAG1187581% 2Findex.htm.

Wright, Tom. "Under New Ownership, Newark Bears Hope to Switch Leagues." *Newark Star-Ledger*, October 1, 2010. See: http://blognj./ledgerupdates_impact/print .html?entry=/2010/10/under-new-owner ship_newark_bea.html.

Ziegel, Vic. "Torrez Doesn't Show Up." *New York Post*, April 30, 1977.

Zimmerman, Paul. "Yankees Give Their Series Ticket to the Red Sox." *New York Post*, November 25, 1977.

Oral History Interviews (both by this author and others)

Favila, Rocky. Interviewed by José Angel Gutierrez, March 1, 1998, as part of Tejano Voices, UT Arlington.

Gomez, Albert J. Interviewed by Jorge Iber, October 2011. Copy of interview in author's possession.

Gomez, Bernie. Interviewed by Loren Pennington, April 25, 2006, as part of the Kansas Memory of World War II Project.

Gonzalez, Mike V. Interviewed by José Angel Gutierrez, January 13, 1998, as part of Tejano Voices, UT Arlington.

Lopez, Ambrose. Interviewed by Loren Pennington, April 27, 2006, as part of the Kansas Memory of World War II Project.

Rodriguez, Sylvester. Interviewed by Loren Pennington, March 17, 2006, as part of the Kansas Memory of World War II Project.

Segovia, Martin. Interviewed by Jorge Iber, October 2011. Copy of interview in author's possession.

Silva, Louis. Interviewed by George Walters, April 20, 2006, as part of the Kansas Memory of World War II Project.

Tabares, Antonio. Interviewed by George Walters, April 10, 2006, as part of the Kansas Memory of World War II Project.

Other Sources

Baseball-Reference.com

Retrosheet.org

Index

Numbers in **bold italics** refer to pages with photographs.